Robbery and Restitution

D1557317

Studies on War and Genocide
General Editors: Omer Bartov, Brown University
A. Dirk Moses, University of Sydney

Volume 1
The Massacre in History
Edited by Mark Levene and Penny Roberts

Volume 2
National Socialist Extermination Policies: Contemporary German Perspectives and Controversies
Edited by Ulrich Herbert

Volume 3
War of Extermination: The German Military in World War II, 1941/44
Edited by Hannes Heer and Klaus Naumann

Volume 4
In God's Name: Genocide and Religion in the Twentieth Century
Edited by Omer Bartov and Phyllis Mack

Volume 5
Hitler's War in the East, 1941–1945
Edited by R.D. Müller and G.R. Ueberschär

Volume 6
Genocide and Settler Society: Frontier Violence and Stolen Indigenous Children in Australian History
Edited by A. Dirk Moses

Volume 7
Networks of Nazi Persecution: Business, Bureaucracy, and the Organization of the Holocaust
Edited by G. Feldman and W. Seibel

Volume 8
Gray Zones: Ambiguity and Compromise in the Holocaust and Its Aftermath
Edited by Jonathan Petropoulos and John K. Roth

Volume 9
Robbery and Restitution: The Conflict over Jewish Property in Europe
Edited by M. Dean, C. Goschler, and P. Ther

ROBBERY AND RESTITUTION

The Conflict over Jewish Property in Europe

Edited by

Martin Dean, Constantin Goschler,
and Philipp Ther

Published in Association with the
United States Holocaust Memorial Museum

Berghahn Books
New York • Oxford

CANISIUS COLLEGE LIBRARY
BUFFALO, NY

First published in 2007 by

Berghahn Books

www.berghahnbooks.com

©2007, 2008 S. Fischer Verlag

First paperback edition published in 2008

All rights reserved. Except for the quotation of short passages for the purposes of criticism and review, no part of this book may be reproduced in any form or by any means, electronic or mechanical, including photocopying, recording, or any information storage and retrieval system now known or to be invented, without written permission of the publisher.

Library of Congress Cataloging-in-Publication Data

Raub und Restitution, English.
Robbery & restitution : the conflict over Jewish property in Europe / edited and introduced by Martin Dean, Constantin Goschler, and Philipp Ther.
p. cm. -- (Studies on war and genocide : v. 9)
"Published in Association with the United States Holocaust Memorial Museum."
Includes bibliographical references and index.
ISBN 978-1-84545-082-3 (hbk : alk. paper) -- 978-1-84545-593-4 pbk (paperback : alk. paper)
1. Holocaust, Jewish (1939-1945)--Economic aspects--Congresses. 2. World War, 1939-1945--Confiscations and contributions-Congresses. 3. Aryanization--Congresses. 4. Holocaust, Jewish (1939-1945)--Reparations--Congresses. 5. Jewish property--Europe--Congresses. I. Dean, Martin, 1962- II. Goschler, Constantin. III. Ther, Philipp IV. United States Holocaust Memorial Museum. V. Title. VI. Series: War and genocide ; v. 9.

D804.3.R37513 2006
940.53'1813--dc22

2006013923

British Library Cataloguing in Publication Data

A catalogue record for this book is available from the British Library

Printed in the United States on acid-free paper

ISBN 978-1-84545-082-3 hbk, 978-1-84545-593-4 pbk

The assertions, opinions, and conclusions in this book of collected essays are those of the individual authors. They do not necessarily reflect those of the United States Holocaust Memorial Council or of the United States Holocaust Memorial Museum.

CONTENTS

List of Abbreviations

AAPF	Association des administrateurs provisoires de France [French Association of Provisional Administrators]
ACA	Allied Control Authority
AMZV	Archiv ministerstva zahraničních věcu [Archive of the (Czechoslovak) Foreign Ministry]
ASLK	Algemene Spaar- en Lijfrentekas [(Belgian) General Savings and Pension Bank]
BAL	Bundesarchiv, Berlin Lichterfelde [German Federal Archive, Berlin-Lichterfelde]
BArch	Bundesarchiv, Koblenz [German Federal Archive, Koblenz]
BEG	Bundesentschädigungsgesetz [Federal Indemnification Law]
BGBl.	Bundesgesetzblatt [German Federal Gazette of Laws]
BrüG	Bundesrückerstattungsgesetz [German Federal Restitution Law]
BTG	Brüsseler Treuhandgesellschaft [Brussels Trust Company]
BŻIH	Biuletyn Żydowskiego Instytutu Historycznego [Bulletin of the Jewish Historical Institute, Warsaw]
CAHJP	Central Archives for the History of the Jewish People, Jerusalem
CDJC	Centre de documentation juive contemporaine [Center for Contemporary Jewish Documentation, Paris]
CGQJ	Le Commissariat général aux Questions juives [(French) General Commissariat for the Jewish Question]
CHAN	Centre Historique des Archives Nationales [Historical Center of the French National Archives]
CIVS	Commission pour l'indemnisation des victimes de spoliation [(French) Commission for the compensation of victims of spoliation]
CNRS	Centre national de la recherche scientifique [(French) National Center for Scientific Research]

CL	(Czechoslovak) Collection of Laws
CPC	Communist Party of Czechoslovakia
CRIF	Conseil représentatif des institutions juives de France [Representative Council of French Jewish Institutions]
CZA	Central Zionist Archives, Jerusalem
Dego	Deutsche Golddiskont-Bank [German Gold Discount Bank]
DAE	Direction de l'aryanisation économique [French Office for Economic "Aryanisation"]
DER	Dienst Economische Recuperatie [(Belgian) Office for Economic Restitution]
DO	Dienst Oorlogsschade [(Belgian) Office for War Damage]
EGELI	Ente di Gestione e Liquidazione Immobiliare [(Italian) Office for the Management and Liquidation of (Jewish) Real Estate]
ERR	Einsatzstab Reichsleiter Rosenberg [Rosenberg Operational Staff]
EU	European Union
FRG	Federal Republic of Germany
FRUS	Foreign Relations of the United States
GDR	German Democratic Republic (Communist East German State)
ICE	Independent Commission of Experts: Switzerland – Second World War (appointed by Swiss Government)
ICEP	Independent Committee of Eminent Persons (appointed by Swiss Banks)
JRSO	Jewish Restitution Successor Organization
JORF	Journal officiel de la République française [Official Journal of the French Republic]
KRN	Krajowa Rada Narodowa [(Polish) National Council]
MNR	Musées Nationaux Récupération [(French) National Museums' Recovery Program]
NAGU	Niederländische Aktiengesellschaft für die Abwicklung von Unternehmen GmbH [Dutch Limited Company for the Liquidation of Businesses]
NARA	U.S. National Archives and Records Administration, College Park, MD
NATO	North Atlantic Treaty Organization
NSDAP	Nationalsozialistische Deutsche Arbeiter-Partei [Nazi Party]
OFD	Oberfinanzdirektion [(German) Regional Finance Office]
OKH	Oberkommando des Heeres [(German) Army High Command]

OMGUS	Organization of Military Government of the United States
PAAA	Politisches Archiv des Auswärtigen Amtes [Archives of the German Foreign Ministry, Berlin]
PKWN	Polski Komitet Wyzwolenia Narodowego [National Committee for the Liberation of Poland]
REAO	Rückerstattungsanordnung für Berlin [Restitution Decree for Berlin]
RGBl.	Reichsgesetzblatt [Gazette of Laws for the German Reich]
RSHA	Reichssicherheitshauptamt [Reich Security Main Office]
SA	Sturmabteilung [Nazi Stormtroopers]
SCAP	Service de contrôle des administrateurs provisoires [(French) Service for the Control of Provisional Administrators]
SD	Sicherheitsdienst [Security Service of the SS]
SDP	Sudetendeutsche Partei [Sudeten German Party]
SED	Sozialistische Einheitspartei Deutschlands [Socialist Unity Party of (East) Germany]
SFBD	Société française de Banque et de Dépôts [French Society for Banking and Deposits]
Sipo	Sicherheitspolizei [Security Police]
SOZ	Soviet Occupation Zone (East Germany)
SS	Schutz-Staffel [Protection Squad (of the Nazi Party)]
UB	Urząd Bezpieczeństwa [(Polish) Security Office]
UGIF	Union générale des Israélites de France [General Union of French Jews]
ÚRO	Ústřední rada odborů [(Czecholsovak) Trade Union Central Council]
USHMM	United States Holocaust Memorial Museum, Washington, D.C.
VAP	Vseodborovy archiv Praha [Trade Union Archive, Prague]
VJGB	Verwaltung des jüdischen Grundbesitzes in Belgien [Administration of Jewish Real Estate Holdings in Belgium]
Vobif	Verordnungsblatt des Militärbefehlshabers in Frankreich [Gazette of Decrees issued by the Military Commander in France]
VVRA	Vermögensverwaltungs- und Rentenanstalt [(Dutch) Property Administration and Pension Institute]
WgA LGHH	Archiv des Wiedergutmachungsamtes am Landgericht Hamburg [Archive of the Compensation Office at the Hamburg District Court]

PREFACE

The writing of European history is dependent on the cooperation of historians from many different countries. With regard to the history of the robbery and, especially, the restitution of property belonging to European Jews, it is also an intercontinental history, which can benefit enormously from an open exchange of views not only within Europe but also with colleagues in North America. In this way, a broad spectrum of different approaches, perspectives, and interpretations can be brought together, reflecting the often contrasting and conflicting international views on this contentious subject. Thus, the English-language edition of this volume represents an important step in summarizing, analyzing, and interpreting the results of much recent research on the topic of robbery and restitution, taking it beyond the bounds of narrow national historiography and disseminating it more widely to an international audience.

For this considerable achievement it is necessary to thank a multitude of sponsors and mentors who made this project possible. First of all, Klaus-Dietmar Henke and the Hannah-Arendt-Institut in Dresden, as well as Ulrich Herbert (Freiburg), must be mentioned for their support of a conference in January 2002, which laid the groundwork for this volume. The conference, which was generously hosted by the Center for Comparative European History in Berlin, was entitled: "'Aryanisation' and Restitution in a Comparative Perspective: The Question of Jewish Property Stolen under Nazi Occupation in Europe," and gathered academics from more than a dozen countries. The conference was also supported generously by the Kurt and Marga Möllgaard Foundation, which also contributed to the publication of the German edition and to part of the translation expenses for this volume. Warm thanks go also to the Volkswagen Foundation, which has supported not only the conference and the German publication, but also made an indispensable contribution by their funding of the Center for Comparative European History over a number of years.

In addition to those institutions that participated were also many individuals, without whom the project would not have been realized. Włodzimierz Borodziej, Gerald Feldman, Klaus-Dietmar Henke, Ulrich Herbert, Manfred Hildermeier, and Jürgen Kocka all contributed sound advice and constructive criticism to the project from its inception through to its completion. Not to be forgotten also are the individual authors, who have given us not only the product of their research, but have responded tirelessly and promptly in clarifying specific translation queries and checking their manuscripts. In addition, much deserved thanks goes to Charlotte Kreutzmüller and the other translators for their precise rendering of difficult financial terms and concepts. Also present at the conference were numerous scholars, from all over Europe, who made insightful comments on the various papers, some of which have been included in the present publication. For her great efforts in organizing the conference in Berlin, we thank also Heike Emmrich of the Center for Comparative European History.

With specific regard to the English-language edition, we thank Paul Shapiro and his staff at the Center for Advanced Holocaust Studies at the United States Holocaust Memorial Museum, which was the main sponsor for both the costs of translation and the editorial work on this publication. Special thanks must go to Michael Gelb of the Center for his careful review of the entire manuscript. Finally, we are grateful also to Frank Bajohr and Constantin Goschler for contributing their essays from the earlier volume entitled: "*‚Arisierung' und Restitution: Die Rückerstattung jüdischen Eigentums in Deutschland und Österreich nach 1945 und 1989*," edited by Constantin Goschler and Jürgen Lillteicher, which filled the gap on Robbery and Restitution in Germany itself, and also to Regula Ludi for contributing an additional piece on Switzerland to round out this English-language edition most effectively.

Martin Dean, Constantin Goschler, Philipp Ther
July 2006

– Part I –

INTRODUCTION

A History without Boundaries

The Robbery and Restitution of Jewish Property in Europe

Constantin Goschler and Philipp Ther

The robbery of Jewish property during the Nazi era has attracted dramatically increased interest from the public and from scholars during the past few years. Historical perspectives on the Holocaust and its consequences have changed at the same time. From the rising number of recent historical studies now emerges a much more detailed picture of the persecution of the Jews in Germany and in Nazi-dominated territories during the war.[1] At the same time these works increasingly raise the issue of the role of the European societies from which the Jews were torn as a result of German policy. The process of expropriating the Jews (and this also includes its "legal" forms) has taken on a central importance, since it took place with much greater participation by, or at least was more clearly visible to, the population than their murder. Stolen Jewish property also linked victims, perpetrators, bystanders, and their heirs again in the postwar years. The conflicts over the restitution of Jewish property—which mainly took place in two phases, after 1945 and after 1990—offer penetrating insights into the values and structure of European societies. This dual and yet indivisible combination of topics, robbery and restitution, is the subject for the essays in this volume, which for the first time brings together authors from eastern and western Europe for a comparative survey, and which in the scope of its subject matter also spans the former division of the continent into East and West.

Even if the massive expropriation of the Jews is examined here from a new, European perspective, the starting point of this crime must not be forgotten. From 1933 the Jews in Germany were progressively expropriated, destroying their economic and social lives.[2] Contemporaries and historians have often simply described this process by using the shorthand term "Aryanization." While this concept with its racial connotations in the narrow sense originally meant only the transfer of property from Jewish to

Notes for this section begin on page 15.

non-Jewish hands, in the postwar years its meaning has broadened to encompass all material aspects of the persecution of the Jews.[3] This lack of clarity unfortunately casts a shadow over the scholarly use of the concept. Nevertheless, there is still no comprehensive and at the same time practical alternative capable of describing the complete process of taking away all the property rights of the Jews. For this reason, care will be taken in this volume in the use of terms to ensure that in each separate case the respective degree of "legality" or the use of direct or indirect force is accurately described. In accordance with the circumstances, therefore, terms such as "Aryanization," "liquidation," "seizure," "spoliation," and "expropriation," as well as "looting" and "theft," will be used.

The Nazis extended their attack on Jewish property in a series of steps, initially to Austria following the so-called *Anschluss*, then to the border regions of Czechoslovakia, and finally to all those regions that directly or indirectly came under German sway during World War II.[4] When the Jews of the occupied territories were expropriated, their possessions were either brought back to the German Reich or they fell into the possession of the local states and the non-Jewish population there. Whereas the radicalization of persecution from expropriation to destruction spanned a number of years within the Reich, in the occupied territories this development was compressed into a much shorter time. In many places the looting of Jewish property took place only in the wake of their murder, but was nonetheless closely linked to it.

Already during the Second World War, the eighteen signatory states of the London Inter-Allied Declaration of 5 January 1943 announced that all expropriation measures in those territories occupied by the Germans were null and void. They also pronounced that all such transfers of property would be reversed after the war, regardless of whether the case was one of outright theft or a concealed, ostensibly legal transaction. In fact many European countries also implemented measures for the restitution of Jewish property immediately following the liberation, sometimes even before the German capitulation. In contrast to the pattern later in Germany, there was no massive, if ultimately unsuccessful, resistance by the Aryanizers against the restitution of Jewish property. Nonetheless, for a variety of reasons, the extent of restitution still remained limited. Many of the dispossessed Jews had been murdered, while others had succeeded in reaching other countries. If there were no surviving family members, there was the question of who the legitimate heir was. The situation was similar in places where formerly large Jewish communities had been shrunk to only a small fraction of their former size. After the war, the respective home states, the reconstructed local Jewish communities, and international Jewish organizations all competed for heirless Jewish property. In this can be seen a development that became increasingly common as the distance in time from the events of the Holocaust expanded, namely, that the property's significance for a collective Jewish identity increased relative to the importance of restoring the individual rights of those who had suffered losses. The difficulties concerning heirless

Jewish property became more acute the greater the percentage of Jews that were murdered. However, even for surviving Jews, getting property back was often difficult. Everywhere in Europe, the principle was established that only citizens of the country in which the property to be restituted was located could make a claim for its return. This excluded from restitution after 1945—and also after 1990—many Jews who had been forced to leave their home countries or who had lost their citizenship.

The political division of Europe into East and West since the end of the 1940s has also exerted considerable influence on the process of restitution. Since restitution is based on the principle of private property, the establishment of mixed or socialist economic systems hindered or blocked demands for restitution in countries like Czechoslovakia, where after 1945 initial steps towards the restitution of Jewish property had been taken.[5] However, even in Western European countries, there was a mixed result:[6] often the surviving Jews encountered great difficulties in recovering their stolen property. This ultimately led to the renewed wave of restitution claims in the 1990s, if during this later phase the actual restitution that had taken place in the immediate postwar years was often overlooked.

The situation in Germany demonstrates well the differences between East and West in handling the restitution issue: while in East Germany the Jewish property confiscated between 1933 and 1945 was generally not restituted, in West Germany, during the period of occupation, the Western Allies ordered the restitution of property that could still be found. Furthermore, in 1957 the German Parliament passed the Law for the Fulfilment of the Restitution Obligations of the German Reich, which also covered the property stolen in the occupied territories.[7] However, this only applied if the property had been taken to the state territory of the German Federal Republic or Berlin. In addition, restitution claims were only recognized for those Jewish victims of National-Socialist persecution who after 1945 were living in the Federal Republic or elsewhere in the Western world. In this way the logic of the Cold War had a decisive influence on the course of restitution policy.

Since the fall of the Berlin Wall in 1989, the question of stolen Jewish property has gained a new actuality throughout Europe. In the wake of the renewed transformation of the structure of property relations in the states of the former Eastern Bloc, the principles established in West Germany for the restitution of Jewish property were initially extended to the newly incorporated eastern states of the German Federal Republic.[8] In Poland, Czechoslovakia, and other countries of the former Eastern Bloc, however, the situation in both legal, moral, and economic terms is much more complicated. Here one has to deal with the consequences of a whole "chain of property revolutions."[9] In some places these started even before the German occupation. In those regions annexed by the Soviet Union after the Molotov-Ribbentrop Pact, quite considerable property transfers took place, which were only interrupted by the German invasion in June 1941.[10] Following the extensive reordering of property relations during the German occupation, which affected not only Jews, between 1945 and 1948 a considerable portion of the local economies in East-Central Europe was nationalized, and in addition the property of former wartime enemies and occupiers was seized by the state. Then in the course of the Sovietization of this region, the whole principle of private property was also called into question. In the era of state socialism that followed, in contrast to the experience in the West, these societies had only limited possibilities to discuss in public their relationship to the Jews and the fate of Jewish property in the past.

For these reasons, the restitution of Jewish property is closely linked to the more general program of reprivatization and the privatization of state property, structural economic reform, and even the treatment of religious communities and other issues that are central to creating a new economic and social order. The return of Jewish property in East-Central Europe encounters greater resistance of a different nature than that in Western Europe, as it is seen as a Pandora's box that, once opened, might result in other massive property changes—for example, changes concerning the property of German refugees and those forcibly resettled at the end of the war.[11] Restitution is closely tied to the national and historic identities of these countries, as the question of Jewish property touches also on their own role during the Second World War and the extent of external influence in the establishment of the socialist system. In a broader sense, however, this applies also to the Western European countries, insofar as the issue of restitution raises questions everywhere concerning a country's role during the war and has an impact on a nation's self-image.[12]

Alongside the World Jewish Restitution Organization, a collective body founded in 1992 to represent the interests of various Jewish organizations (in which, however, the representatives of those Jews who remained in Eastern Europe play only a marginal role) the European Union (EU) and other international actors have exerted considerable direct and indirect pressure on the East-Central European states that are applying to join it, urging them to restitute remaining stolen Jewish property still in their countries. The principles of private property and the free movement of capital play key roles in the convergence of legal systems, which has been an important prerequisite for the acceptance of new states into the EU. While privatization in favor of their own citizens has made great progress among the new EU states and remaining applicants, questions concerning the property of emigrants who had lost their citizenship remain unresolved. Apart from the Jewish victims of the Nazis, this also affects other groups, such as the German, Austrian, and Hungarian refugees and victims of forced resettlement, as well as the political refugees of the postwar period. For this reason, the specificity of the Jewish case has to be most carefully stressed in order to prevent it from being exploited for political purposes.

The West European countries, whose political systems and social values appeared to have been clearly confirmed by the collapse of the Eastern Bloc, have also been pulled along behind the former Communist states. Courts in the United States and also governmental and nongovernmental organizations in the United States have increasingly put pressure on European businesses and governments on account of their participation in, or their role as beneficiaries from, the expropriation of Jewish property during the Second World War. At the start of the new campaign for the restitution of Jewish property, the first targets in 1996 were the Swiss banks.[13] The public debate centered above all on the fate of bank accounts, insurance policies, and artwork belonging to victims of the Holocaust. The American legal instrument of the class-action lawsuit, which was previously unheard of in Europe, became a very powerful weapon, because so many European companies who wanted to continue doing business in the United States saw themselves threatened with massive financial risks. Therefore, the resurgence of the restitution debate can be seen as an indirect consequence of economic globalization, and also as both reflecting and intensifying the ever-expanding cultural recognition for the victims of historical crimes.

In response to the new restitution campaign, which reached its zenith in the 1998 Conference on Holocaust-Era Assets in Washington, DC, more than twenty-three countries established historical commissions. Among them were not only countries occupied by Germany during the war, but also former neutral states and even wartime enemies of the Nazis. The commissions investigated what happened to Jewish property during the war and thereafter. Already in 1944 the total value of Jewish property losses was estimated to have exceeded U.S. $8 billion (using 1944 currency values).[14] More recent investigations estimate that the property of the approximately 4.95 million Jews who lived in Germany, Austria, the Netherlands, France, Poland, and Hungary before the war, according to exchange rates at the time, was worth about U.S. $12.9 billion. Of that, minus the flight capital that was saved, some $10 billion was lost.[15]

Such value estimates, however, can only approach the true figure on account of the incomplete nature of the data and, above all, due to the dramatic changes in the overall economic and political framework between 1933 and today. This criticism is not meant to belittle the enormous financial dimensions of the expropriation of Jewish property. In reality, much more was destroyed than was robbed, as many of these values were inseparable from the physical existence of the Jewish property owners or Jewish communities. In addition, it must be borne in mind that property often has a symbolic value also alongside its material worth. The nonmaterial value of photograph albums and similar personal items explains why the last possessions of Holocaust victims have almost achieved the status of religious relics in some historical exhibitions. From the perspective of the non-Jews there had always been wild "fantasies of Jewish wealth,"[16] that in the postwar era above all were still shamefully exploited by the Communists for their own ends. But a subsequent generation is also not willing to forget that wealth. So it is not a surprise that recently the memory of stolen Jewish property has been used as the occasion to view the Holocaust as the inherited sin of Europe, which should serve as the negative reference point for the construction of a new European identity.[17]

In view of the multiple historical layers to the issue of stolen Jewish property, there emerges the question whether the concept of property itself should not be more carefully defined and examined in the light of the changing historical context. Precisely with respect to a Europe-wide comparison, this step appears to be a historiographical necessity. According to Hannes Siegrist and David Sugarman, "property is a 'package of rights and entitlements,' which regulates the relationship between people, institutions and goods."[18] As a historical category, therefore, property remains dependent on specific social and economic structures, and the time-related normative understanding of this concept is linked to the respective language and culture. This oscillates between the anarcho-socialist slogan "property is theft" (Pierre Joseph Proudhon), which historically can be found in its national-socialist version in which "Jewish property is theft," and the liberal formulation that "Socialism is theft" (Gerald D. Feldman). Not only in the People's Democracies was the sanctity of private property contested, but also in Western Europe after 1945. On the other hand the current interest in the question of restitution is probably linked to the success of a liberal economic world order after 1990, that has made private property into its own iconic symbol. Addressing the treatment of stolen Jewish property after 1945, therefore, demands that one also consider the historical transmutation of values, both in material and conceptual terms.

Robbery and restitution are inextricably intertwined, but nevertheless they each need to be examined in a separate analytical framework. With regard to Aryanization, German direction and also active participation frequently stands in the foreground. In the context of a Europe-wide comparison, therefore, it is necessary to examine the relationship between the German Reich and the territories it ruled or occupied. Here the great differences in the treatment of the allied states, and above all between the occupation policies in the West or North by comparison with those in the East, are most striking, as the persecution and destruction of the Jews took on completely different forms in these respective regions. During the war the status of countries falling within the German sphere of control varied from that of Poland, where almost no local participation in the occupation regime was permitted, to that of Vichy France, Slovakia, or Romania, which all retained control over most of their own internal affairs. In addition, some countries changed status during the course of the war from allies of Germany to occupied territories, as was the case with Hungary and Italy. The degree of independence or participation is decisive, therefore, in assessing the role played by the local society, administration, or government in the persecution and expropriation of the Jews.

With regard to the process of Aryanization in Europe, three linked perspectives can be differentiated. A first aspect is the expropriation of the Jews as a political process. In this case it is a question of political responsibility, which is closely tied to the respective freedom of action of the local administrations in the various territories dominated by the Germans. Admittedly, in most instances the process consisted primarily of applying an already-tested model for the robbery of Jewish property borrowed from the German Reich. However, occasionally, as in the case of Austria,[19] there were also some reverse transfers and radicalizing effects "from the periphery to the center." Aryanization in the occupied territories should be understood as an "overdetermined process"[20] in which different contributory factors could lead to the same result, making the identification and weighting of the precise causes even more complicated.

This can also be applied to the old dispute between the relative importance of ideology and economics: were the Jews robbed mainly on the grounds of antisemitism or rather for utilitarian motives, in order to meet the escalating demands of the Nazi war economy? The dispute, which was conducted so bitterly just a few years ago—at that time focused, however, more on the role of labor rather than of capital—has recently been reopened. Several years ago Götz Aly together with Susanne Heim had proposed the provocative thesis that Aryanization could be viewed as part of a "*Flurbereinigung*" (reallocation of agricultural land within a community) in Eastern Europe.[21] Most recently he has made another argument that shares, however, the emphasis on an economic rationale for Aryanization. Since in Aly's view the German assault on European Jewry constituted robbery with murder, for him the spoliation of Jewish property no loger appears as a so-to-speak ephemeral aspect of the Holocaust, but rather as part of its essential driving force. According to Aly, the property of European Jewry was used to stabilize the local currencies in countries occupied by the Wehrmacht that came under pressure due to the extortionate German occupation costs. These exploitative payments also served the purpose of shifting the financial burden of the war away from German taxpayers and onto the occupied and allied territories.[22] Aryanization in Europe, therefore, can be placed within the familiar interpretation that the Nazis did everything possible to avoid a repeat of the collapse of the "home front," that occurred during the First World War. By ensuring a secure food supply at the expense of the occupied territories, the Nazis assured themselves of the continued support of the German population.

While it must been conceded that Aly has offered a fresh synthesis of the German policy of spoliation of Jewish property in Europe during the Second World War, he has been rightfully criticized for driving his point too hard. Even worse, he has also been severely criticized for neglecting well-established historical knowledge both on Nazi occupation policies and on domestic social policy for the sake of his argument, which largely reduces the explanation for the spoliation of Jewish property to a prerequisite for what he describes as a Nazi "dictatorship of favors" (*Gefälligkeitsdiktatur*): thus, Jewish and other stolen property became key instruments for relieving the *Volksgemeinschaft* [German People's Community] to a large degree from the financial burdens of war.[23] Thereby Aly is not only overestimating the financial benefits for German society to be gained from the robbery of Jewish property but also underestimating more complex explanations for this process, which try to integrate a multitude of individual and structural factors—not least antisemitism, which is barely mentioned in his account.[24]

Aly's argument is very much focused on bureaucratic and political elites—mainly the financial administration of the German Reich. However, his question regarding the role of stolen Jewish assets—and also other stolen property—in the integration and stabilization of the Volksgemeinschaft is also closely linked to a second aspect of our topic, that of Aryanization as a social process. In this respect the wide variety of participants and the dynamic self-radicalization of party and state institutions at the local level, in contrast to the policy of the Reich, has to be examined. How far can this interpretation, which Frank Bajohr presented very convincingly using a case study from the German Reich,[25] be transferred to the European level? Naturally the societies in those countries ruled by the Germans during the war had a considerably lower possibility of influencing events than the German population. In some countries, such as in the apparently sovereign state of Croatia or in the German-occupied Banat, however, the local ethnic German population played a central role in the Aryanization of Jewish property and thereby muddied such a clear differentiation between German and local participants.[26] Whereas in the occupied countries of Western and Northern Europe, as well as in Bohemia, the Nazis made an effort at least to secure a certain degree of loyalty from the local population, such concerns were almost completely absent in Poland, Serbia, and the occupied parts of the Soviet Union. Although the German Reich was involved in one way or another in almost all Aryanizations and frequently controlled them completely, nonetheless the collaboration of local institutions and offices also played a considerable role. Their relevance for the different expropriation processes depended both on the respective status of the countries and also the timing of events. The local institutions and offices, however, could not operate in complete isolation from their respective societies and the prevailing attitudes in them. The expropriation of the Jews, therefore, was not limited simply to the implementation of German orders, but was also linked to the behavior of local societies towards the Jews, that is, to the different forms of antisemitism. As in the German Reich, the corruptive influence that spread with enrichment from Jewish property in the occupied territories could also lead to various forms of accommodation to the policies of Nazi Germany.[27] The robbery of Jewish property is therefore also a useful barometer for the relations of various local populations toward Nazi Germany, to the German occupational authorities, and also toward the Jewish population of their own countries.

Aryanizations in the German Reich and in the occupied Western countries—with regard both to their quality and their quantity—constituted a unique historical event. It is not so clear whether the same can be said with regard to those countries, such as Poland, where the expropriations under German occupation also widely affected the non-Jewish population. Such a comparison could help to resolve the conflict between two competing interpretations. In one explanatory model, which Jan Gross applied to Poland, indigenous antisemitism is accorded a very important role in this connection.[28] According to another explanatory model, the conduct of Polish society is seen as a more complex phenomenon. The proven participation of the local population in robbing their Jewish neighbors is seen as a product of an increasing radicalization and loss of restraint resulting from the breakdown of social ties along ethnic lines that can be found repeatedly in reports from the occupation period.[29] Both the role of the local population as witnesses to the Holocaust and also the impact of radical German economic exploitation in the occupied territories, which led to bitter social conflicts over scarce resources, contributed to this development. In general, when trying to explain and thereby also make a moral assessment of the looting and other property crimes, the fact cannot be ignored that during a period when all laws were being broken and people were being deliberately murdered, property laws must have been viewed with much less respect than today.

This brings us to a third aspect, namely the possibility of establishing a typology for Aryanization and its consequences in Europe. In contrast to the murder of the Jews, where there are considerable differences in the proportion of Jews killed from one country to another, with respect to the robbery national differences existed more with regard to the process than the end result: Jewish property everywhere was stolen as comprehensively as possible. Those delays that occurred resulted mainly from the self-interest of the participating bureaucrats, who sought to keep themselves occupied in comfortable jobs well away from the dangers of the front.[30] The respective form of German rule—direct or indirect—was only a secondary consideration with regard to the form of Aryanization applied. The decisive factor emerging from the comparison was undoubtedly the different methods applied for implementing the murder of the Jews in various regions,[31] which itself in part reflected the respective harshness of German rule.[32] In areas such as Poland and the occupied parts of the Soviet Union, where the Jews were murdered inside the country or even locally, close to their homes, the robbery was more directly linked to the murder than in places where the deportation of the Jews put considerable distance between these events. Furthermore the different forms of robbery also reflected the pace of destruction, as generally Jewish property was used initially to support the Jews prior to their murder.[33] Therefore, a comparative analysis of the robbery measures reveals a clear difference between Western and Eastern Europe, as in the West (and the North) greater care was taken to preserve at least the appearance of measures based on a legal framework. The West and the East, of course, were defined quite differently during the Second World War than they were after 1945—namely in accordance with the Nazis' own racial criteria, which again confirms the conditional nature of these apparently objective geographic categories. Both the Czech lands and Hungary, while under German occupation, still belonged to some extent to the West, whereas soon after the end of the war they became part of the East.

Differences existed also with respect to the impact of the robbery of Jewish property on the economic and social structures of the various countries. In Western and Northern Europe, but also in Southeastern Europe and the Czech lands—in contrast to Poland and the western part of the Soviet Union—the Jews comprised a relatively small proportion of the total population and therefore their despoliation had a much smaller impact on the overall national economies of these regions. But other consequences of the war were also different: in Western and Northern Europe the old borders remained intact, whereas the war in Central and Eastern Europe resulted in large-scale border changes that continued after 1945. The extent of war destruction also presents a differentiated picture, as the destruction of the economic and social structure in the East was generally much more radical. These key contrasts also contributed significantly to subsequent differences in how the restitution of Jewish property was handled.

The analytical framework for a comparison of restitution in Europe is shaped by the fact that German responsibility for the theft is of quite a different quality than that of other European countries, and by the fact that only in West Germany was restitution initiated as an integral part of Allied occupation policy. These reasons alone produced certain key contrasts to both the course and nature of restitution in Germany compared with other European countries.[34] Despite these differences, the current rapidly expanding research on how to deal with historical crimes often draws upon "German compensation payments" as a possible model,[35] if at the same time the issue of restitution has so far attracted less attention.

Restitution faces a dilemma: restitutions, compensation and reparations all aim by definition at righting historical wrongs, which, in the case of Nazi crimes, however, can at best only be alleviated.[36] Therefore, the question of what the restitution of Jewish property means in the context of justice for historical crimes produces some quite divergent responses. Research so far has produced five, partly overlapping, explanatory approaches. One approach stresses above all the role of external political pressure, in which the United States is seen as the decisive actor. This argument, which previously was developed mainly in reference to the Federal Republic of Germany (FRG),[37] has found renewed application in the course of the recent wave of restitution demands directed at various European states. The political and economic power of the United States was seen as playing a central role during the first phase of restitution in Germany and Austria after the war, and the same can be said with respect to the other European countries in the period after 1990. Yet the examination above all of Western European states, such as France, Belgium, and the Netherlands, after 1944, reveals that political pressure from the United States at this time was not sufficient on its own to explain the efforts for restitution.[38] Rather, the restitution of stolen Jewish property resulted here initially from the great concern with restoring those legal rights that had been violated by the German occupation authorities.

This raises the question of the link between restitution and the structure of civil property rights. According to Ulrich Herbert the restitution of

Jewish property provides the basis for the reestablishment of trust, which is a vital resource for the functioning of an economic system based on private property.[39] This is linked to the apparent paradox of liberal economic theory known as the "Adam Smith problem," in which the fairness and the realism of the market are inextricably linked. Adam Smith argued that a market economy functioning largely without regulation could only be successful if the participants had faith in the justice of society and the fairness of the other traders in the market.[40] Without doubt, a liberal economic order based on private property has always been a necessary prerequisite for the restitution of Jewish property. Of course, this would in all cases neither have prevented the theft, nor was it subsequently a sufficient condition on its own to ensure that restitution took place. Restitution was most likely in countries such as France, where a relatively large proportion of the victims survived to make their own claims after the war. The problem with arguments based on the central significance of the resource "trust" for the functioning of a liberal economic order becomes clear when it is noted that those who had acquired Jewish property under the circumstances of a general persecution of the Jews later insisted that they had acted in "good faith." However, the reintroduction of a liberal economic system based on private property in the countries of the former Eastern Bloc after 1990 demonstrates that even though a clear connection can be seen, it is not guaranteed that this change will necessarily lead to the restoration of Jewish property.

A third argument also sees a link between restitution and the existence of a civil society as an important prerequisite for the constructive solution of property issues.[41] This draws upon the recent appreciation of the role of "civil society" as an instrument for overcoming dictatorship, that is, coping with the consequences of dictatorship in the postcommunist countries of the former Eastern Bloc. In fact, only in those places where a civil society existed did restitution take place. On the other hand, where groups organized themselves in connection with the conflict over stolen Jewish property, it was mostly directed at blocking or at least restricting the scope of restitution. The restitution of Jewish property therefore provides an important case study for examining the question of how well civil societies are able to handle the historical exclusion and discrimination of minorities. The strong historical link between the nation-state and civil society that in many ways made its emergence possible can also be a factor that contributes to some limitations of civility. The conflicts after 1945 and 1990 over stolen Jewish property thereby point to a certain ambivalence that is built into the concept of civil society.[42]

These interpretations of the restitution of Jewish property, which appeal to the principles of civil society, also run into some other more fundamental limitations: even the most successful restitution would not be able to bring back to life those who were murdered. At this point, interpretations based on compensation for individuals run up against other models based on group rights.[43] Elazar Barkan, who views restitution not as a legal category but rather as a cultural concept, focuses on the question, whether the notably increased importance attached to the recognition of historical guilt during the last century also reflects the development of new international moral standards.[44] For him restitution is primarily "negotiated history" in which different groups that are linked by an "historical crime" seek to overcome the conflict in their search for a common narrative, thereby also changing their own identity. Denying the assumption of universal standards of justice, in this way Barkan views justice as the outcome of a negotiation between different communities, with reference to somewhat vague international standards of justice. However, it should be noted that the restitution of Jewish property in Europe generally has not entailed a new negotiation of social identity connected with the inclusion of a previously disadvantaged minority, as was the case with most postcolonial conflicts. In addition, with respect to such an "intercommunicative history" one also has to examine closely who is conducting the negotiations with whom and on whose behalf, and especially to assess how far the individual victims themselves are involved at all in the creation of such a narrative.[45]

The question of the connection between property and memory also arises here, which leads to a fifth point. In the historical and anthropologically-oriented explanation of Dan Diner, restitution not only leads to a reawakening of the memory vested in property; rather, restitution itself is the result of a rediscovered memory.[46] Here Diner is refering above all to the latest wave of restitution claims, which should be seen against the background of a vast increase in the public and private memory of the Holocaust over recent years. That restoring property to its previous owners reawakens associated memories is more or less to be expected. It is much harder, however, to prove the reverse proposition that historical memory has directly contributed to the restitution process. In this respect, one has to differentiate between separate phases and regions. In any case it becomes clear that the element of memory made a greater contribution to the process of restitution the longer the time since the events being remembered and also the less this memory had to compete with other painful memories arising from the consequences of the Second World War. This process was not the same throughout Europe. Rather the memory of stolen Jewish property is part of a complex European history of property losses, since the forced expulsion of ethnic minorities and the property transfers linked thereto were central elements in the creation of ethnically homogeneous nation-states in Europe. The integration of these events within an overall historical framework remains a long-term project for the history of the twentieth century, in which historians from both sides of the former Iron Curtain can also learn a great deal from one another.

However, one further problem remains unsolved for the moment: at least for the period after 1945, the perspective of the Jewish victims, over which the bitter conflicts regarding lost property have cast a dark shadow, cannot simply be integrated within a broader European history of how postwar societies dealt with the legacies of the Nazi past. Rather, this must be contrasted with the story of the reconstruction of Jewish life after the war that took place largely outside of Europe. The attempt to integrate the German or the European perspective on the one hand, and the Jewish or intercontinental perspective on the other hand, in researching the issue of how stolen Jewish property was handled, reinforces the need to dissolve social history from its long-term connection to the unit of the nation-state and to pay much more attention to transnational processes. Otherwise the transnational and even transcontintental history of European societies in the twentieth century, itself in large part unleashed by Nazi Germany, cannot be successfully addressed.

Translated from German by Martin Dean

Notes

1. See the overview of recent research by U. Herbert, "Extermination Policy: New Answers and Questions about the History of the 'Holocaust' in German Historiography," in *National Socialist Extermination Policies: Contemporary German Perspectives and Controversies*, ed. U. Herbert (New York, 2000), 1–52.
2. See especially H. Genschel, *Die Verdrängung der Juden aus der Wirtschaft im Dritten Reich* (Göttingen, 1966); A. Barkai, *Vom Boykott zur "Entjudung". Der wirtschaftliche Existenzkampf der Juden im Dritten Reich 1933–1943* (Frankfurt a.M., 1987); F. Bajohr, *'Aryanisation' in Hamburg. The Economic Exclusion of Jews and the Confiscation of their Property in Nazi Germany 1933-1945* (New York, 2002); I. Wojak and P. Hayes (eds.), *"Arisierung" im Nationalsozialismus. Volksgemeinschaft, Raub und Gedächtnis* (Frankfurt a.M., 2000).
3. On the problems of definition see especially, F. Bajohr, "'Arisierung' als gesellschaftlicher Prozeß. Verhalten, Strategien und Handlungsspielräume jüdischer Eigentümer und 'arischer' Erwerber," in *'Arisierung' im Nationalsozialismus*, 15–30; and for a critical view on the use of the term "Aryanization," see L. Herbst, et al., Einleitung, in *Die Commerzbank und die Juden 1933–1945*, ed. L. Herbst and T. Weihe (Munich, 2004), 9–19, esp. 10–13.
4. See the contributions of Jean-Marc Dreyfus, Tatjana Tönsmeyer, and Dieter Pohl in this volume, as well as R. Hilberg, *The Destruction of the European Jews*, 3 vols. (New Haven, CT, 2003); M. Dean, "The Plundering of Jewish Property in Europe: Five Recent Publications Documenting Property Seizure and Restitution in Germany, Belgium, Norway, and Belarus," *Holocaust and Genocide Studies* 15 (2001): 86–97.
5. See the essay by Eduard Kubůand Jan Kuklík in this volume.
6. See the essays by Claire Andrieu, Rudi van Doorslaer, and Ilaria Pavan in this volume.
7. See the essay by Jürgen Lillteicher in this volume.
8. J. P. Spannuth, "Rückerstattung Ost. Der Umgang der DDR mit dem 'arisierten' und enteigneten Eigentum der Juden und die Gestaltung der Rückerstattung im wiedervereinigten Deutschland," (PhD diss., Freiburg i. Br., 2001), 270–71; C. Meyer-Seitz, "Die Entwicklung der Rückerstattung in den neuen Bundesländern seit 1989. Eine juristische Perspektive," in *"Arisierung" und Restitution. Die Rückerstattung jüdischen Eigentums in Deutschland und Österreich nach 1945 und 1989*, ed. C. Goschler and J. Lillteicher (Göttingen, 2002), 265–79, here especially, 266–72.
9. H. Leber, "Eine Kette von Eigentumsrevolutionen," *Berliner Zeitung*, 14 January 2002.°

10. On the Sovietization of this part of Eastern and Central Europe, see J. Gross, *Revolution from Abroad: The Soviet Conquest of Poland's Western Ukraine and Western Belorussia* (Princeton, NJ, 1988).
11. M. Henry, *The Restitution of Jewish Property in Central and Eastern Europe* (New York, 1997), 20–21.
12. On France, Belgium, and the Netherlands, see P. Lagrou, *The Legacy of Nazi Occupation: Patriotic Memory and National Recovery in Western Europe 1945–1965* (Cambridge, 2000).
13. See, for example, J. Authers and R. Wolffe, *The Victim's Fortune: Inside the Epic Battle over the Debts of the Holocaust* (New York, 2002).
14. N. Robinson, *Indemnifications and Reparations: Jewish Aspects* (New York, 1944), 83.
15. H. B. Junz, "Report on the Pre-war Wealth Position of the Jewish Population in Nazi-Occupied Countries, Germany and Austria" prepared for the Independent Committee of Eminent Persons and included as Appendix S in their *Report on Dormant Accounts of Victims of Nazi Persecution in Swiss Banks* (Bern, 1999).
16. See the contribution by Ron Zweig in this volume.
17. D. Diner, "Gedächtnis und Restitution," in *Verbrechen erinnern: die Auseinandersetzung mit Holocaust und Völkermord*, ed. V. Knigge and N. Frei (Munich, 2002), 299–305, here 301 and 305; see also B. Giesen, "Europäische Identität und transnationale Öffentlichkeit. Eine historische Perspektive," in *Transnationale Öffentlichkeit und Identitäten im 20. Jahrhundert*, ed. H. Kaelble, M. Kirsch, and A. Schmidt-Gernig (Berlin, 2002), 67–84, here 79–82.
18. H. Siegrist and D. Sugarman, "Geschichte als historisch-vergleichende Eigentumswissenschaft. Rechts-, kultur- und gesellschaftsgeschichtliche Perspektiven," in *Eigentum im internationalen Vergleich (18.–20. Jahrhundert)*, ed. H. Siegrist and D. Sugarman (Göttingen, 1999), 9–30, here 13.
19. See the essay by Martin Dean in this volume; and also H. Safrian, "Beschleunigung und Vertreibung. Zur Bedeutung des 'Wiener Modells' für die antijüdische Politik des 'Dritten Reiches' im Jahr 1938," in Goschler and Lillteicher eds., *"Arisierung" und Restitution*, 61–89.
20. W. Seibel, "Restraining or Radicalizing? Division of Labor and Persecution Effectiveness," in *Networks of Nazi Persecution: Bureaucracy, Business, and the Organization of the Holocaust*, ed. G. D. Feldman and W. Seibel (New York, 2005), 353–54.
21. S. Heim and G. Aly, *Ein Berater der Macht. Helmut Meinhold oder Der Zusammenhang zwischen Sozialpolitik und Judenvernichtung* (Hamburg, 1986); S. Heim and G. Aly, *Vordenker der Vernichtung: Auschwitz und die deutschen Pläne für eine neue europäische Ordnung* (Frankfurt a. M., 1991); S. Heim, "Gibt es eine Ökonomie der 'Endlösung'? Wirtschaftsrationalisierung und Vernichtungspolitik im besetzten Polen 1939 bis 1945" (Diss., Freie Universität, Berlin, 1991); U. Herbert, "Arbeit und Vernichtung. Ökonomisches Interesse und Primat der 'Weltanschauung' im Nationalsozialismus," in *Ist der Nationalsozialismus Geschichte? Zu Historisierung und Historikerstreit*, ed. D. Diner (Frankfurt a.M., 1987), 198–236.
22. G. Aly, "Hitlers Volksstaat. Notiz zum Klassencharakter des Nationalsozialismus," in G. Aly, *Rasse und Klasse: Nachforschungen zum deutschen Wesen* (Frankfurt a.M., 2003), 230–44.
23. See especially the book reviews by M. Spoerer, *H-Soz-u-Kult*, 05/26/2005, [website last accessed on 05/11/2006]; A. J. Tooze "Einfach verkalkuliert," *taz Magazin*, No. 7613, 03/12/2005; R. Hachtmann, "Eine klassenbewusste Gefälligkeitsdiktatur?" *Sehepunkte* 5 (2005), No. 7/8 [07/15/2005]; F. Bajohr, "Die Beraubung der Juden," *Sehepunkte* 5 (2005), No. 7/8 [07/15/2005].
24. See for example the essays by Dieter Ziegler, Philippe Verheyde, Martin C. Dean, Jonathan Petropoulus, Frank Bajohr, Alfons Kenkmann, Gerard Aalders, Marc Olivier Baruch, and Wolf Gruner in *Networks of Persecution*, ed. G. D. Feldman and W. Seibel; and also the essays by Martin Dean, Jean-Marc Dreyfus, Dieter Pohl, Tatjana Tönsmeyer, and Regula Ludi in this volume.

25. See F. Bajohr, *'Aryanisation' in Hamburg*; F. Bajohr, "'Arisierung' als gesellschaftlicher Prozeß," 15–30.
26. H. Sundhaussen, *Wirtschaftsgeschichte Kroatiens im nationalsozialistischen Großraum 1941–1945. Das Scheitern einer Ausbeutungsstrategie* (Stuttgart, 1983), 245–51; K.-H. Schlarp, *Wirtschaft und Besatzung in Serbien 1941–1944. Ein Beitrag zur nationalsozialistischen Wirtschaftspolitik in Südosteuropa* (Stuttgart, 1986), 294–302; see also the contribution of Dieter Pohl in this volume.
27. See for example F. Bajohr, *Parvenüs und Profiteure: Korruption in der NS-Zeit* (Frankfurt, 2001), esp. 105–20.
28. This view was put forward recently by Jan Gross with respect to the debate on the participation of the local Polish population in the murder of the Jews of Jedwabne. On this debate, see the essay of Dariusz Stola in this volume, and, for example, the German language documentation in the journal edited by the German-Polish Society in Brandenburg, *Transodra* 23 (2001), "Die 'Jedwabne-Debatte' in polnischen Zeitungen und Zeitschriften."
29. See, for example, the very detailed diary of the Lwów doctor, Tadeusz Tomaszewski, *Lwów 1940–1944. Pejzaż psychologiczny* [Lwów (L'viv) 1940–1944. Psychological terrain] (Warsaw, 1996), 17–19, 32 and 84.
30. See the essay by Martin Dean in this volume.
31. Ibid.; see also M. Dean, "The Plundering of Jewish Property."
32. See W. Seibel, "Staatsstruktur und Massenmord. Was kann eine historisch-vergleichende Institutionenanalyse zur Erforschung des Holocaust beitragen," in *Geschichte und Gesellschaft* 24 (1998): 539–69. For an introduction to German occupation policy, see L. Herbst, *Das nationalsozialistische Deutschland 1933–1945. Die Entfesselung der Gewalt: Rassismus und Krieg* (Frankfurt a. M., 1996).
33. See the essay by Martin Dean in this volume.
34. M. Henry, *Restitution of Jewish Property*, 17.
35. See, for example, E. Barkan, *The Guilt of Nations: Restitution and Negotiating Historical Injustices* (New York, 2000); R. L. Brooks, *When Sorry Isn't Enough. The Controversy over Apologies and Reparations for Human Injustice* (New York, 1999).
36. H. Rousso, "Frankreich," in *Verbrechen erinnern*, ed. V. Knigge and N. Frei (Munich, 2002), 253–61, here 260-61.
37. See, for example, C. Goschler, "Die Politik der Rückerstattung in Westdeutschland," in Goschler and Lillteicher eds., *"Arisierung" und Restitution*, 99–125; J. Lillteicher, "Die Rückerstattung jüdischen Eigentums in Westdeutschland. Eine Studie über Rechtsstaatlichkeit, Vergangenheitsbewältigung und Verfolgungserfahrung," (PhD diss., Univ. Freiburg i. Brsg., 2002).
38. See the contributions of Claire Andrieu and Rudi van Doorslaer in this volume.
39. Ulrich Herbert, during the podium discussion on the topic "Did Restitution Achieve Justice?" in Berlin on 11 January 2002.
40. K. Graf Ballestrem, *Adam Smith* (Munich, 2001), 195–98.
41. Jürgen Kocka, during the podium discussion on the topic "Did Restitution achieve justice?" in Berlin on 11 January 2002. On the concept of civil society and its historical development, see M. Hildermeier, J. Kocka, and C. Conrad, eds., *Europäische Zivilgesellschaft in Ost und West: Begriffe, Geschichte, Chancen* (Frankfurt a.M., 2000).
42. See D. Gosewinkel, "Zivilgesellschaft. Eine Erschließung des Themas von seinen Grenzen her," Wissenschaftszentrum, Berlin, Discussion Paper Nr. SP IV 2003-505 (Berlin, 2003).
43. See E. Barkan, *The Guilt of Nations*; J.-M. Chaumont, *Die Konkurrenz der Opfer. Genozid, Identität und Anerkennung* (Lüneburg, 2001).
44. See E. Barkan, *The Guilt of Nations.*
45. See also J. Torpey, "'Making Whole What Has Been Smashed': Reflections on Reparations," in *The Journal of Modern History* 73 (2001): 333–58, here 349.
46. D. Diner, "Der Holocaust in den politischen Kulturen Europas: Erinnerung und Eigentum," in Auschwitz. Sechs Essays zu Geschehen und Vergegenwärtigung, ed. K.-D. Henke (Dresden, 2001), 65–73, here 68.

– *Part II* –

The Robbery of Jewish Property in Comparative Perspective

The Seizure of Jewish Property in Europe

Comparative Aspects of Nazi Methods and Local Responses

Martin Dean

Two of the main questions with regard to the Nazi seizure of Jewish property are how it was organized and what social processes and responses were involved.[1] In an almost historical mirror image, these are also two key questions with regard to property restitution. This chapter addresses the comparative study of Aryanization, confiscation, and plunder, using the results of current research as a starting point. This overview identifies the main issues confronting historians and also the problems they entail.

One important aspect is the close relationship between property seizure and the development of the Holocaust. The considerable differences in the methods of plunder used by the Nazis and their collaborators in Eastern Europe in comparison with Western Europe arose primarily from the manner in which the Holocaust was implemented and the nature of the respective occupation regimes. However, the differences that existed in the structure of property ownership in various Jewish populations may in some respects have influenced the approach taken towards its confiscation and seizure.[2]

The precise chronology of the Holocaust also played a decisive role. In Western Europe the aim was to secure Jewish wealth prior to the deportations, especially in the form of businesses, bank accounts, and securities.[3] Naturally this involved intentional deception to secure as much of the booty as possible. On occupied Soviet territory much of the property collection was done directly at the killing sites; in Latvia, the registration of Jewish property was even conducted retrospectively, in the wake of the grisly massacres, in a largely vain attempt to claw back items from the local population.[4]

This volume deals primarily with the seizure of Jewish property in the occupied territories. However, in order to examine and compare events in both Eastern and Western Europe, it is necessary also to understand the

Notes for this section begin on page 29.

experiences gained and the wide variety of mechanisms first developed inside the Reich in Germany and Austria.[5] For the Nazi leadership these served as a ready-made model that they planned to extend to all areas under their control. Unfortunately the complex structure of competing measures in the Reich does not serve well as a Weberian "ideal type" for the comparative study of Aryanization. There was an important learning process in the application of property seizure measures throughout Europe, which applies to laws, institutions, and even to the transfer of key personnel.[6] For example, certain extensive plans only partially implemented in the Reich were subsequently perfected in the Netherlands.[7] Thus it is necessary for historians to confront not only "unequal comparisons," but also a centrally coordinated system of "mechanism transfers" that varied in intensity over time and space.[8]

Most accounts of Jewish economic persecution begin with the laws passed from 1933 onwards that excluded Jews from the civil service and other professions, and the boycotts applied against Jewish businesses.[9] These two examples demonstrate the combination of legal measures and direct Nazi Party pressure that was applied to drive the Jews out of the German economy. With regard to property rights, however, the bundle of laws decreed in July 1933, authorizing the confiscation of property of "enemies of the people and the state" and also the denaturalization of emigrants, opened the door to the subsequent massive confiscation of Jewish property.[10]

Following a Himmler decree in the spring of 1937 that broadened the categories of persons targeted, increasing numbers of Jews were subjected to denaturalization.[11] This included the seizure of their property as an important aim of the exercise. By this time, the Reich Capital Flight Tax and strict currency restrictions were also extracting a severe financial toll from Jewish emigrants. According to an internal Finance Ministry memorandum from 1935, Jews attempting to transfer remaining funds by legal means suffered a loss of almost 80 percent.[12] The close network of observation and restrictions applied by the police, the currency offices, and the administration developed into the full-scale blocking of Jewish bank accounts by the currency offices in the late summer of 1939.[13]

With regard to the Nazi policy of removing the Jews from the economy—the "Economic Final Solution"—a clear legal framework was required for it to be effective. Potential buyers and middlemen were reluctant to invest in Jewish property without obtaining *Rechtssicherheit*, secure legal title to businesses or real estate. Thus in every country there was the need for an extensive legal and administrative framework to legitimize the theft. This problem was even more critical in occupied and satellite countries during the war, as exile regimes, such as those from the Netherlands and Norway, passed laws outlawing cooperation in German measures of confiscation.[14]

Interestingly it was the wave of spontaneous or "wild Aryanizations" in Austria immediately following the Anschluss in 1938 that gave increased impetus to Nazi legal and institutional measures. Both the registration of Jewish property and the ensuing decrees organizing the compulsory

Aryanization of businesses represented attempts by Göring to reassert state control.[15] The private Aryanization of many Jewish businesses had occurred prior to 1938, permitting some spectacular private profits. During the course of 1938 a network of laws, supervisory institutions, and regulations were put in place that ensured that henceforth the German state would pocket the difference between the lower price paid into blocked Jewish accounts and the actual market price. Many of the institutions and mechanisms used to complete Aryanization in the Reich, such as the Deutsche Revisions- und Treuhand AG, were also adopted and adapted for use in the occupied territories, such as the Protectorate of Bohemia and Moravia or the Netherlands.[16]

Another major innovation in 1938 in terms of economic exploitation was the introduction of the Punitive Tax (Judenvermögensabgabe) in the wake of the Kristallnacht [Reich Crystal Night] pogrom. By 1940 this one measure had raised in excess of RM 1.1 billion for Germany's hard-pressed war finances, representing roughly 25 percent of Jewish taxable wealth at this time.[17] This was only the first and most spectacular of many special taxes or "contributions" imposed on Jewish communities of all sizes throughout occupied Europe from Minsk to Rome.[18] It clearly provided the model for the similar "Punitive Fine" of 1 billion francs imposed on the occupied northern zone of France.[19]

The comparative success of the Punitive Tax and other measures in securing Jewish assets through the regular tax administration calls into question interpretations focused on the Security Police as the main agent of financial exploitation. In practice, financial exploitation relied on the close cooperation between the executive authority of the Security Police and the technical expertise of the financial administration to achieve this complex task. Considerable rivalry and friction still remained, however, between the two branches. This was especially intense in the occupied eastern territories, where new institutions competed openly for jurisdiction without concern for existing structures and norms in the absence of a civil society.[20]

One clear reason for the institutional conflicts that were inherent to the seizure of Jewish property came from differences over aims. Prior to the war the aim of the Sicherheitspolizei [Security Police] (Sipo) and the Sicherheitsdienst [Security Service] (SD) was to encourage Jewish emigration by any means possible. In this respect the extraordinary taxes and strict currency restrictions applied mainly to raise revenue actually proved counterproductive by making it impossible for many Jews to leave. Thus the creation of the Zentralstelle für jüdische Auswanderung [Central Office for Jewish Emigration] in Vienna, and also subsequently the Reichszentrale für jüdische Auswanderung [Reich Central Office for Jewish Emigration] in 1939, were attempts to square the circle by mobilizing the assets of wealthy Jews and even international welfare organizations directly in support of forced emigration. The Security Police used similar methods to extort large sums from the deportees during the war.[21] Nevertheless, the detailed work of winding up Jewish estates was still left to the financial bureaucracy under the comprehensive provisions of the Eleventh Decree to the Reich Citizenship Law, published on 26 November 1941.[22]

Similar conflicts over control of resources and policy were also played out in the occupied countries. For example, in the Netherlands Generalkommissar Hans Fischböck's model of technocratic plunder by decree triumphed over plans to expand the competence of the Central Office for Jewish Emigration set up by the Sipo/SD. This was indeed ironic, as the Central Office in the Netherlands was originally envisioned as a model institution for the whole of Europe.[23]

These questions of the respective role of administrative and police authorities and also the extent to which new institutions were created are important issues for comparative study. They are of particular relevance to collaborating regimes. An examination of these structural components would also be revealing for other key issues ranging from levels of corruption to the responses of officials. Jean-Marc Dreyfus argues, for example, that the French deliberately applied more bureaucratic resources to Aryanization than was the case in the Netherlands or Belgium, in an effort to increase oversight and reduce corruption, responding to previous scandals involving the nationalization of church property earlier in the century.[24]

Emerging from the clashes within the Nazi bureaucracy, one principle that remained important for the Sipo was the need for anti-Jewish measures to pay for themselves. Above all officials were anxious that the increasingly impoverished Jewish community should not become a burden on the state. Thus even deportees faced an extra tax to cover their travel costs.[25] Camps established for Jewish inmates in Serbia and the Netherlands were financed with the proceeds from Jewish property.[26] This principle was even enshrined within the Eleventh Decree itself, which stated that the funds raised were to be used "to serve the furtherance of all purposes connected with the solution of the Jewish Question."[27] Within this framework some funds were used, at least temporarily, to support existing Jewish welfare structures. It is interesting that similar patterns can be detected in the occupied territories, especially in the West, in countries such as the Netherlands and France, if only a tiny fraction of seized property was used in this way.[28]

These key questions of who should control the process of property seizure and what happened to the proceeds took on special importance for regimes collaborating with the Germans. For the occupied territories, the Reich authorities decided that in most cases the proceeds from Jewish property should be applied to the budgets of the respective German-dominated administrations. This meant that the proceeds from Jewish valuables seized in Latvia and sold in Berlin were to be transferred back to the accounts of Reichskommissariat Ostland.[29] However, the actual cash flows require careful study. Often the net effect was much the same. For example, in Serbia payments made into the Serbian State Bank from the proceeds of Jewish property were earmarked to pay off German war compensation claims before they had even been received.[30] In Western Europe the Germans also extracted vast sums from local budgets to pay for so-called occupation costs.[31] Nevertheless this pattern helps to explain how in countries such as Belgium and Norway, for instance, so much of Jewish wealth remained in state hands within the country after the war.[32]

A striking element of the property seizures was the comprehensive nature of the process. In most areas under direct German administration, the aim was to gain control of all the property from all the Jews, with only a few exceptions made for half-Jews or foreign nationals. Only in some satellite countries, such as Vichy France or Bulgaria, were the measures less complete in their aims.[33] In Bulgaria, for example, a certain number of Jewish merchants were permitted to remain in business.[34] A major problem in all areas remained, nevertheless, the question of correctly identifying Jewish property. This led to the widespread registration of Jewish property and its seizure in close conjunction with deportation and destruction measures, for example, by the clearing of vacated apartments. In this way the seizure of property itself became part of the destruction process.

The exhaustive process of administering and selling off Jewish property usually involved a considerable administrative effort, employing hundreds of local staff.[35] In fact it was rarely completed before the end of the war. Even in the Netherlands, generally seen as one of the most efficient cases, some one thousand Jewish businesses had neither been sold nor liquidated by 1945.[36] In most other countries, including Germany, a large proportion of files still remained open at the end of the war. For some officials there was little incentive to finish what was a very desirable job away from the front.[37] Often the high administration costs consumed much of the actual income generated from the property, and a number of organizations and individuals took their cut.[38] These ranged from semiofficial entities such as the Vugesta in Vienna to legions of property assessors, auction houses, trustees, estate agents, notaries, and transport companies.[39] Often the profits were concealed within generous expenses and high salaries.

It is not possible to enumerate all the various kinds of property seized. Only a brief survey of the main categories will be given here, as different types of property required different means of seizure and confiscation that in turn led to clear similarities across regions.[40] Direct quantitative comparisons remain, however, problematic due to the inevitable difficulties in calculating currency conversions (for a controlled economy) and assessing the accuracy of reported economic values, for example, from property registration forms.

Personal property, such as cash, jewelry, and clothing, was frequently secured directly by the police in connection with arrests, deportations, and mass shootings. In other cases valuables had to be surrendered on demand. Furniture and other personal items were also secured in port storage facilities and empty houses and apartments. These items were sold or auctioned off locally, or used to benefit specific groups, such as bomb-damage victims or ethnic Germans. Valuables were frequently sent to Berlin to be sold for foreign exchange or otherwise applied to the war economy.

Many Jewish businesses were Aryanized prior to the deportations, involving a wide range of private and state actors as trustees, evaluators, and approval authorities. Real estate and mortgages, if not sold by the owner, generally took time to liquidate, as land registers had to be amended and restrictions were drawn up on those persons entitled to buy them. Financial instruments—mainly bank accounts, securities, and safe deposit boxes—were wound up in close cooperation with the banks, where most were deposited. These were often the most liquid assets, taken up first to pay punitive fines and cover the Jews' emigration or living expenses.

Similarly, life insurance policies and pensions were generally regulated through the financial administration, with the capitalized values being transferred directly to the state. The existence of outstanding debts and loans was one of the main reasons for the enormous bureaucratic effort involved in maintaining separate files for each victim, as the state still had to regulate outstanding credits and debts. Even intellectual property, such as the proceeds from patents and copyright royalties, were seized.[41]

The special value of cultural property, including artworks, books, and archives, called into existence a number of extraordinary German collecting agencies that operated throughout Europe. For example, the Einsatzstab Reichsleiter Rosenberg [Rosenberg Operational Staff] (ERR) followed the German Army into newly occupied territories to secure some of the most valuable items for the Party's own ideological institutions. Among the competitors for cultural property were the Foreign Office, the Wehrmacht, the Dienststelle Mühlmann subordinate to Reichskommissar Seyss-Inquart in the Netherlands, Himmler's Ahnenerbe, and also various sections of the Reichssicherheitshauptamt [Reich Security Main Office] (RSHA).[42] As several of these agencies, but especially the ERR, acted in a number of countries, they might provide a useful perspective for specific comparative studies.

Jewish communal property was largely handled by the Gestapo, either through direct seizures or the management of communal organizations (such as the Reichsvereinigung) under Gestapo control. For instance, Eichmann organized the liquidation of assets belonging to the Jewish communities in Austria that was largely completed by 1941.[43]

What role did Jewish property play in the development of the Holocaust? Even before the Nazis came to power they used envy and exaggerated claims about the influence of Jewish wealth to stir up antisemitic feelings. In particular, the Nazis viewed Jewish wealth as ill-gotten gains that had to be brought back into the possession of the German people. Jewish property was used to reward Party "Old Fighters" who sought compensation for alleged economic losses in the past.[44] The radicalization of measures taken against the Jewish population from 1938 onwards was closely linked to a full-scale assault on their property rights. Economic discrimination and plunder contributed directly to the Nazi process of destruction in a variety of ways. Ever-diminishing means reduced the opportunities for Jews to emigrate and flee, and ultimately wore down their physical ability to resist.

At the direct level of implementation, the prospect of booty helped to motivate local collaborators in the pogroms and massacres orchestrated by

German security forces in the East.[45] In some cases the names of the victims are even included in property lists sent back to the Reichshauptkasse of the Reichsbank in Berlin, where officials also summarized the accompanying letters noting that some property originated from the shooting of Jews.[46] This demonstrates how the processing of property helped spread a certain awareness of the on-going Holocaust throughout Europe.

What can such detailed property records tell us about the lives of the Jewish victims and their experience of the confiscation process? Detailed property inventories, whether created for the purposes of emigration or listing what remained at the time of deportation, can provide some image of how people lived. For survivors and the relatives of those who died, personal items, such as family portraits, photographs, or even furniture, provide a unique link with the past. The extensive records of both confiscation and restitution can provide valuable clues to the otherwise unknown fate of individuals. Such documents already provide a key resource for genealogists and local historians. The careful work of two scholars in Münster, reconstructing the lives of the local Jewish community with the aid of financial documentation, demonstrates the wealth of detail to be found in these records.[47] Jewish memorial books and survivor memoirs are replete with harrowing descriptions of the progressive seizure of property, often viewed as a clear reflection of local antisemitism.[48]

In most occupied areas the Germans relied to a considerable extent on the cooperation of the local administration, institutions, and population.[49] In the Netherlands, for instance, German officials expressed repeated concerns about the willingness of Dutch banks to comply fully with German registration and confiscation measures.[50] The main problem facing the administration of Jewish property almost everywhere, however, was corruption rather than sabotage. Just as the Nazi Party and its members claimed their share of the spoils in the Reich, so collaborationist organizations, such as the Norwegian Nazi Party or the Belorussian Self-Help Organization, exploited access to Jewish property to reward themselves and their followers and to distribute patronage.[51]

A very important question is the extent to which collaborating regimes initiated confiscation measures themselves. For the French in particular, concerns to defend their own sovereignty with regard to the spoliation of the Jews encouraged them to seize the initiative in order to retain control of the process. In Romania the government introduced indigenous antisemitic legislation and plundering largely without direct German prompting. Many of the mechanisms, however, reflected similar measures in Germany, if there were also certain unique aspects to the "Romanianization" of the economy.[52] In spite of the belated nature of measures taken in Hungary in 1944, the active participation of the Hungarian administration in the economic expropriation of the Jews reveals some autonomy from the Germans in this sphere.[53] The work of Professor Seibel and his team of researchers examining the Holocaust and polycracy in Western Europe demonstrates the insights to be gained from the comparative study of such political horse-trading or "log-rolling" as Seibel calls it, involved in the implementation of the seizure of Jewish assets.[54]

Who were the main beneficiaries from plundered Jewish property and where did the proceeds go? Despite the widespread incidence of private plunder and corruption, there is no doubt that the seizure of Jewish property in Europe was primarily a state-directed process linked closely to the development of the Holocaust. However, the widespread participation of the local population as beneficiaries from Jewish property served to spread complicity, and therefore also acceptance of German measures against the Jews, beyond the smaller circle of immediate perpetrators. In this way the Nazis and their collaborators were able to mobilize society in support of Nazi racial policies to a greater extent than the spread of racial antisemitism alone would have permitted. Thus the existence of "economic antisemitism" and opportunism must be incorporated into interpretations of the Holocaust based on Nazi ideological beliefs alone. Of particular interest might be a comparison of the number and nature of requests for Jewish property from the local population, which are surprisingly numerous in the archives of many countries. These frequently include assertions of one's loyalty and service to the Nazi Party and regime; in Latvia one policeman even boasted of his active participation in anti-Jewish actions.[55]

Interpreting individual motivation is one of the hardest questions to answer on the basis of the available sources. Frequently, it is only possible to surmise people's motives from the evidence of their words and deeds. Nevertheless a comparison of the treatment of Jewish property with other state expropriation policies, such as the treatment of Polish property (also confiscated by the Haupttreuhandstelle Ost) may shed further light both on the development of government measures and also the responses of society.

The main divergences in the nature of property confiscation are those between its implementation in Eastern and Western Europe, derived mainly from Germany's occupation policies. Nevertheless, there remain certain mechanisms and responses that are comparable throughout Europe, not least regarding the strategies followed by allies of Nazi Germany, where political considerations (often linked to Germany's fortunes in the war) played a key role.

In conclusion, what can we learn from a comparative perspective of the plunder and confiscation of Jewish property throughout Europe? The best use of comparative history is often to shed new light or gain a new perspective on aspects of national history that cannot be fully understood in isolation. The international and interrelated nature of property confiscation throughout Europe lends itself to detailed comparison for this reason. The recent work of national historical commissions, company historians, and other researchers has greatly increased our knowledge of the complex processes involved and also the archival resources available on property seizure.[56] Going beyond the raw data, it is now appropriate to develop new interpretations and analyses using a broader comparative approach. Both the implementation of spoliation and the extent of indigenous participation may be assessed more effectively in this international context.

Ironically, just as property restitution cannot be fully understood without first researching the full extent of Aryanization, confiscation, and plunder, so too the study of these topics is now benefitting greatly from the gradual opening of the restitution archives and the intense international interest in resolving outstanding historical legacies. This in turn helps us to understand better the role of property issues within the development of the Holocaust itself. Despite the many obstacles to be overcome, the skillful application of comparative history can provide historians with fresh ammunition to pursue historical debates from a new angle using unconventional means.

Notes

1. The assertions, arguments and conclusions in this chapter are those of the author. They do not necessarily reflect the opinions of the United States Holocaust Memorial Museum or the United States Holocaust Memorial Council.
2. For a rough estimate of Jewish population and property structures for six major European countries, see Helen B. Junz, "Report on the Pre-war Wealth Position of the Jewish Population in Nazi-Occupied Countries, Germany and Austria" in Independent Committee of Eminent Persons, *Report on Dormant Accounts of Victims of Nazi Persecution in Swiss Banks* (December 1999), Appendix S.
3. See, for example, Joseph Billig, *Le Commissariat General aux Questions Juives, 1941–1944*, 3 vols. (Paris, 1955–1957), vol. 1, 46.
4. Martin Dean, "Seizure, Registration, Rental and Sale: the Strange Case of the German Administration of Moveable Property in Latvia (1941–1944)," in *Latvia in World War II: Materials of an International Conference, 14–15 June 1999, Riga* (Riga, 2000), 372-78.
5. With regard to Germany, see in particular the article by Frank Bajohr in this volume.
6. See, for example, the key role of Dr. Hans Fischböck in developing Aryanization and confiscation methods in both the Reich and the German-occupied Netherlands.
7. See Martin Dean, "The Economic Final Solution: The Interrelations of Nazi Emigration, Confiscation and Deportation Policies towards the Jews, 1938–43," unpublished paper prepared for the International Conference "Generations of Genocide," organized by the Wiener Library in London, 26–27 January, 2002.
8. On some of the peculiarities of transfers, see especially Johannes Paulmann, "Internationaler Vergleich und interkultureller Transfer: Zwei Forschungsansätze zur europäischen Geschichte des 18. bis 20. Jahrhunderts," *Historische Zeitschrift* 267 (1998): 649–85.
9. See, for example, *Plunder and Restitution: The U.S. and Holocaust Victims' Assets: Findings and Recommendations of the Presidential Advisory Commission on Holocaust Assets in the United States and Staff Report* (Washington, DC, Dec. 2000), SR-14-16.
10. On the circumstances surrounding the introduction of these laws, which were not in themselves directed specifically against the Jews, see Gerlinde Grahn, "Die Enteignung des Vermögens der Arbeiterbewegung und der politischen Emigration 1933 bis 1945," *1999*, Heft 3 (1997): 13–38.
11. See Bundesarchiv Lichterfelde (BAL), R58/62, Heydrich to Gestapo Leitstellen, 12 April 1937 and RFSS (Himmler) to das Geheime Staatspolizeiamt, Berlin, 30 March 1937; see also Hans Georg Lehmann, "Acht und Ächtung politischer Gegner im Dritten Reich: Die Ausbürgerung deutscher Emigranten 1933–45," in *Die Ausbürgerung deutscher Staats-*

angehöriger 1933–45 nach den im Reichsanzeiger veröffentlichten Listen, ed. M. Hepp, 3 vols. (Munich, 1988), here xiii–xiv.

12. BAL, R2/5977, RFM undated memo 330/35.
13. Gerd Blumberg, "Etappen der Verfolgung und Ausraubung und ihre bürokratische Apparatur," in *Verfolgung und Verwaltung: Die wirtschaftliche Ausplünderung der Juden und die westfälischen Finanzbehörden*, ed. A. Kenkmann and B-A. Rusinek (Münster, 1999), 32; see also BAL, R139II/110–13, for examples of Security Orders issued in the fall of 1939 in Thuringia.
14. See Gerard Aalders, *Geraubt! Die Enteignung jüdischen Besitzes im Zweiten Weltkrieg* (Cologne, 2000), 398; *The Reisel/Bruland Report on the Confiscation of Jewish Property in Norway* (Part of Official Norwegian Report 1997, 22) (Oslo, June 1997), 24.
15. H. Genschel, *Die Verdrängung der Juden aus der Wirtschaft im Dritten Reich*, (Göttingen, 1966), 172.
16. For the files of the *Deutsche Revisions- und Treuhand AG*, see BAL R8135.
17. R. Hilberg, *Die Vernichtung der europäischen Juden* (Frankfurt am Main, 1990), vol. 1, 145.
18. On the extortion of gold from the Jews in Rome, see S. Zuccotti, *Under His Very Windows: The Vatican and the Holocaust in Italy* (New Haven, 2000), 153–55; for Minsk, see Bernhard Chiari, *Alltag hinter der Front. Besatzung, Kollaboration und Widerstand in Weissrusland, 1941–1944* (Düsseldorf, 1998), 261–62.
19. See Republique Francaise, *Mission d'étude sur la spoliation des Juifs de France, Vol. 1 La spoliation financière* (Paris, March 2000), 3–6, L'amende imposée en zone occupée en decembre 1941.
20. See especially Martin Dean, "Seizure of Jewish Property and Inter-Agency Rivalry in the Reich and in the Occupied Soviet Territories" in W. Seibel and G. Feldman, eds., *Networks of Nazi Persecution: Division-of-Labor in the Holocaust* (New York, 2005): 88–102.
21. See H. G. Adler, *Der Verwaltete Mensch* (Tübingen, 1974), 562–71.
22. *Reichsgesetzblatt* (Jahrgang 1941) Teil I, 722–24 (26 November 1941) Elfte VO. zum Reichsbürgergesetz. Vom 25. November 1941. This has been published in *Schriftenreihe des Bundesamtes zur Regelung offener Vermögensfragen Heft* 6, *Behandlung der vermögensrechtlichen Ansprüche der NS-Verfolgten* (Berlin, 1994), 227–29.
23. Joseph Michman, "Planning for the Final Solution Against the Background of Developments in Holland in 1941," *Yad Vashem Studies* XVII (1986): 145–80.
24. I am grateful to Jean-Marc Dreyfus for pointing this out.
25. On the transport costs see, for example, Adler, *Verwaltete Mensch*, 457.
26. On the Netherlands, see A. J. van der Leeuw, "Der Griff des Reiches nach dem Judenvermögen" in *Studies over Nederland in oorlogstijd*, ed. A. H. Paape ('s-Gravenhage, 1972), 211–36, here 233; for Serbia, see U.S. National Archives, College Park (NARA), RG-238, T-75, Records of the Plenipotentiary for the Serbian Economy, roll 68, fr. 683, Report from Belgrade dated 5 March 1942.
27. *Reichsgesetzblatt* (Jahrgang 1941) Teil I, 722–24 (November 26, 1941) Elfte VO. zum Reichsbürgergesetz. Vom 25. November 1941.
28. For the Netherlands, see Aalders, *Geraubt!*, 245–47; for France, see J-M. Dreyfus, "L'aryanisation économique aux Pays-Bas (et sa comparison avec le cas français), 1940–1945," unpublished paper presented at the Center for Advanced Holocaust Studies, U.S. Holocaust Memorial Museum in summer 2001, 24.
29. See *'Nazi Gold' from Belarus: Documents and Materials* (Minsk, 1998), 110–13.
30. See Karl-Heinz Schlarp, *Wirtschaft und Besatzung in Serbien, 1941–1944: Ein Beitrag zur Nationalsozialistischen Wirtschaftspolitik in Südosteuropa* (Wiesbaden, 1986), 297.
31. According to estimates from the archive of the former Reich Finance Ministry, income from these "occupation costs" exceeded RM 47 billion during the war, see BAL, R2 Anh./51, 103.
32. For Belgium, see Services du Premier Ministre, *Les Biens des Victimes des Persécutions anti-juives en Belgique: Spoliation – Rétablissement des droits – Résultats de la Commis-*

sion d'étude [Rapport Final de la Commission d'étude sur le sort des biens des members de la Communauté juive de la Belgique spoilés ou délaissés pendant la guerre] July 2001.
33. Jean-Marc Dreyfus argues that in comparison with the Netherlands the implementation of spoliation in France was less complete and comprehensive; see Dreyfus, "L'aryanisation économique aux Pays-Bas," 22–26.
34. Frederick B. Chary, *The Bulgarian Jews and the Final Solution, 1940–1944* (London, 1972), 63.
35. The Commissariat général aux Questions juives employed over one thousand staff in 1944; see Wolfgang Seibel, "Perpetrator Networks and the Holocaust: Resuming the 'Functionalism' versus 'Intentionalism' Debate," paper prepared for the Annual Meeting of the American Political Science Association, September 2000, 29.
36. Aalders, *Geraubt!*, 202.
37. For an example of concerns about job security, see the criticism of party member Buck of the Nazi Party in Baden to *Generalkommissar Finanzen und Wirtschaft (Reichskommissariat Niederlanden)*, 12 February 1944, in BAL, R177/1245.
38. *The Reisel/Bruland Report*, 15–21; on the high administration costs, see also Dean, "Seizure, Registration, Rental and Sale," 375.
39. On the Vugesta, see Robert Holzbauer, "Einziehung volks- und staatsfeindlichen Vermögens im Lande Österreich, Die 'VUGESTA' – die 'Verwertungsstelle für jüdisches Umzugsgut der Gestapo,'" *Spurensuche* 1–2 (2000): 38–50.
40. For a similar breakdown of property types seen from the perspective of restitution, see NARA, RG-260, 390/44/20/01, Box 3, Berlin Restitution Reports: Loewenthal report to Property Division, 19 December 1949.
41. See, for example, Republique Française, *Summary of the Work by the Study Mission on the Spoliation of the Jews in France* (Paris, April 2000), 37–38 on the confiscation of royalties.
42. For the "polycratic" nature of Nazi cultural plunder, see Jonathan Petropoulos, *Art as Politics in the Third Reich* (Chapel Hill, NC, 1996), 130; for the occupied Soviet territories, see Gabriele Freitag and Andreas Grenzer, "Der nationalsozialistische Kunstraub in der Sowjetunion" in *"Betr.: Sicherstellung": NS-Kunstraub in der Sowjetunion*, ed. W. Eichwede and U. Hartung (Bremen, 1998), 20–66; on the role of the RSHA, see Patricia Kennedy Grimsted, "Twice Plundered or 'Twice Saved'? Identifying Russia's 'Trophy' Archives and the Loot of the Reichssicherheitshauptamt," *Holocaust and Genocide Studies*, 15, No. 2 (Fall 2001): 191–244.
43. BAL, R8135 (80 Re. 3)/69, Bericht der Dt. Revisions- und Treuhand AG Zweigniederlassung Wien über die bei dem Sonderbevollmächtigten für das Vermögen der Israelischen Kultusgemeinden in der Ostmark, 25 September 1940.
44. See Gerhard Botz, *Wohnungspolitik und Judendeportation in Wien 1938 bis 1945* (Vienna, 1975), 120.
45. Martin Dean, *Collaboration in the Holocaust: Crimes of the Local Police in Belorussia and Ukraine, 1941–44* (London, 2000), 97.
46. Martin Dean, "Jewish Property Seized in the Occupied Soviet Union in 1941 and 1942: The Records of the *Reichshauptkasse Beutestelle*," *Holocaust and Genocide Studies*, Vol. 14, No. 1 (Spring 2000): 83–101.
47. Gisela Möllenhoff, Rita Schlautmann-Overmeyer (eds.), *Jüdische Familien in Münster 1918 bis 1945 Teil 1: Biographisches Lexikon* (Münster, 1995).
48. For example, see Martin Dean, "Die Enteignung des jüdischen Vermögens im Reichskommissariat Ostland, 1941–1944," in *"Arisierung" im Nationalsozialismus: Volksgemeinschaft, Raub und Gedächtnis*, ed. I. Wojak and P. Hayes, *Jahrbuch des Fritz Bauer Instituts*, Band 4 (2000).
49. For France, see Billig, *Commissariat General*, vol. 1, 25.
50. Aalders, *Geraubt!*, 315–16. Nevertheless there was considerable cooperation by Dutch financial institutions in German Aryanization policies, for example with regard to the sale of confiscated Jewish shares.
51. See *The Reisel/Bruland Report*, 19 and Chiari, *Alltag*, 114–22 and 259.

52. See Jean Ancel, "Seizure of Jewish Property in Romania" in *Confiscation of Jewish Property in Europe, 1933-1945: New Sources and Perspectives* (Washington, DC: Center for Advanced Holocaust Studies, U. S. Holocaust Memorial Museum, 2003), 43–55.
53. For a very brief summary of the measures taken to dispossess Hungarian Jews in 1944, see Gabor Kadar and Zoltan Vagi, *Holocaust Looted Assets of Hungarian Jewry: A Case Study on American Policy* (Budapest, 2000), 16–20.
54. See Wolfgang Seibel, "Perpetrator Networks and the Holocaust: Resuming the 'Functionalism' versus 'Intentionalism' Debate," paper given at the 2000 Annual Meeting of the American Political Science Association (September, 2000).
55. Martin Dean, "Seizure, Registration," 373.
56. See, especially, the recent French and Belgian reports for detailed reviews of the archival sources. Good examples of company histories include Gerald Feldman, *Die Allianz und die deutsche Versicherungswirtschaft 1933–1945* (Munich, 2001) and Jonathan Steinberg, *The Deutsche Bank and Its Gold Transactions during the Second World War* (Munich, 1999); in both cases the authors were supported by teams of able researchers.

ARYANIZATION AND RESTITUTION IN GERMANY

Frank Bajohr

Aryanization as a Political Process

The concept of Aryanization after 1933 signified more than just the transfer of property from Jewish to so-called Aryan ownership. In its broader sense, it also encompassed the gradual expulsion of the Jews from economic life, a process that usually preceded the transfer of assets and their ownership.[1] In its entirety, Aryanization constituted one of the largest transformations in property ownership in modern German history. It is true that the great majority of the approximately 100,000 Jews who were self-employed in Germany liquidated their shops or firms, dissolving them either voluntarily or by official order. The consequence was that less than half of Jewish firms passed intact into Aryan hands. But even the liquidation of a Jewish business involved a massive transfer of assets, since the warehouse stock, shelf inventory, and market share of a Jewish firm were channeled to its competitors. The Aryanization and liquidation of Jewish firms in the German Reich after 1933 was not a sudden phenomenon; not until 1938 did it take on uniform and systematic bureaucratic features. Aryanization in Germany within its 1937 borders was a prolonged political process. It began slowly, reaching its high point in 1938–1939 after several radical shifts of gear. This was in marked contrast to practices in the territories annexed or incorporated into the Reich in 1938–1939, where Aryanization was characterized by a bureaucratic centralism, mixed in part with violent and anarchic forms of property appropriation that assumed extreme proportions in Austria in the spring of 1938.

The boycott actions of the NSDAP in the spring of 1933 had clearly underscored the long-term goal of the new rulers: namely, to destroy the economic existence of the Jews in Germany. At the same time, however, for years the Reich Interior and Economics Ministries in particular sought to maintain the fiction in their pronouncements that Jews enjoyed "freedom

---

Notes for this section begin on page 50.

of economic activity" in National Socialist Germany. While antisemitic activists in the Party and in some, especially medium-sized, businesses pressed for the elimination of Jews from the economy, the government took a more reserved line in the early years of Nazi rule. This was primarily for tactical reasons arising from concern for the broader economic situation, foreign public opinion, and calls abroad for the boycott of German goods. Ultimately this reserve also had deep-seated ideological motives, as the National Socialists initially wanted to avoid a head-on confrontation with the purported "power of international Jewry." Once the economic recovery forged ahead rapidly after 1933, accompanied by concerted efforts for rearmament and the fast-paced consolidation of the National Socialist regime domestically and in foreign policy, the reasons for this tactical reserve gradually evaporated. Now the process of expelling the Jews from the economy was radicalized in a series of phases.

Remarkably, Aryanization in the Altreich (1937 borders) did not emanate from some central law on Aryanization or expropriation, nor was there any national authorizing body that orchestrated the process. The national government concentrated essentially on fiscal and monetary aspects, seeking to confiscate Jewish assets by means of taxes and special levies. It chose to delegate the concrete procedures of Aryanization, however, mainly to regional decision-makers. Consequently, even at the high point of Aryanization in 1938–1939, the Reich Economics Ministry continued to play only a marginal role, functioning exclusively as an institution where complaints could be lodged. It reserved the right to decide only in the case of firms with more than one thousand employees. Instead, Aryanization was distinguished by its multifaceted architecture; there were a large number of decision-makers and participating bodies, which also varied according to local conditions in each region. Outside the large urban centers, it was often mayors, district administrators and representatives of the local party organizations that concerned themselves with Aryanization. In the large cities, the local economic authorities dominated the decision-making process, in particular, the Gau economic advisers of the Nazi Party bureaucracy. In some towns such as Munich or regions like Thuringia and the Saar-Palatinate, the Gau Party leadership set up its own Aryanization offices or private property associations. These pursued the Aryanization of Jewish property with singular ruthlessness, pocketing "forced contributions" to augment the covert financing of regional and local party organizations and their functionaries. The practice of these newly created institutions, such as the Hamburg Real Estate Administration Corporation of 1938 Ltd., the Foundation Wirtschaftsdank Württemberg, the Saarpfälzische Vermögensgesellschaft, the Erich Koch Foundation, and similar obscure Nazi front organizations, was a clear demonstration that Aryanization was also a field in which National Socialist corruption crystallized and flourished.[2]

Creeping radicalization and the multiplicity of diverse institutions involved created a wide variety of conditions for the Aryanization of Jewish enterprises, which changed especially over time. In retrospect it is possible to identify at least five stages of radicalization: (1) the inclusion in 1935–1936 of the NSDAP Gau economic advisers as responsible for the authorization of Aryanization contracts; (2) the tightening of legislation on foreign exchange and also of its implementation in 1936–1937; (3) the increasingly anti-Jewish activity of the Reich Economics Ministry in 1937–1938; (4) intensified Aryanization by government decree from May 1938; and (5) the open transition to compulsory Aryanization after the Kristallnacht pogrom in November 1938.

In the early years under National Socialism, it was still possible to negotiate a halfway decent sale price for a Jewish-owned firm. Despite the oppressive political context and the conditions imposed on Jewish property owners, they frequently managed to sell their firms at prices that included not only the value of inventory and warehouse stock but also the nonmaterial value of the firm, its so-called good will. The latter consisted of the market position and reputation of the enterprise, its range of products, clientele, business relations, and distribution network. Of course, right from the start, the foreign exchange policies of the Reich severely restricted the ability of Jewish owners to transfer abroad more than a fraction of the proceeds from sale. Thus, the Reich Flight Tax, introduced in 1931 under Chancellor Brüning in connection with reparations policy, evolved under the influence of subsequent amendments into an anti-Jewish compulsory levy. From May 1934 on, it was applied to all cases involving property in excess of RM 50,000.[3] In addition, emigrants transferring funds abroad were required to pay a special levy to the German Gold Discount Bank (Dego). In August 1934, this amounted to 65 percent of the total sum transferred. By 1939, the levy had been increased in stages to a staggering 96 percent. There was one important exception: emigrants to Palestine were permitted to transfer a relatively large proportion of their assets to Palestine. This arrangement had been made possible in the summer of 1933 by the Ha'avara Agreement between the Reich Economics Ministry and Jewish organizations.[4]

In 1935–1936, the Gau economic advisers appointed by the Nazi Party took on a new set of functions, becoming directly involved in Aryanization.[5] They were subordinate to the Commission for Economic Policy under the NSDAP senior official Bernhard Köhler in Munich. Among other things, Köhler championed the idea of a "race war in the economy." Throughout the Gau districts, the economic advisers moved to gain control over sales contracts between Jewish entrepreneurs and Aryan buyers, making them subject to their formal approval. In this way they tried to steer Aryanizations in accordance with the aims and interests of the Party. In concrete terms, that meant favoritism toward Nazi Party members among potential purchasers, preventing the "formation of large combines," promoting the younger entrepreneurial generation, and the elimination of "typically Jewish" business names. In particular, these Gau advisers tried to ensure, as the Hamburg representative phrased it, that "the Jew did not receive an inappropriately high price" for his property. Consequently, it was rare for any amount to be allotted for the firm's good will. Shelf inventory and warehouse stocks were intentionally undervalued, thereby arbitrarily depressing the final sale price. Frequently, this price-shaving occurred in close cooperation with the purchaser, who naturally had scant interest in a high final price. In some Gau districts such as Hamburg, the Gau economic advisers were able to establish themselves as the sole authority for authorization and inspection. In others, such as Westphalia-South or Baden, they were able to achieve only a more limited right of mere participation in the final decision.[6] In any event, this activity by Nazi Party Gau economic advisers put a formal end to the previous official freedom of contract for Jewish entrepreneurs.

In 1936–1937, the creeping exclusion of Jewish entrepreneurs reached a new level of escalation when the government drastically altered its foreign exchange policy.[7] In their ultimate effect, the establishment of a Foreign Exchange Investigation Office headed by Reinhard Heydrich on 1 August 1936, the expansion of checks on foreign exchange transactions, and the revision of the foreign exchange law on 1 December 1936 were all aimed at Jewish entrepreneurs in particular. Jewish import/export firms were especially hard-hit by tightened restrictions aggressively applied by the Foreign Exchange Control Offices of the Regional Finance Administrations. Paragraph 37a of the foreign exchange law permitted these offices, in the case of even the slightest suspicion of a capital flight violation, to strip owners of all their rights to dispose over their assets, and to appoint trustees to take over the running of the firm. Since according to an instruction issued by the Reich Economics Ministry, Jews were to be viewed fundamentally as under "suspicion of capital flight," paragraph 37a in the foreign exchange law developed into a veritable lever for implementing expropriation, arbitrarily defined and interpreted. Beginning in 1936–1937, numerous Jewish firms active in import and export fell victim to this section of the law. The functionalization of policy on foreign exchange against Jewish firms also made it clear that the intensification of anti-Jewish policy did not stem solely from the actions of the Nazi Party or the "prerogative state" (*Maßnahmenstaat*). The "normative state" also contributed to this development in the form of the Foreign Exchange Control Offices. These tended to divorce themselves from behavior anchored in binding norms, even perceiving this to be a welcome liberation from the constraints of the rule of law.[8]

In the older research literature, the dismissal of the Reich Economics Minister Schacht in the autumn of 1937 and the subordination of the ministry to Hermann Göring, Plenipotentiary for the Four-Year Plan, is sometimes viewed as the "decisive turning point" in anti-Jewish policy.[9] This is doubtless exaggerated, since on the whole the supposed "change of course" was more a shift in mood and symbolism; the person of Göring at the helm of the Reich Economics Ministry tended to embolden local and regional party functionaries to step up anti-Jewish measures. Under Göring's direction, an office in the ministry, whose official function was to "prevent inadmissible interference in the economy" and was unofficially called the "Section for Protection of Jews" was transformed into the "Jewish Section."

It no longer intervened in favor of individual Jewish entrepreneurs, but rather set about the task of "ridding" the German economy of its Jews (*Entjudung*). When the Reich Economics Ministry gave a binding definition to the term "Jewish commercial enterprise" on 4 January 1938, it became clear for the first time that the central government had begun to abandon its previous more passive role in Aryanization.

This was amply manifest in the Decree on the Registration of Jewish Property, signed into law by Göring on 26 April 1938. The Decree obligated all Jews as defined by the Nuremberg Laws and whose assets exceeded RM 5,000 to report, list, and value their possessions. This move toward tighter government control over Jewish assets emerged primarily in response to events in Austria following its annexation by the German Reich. After the Anschluss, violence had erupted, especially in Vienna, marked by excesses against Jews and the uncontrolled appropriation of their property by Nazi Party members and others who jumped on the bandwagon. This was a warning sign, threatening to undermine the exclusive claim of the state to confiscate Jewish assets. All decrees issued in the following months were intended primarily to reassert this claim. By contrast, the government continued to be disinterested in the concrete details of Aryanization and the question of who received which Jewish firm and for what price. In the main, it still delegated responsibility in these matters to the regional institutions and authorities.

The final stage in the radicalization of Aryanization was reached in the aftermath of the November 1938 pogrom. It marked the transition to compulsory Aryanization imposed by the state. The first Decree on the Exclusion of Jews from German Economic Life of 12 November 1938 prohibited all Jewish retail shops and instituted a ban on artisan workshops, effective 1 January 1939. The Decree on the Utilization of Jewish Property of 3 December 1938 introduced the liquidation or forced sale of all other Jewish commercial establishments. In the wake of the November pogrom, thousands of Jewish businessmen had been arrested and confined in concentration camps. The trustees appointed to oversee the orphaned businesses were now able to sell these companies without the agreement of the owner, whose rights had basically been reduced to putting his signature on the sales contract. In some cases, the Jewish businessman was even marched in to sign the contract in his prison uniform.

In the wake of the November pogrom, the market value and selling price of Jewish firms plummeted. The National Socialist state still showed little interest in the nitty-gritty details of individual Aryanizations. Instead it pressed ahead with the confiscation of Jewish assets, employing new taxes and levies to this end, such as the November 1938 Jewish Property Levy, a compulsory contribution of more than one billion Reichsmark to the coffers of the Reich imposed after the pogrom. Jews were required to offer the German Reich jewelry, precious stones, and art objects "for sale." As a rule, the government paid Jewish owners less than a sixth of the actual market value of such assets.[10] In the case of emigration, Jews after 1938–1939 were in fact plundered by the German Reich. After stripping the person of citizenship, any assets unsold fell to the possession of the Reich. This was a measure made obligatory by the 11th Decree to the Reich Citizenship Law of 25 November 1941. The assets of deported Jews were also taken over by the Reich. Their remaining possessions were turned into cash by the "Property Utilization Offices" of the Regional Finance Offices, usually by public auction. Without the unscrupulous participation of hundreds of thousands of "bargain hunters" from all segments of the population, the massive "utilization" of property would not have been possible in this form.

Aryanization and German Society

The Aryanization of Jewish firms and the subsequent confiscations of assets were not just a complex political but also a social process. Jews and non-Jews encountered one another in the economy in a variety of functions and roles: as business partners and competitors, as employers and employees, as business owners and customers, as sellers and buyers of firms.[11] It is inaccurate to characterize the prevailing attitude within German society toward Aryanization as acquiescence or toleration. Governance and society did not exist as unconnected parallel spheres, but rather they interacted in numerous ways within Aryanization. National Socialist rule was not a mere dictatorship from above—it was a social practice in which German society was directly involved in many ways. Precisely the example of Aryanization demonstrates how a process that was essentially ideological came to incorporate highly diverse motivations and interests, especially material ones. These then contributed to a progressive and deepening radicalization of the entire process. In this manner, the persecution of the Jews in general and Aryanization in particular evolved into an "over-determined set of events" (Wolfgang Seibel).[12] In retrospect, it is not always possible to distinguish clearly between interests and ideological motives. For example, the antisemitism especially among artisans and retail merchants in the medium-sized business sector, directed against Jewish chain stores and department stores, was marked by a specific amalgam of ideology and personal interest.

Already in the spring of 1933, a boycott movement crystallized which was not controlled by NSDAP party organizations and operated largely outside any institutional framework.[13] Owners of medium-sized firms in particular exploited the opportune political climate to denounce Jewish competitors, pressing to augment their share of the market in the wake of the "national uprising." In the advertisement section of the press, many owners of firms, in a display of ardent nationalism, endeavored to present themselves as "true German men": they praised their products to the skies by excessive use of the adjective "German," and an antisemitic mentality of excluding the "other" was common, spliced with highly selfish motives. "True Germans" or the owners of "traditional Christian businesses" proffered their patriotic wares, extolling their "German cash registers,"

"German eggs," or "high-quality German bicycles." Even dealers in oriental rugs praised their carpeting as "German" or "racially indigenous."[14]

The exclusion of Jews from economic and professional associations, often against the express will of the Reich Economics Ministry, was frequently associated with attempts to enhance exclusive privileges of various kinds for the remaining members—for example, with regard to access to markets and trade fairs. Jews were excluded at the initiative of members, not by means of a directive "from above," from the Reich Association of German Realtors, the Reich Association of Commercial Representatives, the Reich Professional League of the German Newspaper and Magazine Agents, and the Reich Association of Traveling Traders. When the regional governor in Düsseldorf noted in a report for March/April 1935 that numerous measures against Jewish firms had been "heavily influenced by economic interests,"[15] he was only giving expression to the fact that for their own personal advantage many people sought to combine their interests with the prevailing political conditions and framework.

The actual process of Aryanization would never had succeeded had it not been for a large number of social go-betweens and intermediaries who helped forge the contacts necessary for making deals while reconnoitering the political terrain. The German banking industry fulfilled a key function here as middleman and financier.[16] The banks supplied numerous contacts between Jewish owners and Aryan buyers and also maintained close ties to the National Socialist institutions involved. By means of commissions and the granting of credit to Aryan purchasers, and partially also by acquiring a share in certain firms sold, the Aryanizations developed into a lucrative segment for the banks. This was true even if the potential profit that could accrue was only one of the motivating factors, as the struggle for gaining political influence took on increasing importance in an economy overdetermined by politics.[17] Also linked to the complexity and decentralized quality of Aryanization was the fact that the Deutsche Bank, for example, did not possess any uniform centrally-formulated strategy. Instead, the initiative of local branch managers, who in many instances subserviently sought to establish a special arrangement with the regional political elite, assumed considerable importance. Here was an example of "radicalization from below,"[18] with hands-on participation by numerous players rather than decisions taken by a small inner circle in some smoke-filled back room.

Realtors, attorneys, and trust companies were also active as intermediaries for Aryanization contracts. This segment of the real estate market was often marked by a high degree of specialization: thus, for example, there were realtors who concentrated on the sale of Jewish-owned pharmacies. The range of behavior by realtors and lawyers involved in Aryanizations was quite broad.[19] It extended from attorneys who primarily sought to represent the interests of their Jewish clients to intermediaries who worked together with government offices and tended to patronize their clients. At the extreme end of the scale were shysters who excelled in servility to the authorities—such as the estate agent who asked the local Gau economic adviser what price he deemed "suitable for the property, to ensure that the Jew would not receive too much for his land."[20]

The network of go-betweens attracted to Aryanization was loosely connected to a criminal milieu of confidence men and dishonest lawyers who lured Jewish entrepreneurs with false promises, often ruthlessly exploiting their distress for their own personal advantage. It extended from criminals who extorted "protection money" from Jewish shops to dubious swindlers who boasted about their supposedly close political ties with highly-placed Nazi functionaries, and then promptly absconded once they had been paid an attractive advance.[21] A Jewish entrepreneur ventured a telling comparison, likening some of the intermediaries with "vultures circling above the head of a man doomed to die."[22]

The Aryanizations imposed by fiat of the authorities from 1938 on extended the circle of those involved in sale transactions by including new groups of individuals and occupations. Experts and assessors appointed by the chambers of industry and commerce now entered the stage. In determining the value of inventory and warehouse stock of Jewish firms, they often participated in the scandalous reduction of the final knockdown price for the assets, which were forcibly sold. Aryanization commissions in the chambers of industry and commerce, which were made up of non-Jewish businessmen, had the power of decision over the sale or liquidation of Jewish firms. In this way, entrepreneurs were able to influence the fate of their Jewish competitors, who in the case of an order to liquidate were not even allowed to hold a clearance sale to recoup some of their losses. Rather, they were required to offer their stock on the shelf and in the warehouse at giveaway prices to the trade association (*Fachgruppe* in Nazi parlance), and thus to their competitors. After the November 1938 pogrom, thousands of trustees and administrators descended on Jewish firms, often granting themselves regal fees for their services. In some instances they even pocketed for themselves the firm they were administering as a trustee.

The accelerated implementation of Aryanization in the Altreich in 1938–1939 would likewise hardly have been feasible without the great "steeplechase for enrichment" among purchasers at the end of 1938, battling to snatch up a piece of the remaining Jewish firms. Almost all purchasers can be classified in behavioral terms into three characteristic groups: (1) the unscrupulous profiteers, who not only knew how to exploit the advantageous conditions of Aryanization to line their own pockets by means such as underpricing the value of inventory and warehouse stock, but also tried to have the selling price knocked down further by taking personal initiatives against the Jewish owners; (2) the "sleeping partners" of the Nazi regime, who tended to pursue their personal advantage in a less conspicuous manner, avoiding personal initiatives either against or in favor of the Jewish owners; (3) well-meaning purchasers who tried to give a proper and fair price to the Jewish owner, sometimes venturing down paths that were illegal in terms of National Socialist law. The behavior of the beneficiaries had a central impact on the accompanying circumstances and conditions of

Aryanization. In particular, the behavior of the "well-meaning" buyers demonstrated the extent to which all of them were free to act independently in their business transactions. This reveals a key dimension: the purchasers were not simply small dependent cogwheels within machinery that was politically driven. But such a typology of buyers should not be understood as some sort of static categorization. The work of Peter Hayes on Degussa and Aryanizations in large-scale industry has shown for example that the same purchaser could behave quite differently in various Aryanization procedures, and a "well-meaning" buyer in 1934 could turn out in 1938 to be an "unscrupulous profiteer."[23] In industry, it was the younger and upwardly mobile large firms such as Mannesmann, Otto Wolff, or Flick which profited from Aryanization rather than the older, more established companies. Other areas of the economy also reflected this, for example export firms, where numerous newcomers took over the export quotas and foreign exchange allotments of the Jewish firms, setting themselves up by means of this windfall. The benefit of Aryanization was especially striking for medium-sized businesses. By eliminating Jewish chain stores, and most especially through the massive liquidation of Jewish retail outlets and artisan shops, they were freed of unwanted competition.

But the conclusion of the sale of firms and forced liquidations in the Altreich in 1939–1940 did not spell an end to the process of Aryanization. It continued in the annexed or occupied territories, opening up additional opportunities for enrichment during the war. In the wake of the auctioning off and distribution of Jewish property that had been collected from across Europe, Aryanization was also expanded, now extending into broad segments of the population that had had little to do with the Aryanization of firms and real estate. These persons now participated quite centrally in the popular hunt for picking up a "bargain" at the public auctions of furniture and household goods.[24] Just in the city of Hamburg and its immediate environs in northern Germany, more than 100,000 people participated in such auctions. The poorest social strata, dependent on social welfare, were able to receive clothing from the storerooms of the Nazi charity organization NS-Volkswohlfahrt (NSV). In many cases, such garments still bore the yellow Star of David worn by their former owners.

On balance, Aryanization generated a growing circle of beneficiaries and profiteers who had a personal interest in not being held accountable for compensation by Jewish owners. In this way, their allegiance to the regime was cemented, or they willingly joined the ranks of its supporters. The instrumentalization of social interests had a radicalizing impact on the process of Aryanization. When so many people were choosing their own interests over moral scruples, one could no longer expect any moral objections. In this way, Aryanization contributed to the weakening of resistance within German society to the broader practice of Jewish persecution. That certainly reflected the strategy of the National Socialist rulers, since they assumed that the Germans would identify themselves more closely with the National Socialist regime, fighting more fanatically for "final victory" the more completely they had burned their moral bridges behind them. Writing in his diary in March 1943, Propaganda Minister Goebbels noted: "Especially when it comes to the Jewish Question, our course is laid out so firmly before us that it is now impossible to deviate from this path. And that is something positive. Experience shows that a movement and people that have burned their bridges behind them fight far more ruthlessly than those who still have an avenue open for retreat."[25] For this reason, it is not surprising when a Jewish entrepreneur from Hamburg who survived the Nazi period in a "privileged mixed marriage" observed in early 1945 that a segment of the population viewed the approaching Allied victory with great apprehension. He wrote in his diary that "many of those who took possession of Jewish homes and other articles are very afraid today that the Jews could return, and might then demand the return of their property. And even call the people to account for robbery and theft."[26]

Economic Exclusion and Social Isolation of Jewish Entrepreneurs

From the perspective of the Jewish owner, Aryanization was only one chapter in a complex personal history of persecution. Even the decision to sell one's possessions did not always spring from economic motives and active measures to drive the Jews from the economy. The situation of a Jewish businessman did not depend exclusively on the balance sheets of his firm. He experienced restrictions on his children's education, taking very personally the pain and humiliation inflicted on them by discrimination at school. The Nuremberg Laws had turned him into a second-class citizen. He was no longer allowed to enter parks, swimming pools, and theaters, and was barred from many vacation resorts. He was excluded from clubs and associations, and he was no longer invited to social functions and gatherings.

As Simone Lässig has shown in the example of the Dresden banking family Arnhold, Jewish entrepreneurs were sometimes harder hit by the social isolation imposed upon them than by economic discrimination.[27] While a member of the Arnhold family was still permitted after 1933 to serve on the board of the Dresden Stock Exchange Association, the Dresden Art Club excluded the Arnholds from membership, even though the family had been significantly involved as donors in building up the art collections in Dresden. That was also the case for social and scientific associations, to which the Arnholds had generously contributed. In the summer of 1935, even the Georg Arnhold Swimming Pool, which had been founded by the family, banned all Jews from its premises. The Arnhold children were no longer allowed to take part in school sports competitions, visits to the theater, or outings into the countryside. The only option open to the family was to visit a resort in Switzerland, while local vacation resorts in Saxony posted antisemitic signs at their gates barring Jews from entry. Such measures were a direct assault on the culturally defined "Germanness" of the Arnholds. Their German identity was undermined and their cultural and social achievements were systematically devalued. This was a process that went hand in hand with the ever more complete exclusion of the banking house from the economy.[28] Economic and social exclusion experienced by Jewish entrepreneurs fused into a complex trauma of persecution, which after 1945 became impossible to disentangle into separate strands of memory.

Moreover, Aryanization was for many not the negative highpoint of their story of persecution. The subsequent confiscation of assets by the Regional Finance Offices frequently took on more severe and humiliating forms, especially when persons did not emigrate until 1938–1939. It then entailed the total financial plundering of the Jewish owners. The Reich Flight Tax, Dego Levy, Jewish Property Levy, "compulsory contributions" to Nazi party institutions, and the emigration fund of the Gestapo added up to a crushing burden equivalent to their complete financial expropriation. Thus, for example, the Jewish entrepreneur Albert Aronson, who emigrated in September 1938 from Hamburg to Great Britain, was able to transfer abroad only 1.7 percent of his total worth of millions of Reichsmark. The German Reich expropriated 98.3 percent of his total assets.[29] Even the household effects of Jewish emigrants were searched in a humiliating ritual, as officials sifted through belongings looking for newly purchased goods. There was a heavy surcharge for such items, if found. Although the majority of Jewish entrepreneurs in Germany were able to emigrate up to 1939, and thus were spared deportation and murder, almost all of them lost family members, friends, and relatives in the Holocaust. Such personal tragedies were doubtless a far graver blow than the material losses they suffered.

Even those who had been able to save their lives by emigration often suffered for many years under the weight of the cumulative effects of persecution, which also cast a shadow over their new life in their land of immigration. An emigrant had to adapt to a totally strange and alien environment, and often experienced a steep decline in social status. Thus, after his emigration to the United States, the formerly prosperous owner of the Köhlbrand Docks, Paul Berendsohn, was obliged to work, at the age of 65, as an unskilled laborer in an American plastics factory.[30] The owner of the optical company Campbell & Co., Julius Flaschner, migrated to London in early 1939. The entire furnishings of his Hamburg villa were subsequently sold at public auction and the proceeds disappeared into the coffers of the German Reich. His property included a "French music salon in the style of Louis XVI," a "gentleman's room in oak," and a "living room in original Biedermeier style." Flaschner meanwhile lived in his London exile in the most destitute condition, especially since he was not granted a work permit and had no regular income of any kind. He eked out a bare existence with his wife in an unfurnished garret, lunching every day at his son-in-law's in order to save money on food.[31]

The loss of property and possessions was coupled with diverse psychosocial costs and nonmaterial losses for the Jewish owners. In a recent research report, Harald Welzer has stressed that material goods form an important constituent in the construction of personal identity.[32] Who can measure and assess the psychosocial burden for an individual forced to sell a family business handed down for generations, who now must view himself as a failure compared with the proud gallery of his successful forebears? Ultimately, the total worth of a company was not measured solely by its monetary value. In his cultural-sociological analysis of power, the French sociologist Pierre Bourdieu has pointed out that economic capital often serves as a means to acquire social and symbolic capital: social connections, status, recognition, and respect.[33] This was all the more true for a minority group that was never really fully accepted and integrated within German society. Consequently, many Jews associated economic and professional success with the desire for recognition and social integration. Aryanization put a sudden end not only to all hopes for integration. It also shattered one's personal sense of self-esteem and identity. After National Socialist racism had excluded Jews from the German racial People's Community, Aryanization eliminated any basis for the bourgeois identity, moored on material wealth, which many Jewish businessmen had nurtured. It was that amplified sense of self that had enabled them for a time to delude themselves about the real impact of Nazi racism.

Thus, for example, up to 1938 the Hamburg export merchant Edgar Eichholz possessed all the external regalia of a well-to-do entrepreneur, with his own firm, villa, servants, and luxury automobile.[34] He was long spared the experiences of profound humiliation and antisemitic violence, which since 1933 had been part of everyday life for many Jews, especially from the lower social strata. That is why Eichholz perceived his arrest after the November 1938 pogrom not only as a massive intrusion into his life, but also as a double degradation. Not only did he have to endure being ordered around by callow Schutzstaffel [Protection Squad] (SS) youths, 22-year-olds, who from his privileged perspective were far beneath him in social standing. On top of this, in his memoirs he comments bitterly that he was forced to share a cell and the same prison conditions with a young Jew, a "lousy petty cash boy." Eichholz, who felt he belonged to the mercantile elite of Hamburg, was now treated like a member of a criminal group, harassed by men whom National Socialism had elevated from the very dregs and periphery of society to the center of power. These young SS men had a sadistic glee in relishing this reversal in social relations. They relished making persons who resembled the cliché image of the "Jewish bigwig" the targets of their mockery and torments.[35] A report from the Sachsenhausen concentration camp noted significantly:

> The SS men, of whom almost none was older than 21, took a special pleasure in tormenting older, corpulent Jews who had a Jewish appearance and were of a higher social status, such as rabbis, teachers, lawyers. They were more lenient in their treatment of younger Jews with a more athletic look about them. Thus, a former high-ranking legal official, who had reported by announcing his title, was treated with especial harshness, and along with him the proprietor of a large restaurant was subjected to similar abuse.[36]

Education and possessions had determined the position of Jewish entrepreneurs in the pre-Nazi period, providing them with social standing and respect. By contrast, after 1933 they largely lost their former status in German society, itself transformed into a racist "folk community." Now declassé, they had become social outcasts, even members of a stigmatized pariah group that was no longer accorded any social prestige.

Take the example of Edgar Eichholz. Although he was able to survive in a "privileged mixed marriage," he was not spared further experiences of extreme humiliation and degradation. In 1943, after the maximum age for Jewish labor deployment had been increased from 55 to 65, he was made to do forced labor. The 63-year-old Eichholz, deployed as a laborer in the factory of a former friend and business colleague, had once been the director of a large-scale enterprise. Now he was forced to knead and pack rat poison with his bare hands. His other option would have been to work sweeping the streets.[37] The less wealthy Jews suffered smaller material losses, and thus comparatively less loss of symbolic social status. But as cherished objects were taken away, they too lost focal points of personal orientation of central importance for memory and identity. Consequently, the few objects that Jewish emigrants were permitted to take abroad with them were often preserved like personal relics. Almost all Jewish children permitted to migrate to Britain in 1938 as part of the children's transports still have the silver spoon they were allowed to take with them. And the tattered remnants of a childhood doll were also cherished and preserved if, as a gift from murdered family members, it remained one of the few objects that still reminded their owner of his or her lost loved ones.[38]

Problems of Restitution in the Atmosphere of the Postwar Years

After 1945, the legacy of Aryanization provided almost insurmountable difficulties for restitution.[39] It had been a complex political and social process accompanied by diverse material and nonmaterial losses, and entangled within a complex history of persecution. For this reason alone, it would be both naive and questionable to seek to assess the success or failure of restitution solely in terms of the material amount transferred. In this connection, five problems of restitution will be briefly sketched.

External Pressure and German Self-pity

Restitution after 1945 was limited to the territory of the Western zones of occupation and the Federal Republic of Germany (FRG), since the Soviet Union and the Communist German Democratic Republic (GDR) had no interest in compensating "Jewish capitalists" for material losses. Therefore, restitution in Eastern Germany could not begin before German reunification in 1990.[40] The whole process would not even have come about had it not been for the political pressure applied by the Western Allies, given that the social climate after 1945 was influenced by the previous widespread participation in Aryanization. A self-critical encounter with their own complicity was not on the agenda of most Germans at this time. Nor were they concerned with the social rehabilitation of the Jewish owners, whose property had been stolen. That would have presupposed a powerful break with the mentality and traditions of the National Socialist People's Community. On the other hand, persons who in the wake of the onslaught of National Socialism had profited in an especially flagrant manner from the expropriation of Jewish property could not expect much sympathy or even social solidarity from their compatriots. Yet more characteristic of the prevailing social atmosphere in the 1950s is that even a well-known party boss and Aryanization profiteer like Fritz Kiehn, owner of the Efka Works in Trossingen/Württemberg, was, after a few short years of social ostracism, rehabilitated and reintegrated into society, and even awarded the honorary citizenship of his hometown.[41] At times, it was not the original Jewish owners but the Aryan beneficiaries who claimed before the restitution courts that they themselves were "victims" of circumstance. This was a mental attitude with a long tradition in German history, as the National Socialists had portrayed themselves as victims of a Weimar system controlled by Jews and progressives, and after 1933 they had been vehement in their demands for due "compensation."[42] After 1945, self-pity often supplanted any sense of empathy with the Jewish victims of Aryanization.

Thus, shortly after the war, the managing director of the cigarette factory Garbáty in Berlin contacted the former Jewish owners who had emigrated to the United States, noting: "I suppose it goes pretty much without saying that in the meantime over here, we've gone through some difficult times."[43] Yet what the Jewish owners had suffered, stripped of their possessions and forced to leave the country—what truly difficult times they had endured—was not worth either a comment or even a question from this director of their former enterprise. This sheer ignorance vis-à-vis the material and nonmaterial losses of the Jewish owners—including especially the loss of their homeland and social standing—is all the more noteworthy since German society did not remain silent when it came to the fate of the expellees from the East, the *Heimatvertriebene,* who likewise in most cases had lost their native land and social position. The exclusion of the Jews from the national discourse of suffering after 1945 was a kind of extension of their previous social exclusion from the National Socialist People's Community.

Material Reductionism

Restitution also totally excluded the various non-material losses of the Jewish owners from consideration, reducing the complex experiences of persecution that Jewish owners had suffered to individual material aspects, even though the concept of *Wiedergutmachung* misleadingly suggested measures that went much further.

This material reductionism was further strengthened by the legal and procedural distinction made between compensation on the one hand and restitution on the other. In this way, compensation and restitution were often obscured, bogged down in the bureaucratic paperwork of precise point-by-point listings of individual material losses, which had to be painstakingly substantiated by the Jewish claimant. The dissatisfaction of many a Jewish claimant with this persnickety procedural maze was expressed in complex narratives that were in fact "autobiographies" of their persecution, appended by a number of claimants to their applications for restitution. In these narratives, they integrated the material losses into a description of numerous and painful experiences of persecution. In so doing, they shattered the frame of a routinized bureaucratic procedure, in which there was no provision for the full story of their persecution; on the contrary, within that procedure, individual material aspects were torn from the complex overall experience of persecution in which they were embedded.

One striking but representative example in Hamburg is the case of the Aryanization of a plot of land, in which the original Jewish owner reported in detail how he had emigrated in 1940 after selling the property. His plan was to create a new basis for his own existence and that of his family in his land of immigration. Though he intended to have his family join him, this plan proved impossible to realize after the prohibition on further Jewish emigration in October 1941. Instead, his wife, his two sons, seven and nine years old, and his elderly parents-in-law were deported at the end of 1941 to Riga, and murdered there shortly after their arrival. Here was a claimant who refused to bargain bureaucratically for the restitution of a plot of land without at least mentioning the fact that he had lost his entire family.

Underestimation of the Extent of Social Involvement

It is true that restitution turned the spotlight onto those who had acquired Jewish property, thus revealing the social context and complicity that Aryanization entailed. Yet numerous social intermediaries and profiteers were given scant consideration at this time. Only more recently has interest come to focus on them and their role, as for example in the case of the banking industry. The Allies likewise underestimated the extent of social involvement, proceeding from a view of dictatorship that concentrated on the role of the state; in their conception, Aryanization had been primarily the product of laws and ordinances of the Nazi state, and far less the result of a synergy between regime and society. That was evident for example in the central role accorded to the Nuremberg Laws of September 1935 for challenging the legality of the Aryanizations after the fact. This greatly overestimated the importance of the Nuremberg Laws, which actually had little concrete impact on Aryanization.

At the same time, most of the perpetrators behind Aryanization slipped into the shadows and vanished into the darkness of history. Aside from Munich, where the staff had physically manhandled Jews summoned to the local Aryanization Office and had been brought to trial for these offenses after 1945, I am unaware of any other cases in which an especially brutal or vicious treatment of Jewish owners was punished by the courts—or where, for example, the Aryanization experts of the Gau economic advisers were prosecuted. Even spiteful recipients of Jewish property, who were probably regarded in the main by the Allies as passive beneficiaries, were not held legally accountable for their behavior, at least not in the FRG.

Restitution as a Reenactment of Aryanization

Among the special features of many restitution cases was the circumstance that restitution reenacted to some extent the original scenario of Aryanization for those involved, though now with the players in different roles. Jewish former owners and Aryan beneficiaries now faced each other as parties "entitled to restitution" and "obligated to provide restitution." Many persons who had participated in some way in Aryanization were now summoned to the restitution proceedings as witnesses or experts—for example, assessors and tax experts, who during Aryanization had been appointed by the chambers of industry and commerce to assess the value of the inventory and warehouse stock of a Jewish firm. They had often given intentionally low estimates, in this way participating in the scandalous price shaving and manipulation. In the restitution proceedings after 1945, they showed little inclination for self-criticism; nor did the officials of the Foreign Exchange Control and Finance Offices. During the so-called Third Reich, these persons had helped organize the confiscation of Jewish assets and their financial plundering, and after 1945 they represented the financial interests of the Federal Republic as the legal successor state of the German Reich. The attorneys for both parties often had a characteristic past history of their own. In many instances, those arguing the case of the restitution claimants were attorneys who themselves had been the victim of political or "racial" persecution in the Nazi period, or who were outstanding representatives of a democratic-liberal group of attorneys.[44] By contrast, the defense lawyers of former Aryanizers were often former National Socialist lawyers who had been dismissed from the judicial service after 1945 and now preferred to represent the affairs of "former party members" and other dubious characters. Many original Jewish owners or their attorneys complained about the widespread denial of any personal culpability and the refusal to recognize the validity both of their claims and the legal basis for them.[45] This was due to a large extent to the personal complicity of so many people in the process of Aryanization in the immediate past. As a result, rather than heal old wounds, the process of restitution frequently gouged open new ones, reawakening traumatic memories of Aryanization.

Inherent Inadequacy of Restitution Proceedings

Numerous such restitution proceedings ended in an "amicable" settlement between the Jewish former owners and the Aryan beneficiaries. This granted the Jewish owners financial compensation but left the German beneficiaries as the now legal owners of the assets or property. In this way, restitution unintentionally served to affirm and validate the results of Aryanization, thus cementing the new distribution of ownership established in the Third Reich. In so doing, the Aryanizers were able effectively to pocket the social prestige, reputation, and tradition of the firms, the product of a long history of economic achievement, which they had acquired through the dubious means of Aryanization. The experiences of persecution and mass murder were too fresh and powerful, and militated against any large number of émigré entrepreneurs considering a permanent return to West Germany. This was compounded by the extent of massive wartime destruction and the problematic economic situation in postwar Germany, which did not encourage Jewish emigrants to return. As a whole, the problems of restitution demonstrate the inherent difficulty of establishing moral justice by legal means. The wheels of history obviously cannot be reversed, but this was particularly the case with regard to restitution.

There could be no *Wiedergutmachung* in the literal sense, nor can one imagine even in theory a legal procedure that could fully achieve this goal. Therefore, despite all criticism of the actual details of implementation, the positive effects of restitution should still not be underestimated. The main achievement was that it occurred at all, providing at least partial compensation for material losses. Since it legally branded Aryanization as an injustice, it may well have made it easier for many Jewish former owners to come to terms psychologically with this difficult chapter in their personal narratives of persecution. Nonetheless, the slow pace of numerous proceedings, the bureaucratic and officious treatment of many of those who suffered a harsh fate at the hands of their persecutors, and the reduction of that suffering to only a few specific material aspects, must in a great number of cases have engendered a sense of bitterness and disappointment. We still know too little about perceptions of people's experiences during restitution and how former Jewish owners came to grips with it over the longer term. Did they perceive the entire event as a credible change of heart by a "new Germany" turning away from its National Socialist past? Or were they painfully reminded in many respects of the unhappy memories of Aryanization and its dark era? Whatever path future research on restitution takes and whatever is brought to light, without the perspective of those actually affected—the subjects of these events—historians will doubtless run the risk of transposing into their own historical analysis the same reduction of human suffering to some material value that is inherent to the concept of restitution.

Translated from German by William Templer

Notes

1. The classic comprehensive studies of Aryanization by Genschel and Barkai are still of value; see Helmut Genschel, *Die Verdrängung der Juden aus der Wirtschaft im Dritten Reich* (Göttingen, 1966); Avraham Barkai, *Vom Boykott zur "Entjudung." Der wirtschaftliche Existenzkampf der Juden im Dritten Reich 1933–1943*, (Frankfurt, 1987) (English trans.: *From Boycott to Annihilation, The Economic Struggle of German Jews 1933–1943* [Hanover, 1989]). For more recent studies, see, *inter alia*, Frank Bajohr, *"Arisierung" in Hamburg. Die Verdrängung der jüdischen Unternehmer 1933–1945*, 3rd ed. (Hamburg, 2002) (English trans.: *'Aryanisation' in Hamburg. The Economic Exclusion of Jews and the Confiscation of their Property in Nazi Germany 1933–1945* (New York, 2002); Petra Bräutigam, *Mittelständische Unternehmer im Nationalsozialismus. Wirtschaftliche Entwicklungen und soziale Verhaltensweisen in der Schuh- und Lederindustrie Badens und Württembergs* (Munich, 1997), esp. 245–336; Alex Bruns-Wüstefeld, *Lohnende Geschäfte. Die 'Entjudung' der Wirtschaft am Beispiel Göttingens* (Hanover, 1997); Barbara Händler-Lachmann and Thomas Werther, *'Vergessene Geschäfte – verlorene Geschichte'. Jüdisches Wirtschaftsleben in Marburg und seine Vernichtung im Nationalsozialismus* (Marburg, 1992); Peter Hayes, "Big Business and 'Aryanisation' in Germany," *Jahrbuch für Antisemitismusforschung* 3 (1994): 254–81; Gerhard Kratzsch, *Der Gauwirtschaftsapparat der NSDAP. Menschenführung – 'Arisierung' – Wehrwirtschaft im Gau Westfalen-Süd* (Münster, 1989); Simone Ladwig-Winters, *Wertheim – ein Warenhausunternehmen und seine Eigentümer. Ein Beispiel der Entwicklung der Berliner Warenhäuser bis zur 'Arisierung'* (Münster, 1997); Dirk van Laak, "Die Mitwirkenden bei der 'Arisierung.' Dargestellt am Beispiel der rheinisch-westfälischen Industrieregion 1933–1940," in *Die Deutschen und die Judenverfolgung im Dritten Reich*, ed. Ursula Büttner (Hamburg, 1992), 231–57; Dirk van Laak, "'Arisierung' und Judenpolitik im 'Dritten Reich'. Zur wirtschaftlichen Ausschaltung der jüdischen Bevölkerung in der rheinisch-westfälischen Industrieregion" (state examination thesis, Essen, 1988); Angela Verse-Herrmann, *Die 'Arisierungen' in der Land- und Forstwirtschaft 1938–1942* (Stuttgart, 1997).
2. On this aspect, see Frank Bajohr, *Parvenüs und Profiteure. Korruption in der NS-Zeit* (Frankfurt a. M., 2001), esp. 112–16.
3. Dorothee Mußgnug, *Die Reichsfluchtsteuer 1931–1953* (Berlin, 1993); Martin Tarrab-Maslaton, *Rechtliche Strukturen der Diskriminierung der Juden im Dritten Reich* (Berlin, 1993).
4. On the Ha'avara Agreement, see Werner Feilchenfeld, Dolf Michaelis, and Ludwig Pinner, *Haavara-Transfer nach Palästina und Einwanderung deutscher Juden 1933–1939* (Tübingen, 1972); Yehuda Bauer, *Jews for Sale? Nazi-Jewish Negotiations 1933–1945* (New Haven, 1994), esp. 8–29; Avraham Barkai, "German Interests in the Haavara-Transfer Agreement 1933–1939," *Leo Baeck Institute Yearbook* 35 (1991): 245–66.
5. Bajohr, *'Aryanisation' in Hamburg*, from 142.
6. See Kratzsch, *Gauwirtschaftsapparat.*
7. On the following, see Bajohr, *'Aryanisation' in Hamburg*, 154–74.
8. On the distinction between the "normative state" and the "prerogative state," which appears increasingly problematic in the light of new empirical insights, see Ernst Fraenkel, *The Dual State. A Contribution to the Theory of Dictatorship* (New York, 1941).
9. See Uwe Dietrich Adam, *Judenpolitik im Dritten Reich* (Düsseldorf, 1972), 173. For a critique, see Albert Fischer, *Hjalmar Schacht und Deutschlands 'Judenfrage'. Der 'Wirtschaftsdiktator' und die Vertreibung der Juden aus der deutschen Wirtschaft* (Cologne, 1995); Barkai, *Boykott*, 69–73.
10. See now Ralf Banken, "Der Edelmetallsektor und die Verwertung konfiszierten jüdischen Vermögens im 'Dritten Reich.'" Ein Werkstattbericht über das Untersuchungsprojekt "Degussa AG" aus dem Forschungsinstitut für Sozial- und Wirtschaftsgeschichte an der Universität zu Köln, in *Jahrbuch für Wirtschaftsgeschichte* 1 (1999): 135–61.

11. On Aryanization as a social process, see Frank Bajohr, "'Arisierung' als gesellschaftlicher Prozeß. Verhalten, Strategien und Handlungsspielräume jüdischer Eigentümer und 'arischer' Erwerber," in *'Arisierung' im Nationalsozialismus. Volksgemeinschaft, Raub und Gedächtnis*, eds. I. Wojak and P. Hayes (Frankfurt a.M., 2000), 15–30; F. Bajohr, "Verfolgung aus gesellschaftsgeschichtlicher Perspektive. Die wirtschaftliche Existenzvernichtung der Juden und die deutsche Gesellschaft," *Geschichte und Gesellschaft* 26 (2000): 629–52.
12. Wolfgang Seibel, "Staatsstruktur und Massenmord. Was kann eine historisch-vergleichende Institutionenanalyse zur Erforschung des Holocaust beitragen?" *Geschichte und Gesellschaft* 24 (1998): 539–68.
13. On the following, see Bajohr, "Verfolgung aus gesellschaftsgeschichtlicher Perspektive," from 631.
14. Bajohr, *'Aryanisation' in Hamburg*, 30.
15. GStA Berlin-Dahlem, Rep. 90P, Lageberichte, 9.5, from 81.
16. Bernhard Lorentz, "Die Commerzbank und die 'Arisierung' im Altreich," *Vierteljahrshefte für Zeitgeschichte* 50 (2002): 237–68.
17. Harold James, *The Nazi Economic War against the Jews: The Expropriation of Jewish-owned Property* (Cambridge, 2001).
18. Ibid.
19. See Kratzsch, *Gauwirtschaftsapparat*, from 239.
20. Quoted in ibid., 242.
21. See Bajohr, *'Aryanisation' in Hamburg*, from 259.
22. Fritz V. Grünfeld, *Das Leinenhaus Grünfeld* (Berlin: Duncker & Humblat, 1967), p. 125.
23. Peter Hayes, "Die 'Arisierungen' der Degussa AG. Geschichte und Bilanz," in *'Arisierung' im Nationalsozialismus*, eds. Irmtrud Wojak and Peter Hayes, 85–123; Hayes, "Big Business," 254–81.
24. See Bajohr, *'Aryanisation' in Hamburg*, 277–82; Franziska Becker, *Gewalt und Gedächtnis. Erinnerungen an die nationalsozialistische Verfolgung einer jüdischen Landgemeinde* (Göttingen, 1994), 77–140; Wolfgang Dreßen, *Betrifft: 'Aktion 3.' Deutsche verwerten jüdische Nachbarn* (Berlin, 1998).
25. Quoted in Elke Fröhlich (ed.), *Die Tagebücher von Joseph Goebbels*, Part II, vol. 7 (Munich, 1993), 454, entry of 2 March 1943. Already in June 1941, Goebbels expressed this attitude in a memorable admission: "Anyhow, we've got so much against us that we had better come out of this the victors." Quoted in ibid., Part I, vol. 9, (Munich, 1998), 379, entry for 16 June 1941.
26. Quoted in the memoirs of Edgar Eichholz (1944/45), private collection, fol. 43. At the end of 1944, a young businessman said something similar to the American officer Saul K. Padover: "At least 80 percent of the Germans committed sins against the Jews. Not as a matter of conviction but due to selfishness, greed, the worst sin. Now their conscience is troubling them, and they're scared." Quoted in Saul K. Padover, *Lügendetektor. Vernehmungen im besiegten Deutschland 1944/45* (Frankfurt a.M., 1999), 55.
27. On the following, see Simone Lässig, "Nationalsozialistische 'Judenpolitik' und jüdische Selbstbehauptung vor dem Novemberpogrom. Das Beispiel der Dresdner Bankiersfamilie Arnhold," in *Dresden unterm Hakenkreuz*, ed. R. Pommerin (Cologne, 1998), 129–91.
28. Quoted in ibid., 164.
29. Bajohr, *'Aryanisation' in Hamburg*, from 244.
30. Archiv des Wiedergutmachungsamtes beim Landgericht Hamburg [Archive of the Compensation Office, Hamburg District Court] (WgALGHH), Z 191-1, fols. 10–12, life history Berendsohn (n.d.).
31. See Bajohr, *'Aryanisation' in Hamburg*, 249–50.
32. Harald Welzer, "Vorhanden/Nicht vorhanden. Über die Latenz der Dinge," in *'Arisierung' im Nationalsozialismus*, Wojak and Hayes, 287–308.
33. Pierre Bourdieu, *Die verborgenen Mechanismen der Macht. Schriften zu Politik und Kultur* 1 (Hamburg, 1997), 49–79.
34. Bajohr, *'Aryanisation' in Hamburg*, from 225.

35. See Bajohr, *'Arisierung' in Hamburg*, 263.
36. Quoted in Wolfgang Benz, "Der November-Pogrom 1938," in *Die Juden in Deutschland 1933–1945*, ed. W. Benz (Munich, 1988), 499–544, here 530.
37. On the biography of Eichholz, see Bajohr, "No 'Volksgenossen.' Jewish Entrepreneurs in the Third Reich," in *Social Outsiders in Nazi Germany*, ed. R. Gellately and N. Stoltzfus (Princeton, NJ, 2001), 45–65.
38. See the corresponding exhibits in the exhibition "Jews in Berlin 1938–1945" in the Centrum Judaicum, Oranienburger Straße, Berlin. The accompanying exhibition guide of the same name was edited by Beate Meyer and Hermann Simon (Berlin, 2000).
39. The following remarks are based on impressions and observations during the study and analysis of restitution files stored in the Reparations Office of the Hamburg District Court. These were evaluated by the author in the context of his research project on Aryanization in Hamburg. Jan Philipp Spannuth was the first to publish an important analysis of these files. See his "Die Rückerstattung jüdischen Eigentums nach dem Zweiten Weltkrieg: Das Beispiel Hamburg," (MA thesis, Hamburg, 1994). On the history of restitution, see Constantin Goschler, *Wiedergutmachung. Westdeutschland und die Verfolgten des Nationalsozialismus 1945–1954* (Munich, 1992); Ludolf Herbst and Constantin Goschler, eds., *Wiedergutmachung in der Bundesrepublik Deutschland* (Munich, 1989).
40. Jan Philipp Spannuth, "Rückerstattung Ost. Der Umgang der DDR mit dem 'arisierten' und enteigneten jüdischen Eigentum und die Gestaltung der Rückerstattung im wiedervereinigten Deutschland," (Ph.D. diss., Freiburg, 2001).
41. Hartmut Berghoff and Cornelia Rauh-Kühne, *Fritz K. Ein deutsches Leben im zwanzigsten Jahrhundert* (Stuttgart, 2000).
42. See Bajohr, *Parvenüs und Profiteure*.
43. Quoted in Beate Meyer, "'Arisiert' und ausgeplündert. Die jüdische Fabrikantenfamilie Garbáty," in *Juden in Berlin 1938–1945*, ed. B. Meyer and H. Simon (Berlin, 2000), 77–87, here 85.
44. In the Hamburg restitution proceedings, this holds true, for example, for the attorneys Friedrich Rosenhaft, Conrad Baasch, Clara Klabunde, Gerd Bucerius, or Hanns-Harder Biermann-Ratjen.
45. Symptomatic of this basic attitude was the position espoused by an Aryanizer who denounced restitution legislation as "immoral and illegal"—not the fact of Aryanization. See WgALGHH, Z 3350–1, Letter of Julius Mehldau to the Hamburg District Court, 17 February 1953.

THE LOOTING OF JEWISH PROPERTY IN OCCUPIED WESTERN EUROPE

A Comparative Study of Belgium, France, and the Netherlands

Jean-Marc Dreyfus

The study of the looting and expropriation of Jewish property by the Germans during the Holocaust has witnessed a remarkable series of developments since 1996, particularly with the creation of numerous official commissions in European countries, Israel, and the United States, established not only by governments but also by a number of large industrial and financial companies. Since these studies developed within a national context, they only rarely included efforts at international comparison. The Holocaust was nonetheless a Europe-wide phenomenon, which affected the entire continent and had consequences for every segment of society. The renewed interest in the question of expropriation has also had the advantage of revealing the separate steps (whether or not they preceded the massacres), and therefore the "complicity," however limited, of numerous economic actors and institutions. In the economically developed societies of Western Europe, where Jews were largely integrated within all social classes, the implementation of the Holocaust required an enormous bureaucratic effort, in terms of identification (both of people and of properties), confiscation, concentration, and finally deportation to the death camps.[1] This scheme developed by Raul Hilberg provides a centralized German perspective, which can only with difficulty be transferred to the respective national administrations in Western Europe. It is especially difficult to apply to the French Vichy government, whose antisemitic policy did not plan for the murder of the Jews. Nevertheless, the Vichy policy of "collaboration" also made it an accomplice in the so-called Final Solution.

This chapter seeks to apply a comparative approach to the analysis of the expropriation and robbery of the Jews in three countries that were

---

Notes for this section begin on page 64.

occupied by German troops: Belgium, France, and the Netherlands. A direct comparison between these three countries is feasible, as they were all occupied for roughly the same time span, from May or June 1940 up to at least June 1944. The complete liberation of these three countries covered a period of some nine months, but by the end of the war the Germans only controlled the northern tip of the Netherlands and a few other isolated pockets of resistance.[2] In any case, with regard to the subject of interest, namely the expropriation of the Jews, there were no further developments of significance during the last year or so of the occupation.

It is out of the question here to examine the three countries in their entirety or to compare one national history directly with another. The more modest aim is rather to define certain precise points of comparison that may permit one to draw some firm conclusions. For if the comparison is to be legitimate, it is necessary to define precisely what is to be compared and also to remain strictly within this limited framework during the course of the investigation. Here we will only be examining economic Aryanization—that is, the confiscation of Jewish-owned businesses, of Jewish bank accounts and share portfolios.[3]

If the level of economic development in the three countries under consideration was similar in 1940, the extent to which the Jews were integrated within society was not the same, and furthermore the Jewish populations were also not of the same origin. If in France more than half of the Jews living on French territory when the German forces invaded the country were French citizens (55 percent),[4] in Belgium only 6.6 percent were citizens, and in the Netherlands the figure was 80 percent. There were, therefore, certain quite sharp contrasts, reflecting the diverging respective histories of the Jewish communities in the three countries.

It is inaccurate to state that no direct comparison has ever been attempted between Belgium, France, and the Netherlands with regard to the Holocaust, but so far such comparisons have focused primarily on the respective proportion of Jews who were murdered, rather than on the question of expropriation. In fact, even shortly after the liberation, the marked differential in the "deportation rates" for Jews attracted attention. Whereas 25 percent of the Jews living in France were deported to death camps, most of them to Auschwitz, 83 percent of Jews in the Netherlands were arrested and murdered. For Belgium the rate lies in between these two figures at 46 percent.[5] Of the 140,000 Jews in the Netherlands, 107,000 were deported. Some partial attempts to explain these discrepancies have been made,[6] but none of them has included an examination of confiscation as a further yardstick for measuring the respective intensity of persecution.

The structure of the German occupation authorities (and their relationships with the national and local administrations) was utterly different from one country to another. If France and Belgium were subjected to German military administration (the Militärbefehlshaber in Paris and the Militärverwaltung in Brussels), the Netherlands had to endure the more stringent rule of a civil administration. Whereas the Belgian and Dutch governments both fled to London, France experienced a new regime and a new policy directed by a French government dedicated to state collaboration. In all three countries, the Germans found almost intact national administrations. The role played by the SS was also quite different from one country to another. It was immediate and massive in the Netherlands, as the SS was directly represented among the four German General Commissars with H. A. Rauter receiving the portfolio for security matters.[7] In France, a Higher SS and Police Leader (*Höhere SS-und Polizeiführer*), Carl Albrecht Oberg, arrived in Paris in May 1942 and assumed authority on 1 June 1942.[8] In Belgium, the struggle of the SS to impose a Higher SS and Police Leader was not successful before the end of the occupation.[9]

In this chapter, three precise elements of the expropriation will be considered and compared in each of the three countries: the chronology; the agents—both people and institutions—in charge of the Aryanization and the looting; and the respective end results of the process.

The Chronology of Expropriation

It is interesting to compare the various steps in the Aryanization and looting of Jewish property in the three countries, as there were significant differences in the sequence of events. In July 1940, the Germans started the looting of works of art. In the Netherlands, the Dienststelle Mühlmann was in charge of the robbery.[10] In France and Belgium, the ERR tracked down Jewish art collections, sorted them and placed part of them at the disposal either of Hermann Göring's private collection or of Hitler's planned Art Museum in Linz.[11] The search for artworks continued into the fall of 1940. The first anti-Jewish decree promulgated by the German occupation authorities in the West was published in France on 27 September 1940.[12] A month later, similar decrees, defining who should be considered a Jew and which firms could be confiscated, were promulgated in the Netherlands (on 22 October) and in Belgium (on 28 October). A "competition" between the Vichy government, which was preparing its own antisemitic policy at this time, and the German military government may have led to the early timing of this escalation in anti-Jewish measures. The implementation of Aryanization did not commence immediately following these first decrees, but they established the necessary legal framework. For the purposes of this comparison, it is necessary to define, somewhat arbitrarily, when the widespread confiscation of businesses really started in each country. Toward this aim, it is helpful to establish an outline of the main steps involved in economic Aryanization. These steps went roughly as follows:

1. Definition of a Jew;
2. Definition of a "Jewish" business;
3. Appointment of a provisional administrator;
4. Decision whether to sell or liquidate the firm;

5. Implementation of this decision;
6. Blocking of assets belonging to the enterprise, including bank accounts and revenue from the sale of assets;
7. Centralization of the assets at a specific financial institution;
8. Centralization of all assets on a single collective bank account (*Sammelkonto*);
9. Formal confiscation of these assets.

If the beginning of economic Aryanization is defined as the moment when a firm could be placed under provisional administration, thereby depriving the owners of their property rights, it started in France with the second German anti-Jewish decree on 18 October 1940.[13] In the Netherlands, this process was started only on 12 March 1941, so five months later. In Belgium, the law on provisional administration was decreed on 31 May 1941 with the third anti-Jewish decree,[14] six weeks later than in the Netherlands.[15] These dates nonetheless conceal certain additional disparities, as the appointment of provisional administrators in France rapidly led to the sale and liquidation of firms, largely implemented from the spring of 1941 onwards.[16] On the other hand, the provisional administrators in Belgium carried out their duties without conducting any forced sales, except for a handful of major companies, up until March 1942, when the liquidation of all Jewish-owned firms was commenced in order to meet a deadline set for its completion on 31 May 1942.[17]

The second important indicator in assessing the chronology of the expropriation was the imposition of government controls over Jewish valuables, bank accounts, and shares. In France—but only in the northern, occupied zone—the bank accounts of firms under provisional administration were blocked on 26 April 1941,[18] whereas the bank accounts of individual Jews were blocked on 28 May 1941.[19] Subsequently, a French law of 22 July 1941,[20] which was the result of lengthy negotiations between the French and German officials and of pressure exerted by the French government from February 1941, extended the appointment of provisional administrators to the nonoccupied zone and also started the process of confiscating Jewish share portfolios.[21] In Belgium the above-mentioned decree of 31 May 1941[22] required the deposit or eventual transfer of all Jewish accounts to foreign currency banks. Transfers theoretically had to be made by 15 July 1941.[23] This law, however, was not implemented systematically. Jewish-owned securities in Belgian banks were blocked on 16 July 1941.[24] Numbered accounts, however, remained unblocked for a while longer. It appears that in practice the measures were progressively tightened, so that the decree of 21 September 1942, which required that the sale of transferable securities be authorized by the Feldkommandanturen, only confirmed an already existing situation.

In the Netherlands, Jewish-owned assets were blocked on 8 August 1941 by the First "Liro" Decree.[25] According to this law, Jews were obliged to open a bank account at the recently created mock bank of Lippmann,

Rosenthal & Co. (or Liro).[26] All Jewish assets, such as bank accounts, savings deposits, cash, or securities, had to be transferred onto these new Liro bank accounts.[27] Dutch financial institutions were also ordered to transfer all Jewish assets, obliging them to determine which of their customers were Jewish, so that they sent out forms to all of their customers. Notaries responsible for Jewish assets were also obliged to transfer them to the Liro Bank. The sale of Jewish securities started in January 1942, following an order by Reichskommissar Seyss-Inquart. In France, the sale of Jewish securities had started earlier in September 1941.

By the end of 1941, the main infrastructure for the expropriation was in place in France, in particular, a collective fine (*l'amende*) of one billion francs imposed on the Jews of France, officially as a reprisal for attacks on German soldiers carried out by the Resistance.[28] In March 1942, the last major step toward confiscation was decreed in Belgium with the order to liquidate those Jewish businesses not yet Aryanized. On the other hand, the German civil administration in the Netherlands went one step further in May 1942, with the promulgation of the Second Liro Decree.[29] Unique in occupied Western Europe, this law took the practice of financial looting to a terrifying new level of detail. The decree required the declaration and transfer to Liro of all forms of Jewish property rights. This included insurance policies, contracts, diverse loans, leases, mortgages, salaries and stipends, pensions, honoraria, copyrights, patents, inheritances, and concessions. These property rights also included current and future obligations toward individuals or legal entities, inside the country or abroad. Works of art, collections of any kind, gold, platinum, or silver objects, gems or semiprecious stones (mounted or unmounted), stamps, books, coins, china, and so forth were all to be delivered to Liro as well. All means of transportation, including bicycles, were also confiscated.

The only step taken at exactly the same time in all three counties was the confiscation of furniture, in the so-called Furniture Operation (Möbel Aktion), decided in December 1941 and starting in January 1942 in Paris. Against the background of considerable tension following attacks by the Resistance, the military command in Paris introduced a tougher occupation policy involving the killing of hostages, while at the same time trying to avoid an adverse reaction among the majority of the French population, which up until then had remained relatively calm and subdued.[30] The collective fine of one billion francs was imposed in this context. This escalation in the anti-Jewish measures taken and the competition that it provoked between different branches of the German administration contributed to the development of the Furniture Operation,[31] which was proposed by the chief of the ERR in Paris, Baron von Behr. On 18 December 1941, Alfred Rosenberg sent a note to Hitler requesting permission for the ERR in Paris to confiscate the furniture from Jewish apartments that were no longer occupied.[32] Once the authorization was given, the Oberkommando des Heeres (OKH) [Army High Command] gave instructions for the operation to be expanded to cover Belgium and the Netherlands as well. Hitler himself decided that no public decree was necessary to legitimate this operation and also that the implementation of the operation should be intensified.[33] In the Netherlands, the looting of apartments was supervised by a separate administration, the Zentralstelle für jüdische Auswanderung[34] (the Central Office for Jewish Emigration), established by the Security Police in Amsterdam and modeled according to the institution of the same name in Vienna. In Belgium, the looting of apartments was directly coordinated with the arrest of the Jews. When a roundup was being planned, the ERR was informed so that its officials could secure the remaining property.[35] The Furniture Operation was the only looting operation that was officially coordinated by a single administration in all three occupied countries, although the operation in the Netherlands remained more independent, as the central office of the ERR in Paris only issued detailed instructions for France and Belgium.

If in terms of chronology, the expropriation and robbery started first in France in terms of legislation, it was actually implemented from the spring of 1941 in all three countries. It is difficult to find specific instructions issued from Berlin ordering the confiscation. Even if a more general order for the extension to the West of the anti-Jewish policies that had been progressively applied within the Reich can be assumed, this order was still implemented differently by the particular administrative and political structures in each occupied country. It should be noted that the existence of two parallel antisemitic policies in France (directed by the Germans and by Vichy) resulted sometimes in slowing down and sometimes in speeding up the drafting and implementation of the various expropriation decrees. Measures against the Jews were generally promulgated later in Belgium. However, in the Netherlands the policy of expropriation was directed and implemented in a much more radical and comprehensive fashion, reflecting the political will demonstrated by the four German General Commissars who could concentrate nearly all power in their own hands due to the almost complete absence of counterveiling forces; their ideological radicalism was not matched among the military commanders administering Belgium and France. The thoroughgoing nature of the Second Liro Decree reflected a clear qualitative difference between the policy implemented in the Netherlands and those carried out in the two countries to the south.

If chronology is one of the main differences in the respective expropriation policies, a study of the agencies responsible for the looting also demonstrates certain key similarities and discrepancies between the three countries. The very wide diversity among the institutions and individuals who played a role in the process cannot be described fully within the limited space available here, but some salient features can nonetheless be outlined.

The Actors in the Expropriation

The Aryanization and robbery was initiated everywhere by the German occupation authorities. Even in France, where state collaboration began in

October 1940, there was no independent initiative by the French government or its administration. (The first anti-Jewish Law of 3 October was a French initiative, but it did not attack any private property rights.)[36] The expropriation commenced with a decree issued by the German military commandants in April 1941. But following the usual tactical maneuvering, the collaborating French administration adopted as its own the steps mandated by the Germans, thus demonstrating its independent will, especially between April and July 1941.

If one considers the officials responsible for the expropriation of the Jews, one has to establish their exact status: Were they working for preexisting or for newly created bureaucracies? Were these authorities created only for the purpose of implementing the robbery or did they have a more general purpose, such as supervising the economy? The functions of the provisional administrators in the process of Aryanization represent an interesting case. Provisional administrators were employed in all three countries, as already shown. In France the first appointments by the German authorities commenced in October 1940. In December the French Ministry for Industrial Production took over the task of appointing the provisional administrators. Its intention was to protect against the appointment of German administrators, as these might have become a "Trojan horse" for the furthering of German interests within the French economy.[37] For the French administration and especially for Jean Bichelonne, the General Secretary for Industrial Production, it was most important to check the status of the new appointees—were they loyal state officials or trustees acting for the Jewish owners? For this purpose a new office was created on 9 December 1940, initially subordinate to the Ministry for Industrial Production: the Service de contrôle des administrateurs provisoires [Office for the Supervision of Provisional Administrators] (SCAP). This office expanded considerably after April 1941, ultimately becoming a part of the Commissariat général aux Questions juives [General Commissariat for the Jewish Question] (CGQJ).[38] In due course it became the principle agency for carrying out Aryanization,[39] especially following its reorganization in May 1942, becoming the Direction de l'aryanisation économique [Office for Economic Aryanization] (DAE) within the CGQJ.[40]

During the occupation some eight thousand provisional administrators were appointed, all French and almost all male.[41] The emergence of this large new occupational group was unique to France with regard to Aryanization. According to the initial plans of the French authorities, a large number of businesses in a particular branch of the economy that were to be liquidated quickly were supposed to be placed in the hands of a single provisional administrator experienced in that same branch; however, in practice, the large number of administrators appointed throughout the country generally undermined this simplifying intent. The appointment of provisional administrators, that is, officials, who on account of their experience were most adept at liquidating Jewish businesses was tried out initially in Vienna after the Anschluss. The application of the "Vienna Model"[42] can be clearly recognized in the appointment of provisional administrators for the administration and liquidation of Jewish businesses. In the Netherlands only a few dozen were appointed. In Belgium in the summer of 1942 only 129 provisional administrators were active, of whom only nine possessed Belgian citizenship.[43] But the French authorities appointed thousands of these Aryanization specialists, giving the "Vienna Model" a new twist.

In reality France was an exceptional case, as apart from the SCAP, traditional administrative institutions were entrusted with implementing Aryanization. In this respect, alongside the Ministry for Industrial Production, the Finance Ministry was very active, especially its Domains Administration (responsible for the management and sale of Jewish securities) and the Caisse des Dépôts et Consignations (where the revenues from the sale of assets were concentrated). The Prefects (especially in the Occupied Zone), among other established state institutions were also active. Whereas in France the SCAP centralized and coordinated the Aryanization measures in its own hands, in Belgium Group 12—a section of the German military administration responsible for "enemy" and Jewish property—was entrusted with coordinating the Aryanization effort.[44] It delegated much of this work to the Brussels Trust Company (BTG), an office established in accordance with German law. In the Netherlands the most important instrument in the expropriation was the disguised Liro Bank. In July 1941 the latter was established from scratch and assumed the name of an old-established Jewish private bank that enjoyed a good reputation, in order to deceive not only Jews, but also the Dutch and international financial community.[45] With a limited staff of not more than 511 employees, this disguised bank collected nearly all Jewish property and organized its expropriation. In this it carried out functions assigned to many different offices in France and Belgium.

The Germans also created other new organizations in the Netherlands, which, however, were each entrusted with only specific component tasks in the robbery. These organizations were possibly also intended to operate in occupied France as well, but they never became active there, as responsibility was assumed instead by the French administration. As a result, the Trustee Office (Treuhand) and the Review Office (Revisionsstelle), which were established in Paris in the offices of Barclay's Bank (which had been placed under compulsory administration as "enemy property"), played only a marginal role in the expropriation of the Jews. They conducted assessments of some companies and collected an Aryanization tax of one month's wages from each Jewish company for a provisional administrator. In Belgium and the Netherlands a series of trustee offices was established, mostly in accordance with German law (in order to get around local legal restrictions). In Brussels the BTG was entrusted with the administration of many Jewish companies. In the Netherlands the Niederländische Aktiengesellschaft für die Abwicklung von Unternehmen [Dutch Limited Company for the Liquidation of Businesses] (NAGU) was created as a Trustee company.[46] Staffed by employees in the private sector and operating like a business accountancy office, it administered and Aryanized large Jewish companies. The Omnia Treuhandgesellschaft GmbH [Omnia Trustee-Society Ltd] (OMNIA) established an office in the Hague in 1941 and subsequently branch offices in ten other cities in the country.[47] This private company employed fifty people in its main office, one third of whom were Germans. In France all of the Aryanization procedures were carried out by the national and local administration; with the intention of gaining maximum control over the whole process, the government made the participation of private companies impossible. But even in the Netherlands, NAGU, OMNIA, and other companies established by the state, such as the Vermögensverwaltungs- und Rentenanstalt [Property Administration and Pension Institute] (VVRA), were only able to convert a fraction of their overall Jewish assets into cash before the end of the occupation.

In the Netherlands, the Aryanization process and the plundering of the Jews was most strongly centralized. This can be explained above all by the structure of the occupation apparatus itself, with its limited (if not entirely absent) friction and competition between the civil administration and the military authorities. In France the centralization of the expropriation was less marked, not really because the political will was lacking or because the administrative model opposed it, but rather on account of the geographical division of the country into several separate administrative zones. In Belgium the field commandants (Feldkommandanturen), whose power derived from German decrees, played a very large role in these operations. The final outcome of the expropriation reflects in part the degree of centralization. It also reveals significant differences in the aims of the respective political measures taken toward the confiscation of Jewish property.

The Final Outcome of the Expropriation

To the Jews the robbery appeared to have been total, thanks mainly to the energy and persistence displayed by their persecutors. And in reality those Jews that remained in the country and managed to evade deportation had lost almost all of their property by the time they were liberated. Nevertheless, a comparison of the three countries permits us to differentiate between the respective degrees of resoluteness displayed by the German occupation authorities and, especially, with regard to the different categories of property that were confiscated. In Belgium and France, for example, insurance policies were not confiscated. Rather they were only affected insofar as they were caught up in the more general blocking of financial accounts. In Belgium the German decree of 31 May 1941 instructed that all property be deposited in a blocked account, including insurance policies.[48] The latter requirement was rarely enforced, as the general blocking of all Jewish assets made it impossible for the companies to pay out on such policies in any case.[49] An office for the processing of some payments on Jewish insurance policies was created, but this also required the identification of those policies in Jewish hands. The control over this was not as strict in Belgium as in

France, where the bureaucratic tradition was more deeply embedded and the CGQJ had imposed particularly sharp restrictions on capital flows in August 1941.[50] In France, as in Belgium, insurance policies belonging to Jews were not explicitly confiscated. The paying out of insurance policies was blocked by a law that was subsequently revised several times.[51] Of the three countries under examination, only in the Netherlands did the Second Liro Decree lead to the direct theft of insurance policies.[52] In accordance with a further decree (54/1943) of 11 June 1943, all Jewish insurance policies had to be dissolved and the proceeds transferred to the Liro Bank.[53]

In France the expropriation of the Jews left open certain loopholes, which demonstrates also that here the confiscation measures were less effective than in Belgium, and especially in comparison with the Netherlands. Accordingly, the private bank accounts of Jews were not blocked if they were in the Southern Zone, even after it was occupied by German troops on 11 November 1942. While the property of Jewish communal organizations in the Netherlands,[54] which were all forcibly liquidated, fell victim to the confiscation measures, this cannot exactly be said for Belgium, or for France, where in November 1941 a law was passed creating the Union générale des Israelites de France [General Union of French Jews] (UGIF),[55] which decreed that the property of dissolved organizations would be transferred to the Union.

In Belgium and the Netherlands there was a special form of confiscation within one particular economic branch of considerable interest to the Germans. This was the diamond sector, exceptionally important in Antwerp[56] and Amsterdam, and which was dominated to a great extent by Jewish traders and craftsmen.[57] The confiscation institutions that operated in this sector had no equivalent in France.

Even if the overall extent of the robbery is very difficult to quantify on account of the large number of measures and actors, and especially the almost insurmountable difficulties preventing the accurate conversion of past values into their present-day equivalent, nevertheless, some statistics may assist in measuring the key differences in how the plundering was implemented. The above-stated abstract model laying out the individual stages of economic persecution was not applied in its entirety in each country. For example, the final stage of simply confiscating "liquid" property values did not take place in Belgium, where the sums remained in blocked accounts. In France the total sum of confiscated assets was at least one billion francs, the amount of the Collective Fine that was imposed in December 1941. In the Netherlands, the assets blocked during the course of the Aryanization measures still "legally" belonged to the owners. In theory at least, the Jews were supposed to receive four percent of their blocked liquidated assets per year over a period of twenty-five years as a form of pension.

The concentration of all blocked Jewish accounts at a single financial institution was not pursued with the same energy in all three countries. In France about four billion francs were assigned to individual blocked accounts at the Caisse des Dépôts et Consignations. The bulk of securities remained blocked in the financial institutions and untouched until the end of the occupation. In Belgium the same process was only started at the end of 1942, when, after a change of mind by the German authorities, instructions[58] were issued for all Jewish assets to be transferred to the Société française de Banque et de Dépôts [French Society for Banking and Secure Deposits] (SFBD).[59] The concentration took place in fits and starts and was still a long way from completion when Brussels was liberated. The process of concentration was most energetically pursued in the Netherlands. The Liro Bank collected not only almost all Jewish assets and securities in individual accounts, but on the basis of the decree of 21 November 1942 it undertook the transfer of all assets received into a single collective account and dissolved the individual blocked accounts opened in the victims' names. As the culmination of the plunder campaign, the Jews even had their individuality stolen from their bank accounts.

Finally, the "success rate" of the expropriation varied considerably from one country to another.[60] One could draw up innumerable statistical tables, drawing upon the findings of all the recent studies on this topic, including especially those prepared by the official commissions. In the liquidation of Jewish businesses there were great differences. In France, 56 percent of those companies placed under provisional administration were liquidated (the others were to be sold, but most had not received a final authorization and therefore remained under provisional administration).[61] In Belgium this figure was 83 percent and in the Netherlands, where some eleven thousand of the roughly fourteen thousand businesses finally defined as Jewish were liquidated, it was about 78.5 percent.[62] The use of Aryanization to rationalize the economy, voiced by the administrations in all three countries, was only realized in Belgium and the Netherlands. In France competition between the various administrative structures, the poor organization of the CGQJ, and other factors, hindered the realization of this aim.

The percentage of formerly Jewish-owned securities sold also varied considerably. In Belgium no securities were sold unless this was necessary to replenish Jewish accounts at the SFBD that had run into deficit due to the payment of outstanding debts.[63] In France 32 percent of securities were sold.[64] In the Netherlands 80 percent of securities were liquidated, many of them being sold on the Dutch stock market.

Conclusion

A similar Aryanization policy followed by the systematic plunder of Jewish assets took a different course within the framework of the so-called Final Solution in each respective national context, reflecting variations in the institutional structure of the German occupation and also in Germany's long-term political goals for each country. Aryanization and the expropriation associated with it was implemented more drastically in the Netherlands than in France, and above all it resulted there in practically the complete liquidation of all Jewish assets. Belgium remained in most respects somewhere in the middle between these two extremes, which incidentally is also reflected in its "deportation rate."

In Belgium and the Netherlands, the fact that there was no collaborationist government, and therefore no potentially restraining intermediary buffer, can explain some of the differences. But one should also factor in the intentions of the military administration in these countries, which were ready to follow antisemitic instructions from Berlin promptly, but whose own initiatives proved less radical than those of the civil administration in the Netherlands that lay exclusively in the hands of fanatical Nazis. The persistence and thoroughness of the expropriation measures in the Netherlands, and also the "success" in deporting the Jews can, however, only to a limited extent be explained by the personalities of the German administrators.

Therefore, one also has to take into account the long-term aims of the Germans for the occupied territories. Even if the "Final Solution" was conceived for the whole of Europe—at least after the Wannsee Conference—that does not mean, however, that it had the same urgency in all countries. The Netherlands, a region that was to be completely "Germanized," experienced a much more systematic policy of destruction than France, which was assigned rather the role of a dominion within the Nazi sphere of influence; there Jewish influence was also to be eliminated, but economic and political necessities linked to the state policy of collaboration dictated a degree of restraint. In view of German plans to incorporate Flanders into the Reich but only to consolidate their occupational regime over the Walloons, Belgium in this respect also occupied a midpoint between its two neighbors.

Finally, it is possible that the degree of thoroughness with which the expropriation was carried out also corresponds to the level of violence that was applied towards the Jews in each country. Therefore, as Hilberg points out, expropriation should be seen as one of several preceding, but nonetheless contributory, stages in the process of the destruction of the European Jews.

Translated by Jean-Marc Dreyfus and Martin Dean

Notes

1. These are the four stages identified in the seminal work of Raul Hilberg, *The Destruction of the European Jews* (New Haven, CT, 2003), 50.
2. An extensive comparative study of these three countries during the Holocaust has been conducted under the leadership of Prof. Wolfgang Seibel of the University of Konstanz. For an interim report on this research project funded by the Volkswagen Stiftung, see Wolfgang Seibel, ed., *Holocaust und 'Polykratie' in Westeuropa, 1940–1944: Nationale Berichte* (December 2001).

3. The extent of spoliation was much wider than these three categories, as it affected almost all forms of property, from major industrial companies to the more modest objects of everyday life that Jews took with them to the death camps. For a more comprehensive overview of spoliation in France, see: Mission d'étude sur la spoliation des Juifs de France, *Rapport général* (Paris, 2000), or in English: Republique Francaise, *Summary of the Work by the Study Mission on the Spoliation of the Jews in France* (Paris, April 2000).
4. Renée Poznanski, *Jews in France during World War II* (Hanover, NH, 2001), 1–16.
5. Regarding the respective national statistics, see, for example, Wolfgang Benz, ed., *Dimension des Völkermords: Die Zahl der jüdischen Opfer des Nationalsozialismus* (Munich, 1996).
6. Pim Griffioen and Ron Zeller, «La persécution des Juifs en Belgique et aux Pays-Bas pendant la Seconde Guerre mondiale: une analyse comparative,» *Cahiers d'Histoire du Temps Présent/Bijdragen tot de Eigentijdse Geschiedenis*, no. 5 (Brussels, November 1998/ May 1999): 126–64; J. C. H. Blom, "The Persecution of the Jews in the Netherlands: A Comparative Western European Perspective," *European History Quaterly* XIX (1989): 333–51.
7. Bob Moore, *Victims and Survivors: The Nazi Persecution of the Jews in the Netherlands 1940–1945* (London, 1997), 73–79.
8. Michael M. Marrus and Robert O. Paxton, *Vichy et les Juifs* (Paris, 1984), 306–7.
9. Albert de Jonghe, ed., «La lutte Himmler-Reder pour la nomination d'un HSSPF à Bruxelles,» *Cahiers d'histoire de la Seconde Guerre mondiale*, nos. 3, 4, 5, 7, and 8 (Brussels, 1974–84).
10. Gerard Aalders, *Geraubt! Die Enteignung jüdischen Besitzes im Zweiten Weltkrieg* (Cologne, 2000), 85–159.
11. *Contribution de la direction des Musées de France et du Centre Georges-Pompidou aux travaux de la Mission d'étude sur la spoliation des Juifs de France, Le pillage de l'art en France pendant l'Occupation et la situation des 2000 œuvres confiées aux Musées nationaux* (Paris, 2000); *Les biens des victimes des persécutions anti-juives en Belgique. Spoliation – Rétablissement des droits. Résultats de la Commission d'étude, Rapport final de la Commission d'étude sur le sort des biens des membres de la Communauté juive de Belgique spoliés ou délaissés pendant la guerre 1940–1945* (Brussels, July 2001), 133–35.
12. *Verordnungsblatt des Militärbefehlshabers in Frankreich* [Gazette of Decrees issued by the Military Commander in France] (Vobif), 30 September 1940. For the main legal texts regarding spoliation (and also restitution) in France, see Claire Andrieu, ed., *La persécution des Juifs de France 1940-1944 et le rétablissement de la légalité républicaine. Recueil des textes officiels, 1940–1999* (Paris, 2000).
13. Vobif, 20 October 1940.
14. *Les biens des victimes*, 79–80.
15. Maxime Steinberg, *L'Etoile et le Fusil. La Question Juive, 1940–1942* (Brussels, 4 vols., 1983–1987), vol. 1, 51.
16. Martin Jungius, "Der 'Service du Contrôle des Administrateurs Provisoires' (SCAP) zu Beginn der ökonomischen Arisierung in Frankreich (1940–1941)," (Magisterarbeit under the supervision of Prof. Wolfgang Seibel, Universität Konstanz, Oktober 2000), from 72.
17. *Les biens des victimes*, 82.
18. Vobif, 5 May 1941.
19. Vobif, 10 June 1941.
20. *Journal officiel de l'Etat français*, 26 August 1941.
21. Claire Andrieu, ed., *La spoliation financière* (Paris, 2000), vol. I, 34–37.
22. *Verordnungsblatt des Militärbefehlshaber in Belgien und Nordfrankreich*, fasc. 44, No. 1–2.
23. *Les biens des victimes*, 43.
24. Ibid., 44.
25. Verordnungsblatt, 148/1941 (über die Behandlung jüdischer Kapitalvermögens).
26. Aalders, *Geraubt!*, 209–10.

27. For a description of the implementation of the First Liro. Decree, see Aalders, *Geraubt!*, 257–300.
28. Andrieu, *La spoliation financière*, vol. I, 54–55.
29. Jacob Presser, *The Destruction of the Dutch Jews* (New York, 1969), 127–29.
30. Ulrich Herbert, "Die deutsche Militärverwaltung in Paris und die Deportation der französischen Juden," in Ulrich Herbert, ed., *Nationalsozialistische Vernichtungspolitik 1939–1945. Neue Forschungen und Kontroversen* (Frankfurt am Main, 1998), 182–86.
31. On this escalation, see Jean-Marc Dreyfus, "L'aryanisation économique des banques. La confiscation des banques 'juives' en France sous l'Occupation et leur restitution à la Libération 1940–1952," (PhD dissertation, Université de Paris I – Panthéon – Sorbonne, September 2000), 312–19.
32. Annette Wieviorka, *Le pillage des appartements, Mission d'étude sur la spoliation des Juifs de France* (Paris, 2000). For a complete description of the Furniture Operation, see Jean-Marc Dreyfus and Sarah Gensburger, *Des camps dans Paris. Austerlitz-Lévitan-Bassano, July 1943–August 1944* (Paris, 2003), 34–87.
33. Anja Heuss, *Kunst- und Kulturgutraub. Eine vergleichende Studie zur Besatzungspolitik der Nationalsozialisten in Frankreich und der Sowjetunion* (Heidelberg, 2000), 125–26.
34. Aalders, *Geraubt!*, 262.
35. *Les biens des victimes*, 120.
36. The first anti-Jewish Law excluded Jews from holding positions in public life, politics, and the mass media. Beyond this it did not include a single clause that attacked business or private property rights.
37. On the general issue of German-French rivalry within the field of Aryanization, with special reference to large-scale Jewish enterprises, see P. Verheyde, *Les mauvais comptes de Vichy. L'aryanisation des entreprises juives* (Paris, 1999).
38. The General Commissariat for the Jewish Question, a French institution, was created in response to pressure exerted by Theodor Danneker, the representative of Eichmann in Paris. It was established by the French Law of 29 March 1941, *Journal officiel de l'Etat français*, 30 March 1941.
39. Paxton and Marrus, *Vichy et les Juifs*, 151.
40. A. Prost (ed.), *Aryanisation économique et restitutions, Mission d'étude sur la spoliation des Juifs de France* (Paris, 2000), 20.
41. Paxton/Marrus, *Vichy et les Juifs*, 34. Not all administrators carried out their tasks efficiently. Some remained in their positions for several years, others for only a few days; some administered more than 100 businesses, others just a single one.
42. On the question of the export of the "Viennese Model" to the Netherlands, see J. Scheren, "Aryanisation, Market Vendors, and Peddlers in Amsterdam," *Holocaust and Genocide Studies* 14 (2000), 415–29, here 415.
43. Steinberg, *L'Etoile et le fusil*, Vol. II, 59.
44. *Les biens des victimes*, 80–81.
45. Aalders, *Geraubt!*, 221–22.
46. Ibid., 199.
47. Ibid.
48. *Les biens des victimes*, 76.
49. Ibid., 77.
50. Note on the flow of Jewish capital, signed by Faramond (General Secretary of the CGQJ), 25 August 1941, Archives Nationales Paris, AJ 38, 2792. Published in Andrieu, *La spoliation financière*, vol. II, 87.
51. Andrieu, *La spoliation financière*, vol. I, 227–32.
52. Aalders, *Geraubt!*, 320–23.
53. *Verordnungsblatt*, 54/1943.
54. Decree of 28 February 1941, *Verordnungsblatt*, 41/1941. See also Aalders, *Geraubt!*, 192–93.
55. The Law of 29 November 1941 (*Journal officiel de l'Etat français*, 2 Dec. 1941) founded the *Union générale des Israélites de France* (UGIF) after months of pressure from the Ger-

man side. The UGIF did not correspond exactly with the model of the "Judenrat" and offered impoverished Jews economic support ; see Paxton and Marrus, *Vichy et les Juifs*, 157–60; see also *Michel Laffitte, Un engrenage fatal: l'UGIF face aux réalités de la Shoah, 1941-1944* (Paris, 2003).

56. *Les biens des victimes*, 94–118. See also E. Laureys, "The Looting of Antwerp's Jewish Diamond Dealers, 1940–1944," in *Confiscation of Jewish Property in Europe, 1933-1945: New Sources and Perspectives*, Symposium Proceedings (Center for Advanced Holocaust Studies, USHMM, published as an Occasional Paper in February 2003), 57–74.
57. Aalders, *Geraubt!*, 205–9.
58. *Les biens des victimes*, 44–45.
59. The SFBD was dominated by the interests of French banks and therefore was treated as enemy property and placed under provisional administration by the German administration.
60. These differences undoubtedly had consequences for the results of the Restitution and Compensation. For France, see the contribution of Claire Andrieu in this volume.
61. The percentage is calculated according to the table in Prost, *Aryanisation économique*, 264–65, Appendix 9.
62. Of the 20,690 businesses inititially registered as Jewish, some 8,000 were able to escape this status by ousting Jewish partners or board members.
63. *Les biens des victimes*, 52–53.
64. In total, securities valued at 1,815,600,000 francs were sold by the state property administration.

THE ROBBERY OF JEWISH PROPERTY IN EASTERN EUROPE UNDER GERMAN OCCUPATION, 1939-1942

Dieter Pohl

The plundering of Jewish property pales by comparison with the mass murder of the Jews. This is especially true with regard to the Jews of Eastern Europe, who made up the majority of victims of the Holocaust. This crime against humanity cost the lives of about 4.5 million people, including some 1.5 million children, in those Eastern European countries occupied by the Germans by 1942. Horror at these murders may be one of the reasons why historians have been hesitant to investigate the preceding robbery, which also continued during and after the murder campaigns. It is only in recent years that the first detailed studies of the spoliation of Eastern European Jews have begun, as part of the international debate on the restitution of property and compensation for forced labor. In this respect, one must distinguish between the allies of the German Reich, such as Slovakia, Croatia, Romania, Hungary, and Bulgaria,[1] and those lands that the Germans occupied directly themselves. This chapter examines some of the basic principles behind the robbery in the occupied territories without looking in detail into the final whereabouts of the property itself. The investigation is restricted to the Polish, Soviet, and also briefly the Czech lands, as the German occupation of Yugoslavia and Greece requires separate consideration.[2]

First, it is necessary to look at the distribution of property among Eastern European Jews before the war. The economic significance of this minority, of course, went far beyond the mere ownership of property; it extended to shaping cultural values and education, and providing "social capital," all of which was irrevocably lost as a result of the genocide and the effects of the war. The distribution of property among the majority of Eastern European Jews showed certain distinctive features. A number of Jews in Bohemia had achieved rapid social advancement in the nineteenth century, with the result that their living standards were increasingly comparable with those of the

Notes for this section begin on page 77.

majority of the population. In Poland, however, the same can only be said of a small group, which actually formed its own middle class. On the whole, Poland's Jews came from a much broader range of social backgrounds than Polish Christians; there was a pronounced difference between Jewish living standards in eastern and western Poland, and also between Jews living in the cities and those in the small towns. The extent to which Polish Jews were affected by the world economic crisis, which hit Poland particularly badly, remains disputed. Although the overall statistics for income development do not show a decline, the majority of Polish Jews clearly felt that this was the case. Jewish-owned enterprises dealt predominantly in textiles, as well as in chemicals, foodstuffs, building materials, and paper. These encompassed almost 40 percent of the manpower potential of these branches, and about forty joint-stock companies were under predominantly Jewish ownership.[3]

The structure of property ownership in what was to become occupied Eastern Europe can be roughly divided into two categories: East-Central European and East European. The former applies primarily to Bohemia, Hungary, western parts of Poland, and the larger towns of Latvia. The Jews in these countries, as in Germany, were mainly middle class and to a lesser extent upper class or from industrialist families. The East European type describes the larger number of Jews with small businesses, with only small real estate holdings and other possessions mostly only of sentimental value, or who were simply very poor. Agricultural property owned by Jews in Poland was more a regional exception. In most of Poland, eastern Latvia, Lithuania, and generally in the rural parts of Eastern Europe, the impoverished shtetl predominated. Property owned by the Jewish communities in Poland and Czechoslovakia must also be taken into account—their land and buildings, cultural and welfare institutions, which were also expropriated by the German occupying forces. In Poland alone, roughly one thousand four hundred Jewish communities existed before the war.

It is extraordinarily difficult to estimate the amount of property owned by residents of the Soviet Union, who were severely hit by nationalization after the revolution, then again after Stalin ended the "New Economic Policy," and lastly by the shortages imposed during the forced industrialization of the 1930s. Certainly, people of Jewish "nationality" were apparently well represented in the industrial and administrative fields,[4] and in 1939 in Soviet Ukraine and Belorussia, more than half of the Jewish workforce was employed by the State.[5] On the one hand, a relatively large number of Jews had risen to become part of the Soviet elite, but on the other hand, the opportunities for acquiring private property were very small. At present, only very general estimates of the assets held by Eastern European Jews exist: relatively few among residents of the Soviet Union, somewhat more among Polish residents, and considerably more per capita in the Republic of Czechoslovakia. It is correspondingly difficult to compile information on the total substantive loss incurred as a result of National Socialist expropriation measures.[6]

There were massive changes in property ownership in 1940–1941, due not only to the German but also the Soviet occupation. In the Baltic States and eastern Poland, almost all larger-scale enterprises, agricultural businesses and real estate upwards of a certain size fell victim to nationalization. Bank deposits and foreign currencies were effectively expropriated by conversion into rubles; self-employed tradesmen and craftsmen were cut off from supplies. It was only possible to maintain other forms of private property to a very limited extent, if one was not subject to Stalinist persecution, as most industrialist families were. Some tried a last-ditch attempt at saving their property before they were deported (by the Soviets) by entrusting it to friends or neighbors. In 1941, the Soviet authorities had evidently not yet finished confiscating property from the Jewish communities either.[7]

It is currently virtually impossible to ascertain how much Jewish property fell victim to Sovietization, but certainly some sections of the Jewish population were seriously affected. This can be observed by looking at, for example, the eastern part of Poland, occupied by the Soviets in 1939, where a disproportionately large number of Jews were deported in comparison to other sections of society. These deportations were intended to eliminate social and economic elites and clear the way for Sovietization.[8] The nationalization of private property had as its consequence the economic and therefore social weakening of local elites even before the Germans invaded. Nevertheless, it must be noted that a considerable amount of previously Sovietized property subsequently fell into the hands of the occupying Germans.

Yet even under German rule, expropriation practices varied considerably from region to region, according to the specific local occupation and persecution policies. In Bohemia, for a long time the practice was to introduce legal regulations and exert extreme pressure;[9] anti-Jewish policy in Poland and the Soviet Union, by contrast, was characterized from the beginning by the use of murderous violence. While the Protectorate was primarily intended to serve Germany's rearmament needs, western Poland was to be subjected to a program of complete Germanization. For this reason, neither deindustrialization nor the possibility of leaving larger businesses in non-German hands were considered. The situation in the General Government, that is central and southeast Poland, was a different one; while business was to be reduced to a minimum, Polish and even some Jewish-owned medium-sized or, more frequently, small businesses still continued to operate. During the course of the war, the destructive approach to the economy in central Poland changed; in 1942 German companies began to move their businesses there, partly to escape the Allied air raids. The areas formerly annexed by the Soviet Union were dealt with differently again, as the small amount of industry that existed there had been nationalized by 1941.

When considering the actual process of expropriation, one should bear in mind the general context of depreciation in the occupied territories, which was partly caused by the shrinking supply of consumer goods and partly (particularly in the occupied Soviet territories) by ruinous rates of exchange. The occupying powers did their best to extract as much money as possible from local markets.

After the initial chaotic "wild Aryanizations" in Austria in 1938, the occupation of Bohemia was accompanied by a more systematic policy of confiscation, as a number of valuable businesses were located in the Sudeten region and in the so-called Protectorate.[10] The early occupation of Poland, and later of the western Soviet Union, however, involved the intentional destruction of Jewish property in particular. In addition to this, considerable losses were incurred as a direct result of military action, mainly of residential buildings and businesses. The initial short-term plans for the occupied territories foresaw the deindustrialization of whatever areas were not earmarked for Germanization in the near future. In effect, this meant the extensive plundering of stocks and raw materials for the benefit of the German war effort.[11] While this hit non-Jews as well as Jews, the measures introduced in 1939 and 1941 were accompanied by specific waves of anti-Jewish violence. Simultaneously with the first mass shootings, Jewish places of worship were destroyed and areas with a high concentration of Jewish residents were systematically robbed. In Riga in the summer of 1941, for example, no less than 5,800 Jewish homes were plundered.[12] In many cases, the military administrations financed themselves in the short term by exacting enormous contributions from the Jewish communities.[13]

Any attempt at analyzing Germany's occupation of parts of the Soviet Union is complicated by the fact that about one third of the Jewish population of these areas fled or was evacuated before the arrival of the Germans. These were mostly inhabitants of the Soviet Union as it existed before the war. The majority of them were educated people who had worked in key or economic functions or for the administration and generally had somewhat more property than the average Soviet citizen. Of course, most of their property had to be left behind and was subsequently either confiscated or appropriated by other residents.

In the "annexed" parts of Poland, the Haupttreuhandsteelle Ost (Central Trusteeship Agency for the East)[14] took over most cases of expropriation, and the General Government's administration had its own trust agency. The bank accounts of Polish Jews were to a great extent frozen as early as November 1939. In Poland's largest credit institution, the Bank Handlowy, every second account belonged to a Jew, and for those who did not manage to withdraw their funds in time, the losses were considerable.[15] In January 1940, the compulsory registration of all valuables in Jewish possession was introduced.[16] The effectiveness of this regulation seems doubtful, however, despite the severe penalties that threatened noncompliance.[17] Recent Czech research found that 614 kg of gold, 17 tons of silver and silver goods, 5 kg of platinum, and 5,000 carats of diamonds from Jewish hands were registered in the Protectorate.[18] There is only fragmentary evidence of the robbery of valuables in Poland and the occupied Soviet territories, taken either by means of forced contributions from the Jewish councils or during house searches or murder campaigns.[19] While the gold reserves of the Polish State managed to escape Germany's clutches, most privately owned valuables did not.

The seizure of pensions and life insurance funds occurred mainly in Bohemia and Poland, as both countries had relatively well-developed insurance systems. The Italian insurance company Generali was particularly active in Eastern Europe. Polish insurance companies were formally administered by the Central Trusteeship Agency for the East, which urged them not to pay out insurance claims from Polish or Jewish clients, but to transfer the funds to the Reichsbank.[20]

Most Jewish-owned enterprises were confiscated in the annexed areas of Poland as early as 1939; in the General Government this process continued up to the time of the mass murders of 1942. In the latter region alone, 112,000 Jewish-owned businesses, often the smallest microenterprises, fell prey to confiscation; almost 100,000 of them were completely closed down. The approximately 115,000 handicraft businesses in the General Government suffered a similar fate. Expropriation in Poland was initially directed at businesses whose owners had fled in 1939. Thereafter, their property was officially considered "abandoned," as was the property of Polish refugees or the Polish state. Those Jewish-owned businesses that continued to exist suffered considerable discrimination, with barely any capital available to them and severely limited supplies of raw materials. Businesses that were not considered important for the war effort or that could be easily replaced by their Polish or German counterparts were the first to be hit by confiscation. Jewish commercial firms were partly replaced by German district wholesale firms and partly by Polish or Ukrainian cooperatives, which had begun to gain favor before the war. Local governments and chambers of commerce or chambers of handicrafts supported this Aryanization by taking over whole businesses, or at least their equipment and goods. Medium-sized enterprises that were considered irreplaceable were administered by the Trusteeship Agencies, mostly by unqualified or corrupt ethnic Germans. The former owners, meanwhile, became involuntary employees in their own businesses, as the new bosses still relied on their expertise.

On the whole in Poland and the occupied Soviet territories, the tendency was to issue only general regulations on expropriation, in many cases retroactively. Unlike in the Reich, no general directives for the Aryanization of all businesses were formulated as this would not have been practical in Poland or even necessary in the Soviet Union. In these territories in particular, the physical removal of property from its owners was the predominant modality of robbing the Jews. In the areas incorporated into the Reich, this was also the fate of property belonging to Poles who were resettled into the General Government. In the course of these violent resettlement campaigns, which took place in the winter of 1939–1940, the expelled Poles and Jews were forced to leave behind almost all of their property. Measures concentrating sections of the population in certain parts of town, on the other hand, were applied almost exclusively to Jews, but this and the Jews' enforced resettlement out of the countryside into the larger towns had a similar effect.

The process of ghettoization had drastic consequences not only for the lives but also for the property of the Jews. In most towns under occupation, the Jewish minority was forced to move to a certain quarter, which was far too small and lacking in infrastructure. Although not all Polish and Soviet Jews were confined within walled ghettos—Łódź and Warsaw were more the exception than the rule—most Jewish proprietors were nevertheless cut off from their businesses. Only those enterprises that happened to be situated within the ghetto limits could continue to operate. Furthermore, on moving into the ghettos, the Jews had to leave nearly all of their larger belongings behind. By this time, their real estate—mainly houses in small- and medium-sized towns[21]—had to a great extent already been confiscated.

The enforced resettlement of the Jews into ghettos did not, however, mean the end of expropriation.[22] The German civil administration, obsessed with the idea of uncovering huge hoards of valuables, tried to drain the ghettos of all assets. To this end, an entirely unjust exchange deal was made with the Jewish councils, forcing them to "purchase" food at exorbitant prices. In addition to this, even the most minor infringements of German regulations were punished with grotesquely large fines. The introduction of specially printed ghetto money, as in the Łódź ghetto, signified yet another form of confiscation. Ghetto inhabitants were forced to exchange their Złoty for this currency, the only authorized means of payment within the ghetto, which was worthless outside the ghetto walls.[23]

The most direct form of expropriation, the individual pillaging of Eastern European Jews, began in the first days of the occupation of Poland in 1939 and remained an everyday phenomenon throughout the war. German (and Austrian) personnel stole from the local Jews at every opportunity. Very occasionally, victims were permitted to keep belongings if they paid a ridiculously high fee, and even this applied mainly to non-Jews. Later, the Jewish councils had to provide the occupying forces with furniture and valuables and to finance their "colonial" lifestyle. Many occupying officials were not averse to accepting bribes, which were offered in the hope of easing the situation of the Jewish community. When the mass murders began in 1941–1942, there was a brief drastic increase in bribes, as victims made last-resort attempts to save their lives. Some non-Jewish locals were also approached in this way, albeit on a much smaller scale, in order to avert denunciation or in the mistaken hope of protection. Conversely, non-Jewish locals also tried this strategy with the occupying forces, although the results remained ambivalent. In some cases bribery saved lives; in general, however, it merely served to increase the corrupt tendencies of the occupation personnel.[24]

Murder in direct connection with robbery was committed primarily against the Jewish victims of National Socialism, although the murder campaigns against national elites and actual or supposed resistance fighters, as well as the murderous antipartisan campaigns in Poland or Belorussia, for example, were also often accompanied by robbery on a huge scale. From the first days of the systematic genocide in June 1941, the German agencies responsible made every effort to take anything movable from the Jews either directly before their murder or shortly afterwards. The military administration in the Soviet territories regularly sent packages of valuables to the "War Booty Department" of the Reich Main Treasury in Berlin, often with a derogatory note that the previous owners had been "bumped off Jews."[25]

Once a stable SS and police machinery had been established, which implemented the so-called second wave of murders, the robbery was also perfected. Now when ghettos were exterminated, not only the victims were sought out but also their belongings. Small groups of local police, mostly from the Baltic States or Ukraine, but also often Poles or Belorussians, searched the deserted houses of the ghettos for hidden valuables. Sometimes the murderers even searched their victims at the killing site. The men of the Security Police and regular police were out to get every last piece of property they could find. Officially the proceeds were to be delivered to the Reich Department for Precious Metals, but in practice much of it often ended up in the pockets of the (German or foreign) perpetrators.[26] Other official agencies also did their best to secure their share of the booty from the murder and robbery, as is demonstrated by the numerous enquiries, for example, by Wehrmacht agencies requesting household items that had previously belonged to Jews. Victims were made to undress before they were shot so that their clothing was not damaged. Huge lorry-loads of such clothing were transported to warehouses after large massacres such as those in Zhytomyr or at Babi Yar.[27] In eastern Galicia, employees of the so-called Ethnic Germans' Welfare Office joined the convoys of victims to the killing sites in order to collect the leftover belongings as soon as the crime was completed.

Lastly, similar forms of looting took place even in the extermination camps. Before they were transported, Jews were led to believe they could take a small amount of their possessions with them. These were then taken away, sometimes as soon as they got to the station, or at the very latest on their arrival at the camp gates.[28] The concluding report on "Aktion Reinhard" states that assets worth RM 179 million had been confiscated during this murder campaign. In the eyes of organizer Odilo Globocnik, this was fully intended to be a program of robbery as well as murder.[29] Most of the spoils, like those from Auschwitz and Majdanek, ended up with the SS economic administration, and from 1942 all valuables were to be deposited at the Reichsbank.[30] The murderers did not even shrink from looting the corpses next to the gas chambers. When German forces began covering their traces in the East, opening mass graves and burning the corpses, they acted in a similar manner, extracting anything that might be of value.[31]

In general, the expropriation of Jewish assets in occupied Eastern Europe was influenced far more by ideological than economic motives. With the exception of the Czech armament firms and the previously Jewish-owned textile companies that manufactured and repaired uniforms, the confiscations in the East did not play an important role in the German war economy. The expropriation was motivated by the antisemitic assumption of German functionaries that the Jews had acquired their property by improper means, to the detriment of the majority of the population. In these circles, talk of the stereotype of the supposed Jewish "parasites" was virulent. It is difficult to ascertain to what extent the occupation personnel really believed this ideology, but it certainly dominated the discourse on Jewish property. There was in any case a broad consensus among functionaries that the Jews should "disappear" from the occupied areas and that it was therefore absolutely necessary to isolate them within society.

The majority of officials involved in the robbery did not have any extensive knowledge of economics, but they considered the expropriation of "Jewish enemies" to be politically legitimate and necessary. The experts responsible for Aryanization did not think differently, but they acted somewhat more strictly according to economic principles. Some of them developed ideas for modernizing the "backward" Polish market, which they regarded as overcrowded. This policy of rationalization by means of closing down businesses, however, affected non-Jewish as well as Jewish enterprises.[32]

Among the large commercial institutions, the German banks were the first to play an active role in the changes, pursuing primarily the Aryanization of banks in the Czech territories. They contributed to the expropriations in Poland in a more indirect manner, for example by financing business takeovers. Other German companies took over those fields of commerce in Poland that had previously been run by Jewish businessmen. These were generally not whole businesses, as in the Reich, but rather only parts of them, as they were often simply dissolved and carved up.

For its part, the occupation administration hoped to improve its finances by looting Jewish property. There is, however, considerable doubt whether this succeeded to any great extent. Overall, probably only about 5 percent of its income was obtained in this way,[33] with a slightly greater percentage being raised in the early period of the occupation, mainly for local governments. Whatever the actual figures were, the policy of expropriation certainly served to exacerbate the frequent power struggles over resources and fields of responsibility. A running correspondence on the whereabouts of stolen property can be found for all the occupied territories, in some cases persisting even into the last days of the war.[34] While the SS and military administration conducted the confiscations in the early days of the occupation, the civil administrations took over responsibility later on. The SS and police machinery did not try to monopolize the looting until the start of the "Final Solution." In some areas, special administrative offices were set up; in this way, art works stolen from the Soviet Union were divided up between the ERR and the Special Commando Künsberg of the Foreign Ministry. Valuables were to be sent to the Reichsbank, which in turn financed the occupation. Although the SS was eager to take its share of the land confiscated, control over seized real estate came under the jurisdiction of the civil administrations. On the whole, the spoils tended to be concentrated in the hands of the civil authorities, which also gradually centralized their administration.

The occupation authorities used some of the confiscated property to support their racial policies. Ethnic Germans in the newly acquired territories were the first to benefit, especially in western Poland, although they did not receive any valuables or land. Non-German profiteers were the next in line (little is known about the role played by Czech collaborators, who also actively participated in Aryanization).[35] The Baltic States came next in the racist hierarchy, as these peoples, particularly the Estonians and Latvians, and to a lesser degree the Lithuanians, were ranked more highly than other eastern Europeans. Ukrainian Galicians were considered to be somewhat superior to the Poles and other Ukrainians, both of whom were treated extremely badly. The Belorussians and Russians ranked last.[36] Under German occupation, however, the latter had hardly any Jewish neighbors. Special shops sold off whatever Jewish property was not taken by the occupiers or by organized collaborators. Undoubtedly, town residents in Poland and the occupied Soviet territories suffered from desperate shortages. The extreme German occupation policy caused all the markets to be emptied: the death of millions was to be the calculated result of deliberate food distribution policies. Provisions were to be supplied only to those who worked in the interests of the Germans. But even everyday supplies were subject to restricted availability or greatly increased prices. Under these circumstances, people helped themselves to the property of their Jewish neighbors, not unlike the rather better-off residents of the Reich. Antisemitic views also played a role in the willingness of local inhabitants to appropriate stolen property, especially in eastern Poland and the Baltic States.[37]

In this climate of violence, the unrestrained plundering and open circulation of stolen assets led to a consequential degeneration of moral standards. The greed of the occupiers increased their readiness to kill and, in a few cases, even provided the motive for killing. While the robbery and murder caused a blurring of moral boundaries for the German functionaries, it did not remain without consequences for the non-Jewish local population either. Faced with severe shortages, locals supported the expropriations and their solidarity with the Jews diminished.

There can be no doubt then that the confiscations accelerated the course of the mass murder committed by the National Socialists in Eastern Europe. The occupation administration impoverished a minority, which was then all the more perceived to be a burden. In this way, the anti-Jewish policy became a self-fulfilling prophecy: the expropriation of the Jews, as with the confiscation of foodstuffs, caused blackmarket prices to rocket. Cooped up in the ghettos in complete deprivation, the increasingly impoverished Jews gradually fell victim to these terrible, artificially created living conditions. In theory, the Trusteeship Agency administrations should have eased this situation with the aid of the assets that they held in trust. In reality, however, they did not have any interest in doing so.[38] Instead, the Jews in their isolation were forced to conduct black-market trading, which was a criminal offence at the time. Considering the extreme situation in which they found themselves, this was not only a means of survival, but also of self-assertion against their oppressors.

The robbery leveled out social differences among the Jews; almost all were forced to eke out a very meager existence until 1942. The consequences became visible even earlier, with huge numbers of people dying in some ghettos during the winter of 1940–1941. Without any property, it was virtually impossible for people to obtain food on the black market. Life itself in the enclosed ghettos, cut off from work and the help of relatives, was very soon in jeopardy. Expropriation was only one aspect of the economic exploitation of the Jews. Forced labor was the other, which in some territories was probably almost as profitable. However, once the extermination phase had begun, assignment to forced labor could save lives. For this reason, it was vitally important for manual workers to hold on to their tools, or seamstresses their sewing machines, even in the ghetto.[39]

By the spring of 1943 there was almost no property remaining in Jewish hands in occupied Eastern Europe. In Poland and the Soviet Union, hardly any of the victims remained alive. Of course, the survivors and returnees, who had managed to flee into the interior of the Soviet Union, could not pick up where they had left off before the war either. This was, unfortunately, also a question of property. From late 1942, particularly in Poland and the Soviet Union, the question of whether stolen property should be returned to the Jews or not became the subject of debate in the underground press. After the liberation, violent arguments flared up between Jewish returnees and their compatriots who had settled into their residences in the meantime.[40] Not only had the society of the prewar era been devastated, and with it also the brisk economic exchange between Jews and non-Jews that had existed previously in Eastern Europe, but the very basis of property ownership was soon shattered by the nationalization campaigns of the postwar communist period. Returning Jews had to console themselves with the thought that although they had lost their property, they had at least escaped with their lives.

Translated from German by Charlotte Kreutzmüller

Notes

1. On the Axis satellite states of south Eastern Europe, see the essay of Tatjana Tönsmeyer in this volume. On Croatia, see also N. Kisić Kolanović, "Podržavljenje imovine Židova u NDH," [The nationalization of Jewish property in the Independent State of Croatia] *Časopis za suvremenu povijest* 30 (1998): 429–53.
2. See especially K.-H. Schlarp, *Wirtschaft und Besatzung in Serbien 1941–1944. Ein Beitrag zur nationalsozialistischen Wirtschaftspolitik in Südosteuropa* (Stuttgart, 1986), 294–301; E. Völkl, *Der Westbanat 1941–1944* (Munich, 1991), 170–80.
3. J. Tomaszewski, "The Role of Jews in Polish Commerce, 1918–1939," in *The Jews of Poland Between the Two World Wars*, ed. Yisrael Gutman et al. (Hanover, 1989), 141–57.
4. A. Nove and J. A. Newth, "The Jewish Population: Demographic Trends and Occupational Patterns," in *The Jews in Soviet Russia Since 1917*, ed. L. Kochan (Oxford, 1978), 132–67, here 163.

5. M. Altshuler, *Soviet Jewry on the Eve of the Holocaust: A Social and Demographic Profile* (Jerusalem, 1998), from 144.
6. Studies conducted partly still during the war estimate a per capita wealth of $200–300 (at wartime prices) in the Soviet Union, $700–900 for citizens of Poland, and between $3,500 and $5,800 for inhabitants of the Czech lands. According to these estimates the total losses for Soviet Jewry would be in the range of at least $600–700 million, in Poland between $2.2 billion and $3 billion (18 billion złoty), and for the Bohemian lands roughly $420–700 million. See S. J. Zabludoff, "Estimating Jewish Wealth," in *The Plunder of Jewish Property during the Holocaust: Confronting European History*, ed. A. Beker (New York, 2001), 48–65; J. Marcus, *Social and Political History of the Jews in Poland, 1919–1939* (Berlin, 1983), 256; H. B. Junz, *Report on the Wealth Position of the Jewish Population in Nazi-Occupied Countries, Germany and Austria: Appendix S to the Report on Dormant Accounts of Victims of Nazi Persecution in Swiss Banks* (Bern, 1999), from 188. However, these figures remain highly controversial and give only a very rough indication of the scale of Jewish property losses.
7. See B.-C. Pinchuk, *Shtetl Jews Under Soviet Rule. Eastern Poland on the Eve of the Holocaust* (Oxford, 1990), from 43.
8. On the Sovietization of eastern Poland between 1939 and 1941, see J. Gross, *Revolution from Abroad. The Soviet Conquest of Poland's Western Ukraine and Western Belorussia* (Princeton NJ, 1988). For the deportation statistics, see also P. Polian, *Against their Will: The History and Geography of Forced Migrations in the USSR* (Budapest, 2004).
9. See J. G. Lexa, "Anti-Jewish Laws and Regulations in the Protectorate of Bohemia and Moravia," in *The Jews of Czechoslovakia*, vol. 3 (New York, 1984), 75–103; M. Karny, "Die Protektoratsregierung und die Verordnung des Reichsprotektors über das jüdische Vermögen," *Judaica Bohemiae* 29 (1993): 54–66.
10. See R. Hilberg, *Die Vernichtung der europäischen Juden* (Frankfurt a.M., 1990), from 104. On the Aryanizations of businesses in the Protectorate there is now an extensive literature, partly scattered in recent studies on business history. See, for example, C. Kopper, "Die ‚Arisierung' der deutsch-böhmischen Aktienbanken," in *Konkurrenzpartnerschaft: Die deutsche und die tschechoslowakische Wirtschaft in der Zwischenkriegszeit*, ed. B. Barth et al. (Essen, 1998), 236–45.
11. See T. Berenstein and A. Rutkowski, *Grabieszcza polityka gospodarcza hitlerowskiej administracji wojskowej* [The thieving economic policy of the hitlerite military administration], *Biuletyn Żydowskiego Instytutu Historycznego* (*BŻIH*) 42 (1962): 61–87.
12. K. Reichelt, "Profit and Loss: the Economic Dimensions of the Riga Ghetto (1941–1943)," in *Issues of the Holocaust Research in Latvia* ed. Andris Caune, Aivars Stranga, and Margers Vestermanis (Riga, 2001), 168–84, here 172.
13. See A. Dmitrzak, *Hitlerowskie kontrybucje w okupowanej Polsce 1939–1945* [The Hitlerite contributions in occupied Poland] (Poznań, 1983).
14. See J. Dingell, *Zur Tätigkeit der Haupttreuhandstelle Ost, Treuhandstelle Posen 1939–1945* (Frankfurt am Main, 2003); Bernhard Rosenkötter, *Treuhandpolitik. Die "Haupttreuhandstelle Ost" und der Raub polnischer Vermögen 1939–1945* (Essen, 2003).
15. H. James, *Die Deutsche Bank und die "Arisierung,"* (Munich, 2001), 190.
16. *Faschismus – Getto – Massenmord. Dokumentation über Ausrottung und Widerstand der Juden in Polen während des 2. Weltkrieges*, ed. the Jewish Historical Institute in Warsaw (Berlin, 1961), from 165.
17. On Latvia, see M. Dean, "Seizure, Registration, Rental and Sale. The Strange Case of the German Administration of Jewish Moveable Property in Latvia (1941–1944)," in *Latvia in World War II* (Riga, 2000), 372–81.
18. D. Jancík et al., "Der Mechanismus der Enteignung jüdischen Goldes im 'Protektorat Böhmen und Mähren' und seine Funktionsweise (1939–1945)," *Zeitschrift für Unternehmensgeschichte* 46 (2001): 58–76; see also by the same author, for example, *Jewish Gold and Other Precious Metals, Precious Stones and Objects Made of Such Materials. Situation in the Czech Lands in the Years 1939 to 1945* (Prague, 2001).

19. See Y. Arad, "Plunder of Jewish Property in the Nazi-Occupied Areas of the Soviet Union," *Yad Vashem Studies* 29 (2001): 109–48; H. Boryak, M. Dubyk, and N. Makovs'ka, *"Natsysts'ke zoloto" z Ukraïny* -Nazigold from Ukraine, vol. 1, (Kiev, 1998), from 55; *"Natsistskoe zoloto" iz Belarusi – Nazi Gold from Belarus: Documents and Materials*, eds. V. I. Adamushko et al., (Minsk, 1998).
20. See G. D. Feldman, *Die Allianz und die deutsche Versicherungswirtschaft 1933–1945* (Munich, 2001), from 466.
21. On Jewish real estate property in a small Polish town, see R. Lehmann, *Symbiosis and Ambivalence: Poles and Jews in a Small Galician Town* (New York, 2001), from 44.
22. See, for example, J. Adamska, "Grabie mienia mieszkańców getta przez funkcjonariuszy hitlerowskich," [The robbery of the property of the inhabitants of the ghetto by Hitlerite officials] in *Getto w Łódź* (Łódź, 1988), 81–97.
23. See S. Bułkiewicz, *Pieniądz getta lodzkiego 1940–1944* [The money of the Łódź Ghetto] (Pia, 1993); M. Schulze and S. Petriuk, *Unsere Arbeit – unsere Hoffnung: Das Ghetto Lodz* (Schwalmtal, 1995).
24. See J. T. Gross, *Polish Society under German Occupation. The Generalgouvernement 1939–1944* (Princeton, 1979); F. Bajohr, *Parvenüs und Profiteure. Korruption in der NS-Zeit* (Frankfurt a.M., 2001).
25. M. Dean, "Jewish Property Seized in the Occupied Soviet Union in 1941 and 1942. The Records of the Reichshauptkasse Beutestelle," *Holocaust and Genocide Studies* 14 (2000): 83–101; C. Gerlach, *Kalkulierte Morde. Die deutsche Wirtschafts- und Vernichtungspolitik in Weißrußland 1941–1944* (Hamburg, 1999), from 677.
26. *Die Schweiz und die Goldtransaktionen im Zweiten Weltkrieg: Zwischenbericht* (Bern, 1998), 36.
27. See also the cases further south in: Andrej Angrick, *Besatzungspolitik und Massenmord: Die Einsatzgruppe D in der südlichen Sowjetunion 1941–1943* (Hamburg, 2003).
28. See A. Strzelecki, "Der Raub des Besitzes der Opfer des KL Auschwitz," in *Hefte von Auschwitz* 21 (2000): 7-99.
29. *Faschismus – Getto – Massenmord*, 422; see B. Perz and T. Sandkühler, "Auschwitz und die 'Aktion Reinhard' 1942–45," *Zeitgeschichte* 26 (1999): 283–316.
30. *Die Schweiz und die Goldtransaktionen*, 38.
31. A. Strzelecki, "Die Verwertung der Leichen," *Hefte von Auschwitz* 21 (2000): 101–64.
32. See G. Aly and S. Heim, *Vordenker der Vernichtung. Auschwitz und die deutschen Pläne für eine neue europäische Ordnung* (Hamburg, 1991), from 188.
33. M. Dean, "Die Enteignung 'jüdischen Eigentums' im Reichskommissariat Ostland 1941–1944," in *"Arisierung" im Nationalsozialismus. Volksgemeinschaft, Raub und Gedächtnis*, edited on behalf of the Fritz Bauer Institute by I. Wojak and P. Hayes (Frankfurt a.M., 2000), 201–18; Gerlach, *Kalkulierte Morde*, from 682, gives figures for Reichskommissariat Ostland of RM 4.5 million arising from confiscated Jewish property against about RM 300 million of income from taxes.
34. See T. Berenstein, "O podłożu gospodarczym sporów między władzami administracyjnami a policyjnami w Generalnej Guberni (1939–1944)," [On the economic basis of the conflicts between the administration and the police in the General Government] *BŻIH*, 53 (1965): 33–88.
35. See J. Bartos, "Die Arisierung jüdischen Vermögens in Olmütz im Jahre 1939," in *Theresienstädter Studien und Dokumente* (2000): 282–96, here from 284.
36. B. Chiari, *Alltag hinter der Front. Besatzung, Kollaboration und Widerstand in Weißrußland 1941–1944* (Düsseldorf, 1998), 257–63; Gerlach, *Kalkulierte Morde*, from 679.
37. On Poland, see the polemical account in L. Cooper, *In the Shadow of the Polish Eagle: The Poles, the Holocaust and Beyond* (Basingstoke, 2000), 125–36; on the Ukrainians, see K. C. Berkhoff, *Harvest of Despair: Life and Death in Ukraine under Nazi Rule* (Cambridge, MA, 2004), 78–87.
38. S. Steinbacher, *"Musterstadt" Auschwitz. Germanisierung und Judenmord in Ostoberschlesien* (Munich, 2000), 123.

39. An initial overview is provided by H. Kaienburg, "Zwangsarbeit von Juden in Arbeits- und Konzentrationslagern," in I. Wojak and P. Hayes, *"Arisierung" im Nationalsozialismus*, 219–40.
40. See K.-P. Friedrich, "Kollaboration und Antisemitismus in Polen unter deutscher Besatzung (1939–1944/45). Zu verdrängten Aspekten eines schwierigen deutsch-polnisch-jüdischen Verhältnisses," *Zeitschrift für Geschichtswissenschaft* 45 (1997): 818–34; K.-P. Friedrich, "Der nationalsozialistische Judenmord in polnischen Augen: Einstellungen in der polnischen Presse 1942–1946/47" (PhD diss., Cologne, 2003) [available at: http://kups.ub.uni-koeln.de/volltexte/2003/952]; A. Weiner, *Making Sense of War: The Second World War and the Bolshevik Revolution* (Princeton, NJ, 2001), 191–92; M. Altshuler, "Antisemitism in Ukraine toward the End of the Second World War," *Jews in Eastern Europe* 22 (1993): 40–81.

THE ROBBERY OF JEWISH PROPERTY IN EASTERN EUROPEAN STATES ALLIED WITH NAZI GERMANY

Tatjana Tönsmeyer

Jewish minorities lived in all the countries of Central and Southeastern Europe on the eve of the Second World War. They comprised part of the middle classes in these mostly agrarian societies and were destined to become the victims of the Holocaust, most of them being deported to German death camps, but some murdered close to their own homes. Those who survived and returned after the war soon came to realize that there was almost no chance of recovering their stolen property; that which had been "Aryanized" at the beginning of the 1940s was then "socialized" less than ten years later.

Applications for restitution had a realistic chance of success only after the fall of the communist regimes. But by this time, very many of the former owners were deceased and their heirs were confronted with an unclear legal situation and hostile majority populations that did not acknowledge the losses inflicted on the Jewish minority. Even in those cases where all the practical problems could be solved and a former owner (or the heir) got the property back, he or she often discovered that the business consisted of little more than a memory, having lost nearly all value after decades of neglect.

It is not only the restitution of stolen Jewish property that countries in Central and Southeastern Europe have to confront today. An even more difficult task than resolving the technical legal and financial aspects of restitution is that of fostering a realistic understanding of what happened in the 1940s. For without an awareness of the injustices suffered in the past, it hardly seems possible to build a robust civil society in the present. This is all the more important as some people in Hungary, Romania, and Slovakia still believe rather that it was the Jews who had "acquired national property in an illegal manner." Therefore, these people view the expropriation of the Jews in the 1940s as a harsh but not necessarily unjustified measure.

Notes for this section begin on page 92.

The post-communist societies must not only return stolen Jewish property, they must also acknowledge the terrible injustices inflicted upon the Jews. As far as historiography is concerned, this means examining in detail the social climate in which the expropriations took place and answering such questions as: How was it organized and who profited from it? Was the robbery mainly the result of German influence, or was it a policy developed independently by the governments in Bucharest, Budapest, and Bratislava? What role did indigenous antisemitism play in the process?

Expropriations in the Context of Anti-Jewish Persecution

In the three countries examined in this article, expropriation was one step on the road toward the total exclusion of the Jewish minority from the economic and social life of the country. This process was usually achieved in several stages. Usually regulations concerning property followed those that defined who was to be considered a Jew. In Slovakia this was achieved as early as 18 April 1939, only one month after the creation of the Slovak state, by Decree No. 63, which defined Jews mainly in terms of religion.[1] This regulation was drastically tightened in September 1941 by a new law, the so-called Jewish Codex, which was modeled on the Nuremberg Laws with their racist definitions.[2]

The situation in Hungary was quite similar. The first law with a definition in terms of religion was enacted in 1938 and slightly modified the following year. The third Hungarian anti-Jewish law resembled the Slovak one from 1941: enacted the same year in August, it was also modeled on the Nuremberg Laws; indeed some paragraphs were even stricter than the German regulations.[3] In Romania, the situation was slightly different, as a law was already enacted in August 1940 that combined religious and racist elements in its definition.[4]

As a next step the three countries enacted laws restricting the professional activities of Jews and proscribing their ownership of certain types of property. The Hungarian government in May 1938 imposed restrictions on the number of Jews permitted to work in the media and cultural organizations, as well as in the legal and medical professions. Initially the percentage permitted to work in these professions was 20 percent of all those employed, but it was reduced to a mere 6 percent the following year. Furthermore, Jews were to be excluded step by step from the state bureaucracy.[5] The governments in Bucharest and Bratislava acted quite similarly: Jews were excluded from the army and the state bureaucracy; they lost their jobs as publishers, lawyers, physicians, and pharmacists according to laws enacted in the summer of 1940 in Romania, and already in 1939 in Slovakia. In addition, the Romanian government enacted a law on 8 August 1940 that prohibited Jews from purchasing land and industrial property, while in 1939 the Slovak government had already decreed the compulsory registration of Jewish agricultural property.[6]

"Aryanization" was the next step in the exclusion of the Jewish minority from economic life. As a consequence, much of the Jewish population became pauperized, as at the same time social welfare benefits were cut. Thereby the governments in Budapest, Bucharest, and Bratislava created a social problem. The German answer to this problem was "forced labor" and "deportation."[7] Therefore, the expropriations can be seen to have accelerated the pace of anti-Jewish persecution leading towards extermination. What before the expropriations for the three governments had been primarily an ideological question was now a concrete material problem: between 5 and 10 percent of the population, that is the Jewish minority, now had almost no possibility of earning a living by legal means.

The Robbery of Jewish Property

If one studies the persecution of Central and Southeastern European Jewry one realizes that historiography up to now has focused largely on the deportations, but that the robbery of Jewish property has attracted far less attention. In spite of the existence of many divergent aspects that still need to be studied,[8] a number of striking similarities can be discerned in the three countries, which will be examined below.

Farmland and Forests

The three governments made considerable efforts to acquire Jewish farmland and forests. In Romania, regulations for the expropriation of farmland and forests were issued on 5 October and 17 November 1940, respectively.[9] On the basis of these laws, 519,000 hectares had been expropriated by 1943; however, three-quarters of these were in Bessarabia, and only one-quarter within Romania's 1940 borders.[10] Most of the property was taken into state ownership, but regional communities benefited as well. For example the municipal authority of Câmpulung in Bukovina declared all property lying more than three hundred meters from the city center to be agricultural land, thereby expropriating all the Jews living outside this small area.[11] The Slovak government was also highly interested in Jewish agricultural lands and forests. The basis for the expropriations was the law on the compulsory registration of agrarian property, which led to the robbery of nearly 44,329 hectares of Jewish-owned forests and farmland.[12] Most of the expropriated properties went into state ownership, as was the case in Romania.

The Slovak government even proved to be quite aggressive in defending its interests against Berlin. Hermann Göring, head of the Four Year-Plan administration and himself an avid hunter, tried to get his hands on the so-called Weinmann estate in Malacký in Western Slovakia. Through the Reichssicherheitshauptamt [Reich Security Main Office] (RSHA), he tried to confiscate these lands, as the former owner was a Czech Jew. However, the Slovak government prevented this by turning the estate into a "recreational area" for the Slovak president.[13]

The Hungarian government was also interested in seizing land on a large scale. Up to 1942 it had expropriated about 450,000 hectares of farmland and woods, with the lion's share of forests again going into state ownership. Exactly who profited from the farmland has not yet been thoroughly researched. Though the second Hungarian anti-Jewish law justified confiscation "as a means to strengthen the Hungarian farmers,"[14] expropriated farmland not infrequently was given to members of the traditional elite, who were thereby able to augment their already large country estates.[15] Decisions on the fate of any subsequent land expropriations were deferred until after the end of the war, so that a good deal was left fallow.[16] Yet the measures were continued by the Ministry of Food Supply and Agriculture, which expropriated a further 370,650 acres of farmland in the early summer of 1944.[17] It can be concluded that the three governments expropriated farmland and forests on their own initiative. As has been shown by the example of Slovakia, they did not give in to pressure from Berlin, but fought to protect their own interests.

Middle-Class Property

The three governments were also very interested in expropriating middle-class property. As a result, the Hungarian press could report in January 1943 that in many branches there were no Jewish businesses left. This was true with regard to companies and shops trading in food, heating, and construction materials; there were also no more Jewish peddlers, caterers, or traders in church articles.[18] These expropriations continued after German troops occupied the country in the spring of 1944, when the Ministry of Trade and Commerce demanded that Jews close down their shops, offices, and warehouses.[19] Although two-thirds of Hungarian Jews had already become unemployed as a result of the anti-Jewish legislation passed in 1939, the effects of the robbery exacerbated their impoverishment still further. By 1942 some 300,000 people were dependent on Jewish charitable support.[20]

In Slovakia too, the expropriation of the Jewish population gathered momentum. By the end of 1941 nearly twelve thousand shops and handicraft businesses had been expropriated. "Problems" similar to those encountered in the other countries arose, as the new owners frequently lacked the expertise and financial resources required to keep the businesses going. Therefore, Dieter Wisliceny, SS-Hauptsturmführer and an adviser on Aryanization, reported to Berlin that the strict separation of the compulsory administrators from those who purchased "Aryanized" properties, as was usually enforced in Germany, was not possible in Slovakia, since the country lacked sufficient experienced personnel.[21] He faced even more problems on account of the German minority, as they complained to Himmler that they were not getting their share of the expropriated property.[22] On Wisliceny's advice, a joint Slovak-German committee was then established to try to resolve these conflicts.[23]

With regard to Romania, it is noticeable that although the decree of 16 November 1940 ordered the dismissal of all Jews employed in trade and industrial enterprises,[24] no law ordering the compulsory sale of Jewish businesses was enacted. However, there were some expropriations of middle-class shops and handicraft businesses in the country; the Iron Guard, as a part of the government coalition from the summer of 1940, favored so-called voluntary Aryanizations, which were frequently accompanied by brutal attacks on the owners in order to satisfy the appetite of members of the Guard.[25] Altogether, the results were quite chaotic,[26] yet according to Hilberg, up to the spring of 1941 Jewish business ownership remained largely untouched.[27] However, this is not to say that the measures taken to exclude the Jewish population from the economic life of the country did not have any effect. By the middle of 1942 unemployment among the Jewish minority had reached 44 percent.[28]

Until recently there was little reliable information on who were the main beneficiaries from the expropriations of Jewish middle-class businesses. At least the contemporary propaganda of the three governments suggests that they wanted their petit bourgeois Gentile followers to benefit and thereby bind them closely to the regime. Thus the interest of the Slovak middle-class in getting rid of their Jewish competitors was vigorously supported by the government. Its chief ideologist, Štefan Polakovič, even declared in 1941, "By Aryanising we aim to establish a strong Slovak middle class, which owns capital and therefore plays an important role in the life of the nation. It is in the interest of the entire Slovak nation that many entrepreneurs become rich."[29] This is why the expropriations were called Slovakianization or Christianization in Bratislava,[30] and Romanianization in Bucharest.[31]

As far as Hungary is concerned, some researchers argue that the expropriations only developed slowly here, because the Jewish population formed an especially large part of the middle class of the country and therefore the government was worried about the effects of completely excluding the Jews from economic activity.[32] But the figures cited above must cause one to doubt whether the situation in Hungary was really fundamentally different from that in Slovakia or Romania. The non-Jewish middle class was weak in all three countries and one could therefore also argue that the weaker it was, the stronger its incentive to get rid of Jewish competitors. This might be suggested by the example of Eastern Slovakia; in this poorest region of the country, with a Jewish population that was thoroughly pauperized, roughly one-third of all the Slovak expropriations took place.[33]

Even though all three regimes were interested in rewarding their followers with the loot, it is also true that in many cases former Jewish businesses were liquidated rather than sold. For example in Slovakia, by 31 December 1941, some 9,935 businesses had been liquidated (84 percent) and a mere 1,888 (16 percent) "Aryanized."[34] This was mainly due to the lack of know-how and capital among those interested in acquiring the available objects, but by liquidating businesses the Bratislava government also found a means of blocking the demands of the German minority for part of the spoils.[35] At the same time, there is also evidence that, similar to the situation in Hungary, the war contribution demanded by the Germans was also in part financed with money collected from the liquidation of Jewish property. Since the Slovak state's budget expenditure doubled between 1940 and 1944 and German clearing debts even surpassed the state's budget, the extra revenue raised helped to limit the scale of state debt, thereby making possible additional borrowing.[36]

Industrial property

If one examines the policies of the three governments towards industrial property, it is notable that Bratislava, Budapest, and Bucharest all acted quite cautiously. The first laws on Aryanization in Romania[37] and Slovakia[38] did not mention it at all. This was because both governments were afraid that expropriations would only result in further German capital penetration, which would give them majority control over these companies.[39] The Slovak official newspaper *Slovák* put it quite bluntly in 1940: "It is not in accordance with the interests of the state if Aryanisation is carried out with the aid of non-Slovak persons and capital."[40]

In Hungary, the situation was different, as here priority was given to the output of the armaments industry, to which both expropriations and restrictions on Jewish workers were subordinated. There were prominent Jewish armament producers in Hungary, and since Germany desperately needed the war materials produced by these companies, Jewish suppliers were not boycotted and Jewish managers were not forced to resign.[41] Aside from this, intermarriage between Jews and non-Jews also helped to resist or at least defer the expropriations, as demonstrated by the example of the Manfred Weiss company. This was the largest Hungarian armaments company, which was only taken over by the SS in the summer of 1944, after the German occupation of the country.[42]

Other Types of Property

Aside from landed estates, forests, and middle-class and industrial enterprises, the governments in Budapest, Bucharest, and Bratislava also laid hands on other forms of Jewish property, such as real estate,[43] ships,[44] and personal valuables of all kinds.[45] Either the goods concerned were to be surrendered,[46] or extra taxes were collected. Slovakia, for example, issued in September 1941 the so-called decree Z 199, demanding a 20 percent "special fee" on the value of Jewish property compulsorily registered.[47] The Romanian government imposed a special fee even earlier, in July 1941, demanding 10 billion lei. In "return," so the Minister of Finance told the members of the Jewish committee, Marshal Antonescu would guarantee the lives of Romanian Jews.[48] About two years later, in May 1943, the government in Bucharest imposed another special tax, amounting to 4 billion lei, upon the Jewish population, because they were "enjoying their lives" at a time when Romanian soldiers were dying at the front.[49] Aside from these examples there were many other mechanisms by which the governments in these three countries robbed the Jewish population, enabling them at least in part to meet their financial obligations towards the German Reich.

Expropriations: Domestic or Foreign Policy?

There is no doubt that the Jewish populations of Slovakia, Hungary, and Romania were the victims of the expropriations enacted by the three governments under examination. But who were these policies intended to please? Berlin, or the non-Jewish majority in these three countries? Many politicians in Central and Southeastern Europe were firmly convinced that a "Jewish Question" existed. It is true that the historiography has pointed to a form of symbiosis existing in Hungary between the aristocracy and the Jews until the early twentieth century, ending only during the First World War.[50] In contrast to this, Slovak anti-Jewish enmity dates back to the nineteenth century. It was especially the cooperation between the Hungarian aristocracy and the Jews that was perceived as an obstacle to the development of the Slovak national movement. The Jews were therefore labeled as "agents of Magyarization."[51]

The Romanian anti-Jewish enmity, especially that of the Iron Guard, which was notorious for its antisemitism, also included quite strong antimodern features. Traditional antisemitism had been a part of the political mass mobilization of the predominantly agrarian population in all three countries. In the twentieth century, frustration and fear caused by modernization found expression in the conviction that there was a "Jewish problem." Due to their anti-Jewish prejudices, these politicians could not contemplate "integration" as a possible solution. On the contrary, they favored the segregation of the Jewish minority from the non-Jewish majority. The first plans to remove the Jewish population entirely from their native countries were conceived in Hungary as early as 1921. Gyula Gömbös, a convinced antisemite who in 1923 founded a racist party and became prime minister in 1932, demanded, "I think it is necessary that the Hungarian government start talking with the central office of Zionism about resettling some hundreds of thousands of surplus Jews of Hungarian citizenship."[52]

For most of the interwar period, such ideas were not voiced in Czechoslovakia. But in March 1937, Karol Sidor, a confidant of Andrej Hlinka, the leader of the Slovak People's Party, urged at a meeting of the Committee on Foreign Affairs of the parliament in Prague that the Jews should be removed to Birobidzhan (in Siberia),[53] since there was "no space" for them in Czechoslovakia and "in any case, they are all communists."[54] In 1938, after the Iron Guard had been preaching anti-Jewish hatred for years, the Romanian antisemite Alexandru Razmerita criticized the plan of a Romanian priest who proposed that all Romanian Jews should be drowned, because this "total elimination" was not a practical solution, as the country lacked sufficient ships to implement the plan.[55]

Gömbös and Razmerita may well have been "radicals" in their countries, but Sidor was not. However, there was quite a strong consensus among the national elites in all three countries that a "Jewish problem" existed and that it had to be solved not by "integration" but by "exclusion." And they also agreed that dealing with this alleged "problem" was a "just cause."

This can be demonstrated by many specific quotations. The Hungarian prime minister Kálmán Darányi[56] and the Slovak lawyer and member of parliament for the People's Party Karol Mederly[57] (who, incidentally, abjured the use of force as counterproductive), for example, are representative of many other political leaders.

The Slovak president Jozef Tiso, a Catholic priest, even tried to legitimize this idea of a "just cause" in religious terms. In August 1942, at the peak of the deportations from Slovakia, he described the measures against the Jews as a commandment from God and demanded, "Slovaks, go and get rid of those who have done harm unto thee."[58] But it was not only Tiso who could think of Jews only in terms of the enemy. In September 1940, shortly after the Second Vienna Award, Antonescu announced that he was not going to protect the Jews of Romania because he considered them responsible for most of the disasters that had happened to the country.[59] Both politicians, Antonescu and Tiso, represented the conservative majorities who were said to be "moderate" compared to the "radicals" in the Iron Guard, the Arrow Cross, or the Hlinka Guard. And both Tiso and Antonescu were so firmly convinced that they were right with regard to their anti-Jewish measures that they even argued along these lines when defending themselves at their trials after the war.[60]

All this demonstrates that anti-Jewish measures, including the robbery of Jewish property, were policies intentionally pursued by the Slovak, Hungarian, and Romanian governments. These policies were rooted in an understanding of "justice" that was in itself antisemitic. As far as foreign policy is concerned, one should add that until 1944, the three countries were not occupied, but German allies. It is true that there were German personnel based in each of the three countries,[61] but the numbers were quite small and were dependent on the cooperation of the local administrations. This chapter examines the internal arguments and freedom of action of the three governments, in order to help explain the development from robbery to deportation and then murder. There is a need for more research into events outside the capital cities,[62] but as the above-noted example of Câmpulung in Bukovina shows, not all, and maybe not even the majority, of local anti-Jewish measures were the result of German pressure. As far as the robbery of Jewish property is concerned, it can be stated that especially the regimes in Bratislava and Bucharest[63] wanted to proceed in an "orderly" fashion, as they intended to exploit the loot in support of their own "social policies." The robbery of Jewish property can therefore be viewed as a product of the domestic politics of these regimes.

Yet when it comes to the deportation and murder of the Jews, these decisions fall much more within the realm of foreign policy, as they were central to relations with Nazi Germany. This differentiation is quite important, as it illustrates again the essentially multi-causal nature of the removal of civil rights and murder of the European Jews. At the same time this differentiation reveals the freedom of action that the three governments possessed; in July 1944, when extermination was on the agenda, Horthy was able to stop the deportations from Budapest,[64] and Berlin could not persuade Bratislava to restart the transports in 1943.[65] However, these same governments had also used their freedom of action prior to 1943–1944 in order to implement the large-scale expropriation of Jewish property.

Anti-Jewish Measures as "Social Policy"

In a recent publication, Christian Gerlach and Götz Aly have shown how after the German occupation of Hungary, the Hungarian administration—sometimes to the astonishment of German officials[66]—enacted anti-Jewish measures in accordance with their own conceptions of social policy. This was true, for instance, with regard to the expropriation of agricultural land, which was to be reserved mainly for former combatants returning home from the front. Other examples are the distribution of shoes and clothing, or manufactured goods among the rural population after Jewish shops were forced to close down,[67] or the handing over of expropriated apartments and houses formerly owned by Jews to "relieve the housing shortage among workers and state officials."[68] The so-called "people's insurance," enacted in July 1944, also reflects this kind of social policy. The rural population and those working as household servants benefited most from this insurance, which was paid for mainly out of the proceeds from the sale of Jewish property, once the former Jewish owners had been deported to forced labor and death.[69]

There was widespread agreement about these measures among the German occupation forces, the far-right Hungarian government, and the Arrow Cross Men who were still excluded from the government. Furthermore, these measures belonged to a broader context of social policy that included the dissolution of the Social Democratic Party and the "nationalization" of the trade unions immediately after the German occupation. The property of these institutions "was to be used in the interests of the Hungarian workers,"[70] as now "the Jewish poison was going to be eliminated once and for all," all "social differences between the classes" were to be overcome, and everyone would "be judged according to his performance."[71]

This certainly created a new situation in the wake of the German occupation. But the extent to which the Jewish population had already been excluded from society is reflected in local police reports from the early 1940s. These reports maintained that the Jewish population, in spite of "Aryanization," was still very well off. One report written in September 1943 in Carpartho-Ukraine states: "The hatred of the Jewish people has been increasing daily because the public see that they still lack nothing, they are even better off than they used to be, they are acquiring wealth."[72] Furthermore, the reports claimed that the Jewish population was lacking in patriotism, and was even taking sides with the enemy. Nearly every report from 1941 on argues that radios should be confiscated, as the Jews are only listening to "enemy broadcasting stations."[73] And even the synagogues seemed to be dangerous, because they might be used for forbidden meetings instead of worship.[74]

The police reports claim that public opinion was strongly anti-Jewish and that not only the government, but the population in general was deeply convinced that there was a "Jewish problem."[75] A considerable number of Hungarians wanted to profit from solving this "problem": for example, in Sopron in western Hungary, as late as June 1944 3,000 people applied for 150 expropriated Jewish shops; in Cluj (Kolozsvár) in Transylvania there were 1,500 applicants for 400 businesses.[76] Quite often what these people feared most was that they might lose this property after the end of the war.[77] But this pattern was not confined to Hungary. In Slovakia there are also several indications that expropriated Jewish property was being exploited by the government for the implementation of its own social policy.[78]

In Hungary, Slovakia, and Romania the loot gained by expropriating the Jewish minority was intended for distribution among the non-Jewish majority. This was viewed specifically as a "social policy," taking things from "rich Jews" and handing them over to "poor Hungarians" (and Slovaks and Romanians). Since the supposed wealth of the Jews was viewed by the government and much of the public as "unjustly" acquired, the policy of expropriation was perceived as righting some imagined previous wrongdoing. One consequence of the postwar communist regimes in this region was that this conception remained unchallenged for a long time. For example, a Slovak Jewish woman remembers how the man who in the early 1940s had expropriated her father's business, told her thirty years later: "I was one of the decent people. I did not send you to Auschwitz."[79]

Conclusion

In the traditional societies of Central and Southeastern Europe, anti-Jewish attitudes and religious anti-Judaism were both quite widespread. This remained true well into the twentieth century. After the First World War, Hungary belonged to the group of states that had lost the war, whereas Romania and Slovakia (as part of Czechoslovakia) counted themselves among the victors. In Hungary, political and social change ended the "symbiosis" between the Jews and the Hungarian aristocracy. In Romania, educational policies were pursued with the aim of nation-building and integrating the recently acquired territories into "Old Romania" by Romanianizing the elites. As a result the universities became bastions of antisemitism and prime recruiting grounds for the Iron Guard.[80]

During the interwar period, all three countries witnessed an intensification of nationalist sentiment: in Romania through the Romanianization of the new territories, in Hungary under the slogan "revision of Trianon" and in Slovakia in the form of demands for "autonomy" from the central government in Prague. All three societies were involved in different ways in nation-building. Anti-Jewish propaganda was used to exclude the Jewish minority from this process and intensified the already existing traditional forms of antisemitism.

Young academics played an especially important role in this process of political mass mobilization.[81] After completing their studies they had difficulties finding jobs commensurate with their training and ambitions in Hungary, because the loss of territory after the First World War meant that a smaller number of people were needed in the state administration. At the same time young academics had problems finding suitable employment in Romania, as the consolidation of the state administration developed only slowly and widespread corruption remained a great obstacle.[82] In Slovakia, the same group had to face competition from Czech professionals who in the early years of the Czechoslovak state were sent to the eastern part of the republic and still held many of the posts.

Anti-Jewish sentiments were commonplace in all three countries in the nationalistically overheated atmosphere of the interwar period, as a threat that hovered ominously over everyday life. Antisemitism united those social classes that could not solve the problems caused by modernization, nor handle the fears associated with it. Therefore, these predominantly agrarian societies, with weak non-Jewish middle classes, young educated, but often frustrated elites, and churches with an inclination towards traditional anti-Judaism[83] defined the Jewish population as "the others," an alien body within the non-Jewish majority. The majority increasingly perceived this as a "problem" that had to be "solved."

This is the political and social atmosphere in which the laws "legalizing" the expropriation of Jewish property were enacted. As has been demonstrated, the robbery of Jewish property was purposefully implemented by the governments in Budapest, Bucharest, and Bratislava that profited by bringing expropriated forests under state ownership. Middle-class property was mainly liquidated, but part of it was also "Slovakianized," "Romanianized," or "Magyarized."[84] On the other hand, industrial businesses were mostly left untouched, because the governments in Bratislava and Bucharest were afraid that German competitors might exploit this opportunity to buy up a majority holding in these companies. In Hungary, the needs of the arms industry were given priority over expropriation policy.

The perception in all three countries was that thereby a "problem had" been dealt with, a viewpoint so widely and unquestioningly accepted that Antonescu and Tiso even tried to use it as an argument in their own defense during the postwar trials. Obviously, it is absurd to try to use antisemitic arguments as an excuse for criminal acts, but in antisemitism ideology and material interests cannot be separated, as they form two sides of the same coin.

It is this complexity that explains why more recent scholarship increasingly stresses the concept of multiple causality.[85] A variety of separate causes set the machinery of destruction in motion and kept it going once started. It is not in doubt that the Holocaust was primarily a German "project," as this is blatantly obvious. However, it remains important to address the question: why did the governments of non-occupied states such as Slovakia, Hungary, and Romania, which enjoyed a considerable freedom of action, also participate in the Holocaust? This was not merely a result of German pressure, as all three governments enacted their own anti-Jewish legislation, which their majority populations considered "just." But this "justice" could only last if the Jewish population did not come back.

Notes

1. A. Vašek, *Die Lösung der Judenfrage in der Slowakei* (Bratislava, 1942), 27.
2. Ibid., 27–28.
3. C. Gerlach and G. Aly, *Das letzte Kapitel. Der Mord an den ungarischen Juden* (Stuttgart, 2002), 49.
4. R. Hilberg, *Die Vernichtung der europäischen Juden*, (Frankfurt am Main, 1997), 814–15.
5. R. L. Braham, *The Politics of Genocide: The Holocaust in Hungary* (Detroit, 2002), 24; Gerlach and Aly, *Das letzte Kapitel*, 46. The Hungarian Right was especially strong within the country's cultural institutions. See R. L. Braham, "The Holocaust in Hungary: An Historical Interpretation of the Role of the Hungarian Radical Right," in *Studies on the Holocaust: Selected Writings*, ed. Randolph L. Braham, vol. 1 (Boulder, CO, 2000), 69–97.
6. For Romania, see Hilberg, *Die Vernichtung*, 814–15; for Slovakia, see I. Kamenec, *Po stopách tragédie* (Bratislava, 1991), 48–49; and L. Lipscher, *Die Juden im Slowakischen Staat 1939 – 1945* (Munich, 1980), 34–35. A limit on the number of Jewish students entering Slovak universities was introduced in the autumn of 1938, that is, before Slovak independence. See Kamenec, *Po stopách*, 38.
7. For Hungary see R. L. Braham, ed., *The Wartime System of Labor Service in Hungary: Varieties of Experiences* (New York, 1995); for Romania, R. Ioanid, *The Holocaust in Romania: The Destruction of Jews and Gypsies under the Antonescu Regime, 1940–1944* (Chicago, 2000); and for Slovakia, Lipscher, *Die Juden*, 99–136; as well as G. Fatran, "Die Deportationen der Juden aus der Slowakei 1944–1945," *Bohemia* 37 (1996): 98–119. For the number of victims of the Holocaust, see W. Benz, ed., *Dimension des Völkermordes. Die Zahl der jüdischen Opfer des Nationalsozialismus* (Munich, 1991).
8. We still know very few details of the expropriation process and almost nothing about the differences between the capital cities and the regions, about the strategies used by Jewish owners to try to save their property and about the social impact of the expropriations.
9. Hilberg, *Die Vernichtung*, 816.
10. Ibid., 835.
11. J. Ancel, ed., *Documents Concerning the Fate of Romanian Jewry during the Holocaust* (Jerusalem, 1986) vol. I, doc. no. 139.
12. Lipscher, *Die Juden*, 4 and 74.
13. The quarrel was quite long-lasting and ended only in July 1942. Politisches Archiv des Auswärtigen Amtes, Berlin [Archives of the German Foreign Ministry] (PAAA), R 100282.
14. Quoted in Gerlach and Aly, *Das letzte Kapitel*, 67.
15. Hilberg, *Die Vernichtung*, 870–71.
16. This was the case particularly with the so-called heroes' property, reserved for men coming home from the war; see Gerlach and Aly, *Das letzte Kapitel*, 68-70.
17. Hilberg, *Die Vernichtung*, 892.
18. Ibid., 866.

19. Still, out of some 110,000 Hungarian businesses in total, c. 40,000 were considered to be Jewish. Ibid., 891.
20. M. Schmidt, "Provincial Police Reports – New Insights into Hungarian Jewish History, 1941–1944," *Yad Vashem Studies* 19 (1988): 233–67, here 244–45.
21. Wisliceny's report to Eichmann, 17 December 1940. BAL, R 70 Sl./35.
22. H. Kaiser, *Die Politik des Dritten Reiches gegenüber der Slowakei 1939 bis 1945. Ein Beitrag zur Erforschung der nationalsozialistischen Satellitenpolitik in Südosteuropa* (Bochum, 1969), 410–11.
23. Report of Wisliceny, 1 March 1941, BAL, R 70 Sl./157, p. 25.
24. Hilberg, *Die Vernichtung*, 816.
25. Regarding the so-called voluntary Aryanizations and the riots accompanying them, see R. Ioanid, "The Antonescu Era," in *The Tragedy of Romanian Jewry*, ed. Randolph L. Braham (New York, 1994), 117–71, especially 120–22 and 124–46. The Iron Guard was known for being especially violent. See A. Heinen, "Rituelle Reinigung. Politische, soziale und kulturelle Bedingungsfaktoren faschistischer Gewalt in Rumänien," in *Faschismus und Faschismen im Vergleich. Wolfgang Schieder zum 60. Geburtstag*, ed. C. Dipper et al. (Cologne, 1998), 263–72, here 266–71; and A. Heinen, *Die Legion "Erzengel Michael" in Rumänien. Soziale Bewegung und politische Organisation. Ein Beitrag zum Problem des internationalen Faschismus* (Munich, 1986); as well as R. Ioanid, *The Sword of the Archangel: Fascist Ideology in Romania* (Boulder, 1990).
26. Hilberg, *Die Vernichtung*, 816.
27. Ibid., 820. According to Hitchens, the expropriation of Jewish enterprises proceeded quite slowly because of the huge amount of corruption in the office for Romanianization. Therefore, the percentage of trading companies considered Jewish declined only from 38 percent in September 1940 to 28 percent in June 1943, see K. Hitchens, *Rumania 1866–1947* (Oxford, 1994), 484.
28. Hilberg, *Die Vernichtung*, 837.
29. Quoted in Lipscher, *Die Juden*, 40. See also Y. Jelinek, *The Parish Republic. Hlinka's Slovak People's Party* (New York, 1976), 122–23, who states that it was mainly the Slovak middle-classes that were the intended beneficiaries of the expropriation of the Jews.
30. Even if the term "Slovakianization" is rarely used, this was what it was meant to be. See Kaiser, *Die Politik*, 407–9. The sources mostly use the term "Christianization." See Jelinek, *The Parish Republic*, 122; and Lipscher, *Die Juden*, 40.
31. For example, General Antonescu: "The question of the purification of our economy has to be viewed, first of all and exclusively, from the point of view of our duty to Romanize it." Quoted in Ioanid, "The Antonescu Era," 120.
32. Hilberg, *Die Vernichtung*, 866. See also Gerlach and Aly, *Das letzte Kapitel*, 51.
33. This meant that even more expropriations took place in Eastern Slovakia than in the Slovak capital; see Kamenec, *Po stopách*, 106. The situation is quite similar in Carpatho-Ukraine, which belonged to Hungary after 1938 and in those former Slovak territories that were also given to Hungary by the First Vienna Award in 1938; see Gerlach and Aly, *Das letzte Kapitel*, 52. Many of the victims who were deported from Carpatho-Ukraine were later shot in Kamenets-Podolsk, see Gerlach and Aly, *Das letzte Kapitel*, 74.
34. Lipscher, *Die Juden*, 67. See also Kamenec, *Po stopách*, 105 and 112. The ratio between property liquidated and "redistributed," was the same in Belgium and the Netherlands. See the essay by Jean-Marc Dreyfus in this volume.
35. For the protests of the German minority in Romania see Hilberg, *Die Vernichtung*, 817. Berlin instructed the heads of the German minority in Hungary to restrain themselves in April 1944, as "'Aryanization' is a purely Hungarian matter." See Gerlach and Aly, *Das letzte Kapitel*, 204.
36. For Hungary, see Gerlach and Aly, *Das letzte Kapitel*, 212–39. For Slovakia, see the statistics of the state budget given in Kaiser, *Die Politik*, 521–25, and the material in file, BAL, R 70 Sl./60, p. 65.
37. Hilberg, *Die Vernichtung*, 816.

38. Lipscher, *Die Juden*, 42. With Decree No. 303 on Jewish businesses, in 1940 the Slovak government amended the first Aryanization Law (Lipscher, *Die Juden*, 66), but research so far has not dealt with the consequences of this amendment. With regard to the Slovak banks and their role in the expropriations, see Lipscher, *Die Juden*, 71.
39. This was feared because Slovakia was quite aware of the fact that after the destruction of Czechoslovakia, German companies took over the shares of many Czech or Czechoslovak companies. In 1942, 100 percent of oil production, 99.6 percent of mining, 76.5 percent of the chemical industry, and 59.9 percent of metal processing in Slovakia were controlled by German companies. See L. Lipták, *Ovládnutie slovenského priemyslu nemeckým kapitálom 1939–1945* (Bratislava, 1960), 88.
40. Quoted in Lipscher, *Die Juden*, 38.
41. This was true, for example, for Hungarian bauxite production, which was of crucial importance to the German aircraft industry, see Hilberg, *Die Vernichtung*, 869.
42. At the same time, fifty-two members of the family who were classified as Jews were allowed to emigrate to Portugal, see Gerlach and Aly, *Das letzte Kapitel*, 243. For the growing importance of the company during the war years, see Gerlach and Aly, *Das letzte Kapitel*, 27.
43. Up to 1943, about 31,000 real estate properties were expropriated in "Old Romania" and a further 38,000 in Bessarabia. See Hilberg, *Die Vernichtung*, 835–36. As far as Slovakia is concerned, we do not know the number of real estate properties expropriated. For the regulations, see Vašek, *Die Lösung*, 69–70. In the summer of 1944, the occupation of houses became a "mass phenomenon" in Hungary. This mainly affected flats whose occupants had been deported; see Gerlach and Aly, *Das letzte Kapitel*, 202.
44. See the Romanian decree concerning expropriations dated 4 December 1940, Hilberg, *Die Vernichtung*, 816.
45. In Hungary, the decree proposing the compulsory registration of all possessions was dated 16 April 1944. Money and shares were blocked by the banks, such that a maximum of one thousand pengö a month could be withdrawn for personal needs. See Gerlach and Aly, *Das letzte Kapitel*, 191. In Slovakia, a similar regulation was already introduced in 1940–1941, see Kamenec, *Po stopách*, 100–101.
46. On 3 September 1941, the Romanian military commander ordered that the Jewish community had to present more than six thousand beds for the equipment of military hospitals within 24 hours. Two days later, the same method was applied to collect more than five thousand sets of clothing, including socks, underwear, and shoes. See Ancel, *Documents*, vol. III, doc. nos. 53 and 64.
47. Vašek, *Die Lösung*, 76. A similar approach to war finance was taken in Hungary by a decree dated 16 April 1944, see Gerlach and Aly, *Das letzte Kapitel*, 191.
48. Ancel, *Documents*, vol. III, doc. no. 63.
49. Ibid., vol. IV, doc. no. 307.
50. See R. Fischer, *Entwicklungsstufen des Antisemitismus in Ungarn 1867-1939. Die Zerstörung der magyarisch-jüdischen Symbiose* (Munich, 1988); V. Ranki, *The Politics of Inclusion and Exclusion: Jews and Nationalism in Hungary* (New York, 1999); Braham, *Politics*, 19–20; and T. Ungvári, *The "Jewish Question" in Europe: The Case of Hungary* (New York, 2000), 167–84.
51. See M. Podrimavský, "Slovenská l'udová strana," in *Politické strany na Slovensku 1860–1989*, ed. L. Lipták (Bratislava, 1992), 90–96, here 90–93; and L. Rothkirchen, "Slovakia I: 1848–1918," in *The Jews of Czechoslovakia: Historical Studies and Surveys*, ed. Avigdor Dagan (Philadelphia, 1968), vol. 1, 72–84, here 77–78.
52. Quoted in Gerlach and Aly, *Das letzte Kapitel*, 39.
53. Birobidzhan was an "Autonomous Region" in Eastern Siberia in the district of Khabarovsk.
54. Sidor's speech was published the next day in the widely read newspaper *Slovák*. Quoted in Lipscher, *Die Juden*, 15. The head of the Jesuits in Slovakia, Mikus, thought it appropriate to erect ghettos. Lipscher, *Die Juden*, 186.
55. Ioanid, "The Antonescu Era," 121.

56. Gerlach and Aly, *Das letzte Kapitel*, 39–40.
57. Lipscher, *Die Juden*, 27.
58. *Slovák*, 18 August 1942. Tiso's speech had the headline: "We do not give away anything that is ours."
59. J. Ancel, "Antonescu and the Jews," *Yad Vashem Studies* 23 (1993): 213–80, here 213. Similar quotes can be found in Ioanid, "The Antonescu Era," 152.
60. Tiso insisted at his trial that the consolidation of the Slovak state would have been impossible without the "solution of the Jewish problem" (16 December 1946). In: *Pred súdom národa, process Dr. J. Tisom, Dr. F. Ďurčanským, A. Machom v dňoch 2. Dec. 1946 – 15. Apr. 1947* (Bratislava, 1947), 5 vols, vol. 1, 158. J Ancel, "Seizure of Jewish Property in Romania," in *Confiscation of Jewish Property in Europe, 1933-1945: New Sources and Perspectives*, Symposium Proceedings (Washington, DC: Center for Advanced Holocaust Studies, 2003), 43–55, states that Antonescu used very similar arguments.
61. See T. Tönsmeyer, *Das Dritte Reich und die Slowakei 1939–1945. Politischer Alltag zwischen Kooperation und Eigensinn* (Paderborn, 2003). See also C. Steur, *Theodor Dannecker. Ein Funktionär der "Endlösung"* (Essen, 1997).
62. Local initiatives were not restricted to the expropriation of Jewish property. Tim Cole, for example, shows how in the summer of 1944 different levels of the Hungarian administration restricted the hours during which Jews were allowed to shop, without any prodding by the Germans. T. Cole, "Ebenen der 'Kollaboration.' Ungarn 1944," *Beiträge zur Geschichte des Nationalsozialismus* 19 (2003): 55–77.
63. Hilberg states that profit was not the foremost goal of the Romanian measures taken against the Jewish population, see Hilberg, *Die Vernichtung*, 811.
64. See Gerlach and Aly, *Das letzte Kapitel*, 325–44. Jews from "Old Romania" were mostly not deported. See M. Hausleitner, "Rumänien," in *Enzyklopädie des Nationalsozialismus*, ed. W. Benz, H. Graml and H. Weiß (Munich, 1997), 706–7.
65. Quoted in Hilberg, *Die Vernichtung*, 790. Even before this, one cannot speak of German pressure. When the Slovak prime minister and minister of foreign affairs, Vojtech Tuka, asked the German envoy in June 1942 to exercise "strong diplomatic pressure" to restart the deportations from Slovakia, v. Weizsäcker told the envoy he might at "some time" let the Slovak government know that "stopping the resettlement measures had been met with astonishment in Germany"; PAAA, R 29738, fr. 249624.
66. To the astonishment of the German authorities, on 12 April 1944 the Hungarian Trade Ministry closed down all shops with Jewish owners. Gerlach and Aly, *Das letzte Kapitel*, 192.
67. There were examples of similar measures dating back to the end of 1943. While the minister of supply, Szász, announced shortly before the German invasion that the scarcity of goods was a problem that could not be solved quickly, his successor enacted the measures mentioned on 29 April 1944. Ibid., 194–95.
68. Quoted in ibid., 189.
69. Ibid., 198–99. On the Arrow Cross men, see M. Szöllösi-Janze, *Die Pfeilkreuzlerbewegung in Ungarn. Historischer Kontext, Entwicklung und Herrschaft* (Munich, 1989).
70. Quoted in Gerlach and Aly, *Das letzte Kapitel*, 189.
71. Quoted in ibid., 190.
72. Quoted in Schmidt, "Provincial Police Reports," 247. Further examples are on pages 247–48. Many reports complain that the Jews do not have to queue up. The same complaints are known from Slovakia, where a member of the German SD reported that the Jews would push themselves to the front everywhere. SD report dated 22 August 1942, BAL, R70 Sl./208, p. 46.
73. Schmidt, "Provincial Police Reports," 240.
74. Ibid., 241.
75. See A. Cohen, "Pétain, Horthy, Antonescu and the Jews, 1942-1944. Toward a Comparative View," in *Yad Vashem Studies* 18 (1987): 163–98, here 183.
76. Gerlach and Aly, *Das letzte Kapitel*, 193.

77. In the summer of 1944 there were protests in the provinces against the return of the so-called exceptional Jews; ibid., 198. Sándor Márai reports in his diary that a man fleeing before the Red Army advances was most anxious whether he would be allowed to keep the land that had formerly belonged to a Jewish owner; ibid., 200.
78. See the Hungarian police reports, which dealt with Slovakia as well. Schmidt, "Provincial Police Reports," 255–56.
79. Testimony of Ms. R. R. (born in 1929). Quoted in P. Salner, *Prežili Holokaust* (Bratislava, 1997), 47.
80. See I. Livezeanu, *Cultural Politics in Greater Romania: Regionalism, Nation Building and Ethnic Struggle, 1918-1930* (Ithaca, 1995), 211–97; and Heinen, *Die Legion*, 114–27.
81. This is especially true for Slovakia and Romania. As far as Hungary is concerned, Szöllösi-Janze states that because of inadequate sources the social composition of the Arrow Cross men is difficult to determine. Szöllösi-Janze, *Die Pfeilkreuzlerbewegung*, 134.
82. See Holm Sundhaussen on widespread corruption as a pre-modern way of handling matters. H. Sundhaussen, "Die Königsdiktaturen in Südosteuropa – Umrisse einer Synthese," in *Autoritäre Regime in Ostmittel- und Südosteuropa 1919–1944*, ed. Erwin Oberländer (Paderborn, 2001), 337–48, here 347.
83. This is why the churches in most instances only made very belated protests against the deportations. But in Hungary and Slovakia the bishops insisted that baptized Jews not be deported. For Hungary, see Hilberg, *Die Vernichtung*, 865 and 985–86; for Slovakia, see Kaiser, *Die Politik*, 414–16. In a pastoral letter dated 21 March 1943, the Catholic bishops of Slovakia demanded that Jews should not be punished collectively, but only individually if their guilt was proven, PAAA, R100887, fr. 477195–98.
84. It should be noted, however, that the term "Magyarization" is not without problems in this context, because it is generally used to describe minority politics in the late nineteenth and early twentieth centuries. Gerlach and Aly, nonetheless, also use it explicitly in this context, parallel to Romanianization and Slovakianization.
85. See Gerlach and Aly, *Das letzte Kapitel*, 12–13.

– *Part III* –

The Restitution of Jewish Property in Comparative Perspective

WEST GERMANY AND THE RESTITUTION OF JEWISH PROPERTY IN EUROPE

Jürgen Lillteicher

In the late 1950s, a District Court in Berlin had to deal with a somewhat remarkable case of restitution. On behalf of the heirs of the Jewish-Hungarian sugar magnate Ferencz Hatvany, Professor Dr. Hans Deutsch, a successful Hungarian-born lawyer specializing in restitution cases, sued the German government for the return of Hatvany's art collection. According to the magnate's heirs, SS troops had stolen the collection, comprising some 200 valuable paintings, from his Budapest villa during the German occupation of the city, and had later transported it to Berlin.

The restitution laws of the Allied powers as well as those of the Federal Republic of Germany, passed in 1957 and extending the scope of restitution claims that could be brought, made Germany liable for Nazi thefts all over Europe. Hatvany's heirs, however, were eligible for restitution only if they could prove that the collection had been brought to the territory of modern West Germany. Moreover, the claimants were obliged to meet certain standards of residence in order for any award to be paid. Fortunately, the so-called diplomatic clause did not apply to Hatvany's heirs—this clause ruled out the payment of restitution benefits to claimants from most Eastern European countries.

Concerning the whereabouts of the paintings that were seized, former SS Sturmbannführer Friedrich Wilcke declared under oath that Ferencz Hatvany's collection had been brought to Berlin by the SS.[1] If this were the case, Germany would have to pay compensation of between DM 60 and 70 million for the collection,[2] whose value experts had estimated at around DM 400 million. In order to accelerate the proceedings, the judges at the restitution court in Berlin advised both parties to come to some sort of mutual agreement.[3] In any event, the restitution claims were highly unlikely to be paid in full, as there were only limited funds available for the compensation

---

Notes for this section begin on page 109.

of damages arising from Nazi confiscations outside the territory of the Federal Republic of Germany. On 1 November 1962, after lengthy negotiations, the two parties finally followed the judges' advice and agreed on a settlement amounting to DM 35 million. This sum was to be paid to Hans Deutsch, the heirs' representative, in two installments.

A short time after the compromise, Deutsch and his clients got into a dispute over Deutsch's fees. Hoping to receive backing in this quarrel, one of the heirs turned to the Federal Ministry of Finance.[4] The Ministry in turn came to suspect Deutsch of not having handled the case in a proper manner.[5] In the course of the investigations that followed, a friend of Ferencz Hatvany's testified that Hatvany's collection had been stored in the safe of a Budapest bank and had not disappeared until the Russian occupation. This was why Hatvany, according to his friend, had not initially claimed compensation from West Germany after 1945.[6] In any event, Hatvany's claim would not have been successful then, since he would not have been eligible for compensation if he could not prove that the German forces were responsible for the removal of the collection.

Further investigations revealed that, apparently, no one had ever ordered the paintings to be transported to Germany.[7] Moreover, the evidence given to the restitution chamber by Friedrich Wilcke—Deutsch's most important witness—turned out to be false, which prompted the authorities to arrest and prosecute Deutsch.[8] Not until nine years later, on 19 April 1973 (Deutsch had been released in the meantime), did the third criminal division of the Bonn District Court acquit both Wilcke and Deutsch on the charges of fraud and perjury. Nonetheless, the second installment was not paid, because nobody knew exactly where Hatvany's collection had gone.[9]

The legal aspects of the case, then, were never resolved in a satisfactory manner. The intention here, however, is to present an historical rather than a legal assessment of the Hatvany case. Fraud rarely played a major role in restitution cases. But viewed from a historian's perspective, the case highlights well the many difficulties involved in the process of restituting Jewish property stolen outside of the Federal Republic. The majority of such trials hinged on the whereabouts of the stolen goods. A few preliminary questions, however, should be asked: Why was the theft of a Hungarian art collection brought to court in Berlin, and what were the relevant laws that applied? Why was West Germany liable to pay compensation for Nazi thefts in the occupied countries of Europe and also in the satellite states?

In order to answer these questions, this chapter examines in some detail the legal framework for restitution cases from their beginnings in 1947 to the extension of restitution payments in 1957 and the subsequent amendments. It should be stressed that developments in Germany during this period are likely to be of significance for future research on the question of restitution throughout Europe.

Preliminaries: Restitution on the Basis of the Allied Restitution Laws

The fact that the demand for compensation was turned into a legal claim—which made a trial like the one in the Hatvany case possible in the first place—was the outcome of complicated and lengthy negotiations. Moreover, international treaties between West Germany and the Allied powers also had to be taken into account. After all, the Aryanization of Jewish property in Nazi Germany was by far the most significant change in property relations in modern German history.[10] The attempt to reverse the material consequences of such a gigantic crime necessarily entailed a multitude of highly complex problems. On the one hand, such an ambitious aim was bound to be constrained by the limitations of due process in law; on the other hand, the setting in which the return of property was to take place was that of a society still run by many of the same people who had actively participated in Nazi crimes and Aryanization before 1945.

Compensation for Aryanization and fiscal plunder was only made possible because the Western powers forced West Germany to implement an unprecedented program of restitution. Even though West Germany tried to evade coercive measures of this nature, it eventually had to pay back the stolen property of those Jews who had formerly held German citizenship. After the occupation statutes were suspended, international treaties and an extension of the existing legal regulations ensured that West Germany also had to restitute goods that had been taken by German occupational forces abroad, provided that these goods had been transferred to the territory of the Federal Republic. This broader definition of restitution meant that not only Aryanization and fiscal plunder on the territory of the Reich were brought to court, but also the raids conducted by the Nazi regime in occupied countries and the satellite states.

At the outset of the process, the allied powers had different opinions on how stolen Jewish property should be restituted, and whether there should be any restitution at all. France, Britain, and the Soviet Union obviously gave priority to their own demands rather than to the claims of those whose property had been taken away, which was also reflected in the fact that these latter claims were difficult to ascertain. America, however, had not been affected by war damages on its own territory and was therefore largely indifferent towards the question of reparations. However, there was a consensus among Americans that a political claim for the restitution of stolen Jewish property had to be brought forward.[11] After negotiations on common restitution regulations for the three Western zones had been suspended in the Allied Control Council, the American military government decided to go it alone and passed its own restitution law on 11 November 1947. This law was subsequently implemented and is known as Military Law No. 59.[12] Its goal was the restitution of ascertainable property holdings to all persons from whom these had been taken away in the period between 30 January 1933 and 8 May 1945 on the grounds of race, religion, nationality, ideology, or political opposition to the Nazi regime. This was to be achieved to the largest possible extent and with the greatest possible speed.[13] On the same day, another decree on restitution was passed by the French for their occupation zone. This decree was strongly influenced by the French legislation on restitution, and allocated heirless Jewish assets to a fund that was to be used for the payment of compensation.[14] Not until two years later, in May 1949, did the British military authorities decide on a legal regulation for restitution,[15] which, except for a few minor points, was identical to the American legislation.[16]

The German side was, for various reasons, highly skeptical. On the one hand, the laws that the military bodies had passed were regarded as an arbitrary humiliation, and the financial obligations were accordingly seen as an imposed punishment rather than as a fair recompense for the injustices committed. On the other hand, continuities in the personnel of the financial authorities meant that these institutions often had little interest in the reversal of their previous policies. Moreover, the new power relations that had established themselves in the wake of the shifts in property and personal assets proved to be a further hindrance to measures of restitution.[17] This skepticism also had a political dimension: West Germany often opposed or attempted to reduce the scale of Allied plans for restitution, either by pointing to the sorry state of the German economy or by threatening that there would be no support for agreements made without consulting the German government.

Through the Allied restitution laws, all legal transactions with Jews after the Nazi rise to power came under suspicion of having been enforced with the threat of persecution. Likewise, all actions of the government and the Nazi Party directed against Jewish economic existences[18]—whether they were discriminatory taxes, mandatory levies, or the compulsory surrender of precious metals and other valuables—were regarded as improper "deprivations."[19] Consequently, both individuals and the German government had to stand trial for depriving Jews of their assets during the Nazi regime.

The restitution of assets taken away by the Nazi regime was by far the lengthiest and most complex aspect of postwar restitution. Whereas the majority of restitution claims against individuals had been settled by the mid-1950s, at this time the claims filed against the state were very far from having been dealt with satisfactorily. Two main reasons account for the failures in addressing these claims: first, the lack of agreement on the state's liability and on overcoming the inflexibility of traditional legal norms; and second, the resolute opposition of the financial authorities towards the claims of those persecuted under the Third Reich.

Those with claims against the former German Reich naturally turned toward the Federal Republic of Germany, whose financial interests were represented by the Ministry of Finance or its corresponding regional authorities. Here the claimants encountered advocates of the state's financial interests (i.e., civil servants), some of whom had been involved in implementing the very same discriminatory measures before 1945.[20] In Hamburg, for instance, every second trial in which the public treasury was involved ended up before the chamber of restitution.[21] In order to reduce the liability of the Federal Republic to the minimum amount that could still be justified, the officials of the regional finance administration made full use of all the legal instruments at their disposal.[22]

Restitution on the grounds of the Allied legislation was based on the principle of territoriality and only covered property thefts within the territory of the Federal Republic. Compensation for goods stolen abroad was only granted when the aggrieved person could prove that his property had at some point been taken to a specific place within the Federal Republic.[23] Hence, the majority of recipients consisted of persecuted German citizens whose property had been located during the Third Reich in those areas that later became part of West Germany.

Even though some restitution claims were successful in the courts in the 1950s, there was still no consensus as to whether the Federal Republic should be the legal successor of the Third Reich at all. Restitution courts in the American and British occupation zones had passed certain "assessment resolutions" (Feststellungsbeschlüsse),[24] but the final decision whether the sums adjudicated would actually be paid depended on further talks between the German government and the Allied powers.

With the end of Allied occupation, the need for a treaty that regulated and secured the restitution program became apparent. The central points were initially laid down in a transitional treaty (Überleitungsvertrag) of 26 May 1952 in which Allied rights were replaced by a contractually defined commitment by the Federal Republic, and in which Germany was conceded partial sovereignty.[25] The Federal Republic was able to limit its obligation to meet restitution claims against the Reich to a sum of DM 1.5 billion, even though realistic official estimates assessed the Reich's liabilities to be around RM 5 billion.[26]

Additional changes and improvements to the compensation and restitution legislation were introduced during the negotiations with the state of Israel and the Conference on Jewish Material Claims Against Germany (Claims Conference).[27] In Protocol No. 1 of the treaty of 10 September 1952, the principle of territoriality, which had been applied very rigidly, was weakened to a certain extent. Among other things, the Federal Republic promised to assume liability for the household effects and furniture of Jewish refugees, which had been stored for shipment in ports outside the later Federal Republic and were seized there by the German occupation authorities.[28]

While West Germany had a vital interest in the continuation of the restitution program as a prerequisite for partial sovereignty, there was no restitution in the Soviet Occupation Zone (SOZ) and the later German Democratic Republic (GDR). Germany's first restitution law had in fact been passed in the Eastern state of Thuringia in 1945, but this was forgotten once the SOZ/GDR had come into being. With the incorporation of the state into the SOZ, restitution in Thuringia came to a halt. Restitution in East Germany was blocked not so much by the Soviets as by the governing party, the Sozialistische Einheitspartei Deutschlands [Socialist Unity Party of German] (SED), which categorically rejected any restitution of private property to former owners. Figures within the SED who advocated the restitution of Jewish property, such as Paul Merker, were marginalized and persecuted. The idea of restoring private ownership rights stood in fundamental opposition to the SED's plans for restructuring the East German economy and transforming it according to the socialist model. A social welfare program was implemented as an alternative to restitution. However, another consequence of the radical rejection of private ownership was that the socialist successor state in East Germany also transferred property seized during the Nazi regime into state hands.[29] An exception to the rule was the property of Jewish communities, and a large part of their synagogues, cemeteries, and real estate were returned.[30]

The Federal Restitution Law: Restitution Extended to Include Property Thefts Throughout Europe

During the 1952 negotiations with the Claims Conference it was already apparent that the limitation of restitution had saved West Germany billions of marks. By paying DM 450 million, West Germany had met claims to the restitution of heirless property in Eastern and Western Europe without having to acknowledge a legal obligation to restitute property stolen in the territories occupied by Nazi Germany. Moreover, the West German delegation succeeded in reducing the country's liability with regard to the restitution of property in the those areas from which the German population had since been expelled, such as Silesia, Pomerania, and the Sudetenland.[31] This, however, did not mean that the legal issue was put to rest; rather, it reappeared in the context of discussions on the drafting of the *Bundesrückerstattungsgesetz* [Federal Restitution Law] (BRüG). Originally, the BRüG was only to include regulations for payments made on the basis of the "assessment resolutions" already passed by the German restitution courts. Persecuted persons who had received a positive decision on their restitution claim against the German Reich were obliged to wait and see whether West Germany would take over the debts of the Third Reich and in what manner they would eventually receive their money.[32]

The new law, which was passed by the Bundestag without debate on 15 July 1957, included clear instructions authorizing the Oberfinanzdirektionen [Regional Finance Offices] (OFDs) to revise and authorize for payment all of the "assessment resolutions" issued after the implementation of the allied restitution laws in the 1950s.[33] The OFDs now had a dual function, acting both as one of the parties in the legal proceedings and also as a judicial authority. Up to 1 July 1971, about 128,000 payment decisions were issued.[34] Moreover, the BRüG dealt with a second important matter apart from the settling of these older debts. On the initiative of the restitution committee of the German Bundestag, a more generous procedure was to be applied to expropriations that had taken place outside the territory of West Germany.

The new law permitted the restitution of assets, of which the precise whereabouts—within West Germany and Berlin—were unknown. After a thorough examination of the circumstances of each respective confiscation case, however, it had to be proven, or at least not definitely disproven, that the assets in question had actually been taken to West Germany (including West Berlin).[35] In such cases, the fictitious assumption was made that the stolen goods had reached the territory of Greater Berlin.[36] For this reason, it was mainly the Berlin courts that—as, for instance, in the Deutsch/Hatvany case—had to deal with cases of property seizure that were of a completely different quality than those committed in the Reich itself. With the scope of the restitution law being broadened in this manner, the Reich's actions against the property of persecuted minorities throughout Europe also became subject to legal remedy (e.g., during the Furniture Operation in Western Europe and the theft of the property of deportees). West German restitution thereby gained a European dimension.

Although the BRüG had a much wider scope than the previous treaties, its introduction did not change the basic attitudes of the German judiciary and fiscal authorities. Those who interpreted the new law continued to favor the West German public purse, just as they had done in the 1950s. In this context, the Deutsch/Hatvany case played an important role; the popular antisemitic image of careless finance officials hoodwinked by a greedy Jewish lawyer led to even more stringent interpretations of the law in the implementation of restitution.[37]

Some additional restrictions were also added. Persecuted persons might receive a legally binding judgement in their favor, but they still did not receive any money if they lived in a country that did not have diplomatic relations with West Germany.[38] In theory, everybody whose property had been confiscated by the German occupation forces for ideological or religious reasons was entitled to restitution. Whether their claims would actually result in payment, however, depended on whether they were citizens of a Western country. This politically defined condition, essentially a result of the treaty on German foreign debt of 27 February 1953,[39] in turn reduced the percentage of persons entitled to restitution whose claims would actually be fulfilled. With the exception of the Soviet Union, all Eastern Bloc countries were excluded by this clause.[40] After a year-long legal battle and additional negotiations with the Ministry of Finance, Auschwitz survivors who had lost all their belongings before deportation to the concentration camp, and who returned to Czechoslovakia after 1945 did succeed in getting a positive answer to their restitution claims. However, they did not receive any payment, since West Germany and Czechoslovakia did not have diplomatic relations.[41] Hatvany's heirs were lucky in that they had not returned to Hungary.

Restitution on the basis of the BRüG, then, was influenced significantly by the Cold War and the confrontation between the two power blocs. The extension of restitution to include the so-called "Eastern Bloc" was impossible, unless the regulations of the debt accords were to be ignored.[42] Since the German Ministry of Finance estimated that the scope of restitution, if Eastern Europe was included, would be "barely calculable," minds were eased by postponing the question of reparations to the day when a peace treaty would be signed.[43] However, this restriction was politically tenable only as long as the Cold War persisted.

After its proclamation in July 1957 there were several more amendments to the BRüG, but increasing knowledge about the scope of Germany's plunder, especially in Eastern Europe, did not result in any additional legal rights for the persecutees. All they could do was apply for some compensation within the framework of a hardship fund. The argument over whether persecuted persons had a legal right to compensation that could be pursued in the courts or whether these claims should be satisfied solely on the basis of the principles of equity and voluntariness was eventually decided in favor of the latter view.[44]

By 1971 the restitution program had, despite numerous restrictions and difficulties, produced respectable quantitative results. Restitution on the basis of the Allied restitution laws between 1947 and 1949 amounted to a sum of DM 3.5 billion. Following the introduction of the BRüG Laws, an additional DM 4 billion was paid. Under the supervision of the Supreme Restitution Courts of the Allied countries, the German judiciary handed down decisions in some 1.2 million individual trials in the period up to 1975.[45]

However, this did not mean that restitution was brought to a satisfactory conclusion. The end of the Cold War and the collapse of the Soviet Union—events that brought unification to Germany—entailed a reemergence of the restitution issue. The adjustment of the economic order of East Germany to that of West Germany also resulted in a restructuring of property relations. Thanks to considerable political pressure exerted by Jewish organizations, the restitution of property to refugees from the GDR also included the restitution of Jewish property. The Rückerstattungsanordnung [Restitution Decree] for Berlin (REAO) issued in 1949 became part of the new property law (Vermögensgesetzes or VermG) of 28 September 1990.[46]

Conclusion and Perspectives for Future Research

At the outset, the West German restitution program intended to restrict itself to the territory of the Federal Republic of Germany and to claimants of German citizenship. That West Germany was forced to award restitution payments to its own citizens was a novelty in international law. Including the restitution of property plundered by the Third Reich in the occupied countries of Europe was regarded as necessary for various reasons; however, Germany was under no obligation to do this. The Allied powers, whose crucial function was to oversee the restitution process and who repeatedly had to intervene to enforce its correct implementation, had not exerted any pressure on this issue. It was probably the negotiations with the Claims Conference and the increasing weight of new historical evidence that finally caused the restitution committee of the German Bundestag to expand the restitution program.

The BRüG did not develop into a disproportionate financial burden to the federal budget for two reasons: the relatively precise definition of cases in which Germany was liable for property stolen abroad, and the continuing confrontation between East and West. Moreover, the financial authorities took their role as guardians of the federal budget particularly seriously when it came to Jewish claims, and they maintained their traditional pattern of action—dating back to the 1950s—even once the legal framework had changed. The BRüG, which had passed the Bundestag without any debate, was essentially a continuation of Allied legislation, which those responsible for restitution in Germany regarded as an Allied dictate and the product of Allied victors' justice. The trauma of Versailles, after which any cooperation with the Allied powers was regarded as collaboration, was still a potent consideration in the collective consciousness of judges and civil servants.[47] Since Germany saw itself primarily as a victim of the war, the differences between the various victim groups gradually disappeared, and the relationship between cause and effect with regard to war and persecution was even reversed. The gradual extension of the definition of Nazi injustice to include the fields of fiscal plundering and thefts by the German occupation authorities was undertaken only to a very limited extent, if at all. The overall political and ideological development of West Germany, which hinted at a new understanding of the Nazi past, was barely noticeable in the way the restitution program was implemented.

The case of West Germany exhibits several characteristics that are of significance for research on restitution throughout Europe. First, the problems I have sketched here can only begin to demonstrate the discontinuity between the history of the persecution itself and its reconstruction and evaluation by postwar society—a discontinuity that has less to do with the limitations inherent in political and legal responses to mass injustice than with the desire to provide a specific interpretation of the past. In the same context, one might ask how the self-image of the countries occupied and ruled by Germany—and of their roles under German occupation—has influenced the evaluation and treatment of restitution issues in various countries.

On the other hand, the concrete practice of restitution casts a telling light on the view held by European countries of their own role under German occupation or within the German sphere of influence. Austria, for instance, which regarded itself as the "first victim" of German aggression, initially did not see any need for its own restitution program.[48] In France, the general shift in how countries viewed their own past also revived the debate on collaboration with the Nazis under the Vichy regime, resulting in, among other things, a second round of restitution for Jewish property, which started even before world public opinion became aware of the scandals surrounding Swiss bank accounts belonging to victims of the Holocaust.[49]

Second, the robbery and plunder practiced by the Third Reich was to an unprecedented extent linked directly to the Nazi policy of annihilation in Europe. The attempt to reverse the material results of this policy in West Germany stretched the limits of both the judicial and political systems. The treatment of severe and hitherto unknown forms of injustice demonstrated that conventional political modes of compensation and traditional German legislation, such as the Bürgerliche Gesetzbuch [Code of Civil Law], were not well suited for the challenges presented by injustice on this scale. The result was an inability to deal effectively with these matters, which was only partly mitigated by the special regulations and laws introduced; after all, these still had to operate within the existing judicial system. Draconian measures that would not have respected legal traditions and systems, however, could not have received the necessary political support of the Allied powers either. Even those restitution laws that were introduced were widely perceived as unjust, so that more extreme measures would have encountered even greater resistance. Were traditional legal instruments adequate for implementing restitution in other countries, or were special laws also required, which to a certain extent broke with existing legal traditions? Or did governments elsewhere apply quite different measures altogether?

Third, there is the question of the subjective factors that exerted considerable influence on the course of restitution history in West Germany. What kinds of inner conflicts did the key players face, and to what extent were some of them involved directly or indirectly in the preceding Aryanization and plunder? This question raises the problem of the continuities in administrative personnel after 1945 and its influence on the restitution process. Intimately related to this is the question of the role played by former collaborators and their influence on the restitution processes in the respective European countries.

Fourth, there is the question of the significance of restitution with regard to the transition from a dictatorship to a postdictatorial society. West Germany experienced a transformation from a dictatorship to a democratic republic with manifold possibilities of political participation. At the outset, this development was triggered by external forces, such as Allied political pressure and intervention, and the gradual integration of the Federal Republic within the Western community. This also applies to West German restitution policy. Restitution received virtually no support or positive impulses from within West German society. The initiative for the return of Jewish property came mostly from outside or from a small minority. Therefore, restitution cannot be regarded as one aspect of a general movement for the construction of a civil society. Even after reunification caused the merging of East and West German society into one, the only significant impulse for the resolution of outstanding restitution issues came from Jewish organizations such as the Claims Conference. Whenever the West German population took the initiative, its aim was usually not to further restitution but rather to mitigate its consequences, or to stop its progress altogether. In the European context, therefore, we must ask: to what extent in the Eastern European countries has restitution really become a focus for civil participation and the development towards a democratic society?

Fifth, the history of restitution in West Germany, particularly in its final phase, bears the hallmarks of a policy directed towards "overcoming the past" (*Vergangenheitsbewältigung*), which was the attempt to compensate with restitution payments those individuals who had suffered damages due to historical injustices. Therefore, only after a lengthy period of protective silence was the widespread participation of the German population in Aryanization and plunder fully acknowledged. In the European context, then, it would be of interest to examine how those countries occupied or controlled by German forces have developed their own policies for dealing with or overcoming the past. What has been the relationship here between the initial reaction to external political pressure and the gradually increasing awareness of actual injustice?

Regardless of the national context, then, the history of West German restitution bears some characteristics that can give important impulses for examining the history of restitution in other European countries. Of course, this does not bring into question at all the role of Nazi Germany as the chief agent of robbery, plunder, and suffering in Europe during the Second World War.

Notes

1. Statements made on 2 January 1961 and 25 July 1961, respectively. Letter from Féaux de la Croix to the chief prosecutor at the Bonn District Court, Bundesarchiv Berlin (BArch), B 126/68479. The author wishes to thank the Center for Advanced Holocaust Studies at the United States Holocaust Memorial Museum (USHMM) and especially the Revson Foundation for their generous support, which enabled him to complete this article during his time as a Fellow at the USHMM in Washington, DC.
2. Statement made by experts Dr. Herbert Dreyer and Dr. C. Müller-Hofstede, letter from Féaux de la Croix to the chief prosecutor at the Bonn District Court, BArch, B 126/68479.
3. Report of Ministerialrat Fritz Koppe, minutes of the 38th session of the Committee for Restitution 3 December 1964, BArch, B 126/68479, p. 6.
4. Letter from Féaux de la Croix to Martin Hirsch, 8 January 1963, BArch, B 126/68479, pp. 153-54.
5. Deutsch was a member of the Israeli bar association and, as such, not subject to German legislation with regard to contingent fees. See letter from Féaux de la Croix to Martin Hirsch, 8 January 1963, BArch, B 126/68479, p. 155.
6. Testimony of Countess Marie Madleine Bethlen given to the German ambassador in Vienna, 14 August 1964; sound recording made by the Embassy of the Federal Rebulic of Germany in Vienna, 14 August 1964, BArch, B 126/68479.
7. Testimony of retired Police General Karl Pfeffer-Wildenbruch, 15 October 1964, BArch, B 126/68479. The Jewish side, too, had criticized the way the Ministry of Finance handled the affair. See letters from Walter Schwarz to Nahum Goldman, 15 January 1965, Central

Zionist Archives (CZA), Z 6-1239; and from Fritz Koppe to the chief prosecutor at the Bonn District Court, 2 October 1964, BArch, B 126/68479.

8. Letter from Dr. Drügh to the attorney general of the state of Northrhine-Westphalia, 2 November 1964, BArch, B 126/68479.
9. According to Burkhart List, Russian historians Konstantin Akinsha and Grigori Kozlov discovered that the Austrian SS *Sturmbannfuehrer* had had the collection transported to Greater Berlin, from which the Red Army sent the art works to Nizhny Novgorod in Russia in 1945. See B. List, "Hans im Glück, Hans im Unglück," *Süddeutsche Zeitung*, 5 June 2001. It still has to be confirmed whether the Federal Republic of Germany would have been liable for restitution, if this had been known all along.
10. Frank Bajohr, *"Arisierung" in Hamburg: die Verdrängung der jüdischen Unternehmer 1933–1945* (Hamburg, 1997), 9.
11. The genesis of the American restitution law is dealt with in some detail in C. Goschler, *Wiedergutmachung. Westdeutschland und die Verfolgten des Nationalsozialismus (1945–1954)* (Munich, 1992), 106–26. On the genesis of the restitution law in the British zone, see J. Lillteicher, *Raub, Recht und Restitution.* Die Rückerstattung jüdischen Eigentums in der frühen Bundesrepublik (Gröttingen, 2007).
12. *Amtsblatt der Militärregierung Deutschland* [Official Gazette of the Military Government in Germany]—American Occupation Zone, edition G, 1.
13. Article 1 of the Restitution Law passed in the American Occupation Zone. See H. Freiherr von Godin, *Rückerstattung feststellbarer Vermögensgegenstände* (Berlin, 1950), 1.
14. Decree No. 120 (10 November 1947) of the French commander in chief for the restitution of stolen assets, modified in decrees Nos. 156, 186, and 213. See *Journal Officiel du Commandement en Chef Francais en Allemagne*—official gazette of the French High Command in Germany 1949, Nos. 279, 280, 281, and 282, p. 2060.
15. The law took effect on 12 May 1949. *Amtsblatt der Militärregierung Deutschland* (British Occupation Zone), No. 28, 1169.
16. Although general decree No. 10 had frozen assets and made it possible to claim restitution early on, there was no generally binding legislation until 1949.
17. For example, the restitution of the Rosenthal china factory in Upper Franconia; see J. Lillteicher, "Rechtsstaatlichkeit und Verfolgungserfahrung. 'Arisierung' und fiskalische Ausplünderung vor Gericht," in *"Arisierung" und Restitution. Die Rückerstattung jüdischen Eigentums in Deutschland und Österreich nach 1945 und 1989*, ed. C. Goschler and J. Lillteicher (Göttingen, 2002), 127–59, here: 134–44.
18. There was a wide range of government measures against Jewish property and assets. See J. Walk, ed., *Das Sonderrecht für die Juden im NS-Staat. Eine Sammlung der gesetzlichen Maßnahmen und Richtlinien—Inhalt und Bedeutung* (Heidelberg, 1981).
19. The term "deprivation" includes the actual seizure of property as well as the surrender or "sale" of property under duress. See W. Schwarz, *Rückerstattung nach den Gesetzen der alliierten Mächte* (Munich, 1974), 145–46.
20. On these continuities, see G. Blumberg, "Etappen der Verfolgung und Ausraubung und ihre bürokratische Apparatur," in *Verfolgung und Verwaltung. Die wirtschaftliche Ausplünderung der Juden und die westfälischen Finanzbehörden*, ed. A. Kenkmann u. B.-A. Rusinek (Münster, 1999), 15–40, here: 38–39.
21. Report on the activities of the office of restitution in 1952, 8 January 1953, WgA LGHH, 00.11-20.
22. Those responsible in the offices of restitution did not approve of this practice either, since it unnecessarily delayed resitution. See Monatsberichte des Wiedergutmachungsamtes Hamburg vom 31.1.1951, WgA LGHH, 11.00-20; Jahresbericht des Wiedergutmachungsamtes für das Jahr 1950, WgA LGHH, 00.11-20.
23. F. Biella, "Die Entstehung des Bundesrückerstattungsgesetzes," in Biella et al., *Das Bundesrückerstattungsgesetz* (Munich, 1981), 73–122, here: 85.
24. Resolution No. 120, which regulated restitution in the French zone, only dealt with the restitution of property that still existed *in natura*. Only then could the former German Reich be sued for restitution. Claims against the Reich that concerned property no longer

existent—this also included discriminatory taxes—could not be dealt with in the French zone until the BRüG was passed in 1957. In the meantime, persecution victims had attempted to claim financial compensation under the BEG (Federal compensation law). Under this procedure, however, they received far less than they would have on the basis of the BRüG. A subsequent claim under the BRüG was still an option, since the state had confused the claimants by making the legal situation unnecessarily complex. See Schwarz, *Rückerstattung*, 295.

25. On 26 May 1952, Adenauer, Schumann, Acheson, and Eden signed the transitional treaty (Überleitungsvertrag) within the framework of the Deutschlandvertrag. Due to limited support in the French national assembly, the whole treaty could only take effect after further negotiations in 1955. The regulations on restitution were settled in the third part of the treaty. See Goschler, *Wiedergutmachung*, 255.
26. Comment on the statement by Allied experts concerning the German memorandum on Part II, Article 5a of the treaty—Rückerstattungsrechtliche Verbindlichkeiten des Reiches, BArch, B 141/9082.
27. The Conference on Jewish Claims against Germany, founded in October 1951, was the umbrella organization for twenty-three individual Jewish organizations.
28. Regulations on the extension of the restitution legislation, 6 August 1952, II.2, Central Archives for the History of the Jewish People (CAHJP), Claims Conference, New York, 7048.
29. J. P. Spannuth, "'Rückerstattung Ost': Der Umgang der DDR mit dem 'arisierten' Vermögen der Juden und die Gestaltung der Rückerstattung im wiedervereinigten Deutschland," in Goschler and Lillteicher, eds., *"Arisierung" und Restitution*, 241–63.
30. L. Mertens, *Davidstern unter Hammer und Zirkel. Die jüdischen Gemeinden in der SBZ/DDR und ihre Behandlung durch Partei und Staat 1945–1990* (Hildesheim, 1997).
31. Regulations intended for the development of compensation, 6 August 1952, CAHJP, CC, New York, 7048. On compensation, see Goschler, *Wiedergutmachung*, 278.
32. See Lillteicher, "Die Rückerstattung"; also, W. Wirth, "Entziehung von Sachvermögen außerhalb des Geltungsbereichs des Bundesrückerstattungsgesetzes," in Biella et al., *Das Bundesrückerstattungsgesetz*, 272.
33. The manner in which previous decisions had to be changed was prescribed by §§ 15–16 of the BRüG. See Biella, "Die Entstehung des Bundesrückerstattungsgesetzes," 91–96.
34. According to § 38 3. Änd.-Ges. BRüG, the regional financial authorities issued 128,219 (nationwide, including Berlin) decisions, resulting in payments in the amount of DM 2,502,111,622.-. See statistical report on internal restitution, 1 July 1971, BArch, B 136/3318, p. 6.
35. § 5 BRüG.
36. I.e., Berlin within the borders established in Art. 4 of the 1950 Berlin constitution.
37. See Lillteicher, *Roub, Recht und Restitution.*
38. § 45 BRüG, Bundesgesetzblatt (BGBl.) I, 742.
39. On the question of restitution in this context see U. Herbert, "Nicht entschädigungsfähig? Die Wiedergutmachungsansprüche der Ausländer," in *Wiedergutmachung in der Bundesrepublik Deutschland*, ed. L. Herbst and C. Goschler (Munich, 1989), 273–303.
40. § 45 excluded from payment all persons residing in Cambodia, North Korea, Laos, Nepal, Taiwan, and in the Eastern Bloc countries other than the Soviet Union. See Bekanntmachung des Bundesministers der Finanzen gemäß § 45 BRüG vom 26.8.1975 (official statement of the German Ministry of Finance), in *Bundesanzeiger*, No. 168.
41. See Lillteicher, *Roub, Recht und Restitution* for a more detailed discussion.
42. On the efforts of Jewish organizations to break through the "Iron Curtain," see R. W. Zweig, *German Reparations and the Jewish World: A History of the Claims Conference* (London, 2001).
43. Koppe letter to the German Minister of Finance, 19 December 1962, BArch, B 141/14563. See also Goschler, "Die Politik der Rückerstattung in Westdeutschland," in Goschler and Lillteicher , eds., *"Arisierung" und Restitution*, 121.
44. Goschler, "Die Politik der Rückerstattung," 121.

45. See J. Lillteicher, "Rechtsstaatlichkeit und Verfolgungserfahrung, 'Arisierung' und fiskalische Ausplünderung vor Gericht," in Goschler and Lillteicher, eds., *"Arisierung" und Restitution*, 133–34.
46. See J. P. Spannuth, "'Rückerstattung Ost,'" in Goschler and Lillteicher, *"Arisierung" und Restitution*, 241–63; see also C. Meyer-Seitz, "Die Entwicklung der Rückerstattung in den neuen Bundesländern seit 1989. Eine juristische Perpektive," in the same volume, 265–79.
47. See, for instance, Schumacher's defamation of Adenauer as "Chancellor of the Allied Powers," Goschler, *Politik der Rückerstattung*, 110; see also Lillteicher, *Roub, Recht und Restitution.*
48. B. Bailer-Galanda, "Die Rückerstattungsproblematik in Österreich," in Goschler and Lillteicher, *"Arisierung" und Restitution*, 161–88.
49. See Claire Andrieu's article in this volume.

Jewish Property and the Politics of Restitution in Germany after 1945

Constantin Goschler

When in the 1990s new claims for the restitution of Jewish property arose, they were accompanied by disputes over whether earlier attempts at restitution had been adequate or not. Sometimes these disputes were fueled by a lack of knowledge that earlier efforts at restitution had taken place at all. Behind this controversy lie some key shifts in perspective. On the one hand, over the last fifty years the standard of what is considered to be fair restitution has changed dramatically. On the other hand, over the course of time, Jewish property has also changed both its quality and its meaning for individuals and the social composition of communities. Due to the massive destruction suffered by Jews and their belongings during the Third Reich, restitution could not simply aim at restoring the previous status quo; rather, it had to have as its goal the construction of something new. Therefore, restitution has always been an intensely political issue, where different views of interpreting the past and shaping the future have competed with each other.

Bearing these points in mind, this essay will examine the development of the politics of restitution in West Germany.[1] The story of the restitution of Jewish property in East Germany[2]—which basically is a story of non-restitution—will only be dealt with in the context of developments after 1990, when the enlarged Federal Republic had to come to terms with open questions of restitution in its newly acquired Eastern states. My main argument is that since 1945 there has been a cyclical succession of "final settlements" and then reemergences of the restitution issue, which can only be explained by the fundamental changes in the perception of Nazi anti-Jewish policies, by developments in the fields of national and international politics, and changes in the standards of justice. Three sets of questions will be used to develop my argument: First, what different perceptions existed

---

Notes for this section begin on page 129.

among the respective groups that participated on both sides of the argument in the campaign for the restitution of Jewish property? This question refers to their different views on both the past and the future of Jewish property and its former and future owners. Second, what circumstances and patterns of political action most strongly influenced the politics of restitution? What changes in the manner of conducting restitution politics have taken place? And third, what is the meaning of restitution in the wider perspective of overcoming remaining historical injustices? What were the respective roles of German administrations on the one hand and German civil society on the other? And what was the meaning of restitution for the relationship between German society and the Jewish victims? To answer these questions, I will provide a brief survey of the political battles over the restitution of Jewish property in West Germany from the immediate postwar period up to the 1990s.

Competing Models for the Restitution of Jewish Property in the 1940s

The first deliberations on how to undo the spoliation of Jewish property in Germany and the territories occupied by the Wehrmacht began during World War II. Even before the defeat of Nazi Germany, the Roosevelt administration received thousands of claims from former German and Austrian Jews who had become U.S. citizens.[3] However, from a political point of view, these individual claims played only a minor role; from the beginning organized Jewish interests were predominant, although their aims were quite different from those of the individual claimants. Of course, all Jewish claimants insisted that looted Jewish property had to be returned whenever this was possible. But views on how restitution should take place and who should inherit Jewish property varied quite widely. The differences resulted from the tension between the analysis of Nazi persecution on the one hand and the perspective of continuing Jewish life after the end of the war on the other.

In his book *Indemnification and Reparations* (published in 1944), the director of the Institute of Jewish Affairs in New York, Nehemiah Robinson, summarized the differences between the competing views: he distinguished between "restorative" and "constructive" measures. The former were aimed primarily at individual compensation and restitution. The latter, in contrast, considered the Jewish people collectively as a victim and wanted to use the looted Jewish property for a new beginning for them.[4] Already in 1941, Nahum Goldmann, speaking both for the World Jewish Congress and the Jewish Agency for Palestine, had identified the persecution of the German Jews as part of a comprehensive war against the Jewish people and therefore put forward a "collective" reparations claim.[5]

Such differences in outlook were especially relevant to the question of who should be the legitimate heir to Jewish property. Within American

Jewish organizations and the Jewish Agency for Palestine, even before the end of the war, the prevailing opinion was that these assets should be used primarily for the reconstruction of Jewish life in Palestine. However, in the United States there also existed organizations such as the Axis Victims League and the American Association of Former European Jurists, which took a decisive anti-Zionist and nondenominational stance. These organizations mainly represented persecuted Jews from Germany, Austria, and other European countries that had been conquered by Nazi Germany, and they put the persecution of Jews and other groups into a common framework. However, these more universalistic approaches subsequently became politically marginalized.[6]

The Jewish communities in Germany that were trying to reestablish themselves after the war took up a different position again. In opposition to foreign Jewish organizations, which regarded Germany as incurable anyway, they were afraid that aggressive efforts for the restitution of Jewish property might cause a resurgence of antisemitism. For some years, Jewish organizations abroad had disapproved of the reemergence of Jewish communities in Germany at all, which made the conflict even worse.[7] The emigrant German Jews also rejected the claims of German Jewish postwar communities, as they often consisted predominantly of Jews who had immigrated to Germany from Eastern Europe only after 1945: in the eyes of the representatives of the "original" German Jews, the latter could hardly be considered legitimate heirs to the property of prewar Jewish communities.

In his study, Nehemiah Robinson also examined the extent to which German resistance movements were taking the possible restitution of Jewish property into consideration. According to his account, the postwar plans of the German anti-Nazi opposition aimed mainly at minimizing the total financial burden on Germany as much as possible. The German thesis, Robinson wrote, was that it had to prevent the new democratic society from being undermined once again by excessive reparation claims, as had been the case in the Weimar Republic.[8] Actually the German resistance strictly tried to avoid being seen as the proponent of a new Versailles Treaty, which inevitably would have led to its political marginalization. Therefore, even though the whole political spectrum, from conservative to socialist, including part of the communist resistance, accepted the need for the restitution of Jewish property, it remained unclear to what extent restitution should take place. In any case it depended on the respective postwar perspectives of the German political parties.[9]

Differences in interests and perspectives also prevailed on the side of the Allies, who initially set the tone in Germany after 1945. The French Military Government drew upon its own experience with measures already taken in Northern Africa and in liberated France to redress property confiscations and the effects of discrimination upon the Jews.[10] However, in Northern Africa the restitution of confiscated Jewish property had encountered fierce resistance from local beneficiaries, and therefore Nehemiah Robinson had already argued in 1944 for an international solution to this problem.[11] The

British interest in the restitution of Jewish property was also influenced by domestic concerns: primarily, leaders were afraid of placing additional burdens on the British taxpayer. The British authorities were also worried by the possibility that returned Jewish property might be used to finance the conflict in Palestine, where British forces faced a Jewish guerrilla insurgency. Furthermore, based on their colonial experience, they preferred the model of "indirect rule" and therefore would have preferred a direct settlement between Germans and Jews without British involvement.[12]

France and Britain, which had both been severely weakened by the war, always considered the restitution of Jewish property from the wider perspective of their own claims for reparations. On this point they were in agreement with the Soviet Union. Therefore, they repeatedly took a common stance on restitution against the United States, which had suffered no damages from the war on its territory. In contrast, the perspective of the U.S. administration was influenced by the problem of war refugees and the resulting social destabilization of the countries receiving them (at this time the "Holocaust" was not on their agenda). Their main aim was to make Germany bear some of the financial costs of the enormous refugee problem it had created. By the end of the war, the restitution of Jewish property was viewed within the U.S. administration as the minimum acceptable contribution towards this problem. Balancing these claims against the strong U.S. interest in the reconstruction of Germany and its reintegration within a multilateral world economy was the essential premise behind U.S. policy on the restitution of Jewish property.

On 11 May 1945, the Joint Chiefs of Staff issued Instruction No. 1067, which laid down the guidelines for U.S. occupation policy. Within this order, the restitution of Jewish property was declared to be a fixed goal, but the order did not include any specific instructions on how this should be achieved. Behind this lay also the fears of Henry Morgenthau, the head of the U.S. Treasury, that the situation in liberated Northern Africa, where the French authorities had proceeded only very hesitantly with the restitution of Jewish property, could be repeated.[13] So, while the United States became the motor of restitution efforts after 1945, its aim was not just the establishment of a new international moral order, but also its use as a tool in diplomatic and economic relations.

The Conflict over Allied Restitution Legislation

To what extent did the Germans try to settle the restitution issue themselves after 1945? Plans developed by the newly established administrations of the German states (until the establishment of the Federal Republic in September 1949 there was no central authority in Germany) reflected both the inability and lack of will within German society to take this burden upon itself—even though there was no doubt, at least in principle, that Jewish property had to be returned. Restitution was intended to send a signal to the free world that the emerging democratic Germany was ready for the compensation of Nazi victims. At the same time, it was also necessary to remove the insecurity surrounding property ownership that resulted from the decision of the Allied Control Authority (ACA) to block all domestic and foreign property that might have been looted between 1933 and 1945.[14] However, the German authorities generally wanted to return only that Jewish property which had been confiscated as a direct result of the actions of the German Reich. As a result, those cases where Jewish property had come into the hands of non-Jewish owners without the direct intervention of the state or Nazi organizations were to be excluded from restitution. In other words, there was no consideration of the widespread participation of German society in the process of expropriation at all. However, the restitution plans of the German authorities never got beyond the initial planning stages anyway. This reflected both the huge dimensions of the problem and the limited political influence of the individual German states, which made them very reluctant to take on the burdens entailed in restitution.[15] Therefore, the German authorities preferred to wait for the occupation forces to take the initiative.

The main role was played by the Organization of Military Government, United States (OMGUS), which in 1945 had initiated the safeguarding (property control) of former Jewish possessions and had also started to collect restitution claims. In April 1946, OMGUS set up a special committee of the Stuttgart state council (the latter coordinated the four German states within the U.S. zone of occupation). The special committee was instructed to draft a restitution law for individuals and organizations within the U.S. zone. Following earlier German plans, the committee wanted to limit the scope of the law to those cases where Jews had been dispossessed as a consequence of the actions of the German Reich, thereby excluding actions taken by German private individuals.[16]

In general, the German governments tried to limit the scope of restitution, and this collided with the much more far-reaching expectations that had emerged within OMGUS as a result of the pressure from Jewish organizations in the United States. While the latter, through OMGUS, were able to exert considerable influence on the deliberations of the German special committee, German business associations were also lobbying the German administrations heavily at the same time. However, since they could only talk to the weaker partner in the game, their influence was very limited from the beginning. German political bargaining power was based mainly on the threat that the Allies would have to carry full political and financial responsibility for any restitution legislation, which the German side deemed to be unacceptable. Therefore, an analysis of the interventions by German business circles is hardly relevant to the political decision-making. Rather it is important for understanding how postwar German business circles viewed the dispossession of the Jews during the Third Reich. While they accepted the restitution of Jewish property in principle, they advocated the strict limitation of such claims. Consequently, the Economic Council of the Bavarian Ministry of Economics and the Chamber of Industry and Commerce in the British zone of occupation were united in their rejection of "unrestrained restitution."[17]

The image of Jewish suffering during the Third Reich held by these German business circles almost totally neglected the physical destruction of the Jews. Instead they focused on the experiences of those Jews who emigrated successfully, and even tried to argue that those who had left Germany had actually benefited economically in comparison with the losses suffered by other businessmen who had remained in Germany during the war.[18] In this perception, the persecution of the Jews was reduced to little more than a policy of forced emigration, which, unfortunately, had included the use of improper means. Given the fact that most German Jews were now either living abroad or had been murdered, the condition that only those Jews who had returned to Germany or intended to do so should have their property returned served only to reinforce the widespread acceptance of the measures taken by the Third Reich to expel the Jews from the German economy.

In German business circles there was also a broad consensus that only those current owners of Jewish property who had personally enriched themselves in an unfair manner should be liable for its restitution. Again this was based on the assumption that the persecution of Jews generally had been imposed from "above"—by the Nazi state and party—on German society. This was in contrast, however, with the simultaneous threat that a more far-reaching restitution, as promoted by OMGUS, might revive the antisemitic feelings that still existed in Germany. Additionally, there were frequent warnings against doing anything that might destabilize further the seriously damaged German economy. Applying counterfactual history to the issue of restitution and considering what might have happened if the Germans had been permitted to manage the restitution of Jewish property in accordance with their own ideas, it is reasonable to assume that some restitution would have taken place even without Allied pressure. However, the scope of restitution would certainly have been much less than that which eventually resulted from Allied pressure.

Allied restitution politics in the early years of the occupation of Germany bore the strong imprint of the U.S. military governor, Lucius D. Clay, who even went beyond the intentions of the U.S. administration, which tended to be much more cautious. In the autumn of 1946, Clay conferred with five American Jewish organizations in Washington.[19] On this occasion, he gave far-reaching assurances with regard to the scope and implementation of the restitution of Jewish property. However, the governors of the states in the U.S. zone of occupation were not ready to pass a draft restitution law based on the wishes of the American Jewish organizations. Consequently, in the summer of 1946 OMGUS had to accept negotiations at the level of the ACA, which started to discuss common principles for the restitution of property to victims of the Nazis.[20] However, once again the U.S. position, which was tied by the commitments General Clay had given in Washington, did not receive much support.

Three aspects which had already played an important role in the rejection of the draft by the German state governments were vigorously disputed during the ACA negotiations. First, which Jewish property losses should be considered as resulting from unfair actions during the Nazi era and consequently should be liable for restitution? Should one accept the view that even in Nazi Germany, at least in some cases, Jewish property changed hands without any discrimination against the Jewish owner? The U.S. draft proposed that 15 September 1935 (the date on which the Nuremberg racial laws came into force) should be the cutoff date, after which all transactions involving Jewish property in the German Reich should be viewed as liable for restitution; moreover, the current owner should also be liable to return the property, even if he were not personally involved in the respective transaction. Second, there was a conflict over the plan for a supreme Allied restitution court, which had also been one of the original demands of the American Jewish organizations. And third, there was a serious dispute over the desire of the aforementioned organizations to have heirless Jewish property transferred to Jewish successor organizations. By this means, the property would serve the purpose of helping to reestablish Jewish communities outside Germany, especially in Palestine. Again Clay was isolated, as his three allies shared animosities towards Jewish successor organizations, as did not only the German states but indeed the Jewish communities in Germany.[21]

Since OMGUS was not able to obtain the consent of its allies for a common restitution law based on U.S. principles, it eventually had to act unilaterally. On 10 November 1947, Clay enacted U.S. Military Law No. 59, which provided for the restitution of identifiable property taken away under duress for racial, religious, or political reasons.[22] On the same day, the French Military Government enacted Ordinance No. 120 in their zone of occupation, reflecting important input from French restitution legislation and having been drafted without German participation.[23] In contrast to the law for the U.S. zone, heirless Jewish property was to be used not only for the indemnification of the Jews, but all victims of Nazi persecution. The British Military Government followed suit eighteen months later and on 12 May 1949 enacted a simplified version of the U.S. restitution law in their zone of occupation.[24] Soon afterwards, the ACA enacted the British law in a slightly modified version in West Berlin.[25] In the Soviet zone of occupation, however, nothing of this sort occurred.

Only reluctantly did Clay choose the path of proceeding unilaterally with a separate law for the U.S. zone. He had been afraid that there might be a negative response at home, since U.S. taxpayers would notice the comparatively heavy economic burden on the U.S. zone of occupation that resulted from the law. After receiving reports warning of Clay's pessimistic mood, the American Jewish organizations organized a press campaign in the United States enthusiastically praising OMGUS Law No. 59 as "an act of justice."[26] Reactions in Germany, however, spoke of a missed opportunity, or even of a threatened sellout. German business circles even put the U.S.

Military Law No. 59 into the tradition of Nazi legislation: "There is only a slight, but not an essential difference between such a deviation from the objective line and the application of the notorious principle applied by the National Socialist regime, justifying any perversion of the law by claiming that 'justice is what is useful to the people.'"[27]

A fair assessment of West German restitution politics during the occupation period must, however, take into account that after 1945 West German politicians were neither able to speak with one voice, nor with equal rights. Against this background, a common minimum consensus emerged, rejecting the assumption of political responsibility for any restitution measures that went beyond what German society was willing to accept. Without doubt, the arguments over restitution often revealed a considerable disregard for the sensibilities of the Jewish victims of persecution. At the same time, however, the "Versailles trauma" that had already characterized the restitution plans of the German anti-Nazi opposition also played an important role: German politicians were hardly ready to legitimize any Allied *Diktat*, which would have tainted them as in effect collaborators. Therefore, in the first years after the war, German restitution policies were marked by the desire to leave the responsibility for embarrassing legal actions in the hands of the Allies. This went hand in hand with a lack of initiative, except with respect to efforts aimed at reducing the scope of restitution imposed from outside. How did this "attentism" (policy of wait and see) change in the 1950s, as West Germany gradually acquired a greater degree of sovereignty?

Restitution and the "Politics of the Past" in the 1950s

After the establishment of the Federal Republic, most voices spoke out against the restitution of Jewish property. Since the restitution of identifiable property often produced direct encounters between the previous Jewish owners and current owners of property, this particular issue produced much more public unrest than other compensation policies, which only involved the German state rather than private individuals. Owners of former Jewish property who were liable to restitution organized themselves into voluntary associations, which in the spring of 1950 joined together in the Federal Association for Fair Restitution. Their public claims had a strong influence within German society and politics. Initially they pressed for changes in the Allied restitution legislation—mainly to U.S. Military Government Law No. 59, which was criticised for being too draconian. Due to the firm Allied stance, the owners of former Jewish property finally shifted the focus of their demands to the passing of supplementary legislation to provide compensation for those who had been "unfairly" affected by Allied restitution legislation. This remained a constant demand, and the conservative parties repeatedly tried—unsuccessfully—to introduce reforms to the restitution legislation as part of a package deal. Prominent among those who agitated against the Allied restitution legislation were representatives of the retail trade and landlords. Industrial representatives, however, were more cautious about openly resisting it, since they were concerned about the international situation.[28]

The Jewish Restitution Successor Organization (JRSO), which operated as the legal successor for heirless Jewish property in the U.S. zone of occupation, became the main target for complaints against the "outrageous, undeserved enrichment and evil profiteering by means of enforced repeated payment of the once already paid purchase price."[29] While the style of such accusations was not far from the notorious "the Jews are our misfortune" rhetoric, there were other statements that transmitted the same message in a more subtle manner. All in all, the resistance to Allied restitution legislation is an important part of the German "politics of the past" that was aimed at revoking the whole series of Allied measures designed to eradicate the foundations of National Socialism (i.e., de-nazification).[30]

Attempts to weaken Allied restitution legislation also enjoyed much support among the general population. In August 1949 the Allensbach Institute took an opinion poll among West Germans on their attitudes to restitution. The question asked was: "If a non-Jew bought a Jewish shop after 1933, and the former owner now claims its return on the same terms, would you say that the claim is justified or not?" While at least 54 percent answered a more general question on their readiness to compensate German Jews with "yes," answers to more specific versions of the question could be much more hesitant: 39 percent recognized the claim as justified, if the actions of the Nazi regime had been the clear motive for selling, but 28 percent answered that the claim was not justified, while 25 percent answered "it depends," and 8 percent were "undecided."[31]

While German efforts to weaken Allied efforts at de-nazification achieved considerable results, similar pressure against Allied restitution legislation was ultimately unsuccessful—indeed, it may even have caused the Allies to speed up restitution procedures in order to overcome this source of conflict as soon as possible. Therefore, the U.S. High Commission also supported the attempts of some southern German states in the early 1950s to settle some of the outstanding restitution claims by means of global payments to the JRSO.[32] During the era of partial sovereignty after the establishment of the Federal Republic, which lasted until 1955, the Allied High Commissioners strictly enforced the conditions imposed on the Germans. At the same time, the rights reserved to Allies within the statutes of occupation were only given up in exchange for firm commitments by the Federal Republic.

The restitution of Jewish property was one of the issues covered by negotiations, as the U.S. High Commissioner, John J. McCloy, declared it to be one of his political priorities.[33] He combined his interest in the stabilization of the Federal Republic with pressure for the speedy implementation of restitution. In his view, both aims served the stabilization of the Western world, which depended both on economic prosperity and liberal values. As a result of this pressure, by 1957 the restitution of identifiable property had largely been completed. Property with a total value of about 3.5 billion DM had been returned, of which some 300 million DM went to the Jewish successor organizations.[34]

However, already in the early 1950s the United States had reduced its involvement in restitution matters in favor of direct German-Jewish negotiations, which in 1952 culminated in the Hague Treaties between the Federal Republic on the one hand and Israel and the Conference on Jewish Material Claims Against Germany (Claims Conference) on the other. The impact of calls for restitution of Jewish property was reduced not only in the eyes of the German government, but also from the perspective of German society, by German claims that they themselves were "victims of the war." For many years, refugees and expellees, victims of the Allied bombings, POWs, war widows and orphans, and other groups dominated public remembrance of World War II in the Federal Republic.[35]

All in all, the Federal Republic continued its attentism with respect to restitution, which had also marked the attitude of its predecessors during the occupation period. This position of the Bonn administration was not only fostered by the growing economic and political importance of the Federal Republic, but also by tacit support from Washington. While the United States was pushing for the speedy fulfilment of existing restitution claims, at the same time it tried to block the far-reaching claims of France and Britain, who both wanted to weaken the strict separation between German and non-German victims of the Nazis. In the interest of protecting German economic strength, Washington insisted on a strict separation between (internal) restitution and (external) reparations. In pursuing this aim, the U.S. administration mainly had two objectives in mind: sustaining Germany's contribution to Western defense, and preferential treatment of commercial over moral debts (which it successfully achieved in the London debt settlement of 1953).[36] Thus the United States privileged the repayment of American pre- and postwar credits over other claimants, including foreign victims of the Nazis.

The Federal Republic and Restitution Claims against the German Reich

As a result of the negotiations with the Western Allies on the replacement of the occupation statute, and also of the Hague Treaty with Israel and the Claims Conference, the West German government had introduced a number of improvements and extensions of its restitution legislation. Furthermore, in accordance with the Hague Treaty, the Federal Republic paid a lump sum of 450 million DM to the Claims Conference, based on its claim to heirless Jewish property.[37] Certain special aspects of restitution for property losses were also settled by the Bundesentschädigungsgesetz [Federal Indemnification Law] (BEG) of 1953 (amended in 1956). This dealt especially with claims related to special discriminatory taxes and the destruction or plunder of Jewish property. The Federal Republic paid a total sum of about 1.26 billion DM on these claims.[38]

Yet a large share of restitution claims still remained unsettled by the late 1950s: up to this date there was still no legal mechanism for paying the assessed damages for property taken away by the German Reich, the Nazi Party, and equivalent institutions. Legal recommendations had already been made in these cases on the basis of Allied restitution legislation, which had even assessed the value of claims that were upheld. However, apart from partial payment in cases of social hardship, for the moment these claims could not be paid out. During the negotiations for the end of the occupation statute, the Federal Republic had assumed the obligation to settle these claims up to a total sum of some 1.5 billion DM (the total value of all these claims is estimated at between 6 and 7 billion DM).[39] A similar obligation had also been included within the Hague Treaties.

To fulfill these international obligations, in 1957 the Federal Republic finally passed the Bundesrückerstattungsgesetz [Federal Restitution Law] (BrüG),[40] which therefore may be considered only partially a product of German legislative action. For the former owner to qualify for restitution under the BrüG, the respective property had to have been originally located on the territory of the Federal Republic or West Berlin. Furthermore, the claimants had to be from the Federal Republic or a country with which the Federal Republic had diplomatic relations—in practice this meant the exclusion of all claimants from Eastern Europe. However, during legislative proceedings in the Bundestag, an amendment proposed by the Claims Conference was inserted to make property confiscated outside the borders of the German Reich but subsequently removed to an area where the BrüG was now valid, also subject to restitution.[41] This amendment brought a far-reaching extension of restitution, even though it created considerable technical difficulties by requiring claimants to prove that their belongings had been brought within the borders of the Federal Republic. However, since the total amount of compensation provided for by the BrüG was limited initially to some 1.5 billion DM, this extension also intensified the competition between different Jewish claimants.

Originally, payments for any claim exceeding 20,000 DM euros had been limited to 50 percent, and, moreover, this payment was to be spread over several years. As a consequence of the inclusion of Jewish property that had been confiscated outside the borders of the German Reich, the amount that was available for a single claim was reduced still further. As over the years the ability to obtain the necessary evidence on the whereabouts of stolen property improved, the conflicts intensified. This was especially true with respect to two types of cases: first, claims that had been rejected due to a lack of evidence on the ultimate destination of the property; and second, claims that had not been brought forward at all because potential claimants had considered them to be a lost cause from the start due to lack of evidence. In consequence, the Claims Conference pressed for an extension of the already expired registration deadline.

All this clashed, however, with the interests of former German Jews, whose property had been taken away within the borders of the German Reich. These were represented chiefly by the Council of Jews from Germany. The German administration would also have liked to favor the interests of former German Jews. At the same time, however, it was deeply intimidated by the supposed power of "World Jewry," which in their eyes was mainly represented by the Claims Conference, and especially its president, Nahum Goldmann. The Claims Conference was far from interested in destroying this useful myth, as it added weight to its demands, which could not rely exclusively on the moral strength of Jewish restitution and compensation claims to be successful.

And so, while German Jews insisted on an increase in the proportion of the original settlements to be paid ("quota"), the Claims Conference instead pushed for an extension of the number of beneficiaries, widening the distribution of money even at the cost of reducing the size of individual payments.[42] However, there were also Jewish claimants from abroad who were opposed to the existing quota restrictions. Ernst Féaux de la Croix, who was responsible for restitution at the Federal Ministry of Finance, commented: "Behind the large claims are forces that should not be underestimated, for example, the Rothschild family in France."[43] The U.S. administration, at least in this case, did not support the position of the Claims Conference; rather, it wanted a speedy resolution of those restitution claims that had been filed before the original BrüG deadline.[44]

The politics of restitution in Germany were also distinguished by differences of opinion between the Bundestag and the Federal Ministry of Finance. The bottom line of the controversy was a different understanding of the meaning of restitution. In the restitution committee of the Bundestag, there were eloquent adherents of the position that victims of Nazi persecution had civil claims for damages against the German Reich, that is, also against its legal successor, the Federal Republic. Both Franz Böhm and Martin Hirsch—the former a conservative, the latter a social-democrat—insisted that the restitution legislation of the Federal Republic did not create new legal rights, but rather transformed existing civil law claims into public law claims.[45] In 1964, Hirsch commented on this before the Bundestag: "In the sphere of restitution and also in the realm of compensation in general, we find ourselves in a situation that at first sight seems favorable: we can decide for ourselves the size of the debts that we have to pay for the series of robberies committed by the 'Third Reich.'" At least for Hirsch, this presented a moral dilemma, as "maybe one should be more objective in this situation than when one has to decide on behalf of others."[46] The Federal Ministry of Finance was less worried by this quandary: it not only contested the principle that the Federal Republic had an obligation to pay based on civil law, but it also rejected the position that restitution and compensation for Nazi victims should be a privileged category in comparison with other claims for damages arising from the war.[47]

Adding to this conflict between legislative and the executive bodies were also the effects of the democratization of restitution politics that took place after the end of the occupation. Up until 1949 and in some respects even into the early 1950s, the Allied occupation powers frequently used their authority to intervene; later, however, questions concerning restitution became part of the everyday parliamentary battle. During the debate on an amendment to the BrüG in 1963, Martin Hirsch analyzed the effects of this democratization: "Referring to the political aspects, we have to take into consideration that the [Jewish] claimants, in contrast for example to German war victims and other recipients of compensation, do not constitute a substantial and unified group of voters."[48] Since most Jewish victims of Nazi persecution lived abroad, they did not count at the ballot box at all, and hence they were excluded from the well-established mechanisms for the distribution of social benefits within the Federal Republic.

Nevertheless, in 1964 the BrüG payments were significantly increased by a third and final amendment to this law.[49] In exchange for a privileged consideration of the Claims Conference by means of a global settlement, the Federal Republic expected that no further claims would be presented by this organization.[50] Instead of reopening the registration period, Bonn provided additional funds of up to 800 million DM for the settlement of claims concerning Jewish property confiscated in the occupied areas that had not been filed in time. However, the previous limitation of 1.5 billion DM on the total sum to be paid was also dropped, so that claims accepted in the future would be paid out in full, even when they exceeded 20,000 DM.[51] As a result, the final total of all BrüG payments eventually reached about 4 billion DM.[52]

Meanwhile the role of the Allies had changed significantly compared with the first half of the 1950s. Whereas initially they had been eager to make use of their control rights in matters concerning the restitution of Jewish property, in 1964 the Federal Ministry of Finance considered it was sufficient only to propose transmitting the last BrüG amendment to the Allies "just informally."[53] Furthermore, in the mid-1960s the general mood in the Federal Republic with respect to how people viewed the Nazi past was changing profoundly: in 1965, the Christian Democrat Chancellor Ludwig Erhard was in line with the majority of the German people and the political class when he declared before the Bundestag that the postwar era had come to an end.[54] Hence the third amendment to the BrüG in 1964—like the BEG Final Law in 1965—went hand in hand with expectations that a lasting solution had been found, which, as the Federal Minister of Finance Rolf Dahlgrün announced to the Bundestag, "will set the keystone on the compensation and restitution legislation."[55] This conclusion was not unfounded: Nahum Goldmann had nourished such hopes during the preceding negotiations. He successfully convinced the German administration to improve existing restitution and compensation legislation, arguing that then there would be no further claims[56]—thus offering a seductive carrot in the political bargaining process, more effective than purely moral arguments.

As a result, from the German perspective, by 1965 at least the political issue of restitution—and compensation—seemed to have been settled.

However, the stability of this situation depended on a precarious precondition, namely the political division of the world into East and West—which meant the exclusion of victims of Nazi persecution who lived behind the Iron Curtain. Thus there was a tacit admission within the West German administrations that after German reunification it was likely that new restitution and compensation claims would emerge. However, the likelihood of this eventuality became more remote as the prospects for German reunification receded in the 1970s and 1980s—and today we have to remind ourselves that up until 1989 the belief in German reunification had almost vanished both in German society and its political class. Nevertheless, an executive in the restitution department of the Federal Ministry of Finance reminded his boss in 1962: "Behind the entire current compensation, on the horizon remains the prospect of extending our compensation to the East, for example, in the case of the establishment of diplomatic relations. It is known that there are respective claims from Yugoslavia—the extent: hardly possible to assess."[57]

Summary and Outlook: The Return of Restitution after 1990

Following changes in the political landscape of Europe at the beginning of the 1990s, property issues again became much more prominent.[58] They also played an important role within the process of German unification, which also produced a fundamental change of property relations in East Germany, where private property had largely been taken into state ownership. It was mainly as a result of interventions by the Claims Conference, which received strong support from the U.S. government, that the issue of restitution of former Jewish property was once again put on the agenda.[59] However, the East German government headed by Lothar de Maiziére was very reluctant to adopt Western Allied restitution legislation on its territory, as it was afraid of a massive undermining of the property rights of its own population. Therefore, it fought against the principle of restitution in natura in favor of a global compensation settlement for Aryanized Jewish property.[60] This would have resulted in a shift of the burden from actual East German owners to the German taxpayer (including West Germans). However, in the end the conservative West German administration of Helmut Kohl ensured that the whole restitution complex—including restitution of Jewish property—would be dealt with according to the principle of "restitution before compensation." Instead of expanding Allied restitution legislation to East Germany, the law for the regulation of open property questions (the new property law) determined that Jewish property claims would instead be dealt with as part of more general property restitution legislation.[61]

Compared with the postwar American and British restitution legislation, the new property law somewhat weakened the legal position of Jewish claimants. But in the course of later amendments, the differences from the original Allied legislation were reduced.[62] What remained was the general tendency to require Jewish claimants or their heirs to take into account the changes of ownership that had taken place in the meantime. Consequently, in some cases the claimants had to accept financial compensation instead of restitution of their property. The purpose of this was to make restitution more acceptable to East German citizens, who in many cases felt overwhelmed by the legal consequences of German unification.

While restitution legislation was somewhat weakened in comparison with earlier Allied military legislation, the implementation of the property law was much smoother in the 1990s than in the late 1940s and 1950s, when fierce resistance from the subsequent owners of Jewish property was quite common. Restitution of Jewish property in East Germany was handled without the hidden or open obstruction that had frequently marked the actions of West German administrations and courts after the war.[63] Only in those instances where there was a regional concentration of many restitution cases were there public protests—for example, in Teltow-Seehof. Since the filing period stipulated in the property law ended on 31 December 1992—with the important exception of the Claims Conference, which can file indefinitely—most of the cases have in the meantime been decided. To give an impression of the size of the task, one may refer to cautious estimations that in the five Eastern states of Germany and in East Berlin between 1933 and 1945 about 45,000 real estate properties and some 10,000 enterprises had been Aryanized.[64]

The nature of the conflict has profoundly changed, mostly due to the extended time span that has passed since the property was lost. The actual process of Jewish property restitution has been held up much more frequently by problems in determining the legitimate heirs than by resistance from the current owners. Conversely, the large amount of time that has elapsed since the persecution, which in most cases goes hand in hand with a generational change, has also produced advantages. It encouraged a more relaxed attitude to the restitution of Jewish property than was the case in the immediate postwar period in West Germany. Another important element of change was that restitution in East Germany has been handled under public law, and not civil law as in West Germany. So, while in West Germany the former and current owners of Jewish property met face to face during restitution proceedings, in East Germany this type of personal confrontation did not usually take place. And finally, it may have been significant that West German elites—who heavily influenced the implementation of restitution in East Germany—in a way, drew their own historical lessons from the earlier, less successful efforts at restitution in West Germany.[65]

The smooth, almost businesslike atmosphere in which the restitution of Jewish property in East Germany has generally been handled stands in stark contrast to most other recent restitution claims, which reflect the emergence of a new style in the politics of restitution. Since the mid-1990s, not only German companies that used forced labor during the war but also banks and insurance companies have become the targets of aggressive campaigns that were primarily aimed at public opinion in the United States. In addition, now not only German companies but also other European companies and governments have been accused of participating in the theft of Jewish property in Europe during the war.

The changes in political style that lie behind such public campaigns have a lot to do with a generational change within the Jewish organizations involved in restitution negotiations. Nahum Goldmann, to some extent, embodied the attempt to revive the former German-Jewish symbiosis that had been destroyed by the Nazis. Therefore, he was always very fond of striking the right note in his talks with Adenauer, "speaking German, about Goethe and Bach, and God knows what."[66] In contrast, his successors have been much more attached to an American-Jewish perspective. As a result, the question of achieving the restitution of Jewish property for, as we now say, "survivors of the Holocaust," has become directly linked to the complex process of American-Jewish identity construction. Additionally, the German economy has become much more sensitive to the pressure that can be exerted using the American legal system. In particular, class-action lawsuits were instrumental in the unilateral extension of American jurisdiction to international cases—which in part also reflects the growing unwillingness of the United States to accept multilateral legal solutions. Hence the resulting clash of legal cultures has produced new conflicts.

In the realm of restitution politics, it is still true that morality has to be converted into political, legal, or economic pressure to produce practical results. In this respect, the wait-and-see approach that is still predominant in German political and economic circles must bear a large share of responsibility for the, sometimes drastic, methods that the claimants and their representatives have felt compelled to employ. In the transformation of restitution claims from a moral into a political, legal, or economic frame of reference, there has also emerged a change in priorities among these claims, according to claimants' ability to grab public attention and mobilize relevant political support. This might be part of the explanation for the increasing disquiet expressed about the current manner of conducting restitution politics.[67]

Following very difficult international negotiations, in 2000 the foundation Remembrance, Responsibility, and the Future was established in Germany,[68] which provides about 1 billion DM for property claims, while the lion's share of the total of about 10 billion DM has been allocated for payments to former forced laborers. This settlement aims to close the last remaining gaps in existing restitution legislation. In the first instance, this refers to claims from former Iron Curtain countries and also cases in which the claimants had not been able to prove that their property had been brought to the territory of the former Federal Republic. For all of these claims, some 200 million DM were provided. At least 500 million DM were granted to the International Commission on Holocaust Era Insurance Claims (ICHEIC) in order to compensate unpaid, stolen and unreturned insurance policies and also finance a humanitarian fund.[69]

In contrast to the early days of restitution, during these negotiations not only the state but also business circles were actively involved, mainly because of the legal and economic pressure exerted in the United States.

However, soon the business leaders called for the state to assume part of the financial responsibility, and the entire project fell back into the well-established tracks of West German corporatism. It is fair to point out that as a result of his previous negotiations with the Swiss banks, U.S. Special Envoy on Holocaust Issues Stuart E. Eizenstat also pressed for the participation of the German Government.[70] But in the end, this adds to the impression that the problem of restitution is not an encouraging example for the role to be played by civil society in overcoming the consequences of historical injustice.

The establishment of the foundation "Remembrance, Responsibility, and the Future" went hand in hand with expectations that this would be a conclusive settlement of all outstanding compensation issues arising from the Nazi era. Thus at the turn of the millennium, a call for the "final stroke," which had already arisen in the mid-1960s, could be heard once again. It is too early to decide whether this latest attempt at a final settlement to the restitution of Jewish property will be more successful. As we have seen, the standards for illegal confiscation and for fair restitution still depend to a considerable degree on the timing and the interplay of conflicting interest groups—without considering the impact of massive changes in property relations, as was the case in the former Iron Curtain countries. Therefore, in view of the current trends both towards the "Americanization of the Holocaust" and the "Europeanization of Aryanization," it can be expected that the issue of Jewish property restitution still won't disappear completely from the political scene. But what is certain is that the dynamics involved will change again. And maybe the most important metamorphosis will be that the example of Jewish property will serve as a key precedent for restitution claims refering to other historical cases of property loss. So, while the universalization of the Holocaust has been an important prerequisite for the recent successful wave of Jewish restitution claims, it might also lead to the unintended consequence that the persecution of the Jews and the theft of their property during the Third Reich will be viewed as just one among many cases of historical injustice.

Notes

1. See Walter Schwarz, *Rückerstattung nach den Gesetzen der alliierten Mächte* (Munich, 1984); Friedrich Biella et al., *Das Bundesrückerstattungsgesetz* (Munich, 1981); Constantin Goschler, *Wiedergutmachung. Westdeutschland und die Verfolgten des Nationalsozialismus, 1945–1954* (Munich, 1992); Hermann-Josef Brodesser et al., *Wiedergutmachung und Kriegsfolgenliquidation. Geschichte – Regelungen – Zahlungen* (Munich, 2000), 10–16 and 70–81; Constantin Goschler, *Schuld und Schulden. Die Politik der Wiedergutmachung für Verfolgte des Nationalsozialismus in Deutschland nach 1945* (Göttingen, 2005).
2. See especially Uwe Wesel, "Wiedergutmachung für NS-Unrecht und Enteignungen auf der Grundlage sowjetischer Besatzungshoheit," *Zeitschrift für Vermögens- und Investitionsrecht* 2 (1992): 337–41; Hans-Jörg Graf, *Rückgabe von Vermögenswerten an Verfolgte*

des nationalsozialistischen Regimes im Beitrittsgebiet (Berlin, 1999); Jan Philipp Spannuth, "Rückerstattung Ost. Der Umgang der DDR mit dem 'arisierten' und enteigneten Eigentum der Juden und die Gestaltung der Rückerstattung im wiedervereinigten Deutschland" (PhD diss., Univ. of Freiburg-Breisgau, 2001); J. P. Spannuth, "Rückerstattung Ost. Der Umgang der DDR mit dem 'arisierten' und enteigneten Eigentum der Juden und die Gestaltung der Rückerstattung im wiedervereinigten Deutschland," in *"Arisierung" und Restitution. Die Rückerstattung jüdischen Eigentums in Deutschland und Österreich nach 1945 und 1989*, ed. Constantin Goschler and Jürgen Lillteicher (Göttingen, 2002), 241–63; Christian Meyer-Seitz, "Die Entwicklung der Rückerstattung in den neuen Bundesländern seit 1989. Eine juristische Perspektive," in Goschler and Lillteicher (eds.), *"Arisierung" und Restitution*, 265–79.

3. NARA, RG 59, 462.11/7-345, Robert Murphy to James F. Byrnes, 7 July 1945.
4. Nehemiah Robinson, *Indemnification and Reparations: Jewish Aspects* (New York, 1944), from 244.
5. Nahum Goldmann, *Mein Leben als deutscher Jude* (Munich, 1980), 372. See also Leon W. Wells, *Und sie machten Politik. Die amerikanischen Zionisten und der Holocaust* (Munich, 1989), 150–61; originally published as *Who Speaks for the Vanquished? American Jewish Leaders and the Holocaust* (New York, 1987); Goschler, *Wiedergutmachung*, 40.
6. See also Peter Novick, *The Holocaust in American Life* (Boston, 2000).
7. See Peter L. Münch, "Zwischen 'Liquidation' und Wiederaufbau: Die deutschen Juden, der Staat Israel und die internationalen jüdischen Organisationen in der Phase der Wiedergutmachungsverhandlungen," *Historische Mitteilungen* 22 (1997): 81–111.
8. Robinson, *Indemnification and Reparations*, 224.
9. Goschler, *Schuld und Schulden*, 31–39.
10. Schwarz, *Rückerstattung*, from 292; Rainer Hudemann, "Anfänge der Wiedergutmachung. Französische Besatzungszone 1945–1990," *Geschichte und Gesellschaft* 13 (1987): 181–216, esp. 197; Goschler, *Wiedergutmachung*, 187–88; see also the article of Claire Andrieu in this volume.
11. Robinson, *Indemnification and Reparations*, from 248.
12. See Jürgen Lillteicher, "Die Rückerstattung jüdischen Eigentums in Westdeutschland. Eine Studie über Rechtsstaatlichkeit, Vergangenheitsbewältigung und Verfolgungserfahrung" (PhD diss., University of Freiburg-Breisgau, 2003), 33.
13. *Morgenthau Diary (Germany)*, vol. II, prepared by the Subcommittee to Investigate the Administration of the Internal Security Act and Other Internal Security Laws of the Committee on the Judiciary, United States Senate (Washington DC, 1967), from 1243.
14. Bayerisches Justizministerium, Munich (BayMJ), 1101a, H. 1, Walter Roemer, "Entwurf eines Gesetzes zur vorläufigen Wiedergutmachung der aus Gründen der Rasse, Religion oder des politischen Bekenntnisses zugefügten Vermögensschädigungen," 11 October 1945; see also Schwarz, *Rückerstattung*, from 28; Goschler, *Wiedergutmachung*, 96.
15. See Schwarz, *Rückerstattung*, 28–31; Goschler, *Wiedergutmachung*, 91–96.
16. Bundesarchiv, Koblenz (BArch), Z 1, Bd. 1291, Henning von Arnim to Haller, 29 May 1946. Attachment: "Entwurf eines Gesetzes über vordringliche Wiedergutmachungsmaßnahmen (Württemberg/Baden)," 28 May 1946.
17. BArch, B 102/424076, G. Freiherr von Falkenhausen to Bernhard Wolff, 30 October 1946.
18. Bayerisches Hauptstaatsarchiv, Munich (BayHStA), MA 130348, Memorandum from Ludwig Kastl, 9 October 1946; BayHStA, MF 69409, Ludwig Kastl to Wilhelm Hoegner et al., 7 November 1946; BayMJ, 1101 a, H. 2, Albert Glaser to Florian Witzmann, 9 November 1946.
19. Goschler, *Wiedergutmachung*, from 111.
20. Schwarz, *Rückerstattung*, 32–54; Goschler, *Wiedergutmachung*, 106–28.
21. Goschler, *Wiedergutmachung*, 114–22.
22. Gesetz No. 59 (Rückerstattung feststellbarer Vermögensgegenstände an Opfer der nationalsozialistischen Unterdrückungsmaßnahmen) der Militärregierung Deutschland – Amerikanisches Kontrollgebiet – 9 November 1947, published in: *Rückerstattung feststellbarer*

Vermögensgegenstände in der amerikanischen und britischen Besatzungszone und in Berlin: Gesetze der Militärregierungen mit der Verordnung für Berlin, kommentiert von Reinhard von Godin and Hans Frhr. von Godin, 2nd ed. (Berlin, 1950), 1–259.

23. Verordnung Nr. 120 über die Rückerstattung geraubter Vermögensobjekte, 10 November 1947, in *Journal Officiel. Amtsblatt des französischen Oberkommandos in Deutschland*, No. 119, 14 November 1947, 1219–22. See Schwarz, *Rückerstattung*, 292–94; Hudemann, "Anfänge der Wiedergutmachung," 203–4.
24. Gesetz Nr. 59 (Rückerstattung feststellbarer Vermögensgegenstände an Opfer der nationalsozialistischen Unterdrückungsmaßnahmen) der Militärregierung Deutschland – Britisches Kontrollgebiet – 12 May 1949, published in Godin, *Rückerstattung feststellbarer Vermögensgegenstände*, 261–471.
25. Anordnung BK/O (49) 180 (Rückerstattung feststellbarer Vermögensgegenstände an Opfer nationalsozialistischer Unterdrückungsmaßnahmen) der Alliierten Kommandantur Berlin, 26 July 1949, published in: Godin, *Rückerstattung feststellbarer Vermögensgegenstände*, 473–514.
26. See the headline of a comment in the *New York Times* of 11 November 1947, which had been inspired by the American Jewish Committee (AJC). On the media campaign organized by the Public Relations Department of the AJC see Center for Jewish History (CJH), Archive of the American Jewish Committee, Restitution & Indemnification – Germany, AJC, "Summary of Promotion of the Restitution Law by the American Jewish Committee," 18 November 1947.
27. BArch, B 102/424076, G. Freiherr von Falkenhausen to Bernhard Wolff, 17 January 1948.
28. BArch, B 126/12359, "Protokoll über die Sitzung der Vereinigung für loyale Restitution am 29.3.1950 im Hotel 'Monopol-Metropol' in Frankfurt a.M."
29. BArch, B 126/12359, "Offener Brief an die Bundesregierung, insbesondere an den Herrn Bundes-Justizminister, sowie an die Fraktionen des Deutschen Bundestages und verschiedene Herren Abgeordnete, im Namen einer grossen Zahl von Bürgern der Stadt Stuttgart, die Unterzeichneten: Regier. Baumeister Hermann Eckert u. sechs anderen," Stuttgart, 7 February 1951.
30. Norbert Frei, *Adenauer's Germany and the Nazi Past: The Politics of Amnesty and Integration* (New York, 2000).
31. Elisabeth Noelle and Erich Peter Neumann, *Jahrbuch der öffentlichen Meinung 1947–1955* (Allensbach, 1956), 130.
32. Goschler, *Wiedergutmachung*, 175–80.
33. See, for example, public statement of John C. McCloy in Stuttgart, 2 February 1950, in *John J. McCloys Reden zu Deutschland- und Berlinfragen. Publizistische Aktivitäten und Ansprachen des Amerikanischen Hochkommissars für Deutschland 1949–1952*, ed. Erika J. Fischer and Heinz D. Fischer (Berlin, 1986), 67. See also Goschler, *Wiedergutmachung*, 168–72.
34. Schwarz, *Rückerstattung*, 348–55.
35. Robert G. Moeller, *War Stories: The Search for a Usable Past in the Federal Republic of Germany* (Berkeley, CA, 2001).
36. Ursula Rombeck-Jaschinski, *Das Londoner Schuldenabkommen. Die Regelung der deutschen Auslandsschulden nach dem Zweiten Weltkrieg* (Munich, 2004); Goschler, *Schuld und Schulden*, 147–59.
37. Goschler, *Wiedergutmachung*, 266.
38. See "Leistungen nach dem Bundesentschädigungsgesetz (BEG) vom 1. Oktober 1953 bis 31. Dezember 2002 in Mio.," in *Entschädigung von NS-Unrecht. Regelungen zur Wiedergutmachung*, ed. Bundesministerium der Finanzen (2003), 41.
39. BArch, B 126/15199, Koppe to Abteilung VI (Bundesfinanzministerium), 7 November 1961.
40. Bundesgesetz zur Regelung der rückerstattungsrechtlichen Geldverbindlichkeiten des deutschen Reiches und gleichgestellter Rechtsträger (BrüG) in BGBl. 1957, I, from 374.
41. Lillteicher, *Rückerstattung jüdischen Eigentums*, 330–31.

42. BArch, B 141/14560, Protokoll der 11. Sitzung des Ausschusses für Wiedergutmachung, 25 October 1962.
43. Ibid.
44. See footnote 39.
45. Franz Böhm and Martin Hirsch, in *Verhandlungen des Deutschen Bundestags*, 96th session, 14 November 1963, 4415 and 4418–19; BArch, B 141/14432, Martin Hirsch, in Kurzprotokoll der 2. Sitzung des Unterausschusses BrüG des Ausschusses für Wiedergutmachung, 28 November 1963, 11–12.
46. Martin Hirsch, in *Verhandlungen des Deutschen Bundestags*, 132nd session, 24 June 1964, 6429.
47. Bundesfinanzminister Rolf Dahlgrün (Freie Demokratische Partei), in *Verhandlungen des Deutschen Bundestags*, 96th session, 14 November 1963, 4406.
48. BArch, B 141/14432, Kurzprotokoll der 2. Sitzung des Unterausschusses BrüG des Ausschusses für Wiedergutmachung, 28 November 1963, 11; see also BArch, B 141/14433, Franz Böhm, in Kurzprotokoll der 25. Sitzung des Ausschusses für Wiedergutmachung, 5 March 1964, 19.
49. Third revision of the BrüG, 2 October 1964, BGBl. I, 1964, 809.
50. BArch, B 126/15199, Ernst Féaux de la Croix to Abteilung II, Bundesfinanzministerium, 15 November 1960.
51. See H. G. van Dam, "Abschluß der Rückerstattung," *Allgemeine Jüdische Wochenzeitung*, 3 August 1964.
52. "Leistungen der öffentlichen Hand auf dem Gebiet der Wiedergutmachung. Stand: 31. Dezember 2002," *Entschädigung von NS-Unrecht*, 38.
53. BArch, B 141/14434, Koppe in Kurzprotokoll der 29. Sitzung des Ausschusses für Wiedergutmachung, 5 May 1964, 5.
54. *Verhandlungen des Deutschen Bundestags*, 4th session, 10 November 1965, 17.
55. *Verhandlungen des Deutschen Bundestags*, 132nd session, 24 June 1964.
56. "Aufzeichnung über das Gespräch des Bundeskanzlers Erhard mit dem Vorsitzenden Goldmann, Jüdischer Weltkongress," 8 October 1964, in *Akten zur Auswärtigen Politik der Bundesrepublik Deutschland* (1964), vol. II: 1. Juli bis 31. Dezember 1964, ed. Wolfgang Hölscher and Daniel Kosthorst (Munich, 1995), 1131; see also Kurt R. Grossmann, *Die Ehrenschuld. Kurzgeschichte der Wiedergutmachung* (Frankfurt a.M., 1967), 144.
57. BArch, B 141/14563, Koppe to Federal Minister of Finance, 19 December 1962.
58. See also Hans Günter Hockerts, "Wiedergutmachung in Deutschland. Eine historische Bilanz 1945–2000," *Vierteljahrshefte für Zeitgeschichte* 49 (2001): 167–214, esp. 209–13.
59. Hockerts, "Wiedergutmachung," 207; Philip Zelikow and Condoleezza Rice, *Germany Unified and Europe Transformed: A Study in Statecraft* (Cambridge, MA, 1997), 485.
60. Meyer-Seitz, "Entwicklung der Rückerstattung," 267; see also Wesel, "Wiedergutmachung für NS-Unrecht," 338–39; Graf, *Rückgabe von Vermögenswerten*, 67–68.
61. Einigungsvertrag Anlage II Kapitel III Sachgebiet B Abschnitt I nach Nr. 3, in *Bundesgesetzblatt* 1990 II, 885.
62. Meyer-Seitz, "Entwicklung der Rückerstattung," 272–76.
63. Spannuth, "Rückerstattung Ost," 258–59; Meyer-Seitz, "Entwicklung der Rückerstattung," 276–79. See also the more pessimistic assessment by Heinz Düx, "Rückerstattung statt Rückübertragung im Sinne des Vermögensgesetzes bei NS-Verfolgung," in *Zeitschrift für Vermögens- und Investitionsrecht* 2 (1992): 257–61, esp. 259–60.
64. Spannuth, "Rückerstattung Ost," 381–83.
65. Meyer-Seitz, "Entwicklung der Rückerstattung," 278–79; Spannuth, "Rückerstattung Ost," 258–59.
66. CJH, William E. Wiener Oral History Library of the American Jewish Committee, New York, Jacob Blaustein Oral History Project, Interview with Nahum Goldmann, 24 November 1971.
67. See Gabriel Schoenfeld, "Holocaust Reparations – A Growing Scandal," in *Commentary*, September 2000; and also the debate in *Commentary*, January 2001, Holocaust

Reparations. Gabriel Schoenfeld and Critics. See also Jean-Michel Chaumont, *Die Konkurrenz der Opfer. Genozid, Identität und Anerkennung* (Lüneburg, 2001).

68. John Authers and Richard Wolffe, *The Victim's Fortune: Inside the Epic Battle over the Debts for the Holocaust* (New York, 2002); Stuart E. Eizenstat, *Imperfect Justice: Looted Assets, Slave Labor, and the Unfinished Business of World War II* (New York, 2003); Susanne-Sophia Spiliotis, *Verantwortung und Rechtsfrieden. Die Stiftungsinitiative der deutschen Wirtschaft* (Frankfurt a.M., 2003).
69. Gesetz zur Errichtung einer Stiftung "Erinnerung, Verantwortung und Zukunft" vom 2. August 2000, BGBl. I 2000, 1263.
70. S. Eizenstat, *Imperfect Justice*, 215.

TWO APPROACHES TO COMPENSATION IN FRANCE

Restitution and Reparation

Claire Andrieu

The history of the restitution of Jewish property stolen during World War II is both a part of the history of state policy and also of the history of how the past is represented.[1] In France there were two successive phases of compensation policy: one of restitution, which was introduced on liberation, and one of reparation, which began in 1997. The first phase reflected the spirit of the postwar era and the second, the ending of the Cold War. In the postwar era, the state was accorded a decisive role within the democracy and the recent war was considered a political and military matter. Concurrent with this view, the genocide of the Jewish population was seen as just one part of a much bigger event. In the course of the 1970s, however, it came increasingly to be regarded as *the* central event of World War II. Throughout the 1980s, the role of the state in society was called more and more into question, and this tendency increased further with the collapse of the Soviet system.

The terms "restitution" and "reparation" are taken from common French usage. While "restitution" signifies the material restoration of property with no moral connotations, the term "reparation" can also be used in an abstract sense. For French postwar policy, the idea of restitution was central. In January 1945, the Service de restitution des biens des victimes des lois et mesures de spoliation (Office for the Restitution of Property of the Victims of Statutory and other Expropriation Measures) was founded in association with the Ministry of Finance. At that time, as in 1919, the term "reparations" was used to denote all the international measures through which the Allies claimed damages, both concrete and intangible, after Germany's defeat.

Although the idea of reparation was not entirely foreign to French restitution policy, it seems to have had no influence in practice. At that time,

Notes for this section begin on page 151.

people did not distinguish between different degrees of suffering caused by the war as they do today. Jews, resistance fighters, and victims of bombings all had the same entitlement to restitution and compensation. Their claims against the state were treated relatively uniformly as cases of war damage. Since 1997, however, policy has been entirely informed by the remembrance of the Holocaust. This is chiefly moral and emotional and only secondarily material.

The policy of restitution was pursued for more than thirty years, well into the 1970s. The policy of reparation, however, only began in 1997, that is after an interval of more than twenty years. The length of this hiatus in policy raises the question of whether the French Republic resisted restoring the rights of the victims of antisemitic expropriations. If we look back at earlier forms of legalized expropriation by the state, however, we see that it is by no means unusual for the process of restitution to be subject to delays and interruptions.

A dialectic of expropriation and restitution runs through all of French history. In the Middle Ages, the assets of the Knights Templar were confiscated and even modern and recent French history is dotted with similar cases: the expropriation of the property of Protestant emigrants following the repeal of the Edict of Nantes in 1685, of the Church in 1789, of mainly aristocratic emigrants in 1792, of the religious orders in 1901, and of the Church again in 1905 all preceded the expropriations during World War II.[2] There were also forerunners to restitution, namely the explicit restoration of the rights of Reformation- and Revolution-era emigrants. The "religious refugees" were compensated by the revolutionary governments by means of the laws of 1790 and 1793, and refugees from the Revolution benefited from a number of partial restitution measures stretching over a period of twenty years from 1794 to 1814.[3] The culmination of this policy of restitution—the term was already in use at the time—was the passing of a law on compensation in 1825.[4] These two examples indicate a certain continuity: expropriation is always more rapidly performed than restitution. The state is quick to seize property but slow to return it, even when it is well disposed towards the victims of expropriation, as was the case with post-Thermidor governments and, particularly, that of the Restoration (1814 to 1830). Neither the delay in restoring the rightful property of the victims of antisemitic expropriation to its owners nor the ultimate resumption of this policy in the form of final compensation settlements is exceptional. In previous centuries, victims' recollection of offences committed against them was so persistent that they sometimes preoccupied politicians thirty years or even a century later, as in the case of the Protestants. Such enduring periods of remembrance, even outlasting generations, call into question the authentic nature of these memories.

From 1944 to the end of the 1970s, France, and later Germany, carried out a quantitatively successful policy of restitution. In 1997, a policy was instituted that to all appearances seemed to pursue the same goal. Was history repeating itself? What had happened to prevent any recollection of the first phase of restitution? What are the driving forces behind this construction of a new history that supersedes the old view of the past and even renders it invalid? And why is a past that is more than fifty years old suddenly so intensely present? Is the extraordinary violence of the original events sufficient explanation for the return of the past? Will it come back a third time, and if so, in what form?

A Historical Comparison of Restitution and Reparation

The World War II-era restitution phase in France began immediately after the country's liberation, and following the Allied occupation of Germany. In 1957, the German Bundestag passed the Federal Restitution Law (BRüG), pursuant to which further restitution payments were made, including payments to France. In order to evaluate the policy of restitution, one must think oneself back in time to the situation of the 1940s and 1950s. To consider the results of the policy only in terms of figures would be to disregard the experiences of the claimants—their exhaustion, sometimes even bitterness, in the face of a very complex and time-consuming process. Nevertheless, in order to appreciate the size of the task undertaken by the democracies, a quantitative analysis is necessary.

As the expropriation conducted by the Vichy authorities was founded on legal principles, it produced a huge number of files. Restitution was then performed on the basis of these documents, and itself created additional files. These archives enabled the Mission d'étude sur la spoliation des Juifs de France (Study Mission on the Spoliation of the Jews in France), founded in 1997 and often referred to as the Mattéoli Commission after its president, to calculate the rate of restitution. In terms of value, restitution was made with respect to 90 percent of the total value of businesses, real estate, shares, and bank accounts subjected to confiscation measures.[5] In terms of numbers, however, the result was less satisfactory: only at least 70 percent of businesses and real estate properties and between 50 and 100 percent of the deposit accounts and stock accounts were returned.[6] The larger the assets, the more likely it was that restitution was made. The reason for this is of an economic nature: the main value of a workshop lay in the expertise of its master craftsman. Its liquidation value was often almost nothing, so there was no material basis for restitution. For many of the former holders of securities and savings books, which generally had relatively small balances, the situation was similar. When accounts were blocked in 1941, half of the deposit accounts had a credit balance of less than 900 francs (worth 247 euros in the year 2000), while the balance of half of the savings books was even less than 100 francs (about 27 euros in 2000).[7] Moreover, today, more than fifty years after the liberation, many of the documents needed to provide evidence for restitution claims are missing. More than a quarter of the businesses and real estate put under "provisional administration" during the war had still not been sold at the time of the liberation.[8] Initially, they remained in the hands of the acting trustees. If an out-of-court settlement was made, the restitution authority was not necessarily informed. Blocked accounts were legally reactivated.[9] As therefore no formal procedure was necessary, no files exist. Since the number of deportees among the account holders was between 3 and 14 percent, it can be assumed that about 90 percent of them revived their accounts, although this cannot be proven. On the other hand, there is one kind of asset that was almost never the subject of restitution: the cash that people were carrying on them when they were arrested. These sums, which were confiscated and deposited under the victims' names on accounts at the Banque de France or the Caisse des dépôts et consignations remained mostly unclaimed. Less than 3 percent of the accounts that were opened there while the Drancy transit camp was under French administration (1941–1943) were ever restituted.[10]

It is harder to draw conclusions about the restitution performed by Germany, as the documents necessary for assessing the extent of the looting are only partially available. In this case it really is a matter of looting, that is, confiscations made without any formal procedure or inventory. The clearest example of this was the so-called Furniture Operation, during the course of which 38,000 apartments belonging to Jewish families were plundered in Paris alone.[11] No inventories were drawn up. When it came to pillaging works of art, the ERR compiled lists noting the origins of works, but these are incomplete. They contain less than 17,000 entries, although 45,000 objects were returned to their owners after the war.[12] Occasionally, individual works of art plundered from private homes were registered, but no note of the owner was made.[13] In the Occupied Zone, on the other hand, confiscations from safe-deposit boxes containing gold and foreign currency were to a great extent acknowledged with a receipt. Finally, "Reich Jews" were subjected to a specific form of robbery by the occupying forces, the files of which remained in France. In total the "Plenipotentiary for Aryanization and Administrator of Assets transferred to the Reich" processed three thousand cases, concerning both business and private assets.[14] This figure, however, should be considered in relation to the sixty thousand enterprises and real estate properties that were placed under provisional administration by the Vichy government, and in relation to the eighty thousand blocked accounts in the Occupied Zone.

The occupation of Germany also marked the beginning of restitution there: Sixty-one thousand pieces of art were returned to France; of these, forty-five thousand could be restored to their owners. The remaining sixteen thousand were sorted and the less interesting pieces, approximately fourteen thousand, were sold for the benefit of the state. The remaining two thousand were exhibited for four years, from 1950 to 1954, before being provisionally entrusted to France's national museums as part of the Musées Nationaux Récupération [National Museums Recovery] (MNR) program. The origins of MNR works have been the subject of investigations since 1998. In March 2000, 8 percent of those held had been identified as stolen works of art, a further 8 percent were not connected to any robbery, and the history of 84 percent still remains to be clarified.[15] In the case of "monetary gold," the Paris Reparations Agreement of 1946 envisaged a share for each Allied country that had suffered losses, yet the amount of gold secured on German territory fell considerably short of the estimated amount missing. France could only recover half of what was thought to have been lost in the capital alone. Private individuals who claimed damages for lost gold were paid compensation in 1953 and 1958 at a rate of 62.5 percent of the value. Compensation for the plundering of apartments was paid on the basis of the French Law on War Damages of 1946 and later under the German BRüG of 1957.[16] In its original formulation, the BRüG act required evidence from claimants that the stolen objects had been brought to what was now the Federal Republic of Germany or West Berlin. Under pressure from Jewish organizations and the formerly occupied countries, this condition was modified in 1960, and gradually other restrictions on restitution claims were also eased.[17] In the 1970s, works of art and precious metals were added to the list of goods eligible for compensation. The Oberfinanzdirektion (Regional State Finance Office) in Berlin estimates that it has processed a total of forty thousand claims relating to robberies committed in France, and ordered payments to the amount of DM 450–500 million.[18]

By the late 1970s, restitution seemed to have been completed. The proportion of assets restored may not have been 100 percent, but could that ever be achieved by a state policy? To be able to judge the relative success of the restitution policy more precisely, one would have to compare it with a similar policy of the same period. What percentage, for example, was achieved by means of the 1946 Act for the Compensation of War Damages caused by the plundering committed by the occupying forces, including that suffered by non-Jews; and what rate of restitution was achieved for the victims of bomb damage? The 1946 law unleashed a flood of six million claims. How great is the extent of damages for which no compensation was ever made? Yet this technocratic approach does not take into account the crucial fact of extermination. In the case of France, "only" a quarter of the local Jewish population was deported. Although the Jewish community was dealt a very severe blow by this, it was not wiped out. By and large, the legitimate owners or their heirs were able to reclaim their property. Although the level of nonrestitution was increased due to the number of deportees among previous owners, in the case of France there was only a relatively small difference in the rate of restitution between the cases involving deportees and the remainder, amounting to about 15 percent for businesses and real estate.[19]

The evaluation of the second phase, which began in 1997, can only be provisional as the process of reparation has not yet been concluded. The Commission pour l'indemnisation des victimes de spoliation [Commission for the Compensation of Victims of Spoliation] (CIVS),[20] founded in 1999, continues to grant individual compensation when applied for by the victims of spoliation or their heirs. Even the interim results, however, are considerable. The Mattéoli Commission has estimated the value of unclaimed property, on the basis established in 2000, at a maximum of 2.3 billion francs

(351 million euros). The total figure includes the value of all kinds of property, always using the highest reasonable estimate for the benefit of the claimant. Specifically this includes bank accounts and savings books, life insurance policies, businesses, and real estate that remained unclaimed, as well as the cash and assets taken from those interned in transit camps on French territory, and, lastly, the profits acquired by the state from the sale of stolen artworks. When one considers the uncertainty and difficulties entailed in carrying out meaningful investigations decades after the events, taking into account the fluctuating nature of the market value of certain assets, it does not seem to make much sense to compare the maximum value of unclaimed property according to calculations established in 2000 with the figures for restitution paid after the war. This is proved most strikingly by the art sector. Here, in 2000 the state paid out almost twenty times the sum it earned between 1950 and 1953, as the art market experienced a spectacular rise in prices during the 1960s.

Boosted by occasional voluntary contributions, the estimated maximum value of unclaimed property was paid into a foundation set up in late 2000.[21] The Fondation pour la mémoire de la Shoah [Foundation for the Remembrance of the Shoah] was endowed with 2.5 billion francs (394 million euros) and given both a scientific and a social mission: to "carry out research into and disseminate information on antisemitic persecution and human rights violations committed during World War II," and to contribute to the "financing and implementation of expressions of solidarity" towards legal organizations who have helped victims of persecution. With the funds thus collected, the debt of businesses and the state to the victims of expropriation may be regarded as repaid. The Foundation does not pursue exact restitution down to the last penny. An "arithmetical" approach to restitution sixty years after the events is, indeed, for the reasons given above, no longer possible. Calculations inevitably involve an element of guesswork, and, in the present case, the highest value is automatically granted in cases of previous nonrestitution. And as the genocide of the Jewish people has become the focus of public attention alongside the expropriation and robbery committed, proceedings are now approached with extreme caution. The emotional and moral factors that already influenced the generous calculation of compensation payments were instrumental in the reopening of restitution files twenty years after their initial closure. By contrast, the files on war damage caused by bombing raids will not be reopened. Ultimately, the Fondation pour la mémoire de la Shoah is itself an act of reparation for the community. This foundation does not pay compensation to private individuals, but is more a symbol of regret on behalf of the state and private businesses for their participation in the expropriation of the Jews.

Nevertheless, when the founding of the Mattéoli Commission was announced, it was inundated with a flood of individual claims for compensation. In 1999, the government set up the CIVS, which determines the amount of compensation to be paid to private individuals, no matter what their nationality or whether the robbery was of French or German origin.

The only two restrictions are that the robbery must have taken place in France at the time of the German occupation and that no compensation can already have been paid. In spring 2002, the CIVS was still in the middle of processing the 11,500 claims it had received.[22] Almost 2,500 compensation payments had been recommended with an average amount of 21,700 euros, almost 1,900 of which were to settle cases concerning the expropriation of material property (not including bank account assets).[23] These additional remittances were not drawn from the contributions received by the Fondation pour la mémoire de la Shoah as these are inalienable. In respect of all lost assets apart from bank accounts, which the respective financial institutions indemnify following recommendations made by the CIVS, this compensation is paid for by the state, without any budgetary restrictions. For legal reasons, that is, in order to bypass the normal statute of limitations, the CIVS does not have the status of a court and does not adjudicate. The financing bodies are, however, obliged to act on its "recommendations" and so far have done so. The CIVS, like the Mattéoli Commission, works entirely in the spirit of reparations and, if in doubt, estimates the value of payments in favor of the claimant.

Taking into account the generosity of the calculations that both the Mattéoli Commission and the CIVS use as their basis, and of the financial endowment of the Fondation pour la mémoire de la Shoah, the rate of "restitution" is quite possibly higher than 100 percent. This result may be surprising, but as no comparable investigation into another contemporary compensation scheme exists, it is impossible to prove if it is unusual. It remains for us to emphasize the peculiarities of the French approach to restitution and reparation, which have certainly contributed to this result.

The Special Case of France: A Combination of Political and Social Factors

To define the peculiarities of the French process of restitution and reparation, one must make a thorough international comparison. The characteristics of the French case might not be as unique as they appear, and they should be evaluated in their international context. The main elements contributing to the success of the French policy are, in order of their importance: the physical presence of claimants, the political commitment of governments, and the creation of ad-hoc structures outside the established institutions. The almost complete lack of public debate and the restraint shown with regard to publicity has not, paradoxically, detracted from the effectiveness of the program. And finally, the silence or even resistance of the private and public financial institutions—due more to corporate culture than to a culture of antisemitism—has been broken.

The first reason why restitution functioned in France was that those whose property had been expropriated were physically present and able to reclaim it. France and Italy had the lowest percentage of Jews deported from their territory. From France, 25 percent of the population defined as Jewish was deported; from Italian territory, which was not occupied until September 1943, it was 20 percent. In Germany, Austria, Czechoslovakia, the Netherlands, Poland, and the Baltic states, the proportion of Jews who were deported from the population present in 1940 was more than 80 percent. With regard to restitution, this difference changes the very nature of the matter. As we have seen, the relatively high number of survivors made a fundamental difference in France, as here the deportation of asset-holders did not present a great obstacle to restitution. However, one should also bear in mind that the Jews in France were taken by surprise by the events of June 1940, and so most did not have time to emigrate. Neither did they emigrate after the war.[24] The situation was therefore much more favorable for satisfying their legitimate claims than that of German, Austrian, or Czech Jews, of whom 60 percent, 68 percent, and 23 percent, respectively, left their country before the war,[25] or indeed of those who stayed in those countries, 80 percent of whom were exterminated.

The French government's resolute commitment to a policy of restitution and reparation provided a further favorable condition. As early as August 1940, General de Gaulle let it be known that the Free French Movement condemned the antisemitic measures of the National Socialists and their collaborators, and that it would "recompense for the wrongs done to the victims of Hitler's tyranny."[26] In January 1943, France was among those who signed the Allied agreement condemning National Socialist looting activities in London, and added its own commitment to compensate for this injustice.[27] In August 1944, the decree restoring the Republican legal system reiterated the "invalidity" of all actions that were based on or implemented "discrimination on the basis of Jewish identity."[28] In the southern zone, the authorities that evolved from the Résistance referred to this statement of policy in order to proceed immediately with restitution.

Fifty years later, in the reparation phase, the attitude of the heads of government was equally clear. In July 1995, the President of the Republic, Jacques Chirac, made a now-famous declaration acknowledging the French state's responsibility for the persecution of the Jews residing in France. This speech was made as much in response to continuing cultural changes as to the demands of day-to-day politics. In France, as elsewhere, the genocide of the Jews had increasingly begun to take over the central position in people's perception of World War II. Only three years earlier, however, in 1992, the then-president of the Republic, François Mitterrand, had refused to acknowledge the responsibility of the state for the persecution of the Jews. In his view, the Republic did not have to apologize for crimes it could not have committed as it had been abolished by the Vichy authorities. Furthermore, reports concerning Mitterrand's activities during the Vichy era had been a constant source of controversy. In order to put an end to this, the Journée nationale commémorative des persécutions racistes et antisémites commises sous l'autorité de fait dite "gouvernement de l'Etat Français" (1940-1944) (a national remembrance day to commemorate the racist and antisemitic persecutions under the de facto rule of what was known as the "government of the French state") was declared in 1993.[29] In 1994, however, a book was published containing evidence of François Mitterrand's active collaboration with the institutions of the Vichy regime between 1942 and 1943.[30] President Chirac's declaration was, then, a direct response to his predecessor. The founding of the Mattéoli Commission in March 1997 was to some extent also a consequence of this speech.[31] A few weeks later, parliamentary elections led to the installation of a socialist government, which wholeheartedly endorsed this aspect of its predecessor's policy. Thus supported by a right-wing president and a left-wing prime minister, the French policy of reparation benefited from a national consensus that had been reached on the basis of countrywide discussions.

Here one could point to a third, less significant factor. In both phases, of restitution and reparation, the untypical influence of certain—at first glance, minor—figures became evident. Despite their marginal positions in state institutions, these figures played a key role in contributing to the efficacy of the policies. The authorities entrusted with the task of restitution were led, or inspired, by academics and politicians—all of whom had been active in the *Résistance*—rather than by bureaucrats.[32] Again in 1997, investigations were headed by a number of historians associated with the Sorbonne and the Centre national de la recherche scientifique [National Center for Scientific Research] (CNRS). The chief aim of the Mattéoli Commission was to find out the facts: although this approach is time-consuming and unsensational, the moral value of historical truth was more highly prized than a negotiated, contractually agreed settlement. Even the CIVS works on an unorthodox basis: directed by Pierre Drai, the former president of the highest appellate court, the supreme court of *cassation*, and run primarily by senior legal and government officials, the CIVS is nevertheless not a judicial institution. Its position "outside the law" ensures its independence.

One last element among the driving forces behind reparation remains to be mentioned: the press. While it did not play a significant role in the restitution phase, in the phase of reparation that followed, the press succeeded in shaking the government into activity with some alarming and poorly researched articles. The founding of two research institutions in 1996 and 1997 was also partly a response to allegations made by the press. In October 1996, a book was published by a *Libération* journalist accusing the city council of Paris of plundering the apartments of Jews—particularly in "block 16" of the Marais quarter—and of simply keeping the property after the war.[33] The city council responded by asking the Conseil du patrimoine privé de la Ville de Paris (Council for the Private Inheritance of the City of Paris) to investigate. After calling on the assistance of real estate experts, historians, lawyers, and representatives of Jewish organizations, in the year 2000, the Conseil's concluding report showed that the accusations were unfounded.[34] The Mattéoli Commission was also established in part as a reaction to allegations from the press. In January 1997, *Le Monde* initiated an extremely aggressive press campaign concerning stolen works of art,[35] which went on for three years. In this way, the press played a decisive role in the inception of the reparation phase. In April 2000, the concluding report on the Mattéoli Commission was received with universal acceptance by the press and the antagonistic mood of the period from 1996 to 1999 was relieved.

A Peculiarity in the Case of France: the Lack of Public Participation

Among the peculiarities of the French case is the fact that the public played almost no part in events. Apart from the allegations made by the press between 1996 and 1999, in both phases compensation was regulated almost entirely without public discussion. Here, again, the absence of an investigation into a comparable case precludes any proper evaluation of the extent and significance of this restraint. Is it that the French Republic's principle of secularism prevented what is in effect an "ethnic" policy from being pursued in all too public a manner? Or was it the reluctance of the victims of expropriation to have a public fuss made about their property? In France, religion and money are private affairs. Can the restrained use of publicity be attributed to this distinctive relationship between the private and public realms?

It is especially remarkable that there was not even much parliamentary involvement in either phase. The only notable intervention was that by the Assemblée consultative provisoire (Provisional Advisory Assembly) in March 1945, which changed the course of an important government project to the advantage of the victims of expropriation.[36] Yet neither the 1946 legislation on war damages nor the article of the tax law of 1948, in which the state committed itself to reimburse the Punitive Fine (l'amende) imposed by the Germans, sparked debates in Parliament on the restitution of expropriated assets.[37] In the years 2000 and 2001, Parliament was required only to vote on a credit line for the financial endowment of the Fondation pour la mémoire de la Shoah, and it approved the compensation payments recommended by the CIVS. Up to the moment (2006), these decisions have not provoked any serious public debate.

The Jewish organizations involved also avoided the use of publicity. In 1944, in some towns in the South of France—Marseille and Toulouse, for example—the Union de Juifs pour la Résistance et l'Entraide [Jewish Union for Resistance and Mutual Aid] contributed to speeding up the process of restitution. On a national level, the most important organization to exert pressure in support of restitution was the Centre de documentation juive contemporaine [Contemporary Jewish Documentation Center] (CDJC). This organization, founded underground in 1943, acted as a lobbyist after the war without seeking publicity. In the current phase, the Conseil représentatif des institutions juives de France [Council of Jewish Institutions in France] (CRIF) has the function of a pressure group, yet it has not directly and openly criticized the government for its handling of matters. Despite its official involvement, on the whole the CRIF has preferred not to attract media attention. In November 1996, for example, the president of the CRIF called on the government at its annual dinner, attended by the prime minister, to reopen the files on the expropriation of the Jews. This discreet approach was strongly criticized by Jewish organizations in America and Israel, which accused French Jews of passivity in the fight against antisemitism and of an exaggerated desire to assimilate to French society.[38] One should, however, be aware of the actual results of publicity and media campaigns. In the case of reparation for unclaimed bank accounts, a high-profile campaign was pursued in the United States to no avail, while the French method of combining historical investigation and persuasion enabled the facts to be established and the process of reparation to be set in motion. The Presidential Advisory Commission on Holocaust Assets in the United States, under the chairmanship of Edgar Bronfman, gained nothing more from American banks than their endorsement of a guide to researching the assets of Holocaust victims.[39] Perhaps the transnational populism propagated by the World Jewish Congress and the Simon Wiesenthal Centre (itself not entirely devoid of nationalism) is less practiced in dealing with specific national interests.

The principle of secularism, one of the founding principles of the French Republic, was also a factor in the comparative restraint surrounding the debates on restitution and reparation. The especially stringent separation of church and state within French society is a result of the young Third French Republic's conflict with the Catholic Church at the end of the ninteenth century. Since the 1880s, any form of national census on the basis of religious or ethnic categories has been forbidden, and it is officially unknown how many Black or White people live on French territory. The same is true for the number of Catholics, Protestants, Jews, and Muslims. The formulation of a restitution policy after the war was complicated by the fact that official documents could not refer to Jews. For example, the article of the 1948 law on the reimbursement of the Punitive Fine, which the Germans exacted only from Jews, speaks of "persons who, as a consequence of actions, so-called laws, decrees, orders, regulations or rulings by the de facto regime known as the government of the French state, were robbed." Yet since the 1970s, concepts of secularism have progressed and being Jewish is now more often publicly asserted, although Republican institutions remain hesitant in this respect. In 1997, the Mattéoli Commission showed how much progress has been made by referring explicitly to French "Jews." The CIVS, founded in 1999, on the other hand, continued the old habit of avoiding the term "Jew" in its name, replacing it with "the victims of robbery due to antisemitic legislation." In 1978, the ban on publishing lists of names collected on the basis of political, ethnic, or religious criteria was further tightened by a new data protection law. The compilation and publication of such lists now falls under the provisions of this law. For this reason, and because the Vichy government was the only authority ever to publish a list of the Jews residing in France, an official list of victims of Nazi persecution or of the Vichy regime has never been published. Today's reparation procedure takes the opposite approach to private information: any persons who believe that they or their ancestors suffered expropriation are welcome to contact the CIVS.

The relative lack of public involvement in French compensation policy can also be linked to the exclusion of the legal profession from the process. While in the United States the involvement of attorneys was instrumental in bringing reparation into the public arena, in France, this was not the case. This is partly due to the legal situation, partly to the French legal profession's code of conduct, and partly also to a different attitude toward law. French legal traditions prompted the prohibition in 1945 of the engagement of private attorneys by the victims of expropriation, in order to prevent the creation of a market for compensation funds.[40] Lawyers were only called on to mediate in major inheritance cases, such as those concerning important works of art. Furthermore, the French legal profession's code of conduct forbids any kind of advertising; this also helped prevent a market for compensation funds being created. The absence of such a market has not hindered the course of justice; on the contrary, it may even have promoted it.

So far, it has mainly been the failure to attract public attention by those representing the interests of victims of expropriation that has been remarked upon. But the same issue must be addressed in relation to those who participated in expropriation and robbery—whether voluntarily or not—and those who suddenly became obliged to restore property as a result of the liberation. While the ministries and companies concerned acted with obvious hesitation and reluctance at the beginning of both phases, they did not at any time openly protest. Although the founding of an antirestitution or antireparation party would have been unthinkable, pressure groups did their best to undermine the process of restitution in the first months after it was initiated. Among these groups were the Association des administrateurs provisoires de France [Association of French Provisional Administrators] (AAPF), founded in February 1944; a short-lived national union of trade and handicrafts; and two associations of tenants who refused to leave apartments they had rented on favorable terms following the deportation of the previous Jewish tenants.[41] In order to dissolve these two associations, the government amended the 1901 law on the freedom of assembly by inserting a paragraph which allowed the dissolution of groups that "try to cause measures concerned with restoring the legal system in the Republic to fail."[42] Not only here, but also within the government offices that had been designated as owing a debt to the Jews, traces of antisemitism could still be observed in the first months after liberation.[43]

However, the influence of such phenomena was slight compared to the natural forces that influence any organization as soon as the matter of payment arises. After liberation the administration, businesses, and financial institutions were in no hurry to deal with restitution. They handled the problem as if it were business as usual, without consideration for the extreme persecution that their creditors had been subjected to. This is clearly demonstrated by the manner in which in 1944 and 1945 the financial and judicial administrations started drafting the new legislation on the restitution of assets that had been sold.[44]

Again in the 1990s, there was no significant resistance to reparation. Even the extreme right-wing Front National did not openly object. The main obstacle to the work of the Mattéoli Commission in its early days was corporate culture. Loyalty to and identification with their place of work was so strong among employees that the mere notion of their predecessors having been involved in antisemitic policy was unthinkable. This identification reflex cropped up everywhere: in private and public life, and even among senior staff whose families had been victims of persecution. This attitude went so far as to deny facts that were supported by files full of evidence. With time, however, and the help of archival documents and persistent dissemination of the facts, such denial became less frequent. One other factor contributing to this change in attitudes was the pressure exerted by the class actions in the United States. Although these lawsuits did not serve to create a better understanding of the issue—on the contrary, debates were mainly centered around defending national sovereignty or stirring up anti-Americanism—they weakened the position of the companies concerned, which, as a consequence, sought a solution. The first class actions against French businesses—in March 1997 against insurance companies[45] and in December of the same year against banks[46]—were filed shortly after the Mattéoli Commission was founded.

Insight can be gained by considering the relative restraint surrounding restitution and reparation in France in proportion to the effectiveness of these policies. The various bodies involved decided by common agreement to settle their differences without attracting media attention. Maybe it is a sign of the cultural inheritance of a nation that has become prudent, having endured four years of a double dictatorship and become more or less accustomed to surprises of all kinds that such matters are not dealt with in public. Later, especially during the second phase, a consensus emerged that the issue should be settled by common accord, on the basis of historical knowledge, by the political administration. This practice of creating a progressive consensus supported by historical facts is something of an innovation.

From a Policy of Nonintervention to Cultural and Economic Globalization

Although the French restitution and reparation policies display some peculiarities, like every policy, they are products of their time and international context. Between the postwar era and the period following the end of the Cold War, the conditions for developing a policy of compensation changed completely. From the perspective of the history of representation, people's perceptions of the past changed drastically in the 1970s: World War II went from being a political and military event to a huge crime against humanity. Since the end of this decade, both scientific investigations and fictional works in film and literature have focused on the collaboration of the Vichy regime.[47] It is not surprising that thirty years later a new generation that has grown up with a different idea of history is asserting its beliefs. The same development can be observed in the United States, where the Holocaust did not become the subject of discussion until the 1970s.[48] The decision to establish the U.S. Holocaust Memorial Museum in Washington, DC was taken at the end of the 1970s. Up to that time, remembrance of the past had progressed more or less in step in France and the United States. One result of developments in the 1980s and 1990s, however, was the disassociation of these two countries, the deeper reasons for which should be taken into account. While the early postwar period was a phase of agreement between the cultures of both countries, the cultural gulf which opened after the end of the Cold War led to tensions on both sides of the Atlantic.

On a geopolitical level, the change took place in the period between 1989 and 2001. Between the end of the Cold War and the beginning of the "war on terrorism," the international situation seemed peaceful and secure. In this era of peace, the former allies of the free world felt at liberty to express mutual criticism, precipitating the outbreak of a cultural and economic "war" between the United States and some of the countries of Europe. While the United States did not feature in the debates of the restitution phase—at least not in France—the superpower became heavily involved in the reparation phase.

After 1945, the United States proceeded with restitution in their zone of occupation without making it a part of their domestic policy. Here, as in Switzerland, legal requirements concerning unclaimed assets and their restitution were kept to a minimum and passed late (in 1962) in both countries. The American law of 1948 on the regulation of war damages had excluded the question of unclaimed property. In 1950, an amendment to the Trading with the Enemy Act allowed all Americans with dual citizenship who were resident in enemy territory during the war to reclaim their assets. These had been placed under provisional administration in December 1941.[49] The State Department prepared a draft law for the same day, which envisaged the payment of $3 million to the successor organizations of victims of antisemitic deportations.[50] But the bill was not passed until twelve years later and the amount was limited to a maximum of $500,000.[51] In accordance with the prevailing "melting pot" ideology of the time, the term "Jew" did not appear in the wording of the law even if the "successor institutions" clearly denoted Jewish organizations.

During this period there was no apparent American intervention in the French policy of restitution. As we have seen, this was in essence carried out between 1944 and 1954. In 1950, an amendment to the decree of 21 April 1945 on the invalidity of acts of expropriation allowed French Jewish organizations to manage unclaimed assets under the supervision of the administration for state property,[52] but this option was not taken up. This may in part be explained by the compensation agreement signed by Germany and Israel in Luxembourg in 1952. This agreement marked the beginning of

German compensation, to which surviving Jews were entitled. In this instance, the United States had exerted pressure on Bonn to bring about a swift conclusion to the agreement.[53] Possibly as an indirect result of this document, the pressure on France to deal with restitution eased. At this time, however, the process of restitution was already as good as completed. In view of this, the international context does not seem to have played a significant role in France during this phase.

The reparation phase, on the other hand, presents an entirely different situation. Bearing in mind the influence of globalization, it becomes evident how the major global power outside Europe (the United States) exploited European history to further its own interests. The question is: Who put the most pressure on French policy-makers? Was it the government of the United States, U.S. financial institutions, American-Jewish organizations (in particular the World Jewish Congress), or American lawyers? It is too early to say for sure, especially as government archives have not yet been opened, yet one may safely say that the spectacle that unfolded in 1995 regarding relations between the U.S. and Switzerland and the question of unclaimed property met with considerable criticism in France. What course would history have taken if this bilateral crisis had never happened, and would the French government necessarily have proceeded with a policy of reparation? It can only be noted that the declaration made by President Chirac in July 1995, confirming the state's responsibility for acts of violence committed by the Vichy regime, prepared the way for reparation. The day before this speech was made, Serge Klarsfeld, a famous French lawyer, Nazi-hunter, and committed advocate of commemorating the deportees, published information on the whereabouts of unclaimed bank account assets in the Caisse des dépôts et consignations and the Banque de France.[54]

Yet the founding of the Mattéoli Commission was not announced until January 1997, eighteen months later. According to current research findings, it seems more likely that this foundation was a purely French idea which, as we have seen, was influenced by some alarming articles in the press and probably also by the negative example of Switzerland.

When evaluating certain kinds of expropriation, however, the Mattéoli Commission clearly reacted to the situation in the United States. While more than 80 percent of the people who wrote to the Mattéoli Commission claimed compensation for the plundering of private apartments, the most difficult and complex of the commission's investigations concerned works of art and financial assets, the two areas that most preoccupied debates in the United States. The methods applied, meanwhile, remained French. Negotiations, pushed for by American lawyers and financial experts, were deferred until the facts had been ascertained, and reparation was indeed ultimately based on the historical findings. In April 2000, the Mattéoli Commission presented the prime minister with its concluding report, and in the following November negotiations began between the French and U.S. governments. The contract concluded on 18 January 2001 effected a change that amounted to a contravention of the French system.[55] On signing a simple affidavit, petitioners who were convinced that their ancestors had possessed a bank account were in nearly every instance offered an arbitrary sum of $1,500 to $3,000, payable by the financial institution concerned. However, in the hands of the CIVS, this instrument did not produce its own independent repercussions within the French policy of reparation.

In this context, we must look once again at the basic principles of the American policy of reparation. In many respects, they do not seem applicable to the case of France. Firstly, this policy was based on a cultural globalization of European history, which entails a number of misconceptions about French history. The first is the assumption that France has only just begun to uncover the truth about its Vichy past,[56] when in fact this has been something of a national obsession for the last twenty years. The second misconception is the belief that no restitution was performed after the war.[57] The fact of nonrestitution within former Eastern Bloc countries may be indisputable, but in the case of France, the policy of restitution had already achieved some positive results in the mid-1950s. The American policy is, moreover, based on an image of the history of Jews in France that is informed by events in the states of Central Europe. This tends not to differentiate between Jews, deportees, and victims of expropriation, an approach that would have turned the process of restitution more or less into a lottery. In France, probably all those regarded as Jews suffered expropriation in one way or another, either at the hands of the Germans or of the Vichy regime. But, as already mentioned, three quarters of the persecuted population survived and, in addition to the 76,000 who were deported explicitly because they were Jewish, 80,000 men and women of the Resistance were also deported to concentration camps. One may assume that the scale of the deportations and the wide variety of reasons for deporting people from France were among the reasons for the concern shown to deportees by the Republic after the war. After all, hundreds of people in the Free French Movement were robbed by the Vichy authorities, including General de Gaulle. Expropriation was, then, an experience shared by Jews and non-Jews alike, even if the latter group suffered much less. This fact was probably also instrumental in putting restitution on the government agenda.

Not only misconceptions of cultural globalization, but also the process of economic globalization facilitated America's intervention on the old continent. The reopening of the files on restitution in Europe can be partly attributed to the end of the Cold War. The collapse of the Soviet system had a threefold effect. Firstly, it became known that no restitution had taken place in communist countries; secondly, U.S. criticism of European countries was unleashed; and finally, the free market economy was further legitimized. From this last point of view, the current period in France represents the antithesis of the years after the liberation. In 1945, state-owned property was the sign of an efficient, socially-orientated democracy.[58] The concept of "property is theft," as propounded by the socialist Proudhon had widespread currency within society. When in 1998 the World Jewish Congress described the works of art reclaimed from Germany, which had been placed in French national museums after the war as "the last prisoners of war," it expressed a revealing paradox.[59] For in 1954, entrusting unclaimed assets to national museums meant giving them to the people. But seen through the double-filter of the American economy and the liberal revolution of the 1980s, these postwar French ideas were very hard for people in the United States to understand.

The presence of numerous French businesses on American soil also facilitated the intervention of American lawyers in the French process of reparation. As we have seen, the U.S. legal profession's code of conduct allows practices such as advertising and door-to-door selling that are forbidden in France. Furthermore, U.S. attorneys have at their disposal two statutes that do not exist in French law. The first is the Alien Tort Claims Act, which dates back to 1789 and was amended in 1948.[60] This allows non-Americans to bring actions for violations of human rights or property rights even if these took place overseas. The second originates from English law and was adopted by the United States at the beginning of the nineteenth century, where its validity was extended in 1938 and again in 1966. Here, we are talking about the class-action suits that have been filed since the 1970s, mainly by groups of consumers against large businesses. The equity of this procedure is often disputed: allowing groups of clients to take big corporations to court could inhibit the whole vitality of business,[61] and there is only a thin line between the "legal theft" committed by some companies and the "legal blackmail" attempted by certain consumers.[62] This legal instrument played a decisive role in the process of reparation: some branches of French corporations were sued in the U.S. courts. Although the proceedings against French banks were finally quashed, they could have led to a relocation of decision-making to the United States, and thus a denationalization of the issue.

Research findings so far do not allow a formal answer to be given to all the questions raised by the analysis of the two phases of compensation policy. The quantitative assessment of the restitution phase leads to the conclusion that this policy was properly carried out, although "properly" does not imply a 100 percent rate of restitution. In order to establish whether this deficiency is intrinsic to measures taken by the state in this field or rather a general phenomenon, one would have to study other compensatory measures carried out at the same time. In addition to this, the qualitative assessment of restitution should be pursued systematically.

In this attempted evaluation one can also find a history of the emotional reactions to genocide. In the wake of the crime, the predominant wish of most survivors was to get back to normal, and their reintegration into French society was almost like a return to the situation before the war. The desire to assimilate and the rejection of a specific sense of identity characterized attitudes in the postwar years until well into the 1960s.[63] With the coming of age of a new generation in the 1970s, claims to a specifically Jewish history began to be heard. Emotions that had previously been confined to the privacy of the home were increasingly expressed in public and began to reach the rest of the population. With circumstances thus changed, the demand for reparation arose, that is, a new kind of restitution perceived in the light of the victims' acknowledgement of their trauma and the indictment of the perpetrators. In this way, a process which more clearly identified victims and assigned guilt came to influence policy-making.

Although the influence of American-led economic and cultural globalization is evident in the second phase, its extent is nevertheless difficult to gauge. The negative example of Switzerland certainly had an educational effect on France, and the fact that American claims concentrated on bank accounts and works of art meant that these fields of research were given particular attention by the Mattéoli Commission. In addition to this, U.S. class-action lawsuits were a cause for concern among companies, convincing them on the whole to open their files on this issue. But, the "French exception," as former U.S. Secretary of State Stuart E. Eizenstat writes, did not recede. Eizenstat sums up the negotiations he led with his French counterpart with this remark: "The essence of the short, intense French negotiations was a profound cultural divide between two perfectly legitimate but utterly different ways of regarding state public administration, civil rights, privacy, and of rendering justice to the victims of one of history's greatest crimes."[64] French policy stuck to its original line, refusing to publish lists of names compiled on a discriminatory basis, not allowing compensation to become the subject of political-financial negotiations, and basing its strategy on uncovering the historical facts rather than creating a market for reparations.

Translated from German by Charlotte Kreutzmüller

Notes

1. I have written this paper as a professor working at the Sorbonne, but the reader should be informed that since March 1998 I have been a member of the *Mission d'étude de la spoliation des Juifs en France* (Matteoli Commission) and have been working with the sources, especially on financial aspects of these issues.
2. See the Edict of Fontainebleau of 18 October 1685, in which the Edict of Nantes was revoked; the Law of 2 November 1789, which placed church property at the disposal of the state; the laws of February and August 1792, which determined that the property of emigrants would be placed under the compulsory administration of the state and would subsequently be sold; the law concerning the freedom of association of 1 July 1901; and the law of 9 December 1905 separating church and state.
3. A. Gain, *La restauration et les biens des émigrés. La législation concernant les biens nationaux de seconde origine et son application dans l'Est de la France (1814–1832)* (Paris, 1929), vol. 1, from 14.
4. Law of 27 April 1825 "concerning the amount of compensation to be paid to the original owners of property that was confiscated and sold for the benefit of the state on the basis of the Law on emigrants, convicts and deportees."
5. A. Prost, et al., *Aryanisation économique et restitutions. Mission d'étude sur la spoliation des Juifs de France* (Paris, 2000), 173; C. Andrieu, et al., *La spoliation financière* (Paris, 2000), vol. 1, 210.

6. See Prost et al., *Aryanisation économique*, 151; Andrieu, *La spoliation financière*, vol. 1, 208.
7. *Mission d'étude sur la spoliation des Juifs de France, Rapport d'étape, January–December 1998*, 117–18.
8. Prost et al., *Aryanisation économique*, 144. The 26 percent share of unsold properties is the proven minimum (given incomplete data). The actual percentage was higher, but the sources do not permit a precise calculation. The proven minimum percentage of properties legally sold and liquidated is at a similar level of 20 percent.
9. Decision of the Secretary General for Finances, 30 August 1944, published in Andrieu, *La spoliation financière*, vol. 2, 113.
10. A. Wieviorka, *Les biens des internés des camps de Drancy, Pithiviers et Beaune-la-Rolande* (Paris, 2000), 56.
11. A. Wieviorka and F. Azoulay, *Le pillage des appartements et son indemnisation* (Paris, 2000), 18.
12. Isabelle le Masne de Chermont and Didier Schulmann eds., *Le pillage de l'art en France pendant l'occupation et la situation des 2000 oeuvres confiées aux musées nationaux: contribution de la direction des Musées de France et du Centre Georges-Pompidou aux travaux de la Mission d'étude sur la spoliation des juifs de France* (Paris, 2000), 21 and 37.
13. Ibid., 24–25.
14. Andrieu, *La spoliation financière*, vol. 1, 158–59.
15. Contribution by the leadership of the French Museums, *Le pillage de l'art en France*, 74.
16. On this, see also the contribution of Jürgen Lillteicher in this volume.
17. Wieviorka, *Le pillage des appartements*, 62–65; C. Goschler, "Die Politik der Rückerstattung in Westdeutschland," in C. Goschler and J. Lillteicher eds., *"Arisierung" und Restitution. Die Rückerstattung jüdischen Eigentums in Deutschland und Österreich nach 1945 und 1989* (Göttingen, 2002), 99–125.
18. Wieviorka, *Le pillage des appartements*, 67.
19. Prost et al., *Aryanisation économique*, 160–61.
20. The decree of 10 September 1999 founded a commission for the compensation of victims of spoliation, which had taken place on the basis of antisemitic laws during the occupation, in *Journal officiel de la République française* (*JORF*), 11 September 1999, 13633.
21. Decree of 26 December 2000, recognizing the Foundation as a public institution.
22. CIVS, *Rapport public d'activité de la Commission suite à l'accord de Washington du 18 janvier 2001*, 3rd Report, Appendix 3.
23. Ibid., 16.
24. Mission d'étude sur la spoliation des Juifs de France, *Rapport général* (Paris, 2000), 23–24.
25. F. Bédarida, *Le nazisme et le génocide. Histoire et enjeux* (Paris, 1989), 60.
26. General de Gaulle to Albert Cohen (political advisor to the Jewish World Congress), 22 August 1940, published in: Andrieu, *La spoliation financière*, vol. 1, 71.
27. Publication of the "Inter-Allied Declaration Against Acts of Dispossession Committed in the Territories Under Enemy Occupation or Control" (London Declaration), 5 January 1943, in *Journal officiel de la France combattante* (20 January 1943): 4.
28. Article 2 of the decree of 9 August 1944, "On the Restoration of the Republican Legal System in the Continental State Territories," *JORF* (10 August 1944): 688–94.
29. Decree of 10 August 1993, *JORF* (4 February 1993): 1902.
30. P. Péan, *Une jeunesse française. François Mitterrand 1934–1947* (Paris, 1994), 616.
31. Decree on the Mission d'étude sur la spoliation durant l'Occupation des biens appartenant aux juifs résidant en France, *JORF* (25 March 1997): 4721.
32. Among them were in 1945 Prof. Emile Terroine, and in 1997 the Director of the Commission, Jean Mattéoli, and Prof. Adolphe Steg.
33. B. Vital-Durand, *Domaine privé* (Paris, 1996).
34. Final Report of the *Conseil du Patrimoine privé de la Ville de Paris* with the cooperation of its group of experts, *Domaine privé et spoliation (Les acquisitions immobilières de la*

Ville de Paris entre 1940 et 1944 proviennent-elles de la spoliation des propriétaires et des locataires concernés?) (Paris, 16 October 2000) : 10 and 13.

35. "Les Musées nationaux détiennent 1,955 œuvres d'art volées aux Juifs pendant l'Occupation," *Le Monde* (28 January 1997).
36. Debate on the drafts for the legal decrees for the annulment of acts of property theft, 15 March 1945, see on this "Débats de l'Assemblée consultative provisoire," *JORF* (16 March 1945): 493–516.
37. Law of 28 October 1946 on War Damages, *JORF* (29 October 1946): 9191–98; Law of 16 June 1948 on tax relief, articles 42 to 53, *JORF* (17 June 1948): 5868–69.
38. On this issue, see the comments of Edgar Bronfman (President of the World Jewish Congress) and Avraham Burg (President of the Agence Juive). On Bronfman, see W. R. Mead, "Interview with Edgar Bronfman Sr.: Tracking Nazi Plunder into Switzerland's Secret Vaults," *Los Angeles Times* (13 April 1997), cited by A. Colonomos, "L'exigence croissante de justice sans frontières. Le cas de la demande de restitution des biens juifs spoliés," *Les études du CERI*, no. 78 (July 2001): 30. On Burg, see *Depesche de l'Agence France-Presse* (4 February 1998).
39. *Plunder and Restitution: The U.S. and Holocaust Victims' Assets; Findings and Recommendations of the Presidential Advisory Commission on Holocaust Assets in the United States and Staff Report* (Washington, DC, December 2000), 58.
40. Article 47 of the decree of 21 April 1945, with the second amendment to the decree of 12 November 1943 on the annulment of looting activities conducted by the enemy or on his behalf and the decree on the restitution of expropriated property to the victims of these actions, *JORF* (22 April 1945), from 2283.
41. J. Billig, *Le Commissariat général aux Questions juives (1941–1944)* (Paris, 1960), from 307; P. Verheyde, *Les mauvais comptes de Vichy. L'aryanisation des entreprises juives* (Paris, 1999), 380–86; D. Tartakowsky, *Les manifestations de rue en France, 1918–1968* (Paris, 1997), 521; R. Bober, *Quoi de neuf sur la guerre?* (Paris, 1993), 186–92.
42. Decree of 30 December 1942 that amended the law of 10 January 1936 on combat units and private militias, *JORF* (31 December 1944): 2145–46. The law of 1936 was itself an amendment to the law of 1901.
43. P. Verheyde, "Des restitutions incomplètes aux nécessaires réparations. La Caisse des dépôts de 1944 à nos jours," in A. Aglan, M. Margairaz and P. Verheyde, eds., *La Caisse des dépôts et consignations, la Seconde Guerre mondiale et le XX° siècle*, (Paris, 2003), 420–46, here 425 and 439.
44. Andrieu, *La spoliation financière*, vol. 1, 78–79; Verheyde, "Des restitutions incomplètes," 420–46.
45. Class action of Edward Fagan in New York on 31 March 1997 against twelve insurance companies, including Axa (UAP-Vie), Allianz (AGF in France), and Generali, Zurich.
46. Class action brought in New York on 17 December 1997 against Paribas, Barclay's Bank, Crédit lyonnais, Société générale, BNP, Crédit commercial de France, Crédit Agricole, Banque Française du Commerce extérieur, Banque Worms Capital Corp., and John Does 1 to 100.
47. H. Rousso, *Le syndrome de Vichy, 1944–198...* (Paris, 1987), 323.
48. P. Novick, *The Holocaust in American Life* (Boston, 1999).
49. See "Trading with the Enemy Act of 1917," "Amendment of 29 September 1950," *United States Code Annotated*, Title 50, Appendix "War and National Defense," § 1–450 (St. Paul, MN, 1927), 298.
50. S. J. Rubin and A. P. Schwartz, "Refugees and Reparations," *Law and Contemporary Problems* 16 (1951): 377–94.
51. "War Claimants Act of 1948," Amendment of 22 October 1962, *Laws of the 87th Congress–2nd Session, Title II*, 1302–13; *United States Code Annotated*, 296–97.
52. Law of 26 December 1950, which completed articles 14, 22 and 23 of the Decree of 21 April 1945 with the Second Implementation Decree of 12 November 1943 on the Annulment of Looting Activities Conducted by the Enemy or on His Behalf and the Decree on

the Restitution of Expropriated Property to the Victims of These Actions, *JORF* (27 December 1950): 13193–94.

53. T. Segev, *The Seventh Million: The Israelis and the Holocaust* (New York, 1993).
54. A. Lévy-Willard, "Le vol oublié des biens des Juifs déportés," *Libération* (15–16 July 1995).
55. Decree of 21 March 2001 with the publication of the agreement between the governments of the French Republic and the United States regarding the compensation of certain looting actions that took place during World War II (together with three appendices and the exchange of notes), signed on 18 January 2001 in Washington DC, *JORF* (23 March 2001), 4561–64.
56. J. Authers and R. Wolffe, *The Victim's Fortune: Inside the Epic Battle over the Debts of the Holocaust* (New York, 2002), 135 and 153.
57. Ibid., 147–49. The authors reflect here the opinions of the lawyers of the plaintifs and the president of the World Jewish Congress.
58. C. Andrieu, L. Le Van, and A. Prost, *Les nationalisations de la libération. De l'utopie au compromis* (Paris, 1987), 392.
59. Ibid., 135.
60. See "The Alien Tort Claims Act," Section 1350, Title 28, *United States Code Annotated*, from 636.
61. See "Class Actions," "Rule 23," "Federal Rules of Civil Procedure," "Title 28," *United States Code Annotated*, from 375; also "Class Action," in *West's Encyclopedia of American Law* (St. Paul, MN, 1998), vol. 3, 23–24.
62. *Reform of Class Action Litigation Procedures: Hearings before the Subcommittee on Judicial Machinery of the Committee on the Judiciary. United States Senate, 29–30 November 1978* (Washington, DC, 1979), 1–2.
63. A. Wieviorka, *Déportation et génocide. Entre la mémoire et l'oubli*, (Paris, 1992), 506.
64. Stuart E. Eizenstat, *Imperfect Justice. Looted Assets, Slave Labor, and the Unfinished Business of World War II* (New York, 2003), 315.

The Expropriation of Jewish Property and Restitution in Belgium

Rudi van Doorslaer

In view of the worldwide interest in the expropriation of Jewish property, it is remarkable that on an international level, Belgium, unlike its neighbors France and the Netherlands, has not been the focus of a great deal of attention. France was dealt severe criticism by the United States for its handling of various class-action lawsuits, moving the historians of the Mission Mattéoli to defend France's democratic honor. In the Netherlands, where public opinion is very receptive towards Jewish issues, a record number of commissions was set up to process the relevant material. Belgium, by contrast, was the last Western European country to establish a research commission to investigate the fate of stolen Jewish property—which it did in July 1997 under the Christian Democrat prime minister Jean-Luc Dehaene.[1] The commission was led by the former chairman of the Belgian National Bank, Baron Jean Godeaux, until March 1998, when he was asked to resign by the majority of commission members. Dissatisfaction with Godeaux's preferred methods for carrying out investigations in the financial sector provided the ultimate grounds for his ousting, as well as the fact that under his direction inquiries were barely making any progress. His successor, Lucien Buysse, the former major-domo of King Albert I, was expressly approved by the Jewish community and indeed completely changed the commission's approach to the investigation. Financial support from Verhofstadt's government was applied for and granted, enabling the creation of a data bank on Belgium's Jewish population and their property.

The final report of this in-depth investigation was presented to the Belgian government in July 2001.[2] It reveals some interesting aspects of both the theft of Jewish property committed during the German occupation and the compensation paid after liberation in Belgium, which are remarkable in comparison with other European countries.

Notes for this section begin on page 169.

Expropriation in Belgium

The German military administration in Belgium basically pursued two aims: first, to implement the increasingly stringent anti-Jewish measures drawn up in Berlin; and second, to extract as much financial profit as possible for the German war economy. In hindsight, the expropriation of Jewish property can be broken down into the following steps: property was identified; the Jewish economic network was broken up; various material goods (productive equipment, inventory, business capital, real estate, and diamonds) were converted into liquid assets; furniture, household goods, works of art, and items of cultural value were systematically plundered; and finally, bank account balances and securities were concentrated in one bank. The cornerstone of the expropriation operation was undoubtedly the compulsory registration of Jewish property. For the Jewish owners of shops, businesses, or real estate it was extremely difficult to evade this compulsory requirement. One may assume, therefore, that these assets were registered almost without exception. In total, 7,700 businesses and 3,000 real estate properties (in Jewish ownership or part-ownership) were registered.

However, according to the research commission's findings, this high rate of registration did not apply to all other assets. Research has established that liquid assets, bank accounts, securities (in deposit accounts and safe-deposit boxes), gold, jewelry, and ornamental and industrial diamonds were far from completely declared by their Jewish owners. Furthermore, the financial institutions' admittedly scant records demonstrate that they themselves rarely checked and amended these incomplete statements submitted by their clients on their own initiative. Although the banks were instructed by the German authorities to register all customers whom they knew to be or suspected of being of Jewish descent, they did not comply with this (perhaps out of patriotism or self-interest) and confined themselves in practice to those customers who had "spontaneously" registered. Thus on examining the comprehensive archives of the Société belge de Banque (a small but not insignificant merchant bank that was active in the financial market in Antwerp and Brussels), the research commission established that even names or titles that were easily recognizable as Jewish (for example, Joodse vrouwenraad, the Jewish women's council; Dispensaire juif; or Institut israélite pour garçons) were never identified as such.[3] The sources show that this also occurred in other institutions. Those clients who were identified were distinguished in the customer accounting and administration files with a "J," "Jew," or a Star of David next to their name. The total of 17,400 registrations relating to the various assets that came to be, in one way or another, administered by Belgian financial institutions must therefore be regarded as far from comprehensive. This is of crucial significance for both the evaluation of the theft committed in Belgium and the research commission's investigation into "dormant" bank accounts.

The so-called Brüsseler Treuhandgesellschaft [Brussels Trust Company] (BTG) was created by the German military administration to organize and administer the expropriation of "enemy" and "Jewish" property. This company was set up under Belgian law, a fact which may at first seem of minor importance, but actually represents a second peculiarity—alongside the incomplete registration of Jewish property—of the expropriation of Jewish assets in Belgium. For under Belgian law, a trust company was permitted to check, inspect, and manage property, but not ultimately to dispose over it.[4] Because of this limitation, an exceptional situation arose in Belgium regarding the expropriation of Jewish property: the final phase, that is, the actual transfer of ownership of bank account assets, never took place.[5]

With regard to Jewish businesses, however, the outcome was very different. The removal of Jews from economic life, and the liquidation of Jewish businesses that this entailed, was undoubtedly accomplished in a systematic and thorough manner. The occupying forces managed to break up what was in many respects a discrete commercial network, built up primarily by eastern European Jewish migrants in the 1920s and 1930s, and which dealt mainly in clothing manufacture, leather goods, and diamonds. The eight thousand mostly small, family businesses (of which roughly half were commercial enterprises and half small arts-and-crafts businesses) were to a great extent dissolved "voluntarily," that is, under duress, by the proprietors themselves. The proceeds from the sale of inventory, machinery, and business assets—frequently, if not always, sold for less than their real value—were put into blocked accounts in the owners' names. Jews who worked in the diamond sector were subjected to the same treatment, albeit with a certain delay, as the occupation authorities acted more cautiously toward them with the aim of appropriating most of the diamonds.[6]

As the German authorities responsible for expropriation reported, there was a section of the Belgian business world that did not entirely reject the removal of Jews from economic life, as it reduced competition. Nevertheless, it was not a matter of active collaboration, and the administrators working for the BTG had a hard task finding interested buyers for those businesses that were not liquidated. At the end of the occupation period, the BTG was still directly or indirectly administering 637 "Jewish" businesses.

The total sum of the proceeds from the sale of these businesses, deposited in blocked accounts in the Jewish owners' names, was estimated by the Germans to be RM 12 million (at the exchange rate laid down by the German military administration of 1 RM to 12.5 Belgian francs), not including the sums deducted for administration and liquidation expenses.[7] The money from these "administration and liquidation expenses" not only helped finance the occupation administration—as stated in the final report by the so-called Group 12 (of the Economic Department of the German military administration)—but a considerable amount was also transferred to Germany, as the research commission's report demonstrates. The value of the 637 businesses for which the Aryanization process had not yet been completed and which were still controlled by the BTG in late August 1944 was found to be RM 100 million. The Germans could not, however, freely dispose over this sum.

The German military administration had a similar procedure in mind for real estate; first registering the property and then selling it. In accordance with a decree issued on 31 May 1941, compulsory registration was introduced. The BTG provided the legal machinery for administering the property. Initially, the local military authorities assumed the task of administration, but later a special administration authority, the so-called Verwaltung des Jüdischen Grundbesitzes in Belgien [Administration of Jewish Real Estate Holdings in Belgium] (VJGB), was set up under the supervision of the BTG. In Antwerp, management of the property remained in the hands of four private administrators.

The sale of real estate identified as Jewish and placed under German administration was a disaster for the occupying forces, primarily because of resistance by the Belgian notaries and legal authorities, who were not prepared to recognize documents that were not signed by the owners, and who did not prove to be very cooperative when it came to the enforced sales conducted by the German administration. For this reason, the German military administration issued regulations in December 1943 giving German notaries permission to authenticate sales contracts in occupied Belgium, but without much success, as by this time any potential buyers were not inclined to trust the legal validity of this regulation.

The proceeds from foreclosures resulting from defaults on mortgage payments also largely evaded the occupying forces. Creditors received the largest share of the proceeds and the rest was put into private accounts in the names of the Jewish owners with the so-called Deposito- en Consignatiekas (deposit and consignment bank). During the occupation period, probably less than 10 percent of Jewish-owned real estate (taking both "voluntary" and enforced sales into account) was sold in total. Those Jewish-owned properties that were registered did, however, remain under German administration for the whole occupation period. The net rental returns, roughly estimated at approximately 20 million Belgian francs by the end of occupation, were also put into private accounts in the names of the Jewish owners and, in the end, the German administration did not have these sums at its disposal.

Considering the circumstances, the outcome for the victims of expropriation was not entirely negative. If their real estate was encumbered by a mortgage at the time of occupation, it was probably compulsorily sold following court proceedings before a Belgian court. If this was not the case, property was usually still registered under the names of the owners and could be reclaimed after liberation (together with a portion of any possible rental returns) by survivors or surviving dependants.

When the Jewish inhabitants of Belgium were deported, or if they had fled or gone underground, their apartments were cleared out as part of the so-called Furniture Operation.[8] This systematic plundering was organized by the ERR, subordinated to the Reich Ministry for the Occupied Eastern Territories, and the furniture was used to compensate families who had suffered from the bombing in Germany. One year after the deportations began (in summer 1942) almost four thousand apartments had been emptied of possessions and approximately fifty-four thousand cubic meters of furniture and household goods transported to Germany. For those victims who survived, this was extraordinarily hard to bear, as all their personal possessions and family mementos were gone forever.

The ERR was responsible for the expropriation of libraries, including those belonging to Jews, and (in Belgium, to a lesser extent) for the expropriation of works of art. According to conservative estimates, 56,250 books and 885 works of art from Jewish collectors were transported from Belgium to Germany with the help of the ERR.[9]

The ultimate destination for the blocked savings and stock accounts and also for the proceeds from the sale of stolen goods was the Société Française de Banque et de Dépôts [French Society for Banking and Secure Deposits] (SFBD), a subsidiary of the Société générale de France, which had come under the administration of the BTG as "enemy" property. From early 1943, Jewish bank account assets were gradually centralized in the form of private accounts with this bank, which dealt specifically with expropriated assets. First, in January 1943, financial institutions were required to transfer cash balances. This was followed by the transfer of the contents of safes, that is, jewelry, gold, watches, diamonds, foreign currency, and other items of value (shares, fixed-rate notes, and bonds) in March of that year.

As mentioned above, the incomplete identification of Jewish property meant that far from all Jewish-owned accounts with Belgian banks and savings institutes were registered. The extraordinarily small number of savings books with the largest state-run savings bank, the Algemene Spaar- en Lijfrentekas [General Savings and Pension Bank] (ASLK), and of accounts with the Bestuur der Postcheques [Central Postal Giro Office] that were registered is particularly conspicuous. This result is all the more significant when one considers that in 1940, private banks and savings institutes administered 50.8 percent of all deposits belonging to private clients, while 15.3 percent were with the Bestuur der Postcheques and 33.9 percent with the ASLK.

In addition, the financial institutions negotiated various special regulations with the BTG, which enabled them to avoid, or at least put off, the transfer of Jewish-identified accounts. One strategy was the so-called unit principle as applied to bank accounts. Many banks regarded the different accounts held by one client as being inextricably linked (and therefore also providing mutual security), partly for reasons of banking law. On these grounds, they refused to comply with the transfer of cash accounts if these were still receiving income from dividends or other investments. As a consequence of this, some transfers were postponed or split so that not only were some accounts never identified as "Jewish," but also other accounts belonging to Jewish clients were still retained by Belgian financial institutions at the end of the occupation.

At that time, about RM 3 million "invested by Jews" as well as RM 12 million from "administrative measures" (i.e., profits from liquidations and sales, and the estimated equivalent value of items of property, diamonds, and foreign currency) were held by the SFBD according to the BTG. On 31 July 1944, the value of stock accounts was estimated at 216 million Belgian francs. When the German occupying forces withdrew, the employees of the BTG took a considerable amount of foreign currency and various valuable items from safe-deposit boxes with them to Germany. The blocked accounts at the SFBD, however, remained untouched.

In conclusion, it is fair to say that the occupying forces only partly realized their goals with respect to the systematic expropriation of Jewish property in Belgium. Although the politically and racially motivated directives from Berlin ordering the economic destruction of the Jewish population were to a large extent fulfilled, the financial gains were far less than the German military administration had expected. Jews were indeed systematically removed from economic life in Belgium, but the profits for the Reich from the operation remained very limited. Only a relatively small percentage of "Jewish property" was transferred to Germany or used to finance the occupation administration. The only German "successes" were the Furniture Operation and the utilization of stolen diamonds by the German armaments industry. Apart from these cases, most of the money secured by centralizing Jewish financial assets and by removing Jews from business activity remained on blocked accounts in Belgium. Many real estate properties remained under administration without being sold to new owners.

The total sum of RM 225 million given in Group 12's final report takes all stolen property into account, including that which the occupying forces did not have at their disposal. The conclusion may then be drawn that this figure is not definitive and therefore too misleading to be of use.[10]

For the surviving victims of expropriation, the situation was nevertheless dramatic. Those who had owned businesses or shops before the war found nothing left when the occupation ended. Houses had been plundered and were bereft of all furniture and personal possessions. Only those who had put their money in a bank or bought securities before the war could hope for a more positive state of affairs, as most of these assets still existed, even if they were no longer at the original bank. Those who owned real estate that had not been encumbered by mortgages before the war also had a realistic chance that their property had not been despoiled. The situation was less hopeful for surviving dependants (especially minors) of owners of movable or real estate property (particularly with regard to life insurance policies, which the occupying forces in Belgium, unlike in other countries, hardly touched), especially if they remained abroad. How were they to regain possession of their remaining, "dormant" assets?

Ultimately, for the majority of surviving Jews who did not own any property or who had not invested their property in a bank, liberation meant starting completely from scratch and being glad just to have survived. This social distinction, that is, the fact that by comparison those with little or no means faced the greatest difficulties, must also be mentioned in the final reckoning of the expropriation conducted by the Germans.

Restitution in Belgium

Indemnification for expropriation in Belgium involved many different organizations. While some of these organizations were created specifically to deal with the consequences of the war, others simply continued their activities as normal. Among the former category were the so-called Dienst van het Sekwester (Property Custodian), the Dienst Economische Recuperatie (Economic Restitution Office) and the Dienst oorlogsschade bij het Ministerie van Wederopbouw (Office for War Damage at the Ministry for Economic Reconstruction). The second category consisted of two departments of the Administratie van het Ministerie van Financiën (Administration of the Ministry of Finance), the Deposito- en Consignatiekas and the Administratie van Registratie en Domeinen (Land Registry), and the courts of first instance and the private administrators of unclaimed property appointed by them. For many years, from September 1944 to the late 1960s, these institutions and individuals put in a great deal of work and it would be wrong to speak of a failure to provide compensation. Nevertheless, some obvious shortcomings and structural weaknesses of the Belgian compensation process should also be mentioned here.

The institution that certainly played the most significant role in administering compensation for stolen property was the Dienst van het Sekwester.[11] The Belgian government in exile in London set up this office prior to the liberation to administer "enemy" and "suspect" property, drawing on experiences made during the First World War. The aim was to protect this property from alienation or destruction, in order to hold it in trust as security for the damages that the occupying forces were inflicting on the nation. However, this concept made no provision, organizational or legal, for the victims of German occupation. Nevertheless, victim property came under the office's administration when German "enemy" property went into official receivership. By far the most property was sequestered by the BTG, that is, the company that was founded by the occupying forces to administer enemy and Jewish property. In addition, there was an official receiver at the Administration of Jewish Property Holdings in Belgium, and, finally, countless receivers for the property of German and Austrian Jews who automatically came within the law as nationals of an enemy country.

Insight into the extent of the problem of expropriated Jewish property grew only very gradually at the Dienst van het Sekwester. The administrator of the BTG receivership was possibly one of the few Belgians who really had understood what the "Final Solution" had actually meant shortly after the liberation: thousands upon thousands of people, whole families, had disappeared forever; their household goods stolen and any other property systematically taken into official receivership. Today, one might reasonably ask how the rights of the surviving victims could be justifiably restored by a public office that was founded to administer the property of "enemies" and "suspects." A satisfactory solution has never been suggested, let alone found, for this legal, moral, and political problem.

As there was no legal basis for the administration of non-enemy property, the assets of most Jewish victims were reimbursed in tacit disregard of the law by the various official receivers. Case by case, the authorized agents sought individual solutions for the problems at hand. The lack of clarity, and therefore—to a certain extent—of legal security, was compensated for by good will and improvisational talent. This could not, however, make up for the lack of a clear policy and coordination between the various offices dealing with compensation for the loss of property in Belgium. For example, the authorized agent of the receiver's office at the BTG was not aware of the existence of a Dienst voor oorlogsschlachtoffers (Office for War Victims) at the Ministerie van Wederopbouw, whose tasks included the systematic collation of data on Jewish war victims, until six years after he had taken up office.

In December 1944, the receiver's office of the BTG began restitution proceedings. Accounts and securities belonging to Jews that had been centralized at the SFBD were handed back on certain conditions to the entitled parties. However, this release applied only to credit balances on regular cash accounts and holdings of securities, not to the proceeds from the sale of businesses, inventory, business assets, or real estate during the occupation. These sales had been collectively annulled by a resolution passed on 10 January 1941 by the Belgian government-in-exile in London. This meant that owners could not reclaim their property (if it still existed) and at the same time demand the proceeds of sale. These had been transferred to various accounts of the BTG at the SFBD. In this way, the original owners had the choice of either renouncing their property and having their SFBD account entirely at their disposal, or reclaiming their property, which, however, meant that the sale proceeds remained frozen in the SFBD account. The receiver's office of the BTG stressed that it did not share the opinion of those who wanted to give these sums to rightful claimants as compensation: "The Office des Séquestres is not the Office des Dommages de Guerre."[12] As difficult as the situation must have been for the victims, if they wanted their money back, they had first to prove their entitlement.

In January 1945, the government approved the return of accounts to the financial institutions that had administered them before the German occupation (provided they did not contain any profits from German expropriation), without the need for action by the claimants. An inventory was made of the valuables that had been confiscated and stored in the Mechelen Dossin barracks, and they were gradually returned to their rightful owners.

Bank accounts, securities, and other items belonging to unidentified owners were dealt with by the public treasury through the Administratie van Registratie en Domeinen (Land Registry).[13] Those accounts, securities, and (sold) objects of which the owner was known but from whom there had been no sign of life for several years, and for which there did not seem to be any other legitimate heirs (although these may simply not have known of the existence of their property) were transferred in the late 1950s to the Deposito- en Consignatiekas. After thirty years at the Deposito- en Consignatiekas, these assets were transferred to the public treasury.

One exception to this practice was made for German and Austrian Jews. As in May 1940, when German troops invaded and they were arrested and deported by the Belgian authorities, and during the occupation, when their assets were confiscated by the Nazis, German and Austrian Jews once again became dual victims: both as Jews and as Germans. On the initiative of the Allied forces in Germany, German Jews were given back their German citizenship after liberation, which they had lost as a consequence of the Eleventh Decree to the Reich Citizenship Law in November 1941. Regarded and treated for this reason as "enemies" by the Dienst van het Sekwester, all possessions belonging to absent persons (including deceased deportees) passed directly to the ownership of the Belgian state. Survivors' possessions were only gradually released after 1947 (on presentation of written confirmation of their "nonenemy" status).

A further negative consequence of the unorthodox legal maneuvering with which compensation for Jewish war victims in Belgium was handled was the intervention of the courts and the trustees appointed by them. In accordance with the regulations of the Belgian Civil Code, some trial courts appointed trustees to draw up inventories and administer possessions belonging to absent Jews. This was the case, for example, in Antwerp (unlike in Brussels, where the Dienst van het Sekwester assumed responsibility). Although trustees could not, of course, decide what to do with these possessions without judicial consent, locating surviving relatives or heirs was expressly not one of their responsibilities. After a while, however, the custodian involved in the reimbursement of Jewish property eventually began to make modest efforts in this direction.

Many trustees were deputy judges who saw in these administrative activities an opportunity to boost their income as lawyers. Some of them had even been involved in forced sales of mortgaged Jewish properties during the German occupation. Trustees only had to justify their administrative activities if an actual rightful claimant appeared, which, in view of the fact that entire families had been systematically wiped out, did not often occur. Moreover, in Antwerp, they were administrating Jewish properties that had previously been confiscated by the German occupying forces, although private property came under the jurisdiction of the official receivers. This, however, did not prevent the courts from entrusting the task of administration to those attorneys they were familiar with in September 1944. The research commission found it "odd" that these private trustees even had the use of an office in Antwerp's central courthouse. The question of how this administration was paid for remains open, as no accounts were ever submitted—not even to the courts.

A further important step in assessing the effectiveness of postwar compensation for expropriated Jewish property in Belgium is the evaluation of the possibilities available to claimants for restitution or compensation for the loss of assets. The Dienst Economische Recuperatie [Office for Economic Restitution] (DER) and the Dienst Oorlagsschade [Office for War Damage] (DO) at the Ministerie van Wederopbouw [Ministry for Economic Reconstruction] were responsible for this.

The DER was founded in 1944 with the aim of tracking down and repaying all movable property that had disappeared or been unlawfully taken in the course of the war. One section of the DER was responsible for works of art and items of cultural value. This section's results with respect to the restitution of stolen Jewish property were particularly depressing in comparison with the results of Belgium's neighbors France and Holland. Only 1.2 percent of the contents of expropriated libraries and 7 percent of stolen artworks belonging to Jewish collectors were restored to their original owners. Ninety percent of the items of cultural value that were returned from abroad were ultimately placed in Belgian cultural institutions and museums. Many other art treasures were publicly sold in the Paleis voor Schone Kunsten (Palace of Fine Arts) or through the Administratie van Registratie en Domeinen (Land Registry). In this sector, too, coordination between the various administrations, authorities, and municipal offices, which could have promoted the efficient handling of restitution, was sadly inadequate. Investigations abroad were organized in a particularly amateurish manner and were excessively dependent on the goodwill of the Americans and, later, the French.

Under the laws on compensation for substantive war damage of 1945 and 1947, the majority of Jewish war victims were not eligible for compensation. Compensation could only be claimed by Belgian nationals, which effectively excluded approximately 95 percent of the Jewish population in Belgium. Furthermore, the Statuut van de politieke gevangene (Law on Political Prisoners) failed to take the victims of racially-motivated deportation and persecution into consideration.[14] Similarly, the exemption provisions of the Law on War Damages of 1947, to compensate for substantive losses suffered by political prisoners (including the prioritized payment of full compensation for all stolen movable and immovable property), could not be applied to Jewish war victims. For this reason, compensation for the systematic seizure of furniture and household goods from Jewish victims in the course of the Furniture Operation was never paid (this applies to non-deportees as well as deportees) despite the fact that the Law on War Damages makes provisions for this. Thus, for various reasons (the principle of Belgian nationality, the non-recognition of Jewish victims as political prisoners), it is fair to say that Jewish war victims were subjected to discrimination.

This discrimination carried on into the first phase of the application of German reparation legislation in Belgium, when approximately 1 billion Belgian francs were distributed among political prisoners. Although the BEG (1953) explicitly described racial, religious, or political persecution as grounds for substantive compensation, and these criteria were adopted word for word in the Belgian-German agreement of 1960, the Belgian criteria for apportioning compensation did not take Jewish war victims into account. Belgium had, after all, obtained the right to decide on its own distribution criteria. In accordance with the implementation clauses of the subsequent 1961 Belgian Law, only those who fell under the Statuut van de politiek gevangene (Law on Political Prisoners) could be considered for German compensation, and those who had been deported for racist reasons were de facto excluded.

It was only under the second German reparation law, the so-called BrüG act of 1957, providing financial compensation, that Jewish war victims in Belgium received any substantial compensation for the losses they had suffered. A total of thirteen thousand Belgian applications (from both Jewish and non-Jewish claimants) could thus be settled thanks to a total sum of approximately 2.5 billion Belgian francs (in 1960 values). By 1965, those cases settled included 6,500 applications from Jewish victims. This last compensation was paid primarily for household goods and furniture which had been stolen during the Furniture Operation as well as for the expropriations in Antwerp's diamond sector, assets worth a total of approximately 1.6 billion Belgian francs.

Perhaps it is no coincidence that the reparation paid by the Belgian state to Jewish victims in the diamond sector was neither inadequate nor discriminatory. After the American authorities' initial refusal to cooperate, in 1950 the DER managed to get a significant proportion of the stolen diamonds back from Germany, thanks to the persistent efforts of the Belgian state. When the returned diamonds were sold in 1951 and 1952,[15] many SFBD accounts, in which the proceeds from the sale of diamonds (at dumping prices) had been deposited during the occupation, had already been paid out to the original owners or their heirs by the Receiver's Office of the BTG. To enable claimants to assert their right to their fair share in the value of the diamonds it was made possible to reverse the wartime SFBD/BTG transaction. Those who wished to do so could send back the modest sum that they had received from their SFBD "account" and instead claim their share of the proceeds from the new sale of the returned diamonds. The settlement process, under the direction of the Federatie der Belgische Diamantbeurzen (Association of Belgian Diamond Exchanges), began in 1954 and continued until 1966. In some respects, this operation is a perfect example of the Belgian talent for improvisation.

Two aspects of the compensation paid in the diamond sector deserve particular emphasis. First, the principle of Belgian nationality was not applied here, partly under pressure from the United States, so that all victims—foreign nationals and Belgians alike—received the same amount. Second, the responsibility for paying compensation was given to the private Federatie der Belgische Diamantbeurzen. This ultimately saw to it—as the research commission's calculations show—that Belgian compensation, together with that which was paid out on the basis of the BrüG act by the Federal Republic of Germany, just about completely covered the total value of the assets stolen in the diamond sector. The economic and political significance of the diamond sector was no doubt one of the main reasons why compensation proceeded so smoothly here.

In conclusion, one may say that despite the satisfactory work done in certain areas of compensation for Jewish victims of expropriation in Belgium during the postwar period, serious shortcomings and mistakes cannot be ignored. Regarding restitution in the arts sector, Belgium cut a sorry figure. While this certainly did not only affect Jewish victims, the financial compensation provided by Belgium quite simply discriminated against Jewish victims (as it did against a small group of non-Jewish foreign nationals). The sound work done in the diamond sector proved that it was possible, when more vested interests were at stake, to handle compensation differently. With the benefit of hindsight, it is clear that those responsible in politics and the administration lacked sufficient insight into what the genocide of the Jews had really meant and also what consequences it had for the administration of unclaimed property. An administrative institution that assumed responsibility for the assets of victims and entrusted their administration to carefully supervised officials, as in the Netherlands, did not exist in Belgium.

From the end of the war, the Belgian state took over unclaimed estates left by Jewish victims of genocide, worth about 6 million Belgian francs. This modest sum can be attributed to the almost complete lack of control asserted by the Ministry of Finance over the activities of the officials employed by the courts to administer unclaimed assets. The fact that no inquiries were made into victims' unclaimed bank accounts or insurance policies until well into the 1990s demonstrates the complete legal and political inactivity of the Belgian state in this field.

The research of the commission picked up the thread in 1999 at exactly the point where postwar reparation had failed. Checks were made on the extent of assets that had been siphoned off by various channels into the state treasury, the amount of unpaid life insurance policies that were still outstanding, and lastly, the exact situation with "dormant" bank accounts. As mentioned above, some bank accounts had remained with the original financial institutions or had been returned there by the SFBD in 1945. Due to the flagrant lack of records and the complexity of the material, calculating the value of these bank account assets presents a particularly difficult and delicate task.

Conclusion

Was the situation in Belgium regarding the expropriation of Jewish property any different from that in other countries under German occupation? Certainly the guidelines set in Berlin were obediently followed by the military administration in Brussels when handling the "Jewish Question." The deportation of Jews from Belgium was in practice administered by the German Security Police and Security Service and was by no means less drastic or cruel than, for example, in Holland, where a civil administration was in charge.[16] Yet where the property of the Jews was concerned, the German military administration was solely responsible; the policy of expropriation pursued by the Brussels "outpost" was incorporated within the general occupation policy applied to Belgium. Ultimately, the "partial failure" (from the German point of view) described above resulted from this state of affairs.

The Belgian authorities decided to pursue a pragmatic policy of administrative collaboration, which in retrospect was referred to as a "policy of the lesser evil." Bearing in mind the disastrous experiences of occupation during the First World War, the government tried—with the support of the overwhelming majority of Belgium's leading political, financial, and economic circles as well as the trade unions—to do everything possible to keep Belgian institutions in Belgian hands.[17] The crisis of democracy in the 1930s was certainly an important factor. The leading Belgian elite had lost its faith in liberal democracy, which manifested itself particularly in the period 1940-1942. This also influenced its attitude with respect to the Jewish question. One need only recall the registration of Jewish persons carried out by all local governments; or the imposition of the Star of David by Antwerp's municipal authorities (in contrast, the Brussels authorities refused to cooperate in this); or the dedication with which the Antwerp police carried out raids against the Jewish population; but also the refusal of the judicial authorities and notaries to accept documents which were not signed by Jewish owners, and how the BTG was coerced into following the provisions of Belgian commercial law (and the considerable consequences this had for the blocking of Jewish bank accounts in Belgium).

The same ambiguous pictures arise in the postwar period. The extent and significance of the persecution of the Jews failed to penetrate the consciousness of the Belgian political and administrative leadership. It took considerably longer in Belgium than in Holland or France for the Jewish population to be perceived as a specific group of victims of Nazi occupation. Although at least fifteen thousand Jews disappeared from Antwerp's city center in the space of just a few months in 1942, this provoked hardly any public outcry, even after the war. In my opinion, this phenomenon can be explained on the one hand by the weak position of the Jewish community in Belgium, and on the other hand by two contrasting perspectives on the Second World War. Although not smaller in numbers than the Jewish community in Holland, the community in Belgium was split between the mainly orthodox groups in Antwerp and the assimilated, liberal, and left-wing groups in Brussels. These differences put a strain on the process of finding an identity after the war and limited the extent of the community's influence. In addition, the public image of Jews as victims was always juxtaposed to patriotic Belgian war memories (which predominate in the French part of Belgium) and resentment at what is regarded as the unjustly severe punishment of Flemish collaborators (which remains a strong influence on opinion in the Dutch-speaking part of Belgium). The weakness of the Jewish lobby—in comparison with other western European countries and North America—was probably also a factor in Belgium being the last country to establish a research commission to undertake a thorough investigation into the robbery of Jewish assets.

For the above reasons, I would like to place Belgium's attitude to the expropriation of Jewish property in a broader cultural context. What I call a certain "Atlantic culture" has tried since the fall of the Berlin Wall and the end of the Cold War to apply certain symbols of the "free and democratic West" as universal norms for the globalized world. The free-market economy naturally plays an important role in this, as does the tendency rooted in liberal ideology to reject any kind of totalitarianism and to search for "universal moral values," both stances increasingly symbolized by the history of the genocide of the Jews. In the United States, the remembrance of the Holocaust could become a symbol of these universal values because it is apolitical and goes beyond the cultural conflicts that divide American society.[18] In Western Europe, the memory of the genocide of the Jews also plays an increasingly important role for other, often very different, political reasons. Here, however, it must be noted that Europe is well on its way towards following the United States in this respect—European criticism of Israel regarding the Palestinian conflict notwithstanding.

It seems that Belgium will also ultimately align itself with this Atlantic culture—echoing the approach it took to expropriation. Flanders' gaining independence in the new federal Belgian state and the successive electoral victories of the extreme right-wing Vlaams Blok (Belang) there are forcing the traditional parties to look for new symbols of democratic identity. It would seem that the Jewish catastrophe is particularly suited to this purpose, chiefly because resistance during the Second World War (which, if it was not communist-inspired, was exuberantly patriotic) cannot serve as a useful symbol within the context of today's federalized Belgian state. Thus, in my opinion (and bearing in mind the imminent construction of a large Flemish Holocaust museum), in the future the prevailing view of the Second World War in Belgium will shift towards a perspective of greater sensitivity towards the fate of the Jews, not least because this is in the political interest of Belgium's decision-makers.

Translated from German by Charlotte Kreutzmüller

Notes

1. Diensten van de Eerste Minister, ed., *Studiecommissie betreffende het lot van de bezittingen van de joodse gemeenschap van Belgie, geplunderd of achtergelaten tijdens de oorlog 1940–1945. De bezittingen van de slachtoffers van de jodenvervolging in Belgie. Spoliatie, rechtsherstel, bevindingen van de Studiecommissie* (Brussels, 2001). The information on which this article is based, reflects—insofar as not noted otherwise—the results of the investigations carried out by the Research Commission. The analysis and interpretation of the facts are naturally the sole responsibility of the author.
2. The author of this article was a member of the Research Commission from its establishment. In April 1999 he was entrusted with the direction of the research team.
3. A. Godfroid, «Spoliation financière. Étude d'un cas particulier: la Société belge de Banque (1940–1965)» Working paper of the Research Commission.
4. The general occupation policy of the German military administration was to administer the Belgian economy and society with the cooperation of public and private Belgian offices and organizations, as this was likely to bring the maximum benefit to the German war economy. To achieve this goal, the not always apparent adherence to Belgian and international law (Hague Convention) was a necessary prerequisite, which explains why the Brüsseler Treuhandgesellschaft operated within the framework of Belgian law.
5. A partial exception, however, was the Jewish citizens of the Greater German Reich.
6. E. Laureys, "De beroving van de joodse diamantairs in Antwerpen, 1940–1944. Belangen van de Duitse oorlogsindustrie versus ontjoodsingspolitiek," *Bijdragen tot de Eigentijdse Geschiedenis* 7 (2000): 149–87.
7. Certain figures in the final report of Group 12 must be viewed critically. In part, figures from very different sources were put together here, while in addition one must bear in mind that this report was edited in Germany shortly after its compilation in order to put the activities of the German military administration and the BTG in a much more positive light than was actually the case. Abschlußbericht des Militärbefehlshabers für Belgien und Nordfrankreich. Abteilung Wirtschaft. T 13 (Treuhandvermögen), Archives Nationales, Paris, AJ 40.
8. Johanna Pezechkian, «La *Möbelaktion* en Belgique» *Cahiers d'Histoire du Temps Présent* 10 (2000): 153–80.
9. Jacques Lust, «De ERR en de bibliotheekroof in België, 1940–1943» (Brussels, 2000). Working paper of the Research Commission.
10. See note 7.
11. R. van Doorslaer, "De vereffening van de Brüsseler Treuhandgesellschaft" (Brussels, 1999). Working paper of the Research Commission.
12. Brief van Mandatarissen van het Sekwester op de BTG aan het Hoofdbestuur van het Sekwester, 20 September 1945. Archieven Ministerie van Financiën, Fonds Sekwesterarchief WOII.
13. Among others, that was the case with regard to the collective account Mechelen, into which during the occupation the proceeds from the sale of the stolen property collected in the Dossin barracks in Mechelen (the collecting point from which the Jews and Sinti und Roma were deported from Belgium to Auschwitz) were paid. Part of the unpaid wages of the Jewish forced laborers who were employed in constructing the Atlantic Wall in northern France also went into this account. In 1958 this sum was transferred in accordance with a special law via the the Deposito- und Consignatiekas to the National Werk voor Oud-strijders en Oorlogsslachtoffers (National Service for War Veterans and War Victims). See A. Godfroid, «A qui profite l'exploitation des travailleurs forcés juifs de Belgique dans le Nord de la France?» *Cahiers d'Histoire du Temps Présent* 10 (2000): 107–27.
14. The aim of the draft law for the introduction of the *Statuut van de politieke gevangene* (Law on Political Prisoners) in January 1947 was to recognize their suffering (in prison, during deportation, or in death) without differentiating by cause of arrest. The political

majorities in the Chamber approved this draft almost unanimously; in the Senate, however, it was opposed by the Catholic opposition. Racially motivated deportations were no longer included in the compromise that was ultimately approved, since this now demanded proof of "patriotic" activity, that is, political or ideological grounds for imprisonment. The Jewish victims of the war (after all, some 36 percent of all war-related deaths in Belgium during the Second World War) were not taken into consideration by this political compromise. Even more restrictive was the Statuut van de vreemde politieke gevangene (Law on Foreign Political Prisoners), as this could only be applied to foreigners who could prove their active contribution to the resistance. See P. Lagrou, *The Legacy of Nazi Occupation. Patriotic Memory and National Recovery in Western Europe, 1945–1965* (Cambridge, 2000), 221–25.

15. E. Laureys, "Claim 13765B – Industrial Diamonds. De restitutie van industriediamanten aan de Belgische diamantsector en de grenzen van de Amerikaanse goodwill. 1945–1957," in *Bijdragen tot de Eigenijdse Geschiedenis* 10 (2002): 129–52.
16. M. Steinberg, «Un pays occupé et ses juifs. Belgique entre France et Pays-Bas» *Serpinnes, Quorum* (1998); L. Saerens, *Vreemdelingen in een wereldstad. Een geschiedenis van Antwerpen en zijn joodse bevolking, 1880–1944* (Lannoo, 2000).
17. On the German side, the occupation was modeled on the principle of a supervisory administration. In order to save German manpower, the Belgian institutions were supposed to continue their activity under German supervision.
18. See P. Novick, *The Holocaust and Collective Memory: The American Experience* (London, 1999).

INDIFFERENCE AND FORGETTING

Italy and its Jewish Community, 1938–1970

Ilaria Pavan

At the end of the Second World War, Italy's Jewish community found itself facing a dual moral and financial burden. Over the previous seven years, it had lost 40 percent of its members, leaving a mere twenty-eight thousand in 1945.[1] To add insult to injury, despite clear evidence of the trauma suffered by Italian Jews, the topic of racial persecution under Fascism was completely overlooked—whether intentionally or otherwise—by Italian historians for many years. This erasure of Fascist antisemitism was largely the result of a widely shared desire to depict the racial persecution, like the regime that had generated it, as an unpleasant incident in history. It was claimed that Fascist racial policy was mainly an outgrowth of foreign policy; in other words, that the alliance with Germany in 1936 somehow forced an unwilling Mussolini to implement a parallel antisemitic policy in the autumn of 1938.[2] The responsibility of the Fascist government and that of the entire country was thereby brushed aside and diminished, especially with the argument that the racial laws were really quite harmless and weakly enforced, and that Italian society in general had shown considerable solidarity with persecuted Jews.

It was not until 1988, on the fiftieth anniversary of the racial laws, that historians began to reconsider seriously this controversial and dramatic period of Italian history. Since then much new research has been published, leading to a general revision of the previous interpretation.[3] Recent studies have highlighted, for one thing, the total independence of the Fascist government from their Nazi allies in the creation and introduction of racial persecution. These same studies have also demonstrated that the regime was far from lax in enforcing the racial laws throughout the entire period from 1938 to 1945. The mass of documentation examined fails to provide any evidence even of hesitation on the part of officials, let alone protest. On the contrary, there were many examples of overzealous behavior by bureaucrats at all levels and ranks who were eager not only to carry out orders, but also

Notes for this section begin on page 180.

to recommend newer and stricter forms of control. The state's attitude was more often than not reflected among individual Italian citizens, many of whom took advantage of the situation to exploit the practical and legal difficulties facing the persecuted minority. The gradual removal of Jews from the financial life of the country was accompanied by frequent widespread cases of corruption and illegal profiteering, not only by members of the Fascist Party, but also by ordinary so-called Aryan citizens. It can therefore be maintained that the success of the Fascist regime's antisemitic policies stemmed largely from reasons not linked simply to ideology.

The First Five Years, 1938–1943

Racial persecution officially began in August 1938 with the so-called racial census, which for the first time was based on racial criteria alone with no reference to religion. This census counted 46,656 Jews, of whom 37,241 were Italian and 9,415 foreign, making a total of barely 0.1 percent of the entire population of Italy. The census also highlighted the "trade vocation" of Italian Jewry, with approximately 45 percent of all Jews being involved in some form of business. Overall there emerged the prevailing presence of a middle class—independent professionals, white collar workers, and civil servants—and a lower middle class bordering on the poor, if one considers that approximately 25 percent of Jewish traders were in fact street peddlers. During the autumn and winter of 1938-1939, the Fascist regime approved the main legal measures of its anti-Jewish policy.[4] Official publications announced the legal definition of a Jew and the new limits and prohibitions imposed on all areas of their lives—family, work, and property.[5] The laws required the dismissal of Jews from civilian and military state posts; schools and universities; insurance companies and banks; and all structures of the National Fascist Party. Doctors, lawyers, notaries, engineers, architects, brokers, journalists, and all other private professionals were excluded from their respective professional associations and prevented from practicing. Jews were also to be dismissed from all management positions with public and private firms. They were instructed to report to the Fascist authorities their ownership of businesses and shops; any Jewish-owned firms in the field of defense or employing more than one hundred people were to be confiscated and subsequently sold by the state. The same applied to real estate owned by Jews, which—like businesses—was to be expropriated if its value exceeded the limit fixed by the racial laws.

To manage and sell this confiscated property, in 1939 the government established a specific authority named *Ente di Gestione e Liquidazione Immobiliare* [Office for the Management and Liquidation of Real Estate] (EGELI), which until September 1943 seized and managed over four hundred properties and twenty-four firms. This relatively small number of confiscations is misleading in that it gives an erroneous impression of indulgence by the Fascist regime. What this apparently meager data fails to convey is the atmosphere of steadily increasing pressure that Jews experienced as an endless series of new restrictions were introduced. Without going into detail, it is sufficient to say that between September 1938 and September 1943, approximately 180 decrees and circulars were issued by various ministries and other state departments: some prepared the ground for the main anti-Jewish laws, others established how the general rulings were to be implemented in practice, while yet others activated unpublished measures in areas not previously affected by racial legislation. The burden of persecution steadily increased, sometimes in a seemingly haphazard fashion, but precisely for this reason its impact was all the more devastating: only years later would the full effects be appreciated.

Some examples may help to illustrate the atmosphere of endless uncertainty suffered by Jews. While initially there were minimal restrictions on joint-stock companies in which some shareholders were Jewish,[6] later circulars imposed conditions that effectively prevented even firms in which Jews were only minority shareholders from conducting their business.[7] In the sphere of retail and wholesale trade, and also with regard to small and medium businesses, although no laws formally restricted their dealings, the fact remains that by the end of 1940 approximately 20 percent of Jewish shops and other small- or medium-sized businesses had been closed down, sold off, or virtually handed over to "Aryans." This percentage was to grow alarmingly, reaching over 60 percent in the autumn of 1943, just prior to a further bout of racial legislation in the winter of 1943–1944, when all Jewish-owned shops and businesses of all kinds were confiscated. Among the restrictions introduced after 1939, perhaps the harshest were those against Jewish peddlers, which affected about 900 individuals (and also their families).[8] This policy was just as fatal for the less well-off segment of the Jewish community as were the laws directed against its professional middle class.

The remarkable discrepancy between the original wording of the main racial laws and the ensuing circulars—often stricter than the laws themselves—may be considered the key feature of Fascism's anti-Jewish campaign. This discrepancy left ample scope for arbitrariness in the implementation of racial policy, leaving room for maneuver, which institutions, groups, and individual citizens could easily exploit.

Among the first and most blatant consequences of the racial laws was the mass dismissal of Jews from their posts. This sudden unemployment was the first step towards a real personal catastrophe. It eroded both the entire network of relationships on which an individual's life is based and undermined the personal self-confidence of a breadwinner, while also depriving the family of its income. The data available, while neither comprehensive nor definitive, still clearly show that the regulations ordering the dismissal of Jews were rigorously enforced. In numerical terms, by autumn 1938 at least 276 bank employees had lost their jobs, as had 884 bank officials (135 Italian and 749 foreign) working for overseas branches of Italian banks, in addition to 154 employees of insurance firms. Over 400 university lecturers were forced to resign; in the armed forces approximately 105 officers were permanently stripped of their commissions "on the grounds of their Jewish race"; and more than 4,000 Jews working as freelance professionals, office staff, and civil servants were subjected to labor restrictions.

Of particular significance is the reaction of Italian society to the government's antisemitic policy. If one accepts that the antisemitic legislation commenced when Fascism had already passed its height, it does not automatically follow that unease at the persecution was a prime factor undermining support for the government, which then unraveled during the war years. A useful, if rather biased source of insight into the moods and opinions of the public are the reports prepared by the Fascist political police. This documentation was forwarded to the Ministry of the Interior, and, disappointingly, much of the information covering most of the country throughout 1939 appears to show only faint disapproval of the persecutors and very few public demonstrations of solidarity with those persecuted. The general impression created by the reports of the political police is one of basic indifference or at least passivity on the part of public opinion towards the effects of the antisemitic campaign. This picture appears to be confirmed by the reports of local Fascist leaders to the central National Fascist Party, from which no evidence emerges of any reaction to the racial laws—neither of consent nor of disapproval. It is equally significant that during the following year, 1940, both the police reports and National Fascist Party's records contain no trace of any incidents concerning racial persecution, almost as if the "Jewish Question"—a mere year after its introduction—had been mentally stored and digested by a country heading for war and hence in the grip of other worries.

After the collapse of the Fascist regime at the end of July 1943, there came another crucial period for those Jews living in the areas of central and northern Italy, which were still controlled by the remnants of the Fascist government and Nazi German occupying troops. The transition from "persecution of Jewish rights" to "persecution of Jewish lives" meant a journey to the death camps for 8,265 Jews, of whom only 100 survived.[9] Antisemitic legislation became much more aggressive during the autumn and winter of 1943–1944: all Jewish assets—real estate and personal property, firms, businesses, bank accounts, shops, pensions, insurance policies, securities, furniture, works of art—were seized by the state. Specially designated offices were set up within the individual city administrations to organize the confiscations, and there were many cases of initiatives being taken well beyond the limits set by the racial laws. There is ample evidence of incidents of incorrect management, looting, and plunder, which today are still the most difficult episodes to document and assess. Solely in the two-year period from 1943 to 1945, the collaborationist Italian government seized a total of 17,743 assets belonging to 7,920 Jews: 231 firms; land and real estate valued at 1,053,649,611 lire; government bonds worth 36,396,831 lire; stocks and shares to the tune of 731,442,219 lire; and bank accounts totaling 130,597,687 lire.[10]

Postwar Hardship

Research into the postwar situation of the Jews in Italy is far from complete and many aspects remain shrouded in darkness.[11] As mentioned before, a veil was hastily drawn in the late 1940s over both the restitution of property and also the entire topic of antisemitic persecution. The following analysis does not claim to be either complete or conclusive, but rather it aims to provide a general overview. To this day there are still outstanding issues regarding assets (including bank accounts, postal savings accounts, insurance policies, and securities) unclaimed by their rightful Jewish owners after the war. In many cases factors such as death, postwar emigration and unawareness on the part of the heirs hindered or prevented full restitution of that which had been seized. It is, however, also true that no system was established for the automatic return of assets: unless those entitled presented a specific claim, no public body, bank, or insurance company would take the initiative of seeking out the rightful owners in order to return to Jews items that had been confiscated or frozen in previous years.

Perhaps the greatest obstacle to any genuine recognition of the rights of those affected by the persecution was the fact that the Italian legislation in this respect was inadequate and incomplete. It was, if anything, an exercise in blind legal formalism, which offered more safeguards to those who benefited from the persecution than to those who had suffered from it. The decision of postwar legislation to acknowledge across the board the "good faith"[12] of those who had acquired confiscated Jewish property from 1938 onwards was a clear signal that the Jewish assets issue would become subsumed within a blanket acceptance of the transactions conducted during the years of persecution.[13] It is therefore hardly surprising that only one year after the end of the war the Jewish community began to suspect that repeal of the racial laws had in fact only done justice from the moral and political point of view, while completely failing to redress the financial losses suffered.

A striking example of the country's failure to turn a new leaf after the war is the EGELI, the authority set up in 1939 to manage confiscated Jewish assets. Not only was this body not closed down following the armistice, it was actually entrusted with managing the return of the assets[14]—a procedure that was distinguished especially by plodding bureaucracy and red tape. It was not until 1967, twenty-two years after the end of the war, that a report from the EGELI stated that all Jewish property restitutions had been completed. The return of assets in the immediate postwar years was made additionally frustrating by an issue that was not solved for a number of years: EGELI—in other words, the state—required that the persecuted owners pay for all the expenses incurred in administering the confiscated assets between 1939 and 1945. To make matters worse, this was not merely an oversight but simply the application of a specific article of the reintegration legislation itself, which required that "the expenses for normal administration and management fees" were to be met by the owners of the confiscated assets.[15] Last but not least, while the owners were required by law to pay the administration costs, on the other hand there was no provision rendering the state accountable for the manner in which it had administered the assets in its care for these six years. Not surprisingly, the demand for payment met considerable resistance from the victims of persecution, one of whom wrote explicitly in a reply to EGELI in 1947:

> Apart from the moral issue, it is unacceptable that the victims of persecution are made to pay the costs of management planned to their detriment by scavengers whose only intention was to take possession of assets belonging to people doomed to the gas chambers. We draw you attention to the fact that we did not appoint you as the custodians of our property.[16]

For many victims of persecution it seemed hard to distinguish the new democratic state from the past regime, at least judging from the Kafkaesque bureaucracy, which appeared to have refined its talent for overbearing and pettifogging red tape. The majority of Jews refused to pay, even when the state sent them repeated payment demands, warning that otherwise they would lose their rights under the statute of limitations. The question was finally resolved only in the late 1950s when another issue was raised: that of Jewish assets never claimed during the postwar period and still held by the state.

A memorandum from the Ministry of the Treasury in 1958 recommended canceling the demands for payment issued by EGELI over the previous years on "ethical, legal and financial" grounds, pending "the forthcoming statute of limitations set by the Reintegration Laws [December 1958], after which any Jewish assets still held by the state would be forfeited, as a fair refund for the administration expenses previously incurred." In January 1960 the Attorney General's Department drew a final line under the issue of Jewish assets as follows: "we believe that the state has by now acquired the right of ownership of the assets seized and is free of any obligation to return the sale price or to pay any compensation for the use of the items. The state is therefore free to dispose of these assets as it sees fit."[17]

Government bonds, shares, and valuables belonging to twenty-three Jews, nineteen of whom are known to have died as a result of deportation, were confiscated and subsequently sold by the state during the 1960s. Old government bonds, shares, and various other items deemed to be "of no further value," were burned in a fireplace in the Ministry of the Treasury on 6 April 1970.[18]

Sales of Jewish assets by the state during the 1960s were not, however, without precedent. In some northern Italian cities chests were found in 1947 containing silver stolen from Jews between 1943 and 1945. While lengthy negotiations between the state and the Unione delle Comunità Ebraiche Italiane [Italian Committee of Jewish Communities] finally resulted in the return of the religious articles in 1948, the same was not true of items belonging to private Jewish citizens. Despite the obvious origin of these assets, they were nonetheless put on sale at public auction, and it can be estimated that between 1947 and 1948 the Italian state sold over 700 kg of silver, pocketing more than 8 million lire.[19] Perhaps the most absurd case was that of one Jewish citizen who had negotiated in vain to reclaim silver that was his property, but ended up having to buy it back from the state in 1948.

Banks and insurance companies also did not have a very good record concerning the return of frozen assets. Accurate research into the insurance companies in particular is virtually impossible due to the almost total disappearance of the relevant papers. So far the two major Italian insurance companies have been able to produce only sixty-three insurance policies taken out by Italian Jews prior to 1938 that were never cashed or otherwise reclaimed by their legitimate owners after the war. It appears to be extremely unlikely that this was the total number of insurance policies paid into by those persecuted and never paid out afterwards.

The fragmentary nature of surviving records has also hindered investigation into Jewish assets left unclaimed on bank accounts. It is known that in 1950 the value of unclaimed Jewish property—in cash and government bonds—still deposited in banks was 4 million lire, in addition to approximately seven thousand share certificates, whose value was undefined. This figure was in any case incomplete, as a number of banks continued to hide behind bank secrecy laws. A report from the Ministry of the Treasury in 1958 was unable to do more than state that the banks "were biding their time, to allow the statute of limitations to expire in their favor, so that they could take possession of [Jewish] assets."[20] The matter dragged on over the following years and still remains unresolved.

In addition to the fate of their assets or savings, a major problem for many victims of persecution was returning to a normal life in terms of being able to resume their previous occupation. Those who had been forced to give up their livelihoods following the introduction of the racial laws in 1938 and 1939 now wished to return to being teachers, solicitors, or clerks, or to run their shops or businesses in peace and quiet. This was far from easy, however, as is shown by this brief characterization of affairs taken from a report written shortly after the war by an official of the Jewish community in Pisa: "successful businesses destroyed and shops looted; professions left for so long that it is difficult, if not impossible, to start again; jobs lost with no hope of replacement."[21]

The picture was equally depressing for former employees and executives of joint stock companies, many of whom failed to take back Jewish staff dismissed under the racial laws: 348 people are known not to have been offered their old posts, equaling 42.1 percent of all Jews working for joint stock companies before the persecution.[22] If we focus more specifically upon companies with their head offices in Milan, where in the 1930s the majority of joint stock firms had at least one Jewish manager, the figures speak for themselves: in 1949, only thirty-four out of an original 249 Jews who worked there prior to the persecution had returned to their former posts, a mere 12.9 percent. Similar changes can be seen in the small and medium business sector, in which out of 208 firms declared after 1939 by

Jewish owners, 30 percent were no longer working after the war. If we add to this figure the businesses that closed down between 1939 and 1943 and those whose owners perished following deportation, we reach a total of 48 percent. Yet Milan presents an even worse picture: here only 12.1 percent of the small and medium Jewish businesses open in 1939 had resumed work by the end of the 1940s.[23]

For an analysis of the retail trade, an examination has been made of the situation in Milan, Rome, Ferrara, Turin, Florence, and Leghorn, six of the larger Italian cities, which perhaps can be viewed as representative of the general state of Jewish retailers in the postwar period. Although the majority of Jewish retailers managed to pick up from where they had left off, albeit with difficulty, others were closed for good owing to lack of inventory or capital; in some other cases in which businesses used fictitious names of Aryan partners to circumvent the racial legislation they were not returned to their legitimate Jewish owners. The figures show that in the six cities examined, only 22.7 percent, 35.6 percent, 42.6 percent, 43.7 percent, 45.5 percent, and 48.2 percent respectively of Jewish retailers previously in business had resumed trade by 1950.[24] As if the objective difficulties encountered by the business and trade communities were not enough, the Italian Tax Authorities added their own contribution. A number of Jewish retailers—many of whom had already closed down—were asked to pay back taxes for 1943–1945, along with a fine for late payment. Other businesses were asked to pay the tax on wartime profits introduced by the Italian government in 1946. In reply to the protests of Jewish merchants, the Ministry of Finance replied that "a Jewish citizen could have paid the taxes due from wherever he happened to be," and that being out of town as a result of persecution wasn't "a sufficient reason to justify the delay in filing a tax return."[25] The Italian Committee of Jewish Communities wrote to the prime minister on this subject, only to be told in a reply dated February 1946 that: "it was not possible to make an exception for Jewish businesses," since they had already been "granted every possible concession."[26]

Further insight into the Italian Jews' postwar situation comes from an analysis of the legal proceedings brought after 1945 by the victims of persecution.[27] These are a source of much significant information, illustrative of the dynamics triggered by the racial laws, the reintegration of Jews within post-war Italy, and the behavior of the new republic toward them. The identity of the defendants demonstrates, for example, how from 1938 onward it was above all individual Italians who had taken advantage of the newly persecuted Jewish "class": only 7 percent of the lawsuits were brought against the state authorities, the remaining 93 percent being against individuals or firms.[28] This small proportion of claims against the state therefore confirms the theory that after the war, slowly though it may have proceeded, the state returned confiscated assets. The trials that kept Italian magistrates the busiest in the postwar years were those in which the claimants sought to have revoked contracts for the sale of real estate or businesses signed by Jews during the five-year period from 1938 to 1943, which were the grounds for 58 percent of the legal proceedings brought by Italian Jews after the war. This fact also confirms the considerable transfer of wealth caused by the racial legislation.

What is less obvious, however, is the extremely restrictive manner in which the judges enforced the Reintegration Laws dealing with precisely these disputes: verdicts against Jewish claimants made up 64 percent of the total.[29] It has been argued that many magistrates were perhaps unsuited for their position in postwar Italy—for reasons of age, as well as on account of their social, cultural, and political backgrounds; but the establishment had not deemed it necessary to carry out a purge, as indeed was the case in other fields. While it may be the case that some magistrates paid little attention to the values expressed in the new republican constitution and expressed even less sympathy for the fate of those who suffered from persecution, it is, however, also true that the postwar laws that were supposed to redress the injustice were inadequate and ambiguous, rendering their very restrictive application inevitable. On the subject of the sale of property, the Italian Committee of Jewish Communities petitioned in vain the Ministry of Justice to annul all sales of property made by Jews after the antisemitic campaign had commenced, on the grounds that "in those years many Jews had sold their assets either because they had no alternative means of support, or because they feared harsher laws still to come."[30] Since the postwar laws required proof of bad faith on the part of the purchaser—an almost impossible achievement—the lawsuits were, as mentioned above, often decided against the claimants.

It should in any case be noted that only about one hundred Jews actually initiated legal proceedings of this nature, a mere fraction in relation not only to the size of the postwar Italian Jewish population but also to the mass of confiscations between 1939 and 1945. The decision of so many not to appeal to the law was perhaps indicative of the damage done by the racial laws: even after seven years many Jewish citizens simply felt that they could no longer trust the government. An additional reason may lie in the fact that their postwar finances were such that the majority were unwilling or unable to commit themselves to the cost of a lengthy legal action. A third and equally plausible reason might lie in the desire simply to turn the page and put the tragedies of the recent past behind them, thus conveniently lightening the burden of responsibility borne by the Italian nation with regard to antisemitism.

A final consideration concerns the general theme of the oblivion that quickly enfolded both the racial persecution and its more evident social and economical consequences. In Italy, the large cloud of silence that emerged so soon after the war appears to have been created apparently by the mutual consent of all concerned. First, there was the desire—whether subconscious or overt—on the part of the masses to put as much distance as possible between themselves and their collective responsibilities. A classic example of the lack of willingness shown by postwar Italian society and culture is that of the novelist Primo Levi, who spent years trying in vain to find a publisher who would accept the story of his Auschwitz experience. Only in 1958 did he finally succeed in getting *Se questo è un uomo* published.[31] Second, there was also the silence of the former victims themselves, not knowing which way to turn between the therapeutic need to forget and the bitter and growing awareness that they were facing interlocutors—both public and private—who were simply not willing to listen.

Last but not least, there was also a considerable element of political expediency: for the new holders of power the main priority was to reinforce the legitimacy of the infant democracy, and for them forgetting was a most effective means of stabilization. In the ideological clash between totalitarianism and democracy, between Fascism and anti-Fascism, which defined the boundaries and features of Italian public memory after World War II, the victims of racial persecution were an uncomfortable presence—a minority of survivors whose awkward character was difficult to reconcile with a country that wanted to forget as soon as possible.

Notes

1. About 9,000 Italian Jews died during the Shoah; over 6,000 emigrated between 1938 and 1943; approximately 5,500 opted to renounce their Jewish faith after the beginning of the persecution, and only a minority of these reconverted after the war. In addition, 1,000 more left Italy between 1945 and 1955 for Palestine/Israel.
2. This was the interpretation of the first important study—and for many years the only one—dedicated to Fascist antisemitism: R. De Felice, *Storia degli ebrei italiani sotto il fascismo* (Turin, 1961).
3. See M. Sarfatti, *Mussolini contro gli ebrei* (Turin, 1994); M. Sarfatti, ed., *Gli ebrei nell'Italia Fascista* (Turin, 2000); F. Levi, *L'ebreo in oggetto* (Turin, 1993); F. Levi, *Le case e le cose*, (Turin, 1998).
4. Decree no. 1728, 17 November 1938, "*Provvedimenti per la difesa della razza italiana*" (Measures concerning the defence of the Italian race), and Decree no. 126, 9 February 1939 "*Norme relative ai limiti di proprietà immobiliare e di attività industriale e commerciale per i cittadini italiani di razza ebraica*" (Regulations restricting ownership of real estate, industry, or commercial businesses on the part of Italian citizens of Jewish race). September 1938 also saw the blanket expulsion of teachers and pupils from schools and universities through Decree no. 1390, 5 September 1938 (Law regarding the defence of Italian schools), and Decree no. 1391, 7 September 1938 (Measures concerning foreign Jews)—the law for the expulsion of foreign Jews, who were obliged to leave Italy by March 1939.
5. Fascist racial laws were based on the principle of bloodlines: anyone born from two Jewish parents was considered a Jew, even if he or she professed another faith. Unlike the Nazi racial laws, the Fascist regime had no specific category for the so-called mixed people (those born from mixed marriages); as a result the rules were many and complicated, with some children born from only one Jewish parent being classified as Jews and subjected to antisemitic legislation, while others were not.
6. The racial laws concerning joint-stock companies initially required "only" the dismissal of the Jewish chairmen, directors, managing directors, and executives.
7. The restrictions introduced by circulars regarding Jewish joint-stock companies included, among others, a ban on applying for bank loans, obstacles to purchasing raw materials,

and the cancellation of all contracts awarded to Jewish-owned companies by any state authority or public body.

8. See, I. Pavan, *Fra indifferenza e oblio: Le conseguenze economiche delle leggi razziali in Italia (1938-1970)* (Florence, 2004), 133.
9. About 43,000 Jews—35,000 Italian Jews and 8,000 foreigners—were in Italy in the autumn of 1943, before the beginning of the Nazi occupation and the birth of the Fascist collaborationist government, the so-called Repubblica Sociale Italiana. Approximately 6,200 of these escaped to Switzerland, while 500 moved toward southern Italy, which had already been freed by Anglo-American troops. The remainder of the Jewish population lived underground in northern Italy trying to avoid Fascist-Nazi roundups and deportations.
10. See, I. Pavan, *Fra indifferenza e oblio*, 14.
11. For a first description, see G. Schwarz, *Ritrovare se stessi* (Rome, 2004).
12. Good faith is a legal term denoting that the buyer believes he is purchasing an asset from its legitimate owner.
13. This clause was contained in Decree no. 393 of 5 May 1946, "Rivendicazione dei beni confiscati, sequestrati o comunque tolti ai perseguitati razziali" (Reclamation of assets confiscated, frozen, or otherwise taken from the racially persecuted). French postwar laws, on the other hand, determined that all purchasers of Jewish assets would be considered to have acted in bad faith, although they could always appeal for recognition of rights to assets in hand. All sale agreements signed by French Jews after June 1940 were to be considered extorted with violence and thus cancelled. Switzerland passed a "Decree on Looted Assets" in December 1945, which went against the Swiss civil law tradition in order to grant Jews the return of their assets regardless of the good or bad faith of the new owners.
14. The winding up of EGELI began during 1957, but it was not until 1997 that the Ministry of the Treasury, under whose authority it came, declared it to have been definitively closed down.
15. Decree No. 393 of 5 May 1946, art. 6.
16. See I. Pavan, *Fra indifferenza e oblio*, 213.
17. Ibid., 206.
18. Ibid., 207.
19. See. E. Basevi, *I beni e la memoria* (Catanzaro, 2001), 76.
20. See I. Pavan, *Fra indifferenza e oblio*, 200.
21. Ibid., 218.
22. Ibid., 225.
23. Ibid., 231.
24. Ibid., 234.
25. Ibid., 236.
26. Ibid.
27. The analysis covers the period from 1945 to 1965 and is based on data from the "Repertori della Giurisprudenza italiana" (The Italian Law Collections). This is how all the sentences issued by the Italian Tribunals, Courts of Appeal, and the Supreme Court concerning reintegration of the civil, political, and patrimonial rights of the former victims of racial persecution have been traced and analyzed.
28. See I. Pavan, "Gli incerti percorsi della reintegrazione. Note sull'atteggiamento della magistratura repubblicana 1945–1965," in *Gli ebrei italiani in Italia tra persecuzione Fascista e reintegrazione postbellica*, ed. I. Pavan and G. Schwarz (Florence, 2001), 89.
29. Of all legal proceedings brought by Italian Jews after the war, 49 percent were lost by the claimants. See I. Pavan, "*Gli incerti percorsi della reintegrazione*," 91.
30. See I. Pavan, *Fra indifferenza e oblio*, 256.
31. In 1947 the book was published by a minor publishing house, De Silva, Turin. Only in 1958 did Einaudi, one of the major Italian publishing houses, decide to publish it.

"WHY SWITZERLAND?"

Remarks on a Neutral's Role in the Nazi Program of Robbery and Allied Postwar Restitution Policy

Regula Ludi

Allegations and Obligations: The Neutrals in Allied Postwar Planning

In article 8 of the agreement signed at the Paris Reparation Conference in January 1946, a provision was introduced earmarking a share of reparations for stateless and so-called nonrepatriable victims of Nazi action, "in recognition of the fact that large numbers of persons have suffered heavily at the hands of the Nazis and now stand in dire need of aid to promote their rehabilitation, but will be unable to claim the assistance of any Government receiving reparations from Germany." It provided for funds to be raised from three different sources: non-monetary gold found in Germany, German assets in neutral countries, and assets in neutral countries of Nazi victims who had died without leaving heirs (later to be called "heirless assets").[1] These terms were remarkable in several respects and set an important precedent in international law. The Reparation Agreement of 1946 was the first legal document to recognize an individual's right to redress for state crimes (as distinct from the established right of states to war reparations).[2] Moreover, it required that nonbelligerents participate in the general settlement of war-related problems and, as a break with earlier practice, stipulated that neutrals have an obligation to contribute to reparation efforts as well as the rehabilitation of victims of persecution. This can be understood as a response to the transnational character of Nazi crimes, which involved the complicity of nonbelligerents, be it only as silent bystanders. It also suggested that neutrals (and their citizens), by playing the role of receivers or intermediaries, had not only facilitated the realization of the Nazi program of systematic looting but, even worse, also directly benefited from various acts of Nazi expropriation and murder.[3]

Notes for this section begin on page 204.

On account of the innovative and controversial nature of these provisions, their implementation also proved highly problematic. As they suggested a shared responsibility of the neutrals for Nazi crimes, the governments concerned did not exactly embrace them wholeheartedly, reacting instead with protests and obstruction over the years that followed. Overshadowed by the beginning of the Cold War, however, these reparation obligations soon lapsed into oblivion. Allied pressure had faltered by the late 1940s. The London Debt Conference of 1952–1953 lowered the final curtain on the individual reparations claims of non-German nationals.[4] Although the Federal Republic of Germany gradually extended the scope of its own restitution and compensation programs, the issue seemed to lose its international urgency as time passed.[5] Therefore, when similar accusations resurfaced in the 1990s in the context of Holocaust survivors' class action lawsuits, many observers were simply amazed. They were even more surprised that Switzerland was the first country to become the target. That the Swiss had benefited from Nazi murders or prolonged the war by providing financial services to Nazi Germany, as some allegations claimed, seemed too outrageous to believe. But these accusations were not new at all, echoing similar claims made by Allied economic warfare agencies toward the end of the war. At that time, however, such allegations failed to prompt the desired response and did not lead to a sustained and critical grappling with the Nazi-era past after the war, either in Switzerland or other neutral countries.[6] Quite the opposite response was brought by the more recent charges. The affected nations or institutions could no longer afford to ignore allegations of possible complicity. Almost every European country, as this essay collection demonstrates, commissioned intensive investigations into the expropriation of the Jews, examining Nazi policies of murder and robbery as well as domestic collaboration in and profiteering from these crimes.[7]

But why Switzerland?[8] Were the original Allied accusations at all substantiated, or were they merely wartime propaganda? Why did Allied reparations policies pay so much attention to a small and politically insignificant country like Switzerland? And why did the Swiss become the initial main target of the Holocaust assets campaign of the 1990s? Or to put it differently—why should we focus on the role of neutrals in order to understand the full extent of the Nazi program of looting and robbery?

This article will examine recent research more closely in the light of these questions about Switzerland's role as a link between Nazi plunder and its utilization for war purposes. Recent debates suggest that Switzerland is the paradigmatic case of a neutral playing an ambiguous role in a global conflict now increasingly seen as a struggle to preserve civilization, a struggle in which economic resources were mobilized on an unprecedented scale. Götz Aly's book, *Hitlers Volksstaat*, for example, draws our attention to the complex system by which the Nazi regime exploited and despoiled occupied territories in order to meet domestic demand and strengthen its fighting power, employing methods ranging from open robbery to highly sophisticated accounting transactions and currency conversions in favor of the Third Reich.[9] Widespread domestic and international participation was undoubtedly a decisive prerequisite for the implementation of this policy of large-scale expropriation.[10] But the German war economy also depended on the import of raw materials and industrial products from areas not under its control, such as neutrals like Spain, Turkey, Sweden, and Portugal, or satellites like Romania. These countries insisted on payment either in their own or in freely convertible currencies, whose availability rapidly declined with the beginning of the war, for the delivery of strategically important goods and resources. Notorious for its shortage of foreign exchange and gold reserves since the early 1930s, Germany sought to obtain convertible foreign currency, for instance through the confiscation of privately owned assets—works of art, gold, and securities—that could be turned into foreign exchange. This however, required a market offering the opportunity to sell them via intermediary agents or to purchasers who were willing to turn a blind eye to the likelihood that they were stolen property. During the war Switzerland provided both, the market and the currency. Its refusal to introduce stringent currency restrictions or to tighten controls on certain types of business activity clearly worked to the benefit of Nazi Germany.[11]

It goes without saying that the lack of restrictions and the transactions this facilitated were a thorn in the flesh of the Allies. From January 1943 onwards, the United Nations issued a series of declarations against Nazi robbery, including explicit warnings to the neutral countries not to become the receivers of looted property.[12] These warnings were accompanied by press campaigns filled with reproaches to the Swiss for their services to the Nazis, such as gold transactions, money laundering, or arranging capital flight. That Switzerland more than most other neutrals attracted the attention of the Allies was the result not only of its exposed and difficult wartime situation, being surrounded by the Axis powers and therefore highly dependent on German supplies and willing to yield to Nazi pressure. But these allegations were also a reaction to Switzerland's key position in the financial markets. In the early twentieth century, Switzerland had become an international player. Its strong financial sector benefited from legislation favorable to the banks and other vested interests. One example is the law of 1934–1935 that introduced banking secrecy at the federal level. In essence it was simply the codification of a longstanding practice, officially recognizing the banks' concerns for their customers' privacy, for example in the face of requests for legal assistance by foreign governments investigating tax evasion. Revealing customer data to authorities or unauthorized individuals became subject to criminal prosecution in Switzerland. Contrary to some legends, this legislation was neither a response to the rise of Nazism nor aimed at the protection of Jewish savings. Rather it was the international financial crisis that rendered government intervention necessary to prevent the collapse of specific financial institutions. This required the creation of legal regulations that had not previously existed at the federal level.[13]

Even so, associated with utmost confidentiality to protect property holders' interests, bank secrecy granted Switzerland's financial community an additional competitive edge, beyond the country's traditional reputation for stability. As a result, Switzerland became a favored destination for savings from unstable regions in Central and Eastern Europe.[14] Among the foreign customers were a growing number of Jews and other members of minority groups who feared discrimination by their own governments. However, the very same discretion also attracted assets of dubious origin that entailed political risks. With its underregulation that facilitated gray- and black-market activity, Switzerland's financial center was virtually predestined to become the hub for money laundering and other clandestine transactions. Consequently, Holocaust-era assets often ended up in Switzerland, either because they were originally deposited by individuals who would later become the victims of racial or political persecution, or because they found their way to Swiss financial institutions in the form of flight capital deriving from Nazi policies of expropriation, spoliation, and murder.[15]

Allied "Safehaven" policy, aimed at the prevention of Nazi capital flight from Germany and financial penetration of European economies, was particularly concerned with this latter type of assets, as they represented the product of forcible changes in European property relations resulting from Nazi looting. The Allies were very keen to disentangle and eradicate the resulting transnational networks in order to prevent the continued cloaking of German financial interests. This appeared to be essential in order to avert a possible Nazi revival after the war or the reemergence of Germany as a threat to world peace. As a core principle of Allied occupation policy, these goals found their way into various international agreements on postwar reconstruction. At Yalta, the Big Three agreed to link reparations to the elimination of Germany's potential for waging war, declaring that external German assets should become one source of reparations.[16]

This link explains the victorious powers' emphasis on the neutrals' participation in reparations policy. The Allies identified Swiss financial services as an important catalyst for Germany's economic dominance of Europe. Consequently, they expected Switzerland and other neutrals to assist them in unraveling these financial relations. Yet convincing the neutrals to shoulder these responsibilities proved to be one of the major difficulties the Allies faced in their postwar reconstruction efforts. By framing the cooperation of the neutrals in terms of the legal concept of reparations, suggesting both guilt and a notion of liability, Allied postwar policy entailed implications that Switzerland in particular was not willing to accept. This produced an impasse, because the Allies' legal innovation served the Swiss as a pretext for dismissing any obligation to cooperate and enabled them to identify victims' claims with the victorious powers' allegedly unreasonable demands.

Enabling Circumstances: Changing Perspectives on Switzerland's Role in the Nazi Era

The debates of the 1990s have considerably transformed our view of the Nazi era. This went together with ongoing shifts in the understanding of the

Holocaust—from being seen as one, albeit the most horrific, type of German war atrocity to its broader comprehension as the rupture that more than anything else epitomized the threat to civilization embodied by the criminal nature of Nazism. As a result, research is focusing increasingly on the ethical dimension of responses to Nazi genocide and its legacies. New parameters of interpretation have also led to the rehabilitation of actor-centered approaches (often with special emphasis on the question of moral responsibility and political accountability) and conversely engendered new sensitivity toward the victims and their pain.[17] Interpreting wartime history in light of these shifts has encouraged European societies to go beyond the scope of traditional representations that centered on the nation-state as the key historical subject. In Switzerland, this has meant abandoning the previous focus on the country's unscathed survival during the Second World War, which had stressed the country's role as a potential victim of Nazi aggression, promoted an idealized vision of neutrality, and proven very resilient to both political challenges and shifts in the historiography.[18] Evidently the old paradigm had also eclipsed many issues of wartime and postwar history, particularly Swiss responses to Nazi genocidal policies and the plight of the victims, which only resurfaced in the 1990s as a topic of historiography and public debate.[19]

Under these changing circumstances recent debates have been framed by a concept that is quite novel in Swiss historiography (and collective memory): the idea of the Holocaust "bystander."[20] This idea has brought a new sense of moral judgment to the interpretation of the past. Acts that could be considered beneficial from the standpoint of national survival now appeared politically and legally ambiguous at best. Toward the end of the 1980s, diffusion of new knowledge together with the radically changed international environment after the collapse of communism accelerated the disintegration in Switzerland of received interpretations of wartime history.

Such a shift not only encouraged a reevaluation of the existing body of knowledge,[21] but also gave rise to a whole set of new questions and prompted a wave of investigations that were influenced, in their approaches and interpretations, by specific assumptions about Swiss behavior. These have included, for example, the old allegations of prolonging the war, profiting from Nazi looting, and betraying humanitarian principles, as well as the more recent complaints from victim organizations about failed restitution.[22] On a general level, the result has been to promote a more globalized perspective on the past; one that allows for the complexity of economic and cultural interdependencies in modern societies and pays attention to transnational exchange and networks as phenomena that influenced expectations, framed choices, and thereby also had an impact on individual and collective behavior.

The thesis that the Swiss, in providing the Third Reich as well as individual Nazis with special services, created and sustained enabling circumstances for the Nazi policies of robbery and looting has been a key theme resonating through recent research. But although it has produced plentiful findings, the historiography has not yet addressed the question of Switzerland's role as a facilitator of the Nazi robbery program in a comprehensive manner. The following remarks thus remain incomplete in their attempt at interpreting recent findings in the light of the aforementioned thesis.

From the viewpoint of its usefulness to the German war effort and the Nazi regime's utilization of looted property, Switzerland basically fulfilled three distinctive functions. First, it provided the Third Reich with indispensable goods and services in the realm of traditional trade relations. These, however, acquired new meaning under the conditions of war and economic warfare. Second, it served as the focal point for all sorts of (clandestine) transactions, transfers, and business activities, ranging from the highly official gold transactions to the private activity of facilitating capital flight, receiving and selling stolen goods, and cloaking German financial interests. And third, the Swiss marketplace lent its hallmark of quality and good credit to many suspicious activities and thereby offered opportunities to launder assets of dubious origin.

Often these functions overlapped and they cannot be separated very easily. They also differed in their political implications, both with regard to the degree of involvement and approval by the authorities, as well as to their legality. Furthermore, they were mostly embedded in a tradition of services typically offered by the Swiss market and connected to Switzerland's role as a hub for international transactions long before the Second World War.[23]

From the late nineteenth century, Switzerland's economy has been one of those most integrated within international trade. Before the Second World War, investments abroad amounted to almost 150 percent of the country's annual gross domestic product. Also, Switzerland depended on imports for essential resources, while important sectors of its economy were strongly export-oriented, in particular high-tech production and financial services (including the insurance industry). At the start of the Second World War the Swiss government tried to maintain trade relations with all belligerents. In order to safeguard vital supplies and channel them through the blockades and economic warfare restrictions applied by both sides, it had to conduct complicated negotiations with its economic partners—not only Germany, but also the Allies.[24] After the fall of France, however, the authorities had limited choices left. The country was almost entirely encircled by Axis powers and thus vulnerable to German pressure. For political decision-makers this situation meant calibrating economic needs, sociopolitical goals, and strategic requirements while gauging the political price as well as the benefits of yielding to German (or other belligerents') demands. In the end they opted for a course that allowed the Swiss economy to run at full capacity, hence preventing unemployment and the feared attendant social unrest. All of this was all too familiar from Switzerland's experience at the end of the First World War. To meet these goals, however, Swiss negotiators were prepared to make considerable concessions. This resulted in a much higher degree of dependency on Axis supplies and respective Swiss commitments, an outcome that can be interpreted as "economic instead of political integration" in Axis-controlled "New Europe."[25]

In brief, the Swiss federal government radically realigned trade policy in the summer of 1940. Except for 1945, wartime exports to the Third Reich by far exceeded the *courant normal* (customary prewar trade relations), and between 1941 and 1943 they even tripled in comparison to prewar figures. In 1942, at the height of the Nazis' power, Swiss high-tech and weapons manufacturing, watch-making, and other sectors essential for warfare production devoted up to 80 percent of their capacity to fulfilling German orders.[26] The federal authorities also granted Nazi Germany import credits within the bilateral clearing system, starting at 150 million Swiss francs in the summer of 1940 and adding up to over one billion francs by 1945, which allowed the Nazi regime to purchase Swiss goods, mostly weaponry, munitions, fuses, and high-tech apparel, without immediate payment.[27] These credits and supplies directly contributed to Germany's military strength, though their strategic significance is difficult to gauge and, particularly for weaponry, should not be overestimated. (Probably more important were the prewar exports that supported secret German rearmament in violation of the Versailles treaty).[28]

Apart from industrial goods, Switzerland provided a number of services that directly or indirectly benefited the Nazi war effort. The supply of electric power, for instance, was a contribution that has long been underestimated. Another example is the use by the Germans of the Swiss railway system, whose strategic importance increased massively when the Wehrmacht occupied northern Italy and other connections through the Alps became the targets of Allied bombers. The Germans relied on the route through Switzerland for many war-related purposes as well as the transport to Germany of looted assets—valuable objects, raw materials, food, and dismantled factory equipment from Italy. Clearly, since these services benefited only one belligerent they constituted a violation of international law, a fact that the Swiss authorities were not unaware of. Moreover, they assisted the Nazis in their plundering of northern Italy and therefore made a direct contribution to the robbery program. Swiss border controls were not very effective, which reflected the authorities' disinclination to alienate Nazi Germany, even when its defeat was only a question of time.[29]

The intensity of Switzerland's wartime economic ties to the Axis powers has been an issue of debate for a number of years, with controversies focusing on the strategic significance of deliveries and services and on the question of their importance in preventing the Nazi regime from occupying the country.[30] The reappearance in the 1990s of the allegation that these relations prolonged the war has refocused attention on their moral dimension. Similarly, Switzerland's role in the Reichsbank's wartime gold transactions, although known in general terms for quite some time, has acquired new meaning in the light of recent debates. In this context, the question of the country's significance with regard to the utilization of looted property for war-related purposes is of special interest.

During the war, gold was the main means for Nazi Germany to obtain the hard currencies it needed to purchase strategically essential supplies from

Portugal, Spain, Turkey and Latin American countries, as well as from some of its satellites, like Romania. These states refused to accept the German Reichsmark and demanded payment in their own or freely convertible currencies. However, Nazi Germany was notorious for its currency and gold reserve shortages even long before the war. It also did not escape international attention that the Nazi regime had removed monetary gold from reserve banks in annexed Austria, Czechoslovakia, and other parts of occupied Europe. From Belgium, the Netherlands and Luxembourg alone the stolen gold added up to Sfr 1.58 billion (all figures are given in 1940s values). Moreover, looted gold at the Reichsbank's disposal also included an equivalent of Sfr 311 million that had belonged to individuals, as well as the so-called Melmer gold, victim gold with an estimated value of Sfr 12.55 million taken from Holocaust victims in Eastern Europe. In order to serve German needs, this gold had to reenter circulation and be converted into means of payment. To overcome potential concerns about its origin, the Reichsbank covered its tracks by recasting and antedating portions of the looted gold. Using this procedure, not only monetary gold but also bars valued at Sfr 581,899 containing victim gold made their way to Switzerland.[31] Yet the cloaking of the gold's dubious origins largely failed. Suspicions had already been aroused long before the Allies issued their first warnings in January 1943, which persuaded many countries to refuse any further gold from Germany as a precautionary measure.

This was not the case with Switzerland. The officially appointed Swiss historical commission (ICE) instead concluded that Switzerland "was the most important market for gold from the territories controlled by the Third Reich."[32] Almost 80 percent of the Reichsbank's wartime gold transactions went through Switzerland. The Swiss National Bank accepted the equivalent in gold of Sfr 1.231 billion, Swiss commercial banks another Sfr 101 million.[33] Some of these purchases amounted to the actual laundering of stolen gold. Swiss banks acquired it from the Reichsbank in exchange for freely convertible Swiss francs, which the Nazi regime used to pay for supplies from other neutrals or satellite states. These countries, in turn, offered the Swiss currency acquired through trade with Nazi Germany to the Swiss National Bank in exchange for monetary gold (of potentially German origin) or, as in the case of Romania, Swiss weaponry. In this manner some of the "contaminated" gold was laundered and reentered the pool of untainted, freely convertible monetary reserves.[34]

Switzerland not only played a role as a facilitator, but by lending its stamp of approval, it also granted shady transactions a degree of legitimacy. There can be no doubt that in most instances these transactions served war-related purposes, for instance, the procurement by the Nazi regime of strategically important raw materials and key resources for the German war effort. Already by the second half of 1940 the Swiss National Bank faced allegations that its gold policy was favoring the war capabilities of just one belligerent. But neither the bank's leadership nor their political superiors, the Federal Council, felt compelled to change course. After the Allies issued their warnings in 1943 and 1944, Switzerland was almost the only place where the authorities and business circles paid little heed to this admonition, allowing the Nazi regime to make continuous use of illegally acquired assets. Later, when held responsible for their choices, the members of the bank's board explained their behavior with reference to patriotic motives: they claimed that the importance of these financial services for the Third Reich helped convince the Nazi leadership to respect Switzerland's independence.[35]

Private business activity in Switzerland was shielded from political accountability, but this was often accompanied by a high degree of individual commitment to the political process. The privacy of business and commercial activity there has long benefited from a benevolent attitude on the part of the authorities. The tradition of delegating official functions to civil structures has created a system in Switzerland in which business associations are largely permitted to regulate themselves.[36] During World War II, a wide range of illicit economic activities—black-market, smuggling, and trafficking in forbidden goods—only left traces when they became the subject of foreign intelligence, police observation, or criminal prosecution. Altogether these characteristics explain the scarcity of data and source material on this subject. Even the ICE, although vested with special archival privileges, has not been able to reconstruct more than parts of the puzzle.

Nevertheless the ICE did reveal a multifaceted picture with a wide variety of responses to the unique business opportunities (and risks) presented by the Nazi regime and the war. This diversity is reflected, for instance, in the business community's responses to Nazi racial policy. Some German affiliates of Swiss corporations anticipated the antisemitic measures, complying with racial discrimination even before it was officially implemented. Others proved remarkably reluctant when it came to firing their Jewish employees or providing evidence of the purely Aryan nature of their company. Numerous Swiss companies did not hesitate to grasp opportunities offered by participating in the Aryanization of Jewish property. Similarly, Swiss employers in Germany applied for forced and slave laborers, just as their German competitors. During the war, the proportion of foreign labor employed by Swiss companies did not significantly diverge from the German average of about one-third. Their numbers small and their influence insignificant, Swiss businessmen in Nazi-controlled territories nonetheless supported and helped to sustain the regime's racially-based exploitation of foreign workers, Jewish slave laborers, and concentration camp inmates.[37]

With regard to the utilization of looted assets, two economic sectors were particularly important. Due to the ease of trafficking in art and securities, both of which were underregulated in Switzerland, a developing gray market largely escaped the authorities' attention. Already in the early 1930s, observers noticed intensified business activity among some of the better-known Swiss art dealers. Many foreign collectors, driven by inflation and loss of income, were compelled to part with their assets. After the Nazis came to power, antisemitic measures in Germany accelerated the impoverishment of the Jews as the Nazi authorities applied racial discrimination and exploitative taxation policies to destroy Jewish livelihoods. For the victims, selling their valuables was one of the few opportunities left to obtain the cash and foreign currency necessary for emigration, to pay extortionate taxes, or simply to survive.[38] In Germany, the distress of Jewish collectors slashed prices in the art market, allowing foreign collectors and museums to make good bargains. In Switzerland, in turn, a busy market for flight assets emerged. Pieces of art were sold at so-called public emigrant auctions. The well-known Fischer Art Gallery in Lucerne, for instance, hosted forty-seven such auctions between 1933 and 1945, with its peak period between 1939 and 1942. Among those collectors benefiting from the new opportunities was the prominent arms manufacturer Emil G. Bührle, heavily engaged in supplying weapons to Nazi Germany.[39] Given its public nature, the extent of the trade in flight assets was well known, quite in contrast to the business in looted art. Indications of the latter occasionally surfaced, but failed to prompt the authorities into amending the existing legislation in favor of the interests of the victims, to prosecute traffickers, or to prevent the entry of looted assets into Switzerland.[40]

A comparable situation existed with regard to foreign securities. As long as the trade in foreign securities was not completely frozen, they represented a lucrative source of foreign currency for the Third Reich. In Western Europe, particularly the Netherlands, the Germans confiscated securities in large quantities. As an immediate response to the German invasion of Western Europe, the Swiss authorities shut down the stock exchange and banned trading in foreign securities that originated from the occupied countries. But pressure by the banking lobby moved the Federal Council gradually to loosen these restrictions and at the end of 1940 replace them with a system of self-regulation. These rather weak precautions included the requirement for a declaration of Swiss origin, which failed to hamper the sale of looted bonds and, in turn, created a market for fabricated affidavits. A considerable portion of looted securities thus ended up in Switzerland, where a largely free market and well-connected intermediaries catered to the Nazi regime.[41] As long as such activities did not directly harm Swiss interests, the federal authorities did not feel compelled to intervene, being generally disinclined to meddle in matters of civil law. In summary, the largely unregulated nature of the Swiss securities market "favored dubious trading" of all kinds, with the authorities mostly looking the other way.[42] Official inquiries immediately after the war came to the conclusion that the total value of looted bonds and securities that changed hands in Switzerland ranged between 50 and 100 million Swiss francs, an estimate that was probably only a fraction of the actual figure. Because official control was almost absent and none of the agents involved had an interest in leaving behind traces, a fairly large proportion of such transactions remained hidden. Looted securities that had belonged to Jews often were not reclaimed after the war because their rightful owners had died in the Holocaust.[43]

Switzerland's neutrality and its exemption from any direct intervention by the belligerent powers produced conditions favorable for the utilization of looted property. The financial sector and the art trade responded with a "business as usual" attitude to the developments in Nazi-controlled areas. Even with wartime conditions that clearly became abnormal in the eastern territories under German occupation, discretion remained the main guideline for dealing with Axis clients.[44] The same circumstances also provided opportunities for Nazi victims to sell flight assets—jewelry, life insurance policies, art, stamp collections, and other valuables. Yet the boundaries between these two asset categories were often unclear, and for the victims the rapid fall in prices made the necessity to sell valuables at times almost equivalent to outright expropriation. For some Swiss agents, on the other hand, such business could be highly profitable. Though they often operated in legally murky areas, intermediaries and lawyers acting for Nazi clients were not necessarily outcasts or part of the business underworld; rather they were often reputable men with good connections to the establishment. Their long-standing transnational networks allowed for sordid business activity to be carried out within relationships of confidentiality and trust, which often blurred and distorted standards of moral propriety. This was later reflected in the readiness of many Swiss businessmen to provide *Persilscheine* (character references) for their supposedly decent German partners.[45]

Still, Switzerland's role as a hub for gray-market transactions and other questionable business reflected a political system. The authorities displayed a remarkable unwillingness to tighten controls, restrict freedom of trade, or even implement existing legislation effectively. This had several reasons. Due to their strong market position, business associations such as the Swiss Bankers Association or Vorort (the Swiss Federation of Commerce and Industry) had considerable leverage. During World War II, their leading members, Vorort president Heinrich Homberger and machinery manufacturer Hans Sulzer belonged to the diplomatic delegations negotiating foreign trade agreements in Berlin and London, just as other powerful businessmen such as Carl Koechlin (of Geigy, Basel) carried out official functions in the war economy. Also lawmakers and government members, themselves often enmeshed with business, readily yielded to vested interests. For these political and economic leaders, protecting freedom of trade was almost the same as preserving national sovereignty. This direct association with the core values of national identity even created an overtone of heroic resistance when it came to the defense of the free market. The aforementioned Hans Sulzer, for instance, argued against an increase in state control over the economy by equating it with the centralist endeavors of fascist dictatorships![46]

Moreover, by prioritizing the stability of the legal order, the authorities abstained from interfering in matters of civil law, and thereby consistently ignored the dramatically changed circumstances created by the Nazi policies of persecution, expropriation, and genocide.[47] Political decision-makers preferred to turn a blind eye to the fact that the existing legal framework offered many opportunities for perpetrators and their intermediaries to feather their nests, while effective protection of the victims' rights would have required the introduction of special measures. Many examples show that by leaving difficult decisions to subaltern bodies, the political authorities also deliberately shirked their responsibility. In the case of the gold transactions, the federal government gave the board of the Swiss National Bank plenty of latitude and failed to assert itself as the supreme authority. Without interfering, it also let the directors of the state-owned railway take decisions that conflicted with Swiss neutrality. Later this attitude allowed government members, for instance Eduard von Steiger, the Federal Councilor responsible for the restrictive measures applied against refugees, to claim ignorance as a means of escaping accountability for wartime decisions.[48] The retreat to a very narrow understanding of politics thus became a dominant pattern in the authorities' handling of thorny questions relating to neutrality and complicity in Nazi policies. This corresponded with the frequent translation of political issues into purely technical matters, which thereby obscured their moral and legal dimensions. Oddly enough, all this was accompanied by a concentration of power and the development of strong authoritarian tendencies in Switzerland's political, military, and economic leadership. Only a younger generation of historians who questioned the significance of military preparedness have come to see in this ambivalence evidence that Switzerland was more useful to the Nazis as an unoccupied country.[49]

The actual significance of these contributions for the Nazi regime can hardly be gauged, not only due to the lack of precise data but also in part because of the contradictory and confusing statements made by various agencies of the Third Reich. When Germany's defeat became predictable, Switzerland's financial services also assisted with capital flight from the Axis countries. Camouflage and relocation operations benefited from officially sanctioned discretion, although the country no longer needed to pay careful attention to the concerns of the Nazi leadership. At the same time, such operations attracted increasing attention from Allied intelligence. This situation produced the ideal hotbed for all sorts of rumors and conjectures, for which the Interhandel Affair is an exemplary illustration. In the late 1920s, the German chemical giant IG Farben founded a financial holding company in Switzerland, known as IG Chemie until the end of the Second World War and later as Interhandel. Shortly before the Wehrmacht overran Western Europe in 1940, IG Farben transferred its foreign assets in the United States to the Swiss-owned IG Chemie. Nevertheless, its U.S.-based assets were seized in 1942, because IG Chemie's efforts at dispelling U.S. suspicions were unsuccessful. The lack of financial transparency and the board's reluctance to provide information failed to clear the reputation of the holding company after the war, when the U.S. authorities repeatedly refused to acknowledge Swiss claims to Interhandel assets. But even a never fully disclosed Swiss audit harbored reservations about the company's denial of any association with IG Farben. In 1983 IG Farben in liquidation made a claim on assets that, based on a settlement with the Kennedy administration, had been restored to Interhandel, which had been taken over by one of the major Swiss banks. This complicated and opaque story has given rise to conspiracy theories that reflect the confusion left by Nazi cloaking operations, neutral assistance, and Allied attempts at their exposure.[50]

Toward the end of the war, simple market observation often sufficed to reveal the growing intensity of capital flight. In 1944, for instance, the price of diamonds collapsed after the Swiss market was flooded by jewels probably originating in the Dutch and Belgian diamond industries. Similarly, in the last months of the war reports by military intelligence and customs agencies on the smuggling of jewelry, banknotes, and other valuables into Switzerland multiplied. The excess supply of foreign banknotes at times considerably disturbed the foreign currency market, another indication of the German retreat from the occupied territories.[51] But none of these signs prompted official restrictions.

In 1946, the Swiss authorities estimated that German assets in Switzerland amounted to Sfr 1 billion, based on the only inquiry ever conducted after their freezing in March 1945. This figure is now considered far too low. The ICE reckoned that a figure almost double this is more realistic. The Allies, on the other hand, circulated estimates of Sfr 3 to 4 billion by the end of the war, and the most generous calculation arrived at a figure of Sfr 15 billion. This contrasted with Switzerland's net national product of Sfr 13.8 billion francs in 1945.[52] The frozen German assets, however, would soon become a bone of contention between Switzerland and the victorious powers. Together with the so-called heirless assets of victims of the Holocaust, they would come to stand for Swiss entanglement in Nazi policies of persecution and expropriation, and later for failed reparations and restitution.

Reparations Rejected—Restitution Postponed

"We are basically being treated as a conquered and occupied country," Walter Stucki, Switzerland's top diplomat, complained in 1946. "I can imagine much the same tone being used in a communication from the Allies to a German authority."[53] When it came to Allied postwar demands, the author of these lines obviously wore his heart on his sleeve. But more than simply expressing his personal frustration, the statement testified to widespread feelings of irritation in Switzerland. To a growing extent, the Swiss felt victimized by the victorious powers' accusations and demands. When confronted with charges of having benefited from Nazi looting and having prolonged the war by business transactions in favor of the Axis powers, large portions of the Swiss public quickly replaced their relief over Allied victory with resentment and disaffection. In their eyes, Stalin's slurs about the neutrals' pro-Fascist wartime behavior epitomized the Allied approach to wartime neutrality. As a result, Swiss self-representations of wartime policy became highly selective. At the point of their conception, collective memories were being framed through a perceived need to fend off supposedly unjustified demands and protect national independence.[54]

Such a quick change in public opinion could only please those who were most mired in business with the Third Reich and thus vulnerable to foreign restitution claims. The Swiss Bankers Association, for instance, warned government officials that compliance with Allied requests—to identify looted property and introduce legislation to facilitate restitution—would effectively mean "the renunciation of Switzerland's position as a financial market."[55] In concrete terms, they were alarmed that banking secrecy might be lifted temporarily, allowing for official inquiries or, in their worst nightmares, they imagined Allied comptrollers acting on Swiss territory. Such remarks capitalized on popular anxieties that saw in Allied reparations policy an arrant demonstration of power aimed at weakening Switzerland economically. It is no surprise therefore, that Swiss willingness to participate in the reparations program was limited at best. Unequivocally and irrespective of party differences, lawmakers denied any such obligation. A statement in 1962 by the Federal Councilor Ludwig von Moos epitomized this attitude: "Switzerland has nothing to make amends for, either to the victims of Nazi persecution or to Jewish or other organizations, and certainly not to the state of Israel."[56] As a general consensus, this was the official approach to all issues relating to redress.

The Swiss government nevertheless had to yield on several occasions, beginning with the Currie-Mission in early 1945. Negotiations with an Allied delegation headed by the American Laughlin Currie resulted in the freezing of German assets in Switzerland. In the final agreement of 8 March 1945, the Swiss government also promised to fight Nazi capital flight and prevent the concealment of looted property. Eventually, it made a pledge (never fully implemented) to sever economic ties to Germany as far as this was possible and to cease gold transactions.[57] These concessions were hurtful and reflected the country's high degree of dependency on foreign trade as well as the obvious imbalance of power. Toward the end of the war, when the Allies were rapidly gaining economic leverage and almost exclusive control over Swiss supplies while the Third Reich was no longer able to deliver them, the Swiss situation became more and more excruciating. At the same time, concerns of Swiss businessmen about their future market position were growing in accordance with the intensification of Allied economic warfare and Safehaven measures. The number of Swiss companies facing sanctions for trading with the Nazis soared rapidly. Not only mavericks close to the financial underworld, but respected and powerful Swiss businessmen—for instance the aforementioned industrialist and negotiator Hans Sulzer—found their names blacklisted and their companies barred from markets under Allied control. With regard to normalizing trade relations, Switzerland's financial community was also striving for the swift unblocking of assets frozen in the United States.[58]

The Swiss government could achieve these goals only in exchange for a certain degree of cooperation with the Allies and support for their reparations policy. It faced demands in roughly three areas. First, the Allies asked the Swiss authorities to facilitate the restitution of looted assets. This was a multilayered challenge for people in the business community since they had not only acquired but also transferred stolen property and handed victims' assets over to the Nazis (for instance life insurance policies).[59] It was clear that in these complicated cases, often involving whole chains of transactions, civil law protection of the bona fide ("good faith") purchaser would make restitution almost impossible. Elementary fairness thus required legislation to temporarily abrogate conventional legal provisions.[60] The second area included all issues related to the decisions of the Paris Reparation Conference: in concrete terms, the allocation for reparations purposes of German as well as heirless assets in neutral countries. And finally, as a third complex, the Swiss state faced compensation claims by foreign and Swiss victims of Nazi persecution.

Under fire from international accusations and pressurized by the example of Sweden, which had speedily implemented Allied demands, the Swiss authorities hurried to pass their own restitution legislation.[61] The Raubgutbeschlüsse (Decrees on Looted Assets) of December 1945 and February 1946, the last bills to be enacted under lingering wartime emergency powers, fell into the category of special legislation that temporarily overruled existing civil law. They required that even the bona fide purchaser of looted assets renounce ownership (though he could expect compensation from the federal authorities). Still, the decrees were flawed and unsatisfactory with regard to the legal instruments they provided. The deadline for the submission of claims, for instance, expired at the end of 1947, and the government failed to publicize the procedures internationally. The other provisions also fell short, covering only the restitution of works of art and securities. Finally, their application was limited to property transactions carried out in occupied territories and during the war, thereby excluding expropriations within the prewar boundaries of the Third Reich. The number of claims being filed amounted to only 800, for a total of Sfr 3.4 million.[62]

Similarly disappointing were court decisions in restitution cases where no special legislation applied. One of the leading cases dealt with a life insurance policy issued by the Swiss company Rentenanstalt. The latter had complied with Nazi requests and paid the surrender value after the Jewish policy owner had been deported. The victim survived and later claimed restitution in Switzerland. A lower court fully recognized his claim and obligated the company, which in the court's eyes had been far too compliant in paying the German authorities, to compensate the claimant. But the Federal Court reversed this decision. It acknowledged that the confiscation of the policy had violated the claimant's rights and was an infringement of Swiss "public order." But it nevertheless argued that imposing the obligation of double payment on the insurance company was an infringement of the company's rights. The decision referred the claimant to the German courts for redress, thereby subordinating the individual victim's claim to corporate interests. This case also raised the question of the behavior that could be expected from Swiss individuals and corporations acting in Nazi-controlled territories: was it justified for them to bear the costs if they complied with Nazi racial policies and abandoned the principles associated with the ordinary rule of law and democracy; or, conversely, was it unfair to punish them ex post facto for abiding by Nazi laws? The judiciary's message was ambiguous. But eventually, the Federal Court absolved the compromised corporation.[63] In the end, this sent a strong signal to other agencies to absolve Swiss actors of responsibility if they could cite Nazi coercion.

The second group of issues relating to reparations policy was subject to negotiations between the Western Allies and a Swiss delegation headed by the diplomat Walter Stucki. Scheduled for the spring of 1946, these talks were dedicated to an entire bundle of financial problems arising from the war. The resulting Washington Accord of 25 May 1946 became the cornerstone of Swiss restitution policy as well as a precedent for the Allies' dealings with other neutrals.[64] Broadly speaking, it resolved two sets of issues: it specified Swiss obligations and, in exchange, provided for the suspension of economic warfare measures on the part of the Allies. For the Swiss business community, the settlement achieved their full rehabilitation and reintegration into the Western market, heralding Switzerland's orientation to the "Atlantic perspective."[65] But this came at a price: the Allies required that the Swiss government comply with the provisions of the Paris Reparation Agreement, implying the liquidation of frozen German assets and the transfer of 50 percent of the proceeds to the reparations pool assigned for the rehabilitation of stateless Nazi victims. (The Swiss were permitted to keep the other half of the proceeds in payment of outstanding German liabilities). In addition, the Swiss government had to return Sfr 250 million in gold (constituting a sixth of the total gold transactions and a fifth of the purchases carried out by the Swiss National Bank). And eventually—in written correspondence—Walter Stucki also promised that the Swiss government would consider measures by which the proceeds of heirless assets in Switzerland could be distributed for the benefit of Nazi victims.[66]

On the part of the Allies, a consistent policy stemming from the Yalta Conference linked reparations to the goal of disentangling German penetration of other European economies.[67] The Swiss realized that in order to overcome international isolation, they had to comply with these principles, at least on paper. Apart from the restitution of monetary gold, Switzerland was not expected to make any material contributions but instead merely facilitate restitution and permit the liquidation of German assets in Switzerland. Nevertheless, Swiss negotiators expressed their reservations by declaring these commitments a "voluntary" and "humanitarian" contribution to Europe's reconstruction, a formulation carefully chosen to avoid the impression that they officially recognized any wartime liabilities.[68] This sugar coating notwithstanding, the Washington Accord remained a bitter pill and provoked upon ratification much protest in the press and parliament.[69] Its implementation accordingly led to an unrelenting series of disagreements between the signatory powers as well as complaints from Jewish organizations about the Swiss government's failure to meet its promises. For the main commitment, the liquidation of German assets, no precedents existed.

This allowed Swiss lawyers to dismiss such an obligation altogether as being without a proper legal basis. Furthermore, they argued that Allied claims on external German assets signified a breach with established international law, while deeming their liquidation a confiscatory measure not compatible with the Swiss legal system and its respect for property rights.[70]

The Swiss authorities thus obstructed the swift resolution of the problem. Pressurized by the banking industry, they played for time in order to achieve the most favorable compensation for the asset holders. Switzerland and the FRG eventually established a procedure in 1952 that left the German owners with two-thirds of their assets. This was a very generous outcome when compared to the losses suffered by the owners of assets in Germany due to the effects of devaluation, currency reform, and the equalization of burdens (Lastenausgleich). In addition to this successful protection of German interests, the Swiss scored another major victory. They eventually gained Allied consent to their downgrading of reparations obligations to a number of financial questions, mostly of a highly technical nature, that were to be solved bilaterally with the FRG. This was quite in contrast to the original Allied understanding, which emphasized moral and political aspects of the reparations question. Not only did such a redefinition allow the Swiss to shed the odium of their war-related liabilities, but also facilitated the resolution of other financial problems dating back to the Nazi era. The Adenauer government, for instance, rewarded Switzerland's positive attitude with partial repayment of the clearing credit granted by the Swiss government to the Nazi regime during the war.[71]

What did the Swiss finally contribute to the reparations pool established by the Paris Conference? The archives testify to numerous obstructions faced by the International Refugee Organization, which succeeded the Intergovernmental Committee on Refugees in administering and allocating these funds, when it came to collecting the money for the immediate assistance and resettlement of stateless victims of the Nazis. In January 1948, it had received just half of the nominally assigned funds, with Sweden being the only country to pay its share in a timely fashion. In July 1948, the Swiss government finally paid a first installment of Sfr 20 million (out of a total of Sfr 50 million owed) as an advance on the expected proceeds from German assets.[72] It took the Swiss government another four years to settle the rest of the bill, only doing so after the troublesome issue of the German assets had been resolved. The question of heirless assets, on the other hand, was soon swept under the carpet. The Federal Council shelved legislation for years to come. This was in spite of an officially commissioned legal opinion written in 1947 that considered it "morally not justifiable for the state to benefit from the extermination of politically, religiously, or racially persecuted persons," and which therefore called for special procedures for the identification and return of heirless assets.[73]

It was not surprising that business circles and the authorities in Switzerland went to great lengths to defend German interests. With an eye on the buoyant German recovery, and in anticipation of the Federal Republic's future dominant position in the European market, where to place their bets was not an issue for the Swiss business community. They did everything to preserve German confidence in the Swiss financial market and to prevent any possible rupture. This included personal commitments in support of German partners who were eager to whitewash their past.[74] Such favors were less an indicator of political affinities to Nazism (which no doubt existed in Switzerland) than a result of the artificial separation between politics and business that was so characteristic for Swiss attitudes during the Nazi era and afterwards.

As remarkable was the banks' complete frustration of restitution efforts and their reluctance to search for owners of so-called dormant accounts.[75] Given that many foreign account holders broke off correspondence with the banks in order to evade confiscation or taxation, it was not exceptional for banks to go without direct contacts with foreign customers for extended periods. Yet they ignored the reality that the Nazi policy of extermination had dramatically changed the meaning of these broken ties.

Ironically, the Swiss banks now denied the claims of the Nazis' victims with the very same arguments they employed to protect the interests of German property holders. For instance, they decried attempts to establish an official inquiry to identify heirless assets or to search for surviving victims as a violation of bank secrecy, warning that government intervention would undermine legal security as well as damage the trust between banks and their customers. Saving their reputation as being shelters from government intervention and public accountability became the justification for sacrificing their fidelity to one specific group of customers, the victims of Nazi action and their heirs. But then of course the size of this group had been diminished so dramatically that they no longer embodied the prospect of lucrative future business.[76]

But Holocaust survivors could hardly have expected any special sympathy on the part of the authorities. A number of bilateral agreements with Eastern European countries strikingly manifested this attitude. The agreements concerned mostly financial and economic matters, some of which arose from the postwar nationalization of private property in Eastern Europe. The protection of external Swiss investments therefore was one of the central objectives. The 1949 agreement with Poland was the first and served as the model for those to follow. In a secret addendum the Swiss federal government promised to transfer the proceeds of Polish heirless assets in Switzerland to the Polish government in exchange for a global compensation payment for nationalized Swiss property in Poland. The rights of victims of Nazi persecution thus were traded to secure Swiss citizens' property interests. Most probably the bulk of Polish heirless assets had belonged to Jews who had been killed in the Holocaust or to survivors who either were ignorant of the existence of accounts in Switzerland or who preferred to remain silent for fear of sanctions in Poland.

With this deal the federal authorities flouted the claims of Jewish organizations as well as the Allied stance. In recognition of the unprecedented situation created by the Holocaust, the occupying powers had taken precautions to ensure that heirless assets did not devolve to the German state and lead to the awkward situation that the new German authorities became the beneficiaries of Nazi crimes. Restitution legislation instead designated heirless assets for the rehabilitation of Holocaust survivors and assigned them to Jewish successor organizations. Basing itself on the same principle, the U.S. military government in Germany rejected a Polish claim to assets on German territory, while the Swiss authorities endorsed the Polish standpoint that these assets should devolve to the state of the deceased's nationality.[77] With full knowledge of the attitude of the Polish authorities toward private property, the Swiss government also assented to the almost certain loss of assets by any heirs still alive.[78]

Ultimately, it took almost two decades and repeated lobbying and interventions by international Jewish organizations, the small Swiss Jewish community, and the Israeli government for the Swiss authorities to live up to the promise they made in 1946.[79] Before this could happen Switzerland had to experience its own crises of memory politics in the 1950s. Together with international shifts in Holocaust awareness, and prompted by a new wave of criminal prosecutions culminating in the Eichmann trial, Swiss attitudes toward restitution softened and sensitivity toward unresolved Nazi legacies grew.[80] For example, redress for Swiss victims of Nazism whose claims had been sacrificed to the resolution of economic and financial problems acquired a sudden urgency. Rumors about wartime failures in the diplomatic protection of endangered Swiss citizens began to multiply. Stories about Swiss Jews who had been killed in Auschwitz because of a lack of diplomatic protection threatened to unleash another scandal. After putting off victims' petitions for years by referring to a future settlement with Germany, a nervous Swiss government suddenly rushed a compensation bill through parliament in 1957. But primarily a measure of damage control, the new bill on victim reparations did not imply official recognition of wartime failures in diplomatic or refugee policy, but instead constituted a further effort at exorcising their memory.[81]

That the Swiss authorities finally prepared special legislation to tackle the dormant accounts problem must be ascribed to this context of increased official nervousness. A bill on the registration of heirless assets passed parliament in 1962, requiring financial institutions to identify and register heirless assets with a special agency. But official control remained weak and the banks were not required to search for surviving account holders or their heirs. In recent years researchers have unearthed numerous anecdotes of survivors who faced continuing callousness, arrogance, or just plain indifference when looking for their assets in Swiss banks. To prevent double payment banks erected administrative hurdles and required documentation that was impossible for survivors to produce if their personal papers had been lost during the Holocaust. A frequently cited anecdote of one claimant who was asked by a bank official for the previous account holder's death certificate from Auschwitz symbolized the lack of comprehension, or even the cynicism that was common in the responses of many banks to victims' requests.[82] These became the stories that would grab international attention and arouse public outrage in the 1990s. By then, however, the money had gradually trickled away through the many cracks offered by the system of self-regulation and the loopholes in reparations legislation that in any case came much too late. As the Volcker Committee stated in 1999, the near absence of any legal obligations has given rise to malpractice on the part of individual banks, including the "withholding of information from Holocaust victims or their heirs about their accounts, improper closing of accounts, failure to keep adequate records ... and a general lack of diligence—even active resistance—in response to earlier private and official enquiries into dormant accounts."[83] Beyond doubt, the political climate in Switzerland, supported by official and popular representations of history that denied wartime cooperation with Nazi Germany and instead cultivated a resistance myth of its own kind, also created a hostile environment for the recognition of victims' claims.

The Price of Failed Restitution

Legislation on heirless assets was a typical example of a solution to a problem itself becoming the problem.[84] Complaints did not cease, but for the rest of the Cold War era they failed to become a danger for the Swiss financial market. This dramatically changed when the fall of communism released the ghosts of the past. Contentious property rights have since become a catalyst for tackling the legacies of gross human rights violations, as Gerald D. Feldman argues in this volume, and prompted in Europe another round of grappling with the Nazi-era past as well as the Cold War period.[85] Accordingly, the failure to reverse or redress expropriation is being seen in a more comprehensive sense as an attack on human dignity and civil rights.

Against this backdrop, the issue of heirless assets resurfaced in the mid-1990s. With the unscrambling of complicated property relations in former communist countries, the day had finally come for victims' organizations to reiterate their complaints about unresolved Holocaust restitution issues in other parts of Europe. In the early 1990s, allegations that Switzerland had benefited from the Holocaust reemerged. Soon the first reports about the survivors' frustrated search for accounts in Swiss banks appeared in the Israeli, Swiss, and American press.[86] In well-orchestrated media campaigns, lawyers and organizations speaking for the victims, most prominently the World Jewish Congress, seized the opportunity to target Swiss banks. They quickly found resonance with a wider public that was increasingly sensitized about the consequences of the Holocaust and responsive to human rights issues. In the mid-1990s this growing sympathy with the victims, particularly among the American public, coincided with the desire of Switzerland's banking industry to expand its presence in America's booming market, creating a unique window of opportunity for the survivors.[87]

The latter filed a number of class action suits against major banks and insurance companies that took European corporations by surprise as they were still unfamiliar with this legal instrument, in particular when applied to human rights issues. Support from American officials provided survivors with additional leverage.[88]

As of early 1996 disclosures about Switzerland's wartime history and postwar neglect, were making international headlines on an almost daily basis, precipitating a crisis. In the grip of a "retro shock," the Swiss public suddenly faced the pure caricature of previously received representations, with the worst accusations charging the neutral with benefiting from other people's misery in the most unconscionable way.[89] Entrenched Swiss reactions sought refuge in the so-called predicament thesis ("what else could we have done?") to justify wartime behavior, but in so doing they just worsened the situation. At first, official crisis management completely failed. The authorities piled mistake upon mistake and further fueled international outrage.

At the same time, however, the Swiss banks were already in the middle of negotiations with the victims' representatives. In 1996 major Jewish organizations struck an agreement with the Swiss Bankers Association that was deemed a "memorandum of understanding." This settlement provided for an independent investigation into the question of dormant accounts under the auspices of the so-called Volcker Committee (Independent Committee of Eminent Persons under the chairmanship of Paul Volcker). It temporarily lifted banking secrecy to permit the auditing of more than 4 million bank accounts dating back to the Nazi era. The Volcker Committee found some fifty thousand accounts with possible ties to victims of Nazi persecution. On its recommendation, the banks subsequently published these names and paid restitution to individuals who could identify themselves as holders or heirs of these accounts. In 1998, the Swiss banks also concluded a settlement with the plaintiffs of the class action suits in the United States. This resulted in the banks' paying $1.25 billion in exchange for a total release from all future claims arising from the Nazi era. This settlement enabled the banks to continue their business operations in the American market, while for the victims it opened a long and thorny distribution process. In the end the settlement was a makeshift solution to a problem that could no longer be solved with absolute precision due to the length of time that had elapsed since the events. With most claimants no longer alive, documents lost, and assets devalued, the compensation payments could not achieve even an approximation of justice, and left many with a bitter aftertaste. They nevertheless conveyed an important symbolic message that multinational corporations doing business with human rights violators could no longer count on avoiding public accountability.

In hindsight, and considering the economic interests involved, however, this resolution helped reduce the restitution crisis to a minor issue for the banks. The settlement became their entry ticket to the American market and its many lucrative business opportunities. In many respects, the outcome reproduced the situation as it existed in 1945–1946, with Switzerland buying its way out of diplomatic and economic isolation. However, there was one big difference: in the 1990s, the political authorities considered the banks' predicament a civil law matter and evaded direct involvement in negotiations. Nevertheless, they did not hesitate to refer to the settlement's release-clause as a legal basis for the rejection of state responsibility when confronted with the complaint of an Auschwitz survivor who had been handed over to the German police by the Swiss frontier police when seeking refuge in 1943.[90]

The dormant accounts crisis had a more sustained impact on Swiss society, contributing to the polarization of visions of the country's future orientation, with the conservative right capitalizing on feelings of hurt national pride. In one of its rare steps to contain the crisis, in 1996 the Swiss federal government commissioned an independent historical investigation of wartime relations with Nazi Germany and postwar restitution. Restitution claims, accompanying media campaigns, and government-sponsored research all eventually prompted heated debates about collective memory, representations of the past, and the role played by historians in public debate, which all only started to ebb after the turn of the twenty-first century.

From a transnational perspective, Switzerland's involvement with Nazi Germany and its (non)resolution of restitution and reparations issues was an expression of its unwillingness as well as its incapacity to face legal and political liabilities arising from such interdependency. Manifestations of this included, for instance, the conspicuous absence of the political authorities when business activity entailed specific moral and legal risks. The disinclination of the state to assume responsibility was reinforced by a specifically Swiss conception of liberalism that sheltered business from government intervention and endorsed self-regulation. Altogether this opened up a growing discrepancy between the extremely high degree of international interdependency and a myopic world vision lacking categories to assess the political implications of liabilities arising from economic integration. Frozen by the Cold War for almost half a century, this disparity was eventually broken open by the dormant accounts scandal of the mid-1990s, which suddenly revealed a growing desire for public accountability and scrutiny of business activity corresponding with the increasing opportunities offered by globalization, especially where sensitive human rights issues are involved and include the risk of diplomatic and political liabilities. Ultimately, the dormant accounts scandal with all its reverberations may have been more about the challenges of the future than the sins of the past.

Notes

1. Centre Historique des Archives Nationales (CHAN), AJ34, vol. 5: Agreement on Reparation from Germany, on the Establishment of an Interallied Reparation Agency and on the Restitution of Monetary Gold, Paris, 14 January 1946. See also Jörg Fisch, *Reparationen nach dem Zweiten Weltkrieg* (Munich, 1992).
2. On legal questions see Riccardo Pisillo-Mazzeschi, "International Obligations to Provide for Reparation Claims," in *State Responsibility and the Individual: Reparation in Instances of Grave Violations of Human Rights,* ed. A. Randelzhofer and C. Tomuschat (The Hague, 1999), 149–72.
3. For a survey of Allied wartime accusations, *U.S. and Allied Efforts to Recover and Restore Gold and Other Assets Stolen or Hidden by Germany during World War II* (Washington, DC, May 1997), 16–23.
4. See Hans Günther Hockerts, "Wiedergutmachung in Deutschland 1945–2000. Eine historische Bilanz," *Vierteljahrshefte für Zeitgeschichte* 49, no. 2 (2001): 167–214 and Constantin Goschler, *Schuld und Schulden. Die Politik der Wiedergutmachung für NS-Verfolgte* (Göttingen, 2005), 152–59.
5. After a period of "Schlussstrich" rhetoric in the 1960s, which resulted in the German "Schlussgesetz" of 1965 on victim reparation, the subject reemerged in the mid-1980s in the context of renewed grappling with the place of the Holocaust in German history. The ensuing campaign in favor of the "forgotten victims" objected to discriminatory and exclusionary tendencies still present in compensation practice. See Christian Pross, *Paying for the Past: The Struggle over Reparations for Surviving Victims of the Nazi Terror* (Baltimore, 1998), originally published as *Wiedergutmachung: der Kleinkrieg gegen die Opfer* (Frankfurt am Main, 1988). On this point, see also C. Goschler, *Schuld und Schulden*, 293–395.
6. Before wartime neutrality sparked international debate in the 1990s, it failed to attract scholarly attention as an issue of comparative historiography. For a rare exception see Louis-Eduard Roulet, ed., *Les états neutres européens et la Seconde Guerre Mondiale* (Neuchâtel, 1985). Recent comparative research is mostly limited to the period of the Second World War or diplomatic aspects of the postwar handling of Nazi era legacies. See Neville Wylie, ed., *European Neutrals and Non-Belligerents during the Second World War* (Cambrige, 2002); Irène Lindgren and Renate Walder, eds., *Schweden, die Schweiz und der Zweite Weltkrieg* (Frankfurt, 2001); and Christian Leitz, *Nazi Germany and Neutral Europe during the Second World War* (Manchester, 2000); on postwar issues: *U.S. and Allied Efforts*; and *U.S. and Allied Wartime and Postwar Relations and Negotiations with Argentina, Portugal, Spain, Sweden and Turkey on Looted Gold and German External Assets and U.S. Concerns about the Fate of the Wartime Ustasha Treasury* (Washington DC, 1998).
7. For a survey see the regularly updated list on the U.S. Holocaust Memorial Museum's Web site, http://www.ushmm.org/assets/.
8. The provocative title of this chapter is borrowed from Jonathan Steinberg's monograph, *Why Switzerland?* (Cambridge, 1976) on Switzerland's history, identity, and political structures.
9. Götz Aly, *Hitlers Volksstaat. Raub, Rassenkrieg und nationaler Sozialismus* (Frankfurt, 2005). Regardless of the controversy Aly's book has provoked, his work is one of the first attempts at integrating recent findings. The research of the late 1990s still awaits synthesis and comprehensive interpretation transcending national boundaries and the limited focus on highly specialized issues, which is characteristic for many studies on financial and business history published by the official Swiss and Austrian historical commissions.
10. Frank Bajohr, *"Aryanisation" in Hamburg: The Economic Exclusion of Jews and the Confiscation of Their Property in Nazi Germany* (New York, 2002); also the contributions in Constantin Goschler and Jürgen Lillteicher, eds., *"Arisierung" und Restitution. Die Rückerstattung jüdischen Eigentums in Deutschland und Österreich nach 1945 und*

1989 (Göttingen, 2002); and Antoine Prost et al., eds., *Aryanisation économique et restitutions. Mission d'étude sur la spoliation des Juifs de France* (Paris, 2000).

11. Hans-Ulrich Jost, *Politik und Wirtschaft im Krieg. Die Schweiz 1938–1948* (Zurich, 1998), 99–115.
12. The so-called London Declaration of January 1943 (Inter-Allied Declaration against Acts of Dispossession Committed in Territories under Enemy Occupation or Control, *Foreign Relations of the United States (FRUS)*, 1943, I, 444) warned that the Allies would consider all property transactions in territories under enemy control null and void by the end of hostilities. A second warning of February 1944 targeted gold transactions carried out by neutrals. At the Bretton Woods Conference, the United Nations repeated these warnings and announced that accepting and concealing looted property would not go unpunished. See *U.S. and Allied Efforts*, 5–20.
13. Sébastien Guex, "The Origins of the Swiss Banking Secrecy Law and its Repercussions for Swiss Federal Policy," *Business History Review* 74, no. 2, (2000): 237–66; Peter Hug, "Steuerflucht und Legende vom antinazistischen Ursprung des Bankgeheimnisses. Funktion und Risiko der moralischen Überhöhung des Finanzplatzes Schweiz," in Jakob Tanner and Sigrid Weigel, eds., *Gedächtnis, Geld und Gesetz. Vom Umgang mit der Vergangenheit des Zweiten Weltkriegs* (Zurich, 2001), 269-321. On the significance of the Swiss financial market see Marc Perrenoud et al., eds., *La place financière et les banques suisses à l'époque du national-socialisme: Les relations des grandes banques avec l'Allemagne 1931-1946*, ed. Independent Commission of Experts: Switzerland—Second World War (ICE) (Zurich, 2002), 31–152.
14. Apart from saving accounts and deposits, life insurance policies in freely convertible and stable currencies, often called the poor man's Swiss bank account, were assets of some importance for Central and Eastern European Jews. The Swiss insurance industry, earning two thirds of its income abroad, was strongly involved in Central European business. Stefan Karlen et al., *Expansion, Konfiskation, Nachrichtenlosigkeit. Schweizerische Versicherungsgesellschaften im Machtbereich des "Dritten Reichs,"* ed. ICE (Zurich, 2002).
15. Barbara Bonhage et al., *Nachrichtenlose Vermögen bei Schweizer Banken. Depots, Konten und Safes von Opfern des nationalsozialistischen Regimes und Restitutionsprobleme in der Nachkriegszeit*, ed. ICE (Zurich, 2001), 49–63.
16. *FRUS*, 1945 (The Conferences at Yalta and Malta, Protocol of the Proceedings), 979. On postwar planning see James McAllister, *No Exit: America and the German Problem 1943-1954* (Ithaca NY, 2002), 26–73; focusing on Switzerland, see Christiane Uhlig et al., *Tarnung, Transfer, Transit. Die Schweiz als Drehscheibe verdeckter deutscher Operationen (1938–1952)* ed. ICE (Zurich, 2002).
17. See, for instance, the conclusion that Swiss refugee policy had helped the Nazi regime achieve its genocidal goals by denying asylum to Jewish, Sinti, and Roma refugees, in ICE, ed., *Switzerland and Refugees in the Nazi Era* (Bern, 1999), 271. This has provoked much debate, with national-conservatives and many elderly citizens accusing the historians of moralizing and lecturing to the public. Critically on the historians' new role see Henry Rousso, *The Haunting Past: History, Memory, and Justice in Contemporary France* (Philadelphia, 2002).
18. Regula Ludi, "Waging War on Wartime Memory: Recent Swiss Debates on the Legacies of the Holocaust and the Nazi Era," *Jewish Social Studies* 10, no. 2 (Winter 2004): 116–52.
19. Important inspiration came from research by Gaston Haas, "*Wenn man gewusst hätte, was sich drüben im Reich abspielte...*" *1941–1943: Was man in der Schweiz von der Judenvernichtung wusste* (Basel, 1994), Jacques Picard, *Die Schweiz und die Juden 1933–1945* (Zurich, 1994) and Jean-Claude Favez, *The Red Cross and the Holocaust* (Cambridge, 1999).
20. Jacques Picard, "Switzerland as a 'Bystander' of History: On Neutrality in a Time of Global Crises and Genocidal Wars" in *Remembering for the Future: The Holocaust in an Age of Genocide*, vol. 1, ed. John K. Roth and Elisabeth Maxwell (London, 2001), 71–89.

Raul Hilberg, *Perpetrators Victims Bystanders: The Jewish Catastrophe 1933–1945* (New York, 1992).

21. See for example Markus Heiniger, *Dreizehn Gründe. Warum die Schweiz im Zweiten Weltkrieg nicht erobert wurde* (Zurich, 1989), who challenged the prevailing thesis that military preparedness had deterred a German invasion. Instead, Heiniger argued that Switzerland was saved because of its various economic services and the authorities' avoidance of political confrontations with Nazi Germany, for instance through press censorship.
22. As a direct response to these charges, in 1996 the federal government appointed the ICE to conduct research on Switzerland in the Nazi era; see the ICE's Web site at: www.uek.ch/en/index.htm and the detailed survey by Thomas Maissen, *Verweigerte Erinnerung. Nachrichtenlose Vermögen und die Schweizer Weltkriegsdebatte 1989–2004* (Zurich, 2005).
23. Uhlig et al., *Tarnung*, 35 and following.
24. See Michael Bernegger, "Die Schweiz und die Weltwirtschaft. Etappen der Integration im 19. und 20. Jahrhundert," in Paul Bairoch and Martin Körner, eds., *Die Schweiz in der Weltwirtschaft (15.–20. Jahrhundert)* (Zurich, 1990), 429–64; Martin Meier et al., *Schweizerische Aussenwirtschaftspolitik 1930–1948. Strukturen – Verhandlungen – Funktionen*, ed. ICE (Zurich, 2001).
25. Meier, *Aussenwirtschaftspolitik*, 124.
26. See Jakob Tanner, "'Réduit national' und Aussenwirtschaft. Wechselwirkungen zwischen militärischer Dissuasion und ökonomischer Kooperation mit den Achsenmärkten," in Philipp Sarasin et. al., eds., *Raubgold, Réduit, Flüchtlinge. Zur Geschichte der Schweiz im Zweiten Weltkrieg* (Zurich, 1998), 99. *Courant normal* is a category of neutrality law and signifies that wartime exports to belligerents should not exceed prewar figures. See also Jost, *Politik*, 101–2; for import and export figures see Meier, *Aussenwirtschaftspolitik*, 65 and following.
27. Bilateral clearing agreements were part of the protectionist measures introduced by many countries in response to the Great Depression and subsequent currency shortages. Clearing credits served the Nazi regime as a seemingly legal instrument to exploit occupied territories as well as suspend immediate payment for supplies from neutrals. On the German-Swiss clearing system, see Stefan Frech, *Clearing. Der Zahlungsverkehr der Schweiz mit den Achsenmächten*, ed. ICE (Zurich, 2001); Peter Hug and Martin Kloter, eds., *Aufstieg und Niedergang des Bilateralismus. Schweizerische Aussen- und Aussenwirtschaftspolitik 1930–1960: Rahmenbedingungen, Entscheidungsstrukturen, Fallstudien* (Zurich, 1999). For the use of Swiss clearing credits to finance weaponry exports to Germany, see Peter Hug, *Schweizerische Rüstungsindustrie und Kriegsmaterialhandel zur Zeit des Nationalsozialismus. Unternehmensstratgeien – Marktentwicklung – politische Überwachung*, ed. ICE (Zurich, 2001), 615–16.
28. Weaponry of Swiss origin constituted just 1 percent of German production output. However, a much higher degree of German dependency on Swiss manufacturing is evident for some high-tech products in the machinery sector and watch industry, where Swiss products often excelled through their high quality and reliability. For a survey see *Switzerland, National Socialism and the Second World War. Final Report*, ed. ICE (Zurich, 2002), 200–19; Hug, *Schweizerische Rüstungsindustrie*.
29. Alternative routes through Austria were vulnerable to Allied bombing. No evidence could be found that deportation trains or slave laborer transports from Italy went through Swiss territory, as media reports in the late 1990s repeatedly claimed. ICE, *Final Report*, 220–24 (electricity market), 225–37 (railway services).
30. See Heiniger, *Dreizehn Gründe*; Tanner, "'Réduit national.'"
31. ICE, *Final Report*, 238–54. All values given in Swiss francs are based on the calculations made by the ICE. For more detailed statistics see the interim report: ICE, ed., *Switzerland and Gold Transactions in the Second World War* (Bern, 1998) http://www.uek.ch/en/index.htm, updated print version: *Die Schweiz und Goldtransaktionen im Zweiten Weltkrieg* (Zurich, 2001). See also Aly, *Hitlers Volksstaat*, 223–26. Based on a statement

by Auschwitz commander Rudolf Höss, rumors about victim gold from concentration camps ending up in Switzerland began to circulate in 1947, but they were firmly denied by the Swiss authorities. Jost, *Politik*, 216.

32. ICE, *Final Report*, 238 and ICE, *Gold Transactions*.
33. The gold transfers to the SNB from Germany and Italy added up to 1.38 billion Swiss francs; this equaled $320 million (U.S.) based on the then official currency exchange rate of $1 to Sfr 4.3.
34. ICE, *Final Report*, 239–40. One of the first to expose these complex transactions was Werner Rings, *Raubgold aus Deutschland: Die "Golddrehscheibe" Schweiz im Zweiten Weltkrieg* (Zurich, 1985). See also the pioneer study by Daniel Bourgeois, *Le Troisième Reich et la Suisse, 1933–1941* (Neuchâtel, 1974). On the transactions between Germany, Romania and Switzerland, see Aly, *Hitlers Volkststaat*, 271.
35. ICE, *Final Report*, 247–48.
36. Hanspeter Kriesi, *Le système politique Suisse* (Paris, 1998), 264 and following.
37. Lukas Straumann and Daniel Wildmann, *Schweizer Chemieunternehmen im "Dritten Reich"* ed. ICE (Zurich, 2001), 62–87, 196–202, 268 and following; Christian Ruch et al., *Geschäfte und Zwangsarbeit: Schweizer Industrieunternehmen im "Dritten Reich,"* ed. ICE (Zurich, 2001), 217–30.
38. Saul Friedländer, *Nazi Germany and the Jews, vol 1: The Years of Persecution 1933–1939* (New York, 1997). From the mid-1930s, most countries denied refugees work permits. See ICE, *Refugees*, 164–67; Vicki Caron, *Uneasy Asylum: France and the Jewish Refugee Crisis, 1933–1942* (Stanford CA, 1999); Frank Caestecker and Bob Moore, "Refugee Policies in Western European States in the 1930s. A Comparative Analysis," *IMIS-Beiträge* 7 (1998), 55–103.
39. Thomas Buomberger, *Raubkunst – Kunstraub: die Schweiz und der Handel mit gestohlenen Kulturgütern zur Zeit des Zweiten Weltkriegs* (Zurich, 1998). A large portion of the seventy-five artworks claimed by previous owners between 1946 and 1947 had been acquired by the art gallery owner Theodor Fischer and the arms manufacturer Emil G. Bührle. ICE, *Final Report*, 474–75.
40. Legislation served primarily the protection of domestic art production. Esther Tisa Francini et al., *Fluchtgut – Raubgut. Der Transfer von Kulturgütern in und über die Schweiz 1933–1945 und die Frage der Restitution*, ed. ICE (Zurich, 2001), 67–72.
41. Hanspeter Lussy et al., *Schweizerische Wertpapiergeschäfte mit dem "Dritten Reich": Handel, Raub und Restitution*, ed. ICE (Zurich, 2001), 192–217. On Nazi looting in Western Europe: Richard James Overy, ed., *Die "Neuordnung" Europas. NS-Wirtschaftspolitik in den besetzten Gebieten* (Berlin, 1997).
42. ICE, *Final Report*, 269–70, 466. See also Frank Vischer, "Der Handel mit ausländischen Wertpapieren während des Krieges und die Probleme der deutschen Guthaben sowie der nachrichtenlosen Vermögen aus rechtlicher Sicht," in *Die Schweiz, der Nationalsozialismus und das Recht. II. Privatrecht*, ed. ICE (Zurich, 2001), 20–38.
43. Looted securities were subject to the restitution mechanism introduced by the Swiss Decree on Looted Assets of 1945. Of the official estimate of Sfr 50 to 100 million in securities that were possibly looted, less than Sfr 1 million had been returned by 1952. ICE, *Final Report*, 471–72.
44. Perrenoud, *Place financière*, 579. The charge of a "business as usual" attitude was raised by U.S. Undersecretary of State Stuart E. Eizenstat in 1997; see his preface in *U.S. and Allied Efforts*, vii. Similarly Tisa Francini, *Fluchtgut*, 362.
45. Uhlig, *Tarnung*, 217–49; ICE, *Final Report*, 506.
46. ICE, *Final Report*, 178–79.
47. See Vischer, "Handel," 20–21.
48. In the mid-1950s, when these issues resurfaced, he shifted the whole blame onto the senior official concerned, Heinrich Rothmund. Though notorious for his xenophobic stance, the latter had not been in a position to make these decisions alone. See "Stellungnahme des Herrn Bundesrats Eduard Steiger, Vorsteher des Eidgenössischen Justiz- und Polizeidepartements von 1941–1951 zum Bericht des Herrn Prof. Dr. Carl Ludwig," in Carl

Ludwig, *Die Flüchtlingspolitik der Schweiz in den Jahren 1933 bis 1955. Bericht an den Bundesrat zuhanden der eidgenössischen Räte* (Bern, 1957), 378–401. Also ICE, *Final Report*, 516.

49. Most explicitly: Tanner, "'Réduit national,'" and Jost, *Politik und Wirtschaft*, 96–98.
50. See Mario König, *Interhandel. Die schweizerische Holding der IG Farben und ihre Metamorphosen – eine Affäre um Eigentum und Interessen (1910–1999)*, ed. ICE (Zurich, 2001).
51. ICE, *Final Report*, 379 and following pages; Uhlig, *Tarnung*, 119–28.
52. ICE, *Final Report*, 385–87.
53. Walter Stucki, at an internal conference of March 1946, cited in ICE, *Final Report*, 96.
54. Matthias Kunz, *Aufbruchstimmung und Sonderfall-Rhetorik. Die Schweiz im Übergang von der Kriegs- zur Nachkriegszeit in der Wahrnehmung der Parteipresse, 1943–1950* (Bundesarchiv Dossier 8) (Bern, 1998); Luc van Dongen, *La Suisse face à la Seconde Guerre mondiale 1945–1948. Emergence et construction d'une mémoire publique* (Geneva, 1998); also Jost, *Politik*, 171–77 on political and public responses to Allied demands.
55. "Notice: Audience accordée par le Conseil Fédéral aux représentatives de l'Association suisse des Banquiers le mercredi 13 juin 1945," Documents Diplomatiques Suisses, www.dodis.ch/, DoDiS-38:
56. Cited after ICE, *Final Report*, 428.
57. Jost, *Politik*, 153–55.
58. In June 1941 the Roosevelt administration froze assets from most neutral countries in the United States. In anticipation of a German invasion, Swiss banks had transferred considerable sums to the United States before that date. See Marco Durrer, *Die schweizerisch-amerikanischen Finanzbeziehungen im Zweiten Weltkrieg: von der Blockierung der schweizerischen Guthaben in den USA über die "Safehaven"-Politik zum Washingtoner Abkommen (1941–1946)* (Bern, 1984).
59. See Karlen, *Expansion*, 399–438.
60. Kurt Siehr, "Rechtsfragen zum Handel mit geraubten Kulturgütern in den Jahren 1933–1950," in *Die Schweiz, der Nationalsozialismus und das Recht, II. Privatrecht*, ed. ICE (Zurich, 2001), 125–203.
61. On Swedish restitution efforts see Commission on Jewish Assets in Sweden at the Time of the Second World War, ed., *Sweden and Jewish Assets: Final Report* (Stockholm, 1999), 211 and following pages.
62. ICE, *Final Report*, 433–37; Tisa Francini, *Fluchtgut*, 349–414.
63. ICE, *Final Report*, 461–62.
64. See *U.S. and Allied Efforts*, 121–47.
65. Hans-Ulrich Jost, "Switzerland's Atlantic Perspectives," in *Swiss Neutrality and Security*, ed. P. Milivojevic and P. Maurer (Oxford, 1990), 110–21.
66. *Documents Diplomatiques Suisses*, www.dodis.ch/, DoDiS-1730.
67. Allied Control Council Law No. 5 provided the legal basis, relying on the Potsdam decisions in which the Soviets renounced their claim to German assets in neutral countries. See Fisch, *Reparationen.*
68. The introduction to the Washington Accord testifies to conflicting legal opinions. The Allies insisted on their legal claim to German assets in Switzerland while the Swiss denied this claim and merely expressed their desire to contribute to the reconstruction of Europe. *Documents Diplomatiques Suisses,* www.dodis.ch/ DoDiS-1725.
69. Kunz, *Aufbruchstimmung*, 82–87.
70. "Deutsche Vermögenswerte in der Schweiz und damit zusammenhängende Fragen. Verhandlungen mit den Alliierten, 8. März 1946," *Documents Diplomatiques Suisses*, www.dodis.ch/ DoDiS-68. Uhlig, *Tarnung*, 311–33.
71. Ilse Dorothee Pautsch, "Altschulden und Neubeginn. Die 'Clearingmilliarde' und die Aufnahme diplomatischer Beziehungen zwischen der Bundesrepublik Deutschland und der Schweiz," in Antoine Fleury, Horst Möller, and Hans-Peter Schwarz, eds., *Die Schweiz und Deutschland 1945–1961* (Munich, 2004), 17–30.

72. CHAN, AJ43, Organisation internationale pour les réfugiés, vol. 453 (Press Release No. 334 of the Preparatory Commission of the International Refugee Organization, 27 July 1948). The IRO documents often use the term "Nazi assets" when referring to frozen German assets in neutral countries, mirroring the divergence of their perception from that of neutral governments.
73. "Bericht über die in der Schweiz befindlichen erblosen Vermögen der Opfer politischer, religiöser und rassischer Verfolgung," *Documents Diplomatiques Suisses*, www.dodis.ch/DoDiS-6360.
74. Uhlig, *Tarnung*, 217 and following pages, 352–62.
75. ICE, *Final Report*, 442–49. For an in-depth analysis see Independent Committee of Eminent Persons (ICEP), ed., *Report on Dormant Accounts of Victims of Nazi Persecution in Swiss Banks* (Bern, 1999) and Bonhage, *Nachrichtenlose Vermögen.*
76. See Hug, *Steuerflucht*, 305 and following pages; for a very critical analysis of bank secrecy, see Jean Ziegler, *Die Schweiz wäscht weisser: die Finanzdrehscheibe des internationalen Verbrechens* (Munich, 1992).
77. Goschler, *Schuld*, 105–11.
78. See Hug, *Vermögenswerte*, 93–137. Bonhage, *Nachrichtenlose Vermögen*, 244–45.
79. On the lobbying of Jewish organizations and the Israeli government, see Peter Hug, "Unclaimed Assets of Nazi Victims in Switzerland," in Georg Kreis, ed., *Switzerland and the Second World War* (London, 2000), 81–102.
80. Y. Michal Bodemann, *In den Wogen der Erinnerung. Jüdische Existenz in Deutschland* (Munich, 2002), 62–84; Peter Reichel, *Vergangenheitsbewältigung in Deutschland. Die Auseinandersetzung mit der NS-Diktatur von 1945 bis heute* (Munich, 2001), 125–57.
81. On diplomatic protection of Swiss citizens in Nazi-controlled territories, see Frank Haldemann, "Der völkerrechtliche Schutz des Privateigentums im Kontext der NS-Konfiskationspolitik," in *Recht*, vol. 1, ed. ICE, 557–86, and Anton-Andreas Speck, *Der Fall Rothschild: NS-Judenpolitik, Opferschutz und "Wiedergutmachung" in der Schweiz 1942–1962* (Zurich, 2003). On victim reparations, Regula Ludi, "Die Parzellierung der Vergangenheit: Schweizer NS-Opfer und die Grenzen der Wiedergutmachung," *Studien und Quellen* 29, 101–28; Regula Ludi and Anton-Andreas Speck, "Swiss Victims of National Socialism: An Example of How Switzerland Came to Terms with the Past," in John K. Roth and Elisabeth Maxwell, eds., *Remembering for the Future: The Holocaust in an Age of Genocide* (London, 2001), vol. 2, 907–22.
82. Bonhage, *Nachrichtenlose Vermögen*, 278–313. For a reference to the death certificate anecdote see Michael J. Bazyler, *Holocaust Justice: The Battle for Restitution in America's Courts* (New York, 2003), 15.
83. ICEP, ed., *Report on Dormant Accounts*, 13; on the banks' dealing with the problem, see Bonhage, *Nachrichtenlose Vermögen*, 259–348.
84. Jacques Picard, "Über den Gebrauch der Geschichte: Die UEK im Kontext schweizerischer Vergangenheitspolitik," *Jüdische Lebenswelten in der Schweiz*, ed. Schweizerischer Israelitischer Gemeindebund (Zurich, 2004), 391.
85. See Gerald D. Feldman, "Reflections on the Restitution and Compensation of Holocaust Theft: Past, Present, and Future" in this volume.
86. See the popular publications by Itamar Levin, *The Last Deposit: Swiss Banks and Holocaust Survivors' Accounts* (Westport, 1999); Beat Balzli, *Treuhänder des Reichs. Die Schweiz und die Vermögen der Naziopfer. Eine Spurensuche* (Zurich, 1997); and Tom Bower, *Nazi Gold: The Story of the Fifty-Year Swiss Conspiracy to Steal Billions from Europe's Jews and Holocaust Survivors* (London, 1997).
87. Jeffrey C. Alexander, "On the Social Construction of Moral Universals. The 'Holocaust' from War Crime to Trauma Drama," *European Journal of Social Theory* 5, no. 1 (2002), 5–58; Daniel Levy and Natan Sznaider, *Erinnerung im globalen Zeitalter: Der Holocaust* (Frankfurt, 2001).
88. The restitution campaigns against Swiss corporations became the model for similar cases to follow; see Bazyler, *Holocaust Litigation*. Also John Authers and Richard Wolffe, *The Victim's Fortune. Inside the Epic Battle over the Debts of the Holocaust* (New York,

2002), and Stuart E. Eizenstat, *Imperfect Justice: Looted Assets, Slave Labor, and the Unfinished Business of World War II* (New York, 2003); from the Swiss perspective, Maissen, *Verweigerte Erinnerung.*

89. Jakob Tanner, "Geschichtswissenschaft und moralische Ökonomie der Restitution: Die Schweiz im internationalen Kontext," *Zeitgeschichte* 30, no. 5 (September/October 2003), 275.

90. Stefan Keller, *Die Rückkehr. Joseph Springs Geschichte* (Zurich, 2003).

THE HUNGARIAN GOLD TRAIN

Fantasies of Wealth and the Madness of Genocide

Ronald W. Zweig

The relationship between the Third Reich and Hungary was always ambivalent. The revisionist goals of Hungarian foreign policy after the Trianon Treaty of 1920, which Hungary perceived as a humiliation of its sovereignty just as Germany understood Versailles, led to an alliance with Nazi Germany and Italy, two countries that supported Hungarian interests. Hungarian foreign policy was successful, for in the First and Second Vienna Awards of 1938 and 1940 Hungary got back some of the territories it had claimed since Trianon. In return the Hungarians took part in the occupation of Yugoslavia by the German Wehrmacht and declared war on the Soviet Union. But when the tide of war began to turn against Germany in 1943, Hungary edged away from its close alliance with the Third Reich. Using secret diplomatic channels, Hungary sought a separate peace with the Western Allies—a plan that was due to fail, as Hungary did not want to give up the newly gained territories. During that period Hungary showed itself rhetorically compliant towards the Germans while at the same time pursuing delaying tactics. This was especially true for the support of the Germans by Hungarian soldiers in the war against the Soviet Union and also regarding the policy towards the Jews in Hungary.

Antisemitic laws were passed in 1938 and 1939 during the tenure of minister president Imredy and they led to the economic persecution of the Jews and the isolation of Jewish communities. These laws were designed to reduce drastically the prominent role of Jews in the Hungarian economy, and to exclude them from certain spheres of economic activity altogether. The result was the impoverishment of large sections of the Jewish community, but the laws were not as harsh as the legislation that followed in 1944.[1] Hungarian Jews were spared the worst aspects of antisemitic violence for most of the war. And when new anti-Jewish legislation was introduced in 1942, it was justified by Prime Minister Miklós Kállay as part of a tacit deal: "In view of the privileged position of Jews in Hungarian economic life, such

Notes for this section begin on page 220.

measures could assume the character of economic adjustments and could be regarded by the fair-minded section of Hungarian Jewry as their contribution to the national war effort."[2] Kállay was suggesting that the Jews sacrifice their property in exchange for their physical survival, and the arrangement worked. By early 1944, Hungarian Jewry, although increasingly impoverished, was the largest surviving Jewish community remaining in Europe.

The situation for the Third Reich in the war with the Soviet Union was getting more and more difficult. Accordingly the Nazis became quite impatient with their passive allies. As a consequence they began to put pressure on Hungary. The situation of the Hungarian government changed radically in March 1944, when German forces effectively occupied Hungary and imposed a new government more willing to support the Third Reich's goals. The new government of Döme Sztójay was cobbled together from various right wing factions under the direct supervision of Hitler's plenipotentiary, Edmund Veesenmayer.[3] It was both pro-German and violently antisemitic. Almost immediately after it came to power, radical new laws were introduced, compelling Jews to surrender their assets and any valuable personal possessions. This time there was no implied suggestion that by giving up their property the Jews would be guaranteed survival. The regulations, laws, and announcements requiring Jews to surrender their personal property were, as we now know, the prelude to the deportations to Auschwitz.[4]

The confiscation of Jewish property had been an integral part of Hungarian radical right-wing political demands for at least a decade.[5] Hungarian antisemites believed that seizure of physical property was the key to the transfer of economic well-being and prosperity from the Jewish community to the broader Hungarian community. The newly appointed (by the Sztójay government) district governor of the important Székesfehérvár region, Arpad Toldi, articulated the attitude of the new regime in his inaugural speech:

> All of those economic resources that the Jewish plutocracy because of its power has so far used for the nourishment of its racial and power interests will from now on profit, strengthen, and enrich Hungarian life and Hungarian businesses only. The essence of it all: creating a national socialist community of people forming a solid union with the total exclusion of Jews; uniting all moral, financial and mental powers for the war and for work; making social justice prevail; keeping discipline and order.[6]

This policy was implemented with great harshness and rapidity. By the time the deportations to Auschwitz began, in mid-May 1944, Jews across Hungary had been forced to hand over all valuable possessions and savings. Before they were crammed into the deportation trains for slave labor or the gas chambers, Hungarian police brutally searched and interrogated them, looking for hidden loot.[7]

By 8 July 1944, when the deportations were suspended, over half of Hungarian Jewry had been murdered. And throughout the country government warehouses were bulging with Jewish household effects, while government banks held the confiscated jewelry and other valuables taken from 800,000 people. A process of expropriation and asset stripping that had taken years in other parts of Nazi-occupied Europe had been compressed into a few months in Hungary. The process of sorting the items and separating out the most valuable of the loot had only begun when the German army intervened once again and imposed an even more radically right-wing government, in mid-October 1944.

One of the first acts of the new government of Ferenc Szálasi was to hand over to the German Reich the entire economic infrastructure of Hungary. Immediately after coming to power on 16 October, the new government began to implement a scorched earth policy in the territories that were about to fall under Soviet control. Food supplies and agricultural equipment, industrial stock and machinery, hospitals, cars, and even horses—anything that could be moved—were loaded onto Danubian barges or fifty-wagon freight trains and taken across the western border of Hungary into Austria and Germany. The intention was to deprive the advancing Russians while at the same time strengthening the Third Reich in its last stand. From October 1944 until the first week of April 1945, when the Russians completed the occupation of all of Hungary, between three to eight 100-axle trains crossed the border daily. During these six months, Hungary, by its own decision, gave away most of its economic resources.[8]

However, the fate of Jewish assets was different, and ultimately more dramatic. Arpad Toldi, who had articulated the policy of the previous Sztojáy government concerning the expropriation of Jewish property, was now, under Szálasi, appointed the Commissioner for Jewish Affairs. For the next six months, Toldi had all the Jewish valuables concentrated in a few processing centers in western Hungary. Between October 1944 and the end of March 1945, officials of the Jewish property office and other Hungarian government departments sorted the loot into different types of goods. From gold and diamonds to the cheapest fake costume jewelry, typewriters, cameras, tableware, ritual religious silverware, stamp collections, fur coats, Persian carpets, binoculars—everything was collected. The quantities were huge.[9]

At the end of March, as the Red Army approached within 20 kilometers of Hungary's western border and days before it occupied all the country, the expropriated property was loaded onboard a train and taken to Austria. This was the "Gold Train," about which so many myths have evolved. The Gold Train has become a metaphor for the despoiling of Hungarian Jewry, and its trip a symbol of the way in which the material possessions of a thriving community were taken, while the members of that community were forced onto other trains with the destination of Auschwitz.

The train left the border mining town of Brennbergbánya on the night of 30 March 1945. It travelled across Austria, eventually finding refuge in the small town of Hopfgarten, in the mountainous region southwest of Salzburg. At the beginning of May it moved to Böckstein, and was seized by the American forces on 15 May, one week after the end of the war in Europe. Rumors of the fabulous wealth of the train circulated constantly, and grew in the course of time. If the train really did carry the transportable valuable possessions of the 800,000 Jews of Hungary, then it would certainly be an important prize of war. Early postwar Hungarian press reports on the train, like the reports in the *New York Times*, estimated the train's value at an astronomic sum.[10] The postwar Hungarian government endorsed the figure of $350 million (U.S.) in 1945 values (over $4 billion today), and this became the most widely accepted estimate of the worth of the train.[11]

In July 1945 the contents of the train were transferred to an American military warehouse in Salzburg, but a thorough inventory was not begun until the summer of 1947, a full two years later. At that point it very quickly became apparent that the Gold Train was a misnomer. There was very little gold or jewelry amongst the train's cargo. But there was a huge amount of silver tableware and religious items, plus carpets, furs, stamp collections, cameras, watches, wedding rings, and other expensive items.[12] When the saleable items were finally sold at auction and the unmarketable silverware melted into bullion, the final sum realized was just under $2,000,000.[13]

Then, in 1947, and in the years since, the discrepancy between the fabled wealth of the Gold Train and the reality of what was in the U.S. Army warehouse in Salzburg was explained by the alleged theft of the most valuable items by American military personnel. The accusation was made first by the Hungarian communist government in 1948;[14] it was endorsed by the Hungarian Jewish refugee circles in Austria and elsewhere;[15] and it reappeared in press accounts of the unresolved mystery of the Gold Train every few years.[16] It was most recently on the front pages of the New York Times and Washington Post in October 1999, resulting subsequently in a lawsuit in the American courts. But these accusations are grossly exaggerated.[17] As this chapter will argue, the disappearance of the victim loot taken from Hungarian Jewry was mainly due to entirely different factors. Not only was the fabulous wealth on board the Gold Train a myth, but also the basic concept of the transferability of wealth and prosperity in the process of ethnic cleansing is also a myth.

While the expropriated Jewish property was being processed at Brennbergbánya (and other sites close to the Hungarian-Austrian border), part of the work done was to separate out the most valuable and marketable of the items. These were stored separately from the bulk of the goods and packed into specially made crates for future transportation. While the processing (sorting, inventory, and destruction of all evidence of the provenance of the goods) was a time-consuming task on which many Hungarian civil servants (customs officials, tax officers, and employees of the Ministry of Finance) were engaged, care of the most valuable items was restricted to a very small cadre of officials associated with Colonel Arpad Toldi. Toldi was personally present at Brennbergbánya during the months from December 1944 to March 1945, when the Jewish property was being processed, and he personally supervised the work and examined the especially valuable items as they were discovered amongst the mass of everyday pieces of jewelry. It was Toldi who organized the loading of the train, obtained the travel clearances from the German authorities, and got them to honor the fact that the contents of the train were Hungarian state property. But while the bulk items were being loaded onboard the train, Toldi quietly organized a separate convoy of two lorries and a number of passenger cars, and he had the crates of gold, diamonds, and most valuable jewelry loaded onto the lorries. He gave detailed instructions to the Hungarian officials on the train as to their ultimate destination in Austria. But before the train was ready to depart, Toldi, his family, and immediate entourage disappeared with the lorries containing over two tons of the most valuable items. While the train was sent to Hallein, Toldi took the truck convoy directly towards Switzerland.[18]

The rapidly changing political and military situation in Europe in the last weeks of the war, together with an unexpected late snowfall at the Vorarlberg Pass, prevented Toldi from successfully escaping with the real treasure. The goods never made it to Switzerland. Instead, he and his associates buried over forty crates of gold and jewelry at various spots throughout the Tyrol and the Vorarlberg area. Other parts of the treasure were paid as bribes to various Nazi officials whose help Toldi required. Although many important details of the history of the Gold Train are left out here,[19] one thing, however, is clear: the most valuable possessions of the wealthiest members of the Hungarian Jewish community were not on the Gold Train, and were never in American hands.

After the war, France cultivated its commercial and political relations with the postwar Hungarian government independently of Anglo-American allied policies. As France was not a member of the Allied Control Commission in Hungary, Paris considered that it was free to pursue its own interests without being burdened by the broader Cold War concerns of the Americans and British in relations with Hungary.[20] In April 1948, France and Hungary concluded a detailed bilateral agreement which resolved various issues arising from the war. In addition to protecting the commercial interests of French firms operating in Hungary (i.e., protecting them from nationalization by the Communist government), Hungary agreed to return to France over three thousand freight wagons belonging to the French railway system that had been marooned in Hungary at the end of the war. In the circumstances of postwar shortages and economic demands, these freight wagons were assets of very great value. In exchange, France agreed to return the Hungarian Jewish victim loot it had uncovered in the French zones of occupation in the Vorarlberg and Tyrolean areas of Austria. On 24 April 1948 France returned over 1,750 kg of gold, diamonds, and jewelry to the authorities in Budapest. Although the French negotiators stipulated that the Jewish victims' loot be returned to the surviving Hungarian Jewish community, the Hungarian government did not honor this commitment. Only a handful of items were ever returned to the Jews. The rest was retained by the Hungarian government. The surviving Jews (as many as 120,000 in 1948) had the distinction of being the only community to have been robbed twice by their own government—once by the Fascist governments of Sztójay and Szálasi, and once again by the communist government of Mátyás Rákosi.

The unresolved story of the Gold Train continued to attract headlines. From 1964 to 1967 the Hungarian government entered into negotiations with the United States for a settlement of all outstanding claims resulting from the war, the nationalization of American assets by the postwar communist government, and Soviet action forcing a United States Air Force cargo plane down over Hungarian territory in 1951. The total American claim against Hungary was $130 million. The Hungarian government could make only one counterclaim against the United States—for the missing Jewish loot from the Gold Train. The facts of each of these claims were discussed in the course of twenty-five bilateral meetings of junior diplomats in the course of two years. This was one whole generation after the events, and the negotiators tried hard to reconstruct the details from the documents available to them.[21] But neither side was very familiar with the facts, and the archives of the State Department and the Hungarian Foreign Ministry could not provide enough information to illuminate what had really happened. The negotiations reached a dead end in 1967, and both governments decided to allow bilateral relations to develop without reaching a final claims settlement.[22]

Arguments over the fate of the Gold Train assets divided the Jewish community in Budapest in the immediate postwar years. The community was never fully informed of the 1,750 kg of victim loot that had been discovered in the French zone of occupation in Austria, and all of their attention was focused on the contents of the Gold Train, which was in American hands. The potential restitution of this property to Hungary compelled the community to confront directly the options available to it following the destruction caused by the Holocaust and the ruin of 150 years of Magyar-Jewish symbiosis. At an individual level, as in most other countries that had been freed from Nazi or Fascist rule, many Jews decided to speed the process of assimilation and to lose their communal identity. For those who wished to retain their Jewish identity, the options were either to rebuild or to emigrate. The community was split between many shades of opinion, with the deepest lines of division expressing themselves in the conflict between the Zionists and non-Zionists.[23]

As Hungary was moving quickly into the Soviet orbit in the immediate postwar years, the United States soon decided that it would not restitute recovered victim assets to that country, but would instead channel to the leading Jewish organizations that worked in refugee rehabilitation the money raised when the assets were sold off. These were the Jewish Agency for Palestine and the American Jewish Joint Distribution Committee. When the American authorities announced that, unlike the French, they would not restitute the goods to Hungary but would give them to the Agency and the Joint instead, the non-Zionist circles in the Jewish community in Budapest openly accused the Jewish Agency (i.e., the Zionists) of taking control of the last remnants of the looted assets of the pre-war community.[24] Although the

Agency and the Joint had both spent much larger sums (circa $50 million) in their subventions to Hungarian Jewry in the postwar years[25] than they had received from the sale of the Gold Train assets (circa $2 million), until they were each expelled from Hungary by the communist government in 1949, the Hungarian Jews' sense of injustice was not appeased. (The Joint in America was able to send financial support to the community in Budapest until January 1953.) Resentment at the paternalistic attitude of the international organizations then, and now, remains a live issue in contemporary Hungarian Jewish affairs.[26]

The Gold Train has come to personify the vanished wealth of a community that suffered terrible destruction during the war. The facts of the Hungarian Holocaust are well known and are not in dispute here. The same holds for the question of the economic standing of the different Jewish communities that came under the control of the government in Budapest by 1944, when the direct expropriation of Jewish property began in earnest. Other historians have examined this issue at length, and have reached the conclusion that there were rich Jews and poor Jews (that is, there were significant inequalities within the community), and that the economic standing of the Jews in Eastern and south-eastern Europe was closely correlated to their degree of urbanization and education.[27] The Jewish elite in Hungary did play a prominent role in that country's commerce, finance, and industry. Its members were also highly assimilated and many of them totally divorced from the Jewish community by more than one generation. And except for the non-Magyar (Yiddish)-speaking Jewish population that was annexed to Hungary during the war, even the Hungarian Jews that did not convert to Christianity nevertheless saw themselves as entirely Hungarian in their national identity. In this situation, the boundaries between "Jewish" and "non-Jewish" wealth are not very meaningful.

What is far more important are the *fantasies* about Jewish wealth in Hungarian antisemitic circles. The anti-Jewish policies of the Sztójay and Szálasi governments were designed to place the Jews outside the national community while seizing their possessions and "returning" their wealth to the "Hungarian nation." Toldi openly articulated this platform when he was inaugurated as Foispan of Székesfehérvár in May 1944. But fantasies of Jewish wealth confused two separate issues—the material possessions of the Jews, which could be seized and redistributed, and their prosperity and economic well-being, which was based on intangibles such as education, expectations, motivation, professional standing, and experience as much as it was based on the ownership of capital. These are cultural attributes that cannot be seized and redistributed. They can only be destroyed, together with the society that created them and gave them meaning. Whatever *prosperity* was enjoyed by the Jews in Hungary could not have found its way to the Gold Train.

This approach to the "fantasy of wealth" addresses the problem of the vanished prosperity of Hungarian Jewry. But it does not answer the simpler question of where all the diamonds and gold disappeared to. Why was the overall value of the material possessions retrieved after the war so low? The sensationalist accounts of the Gold Train start with the assumption that the looted valuables of 800,000 Hungarian Jews were the cargo of the Gold Train, and since so little was eventually restituted, then it must have been stolen by the Allied armies in Austria, just as it had been expropriated one year earlier by the Fascist governments in Hungary.

But there are many other explanations for the missing wealth. Hungarian Jewry had been subjected to antisemitic legislation of increasing severity ever since 1938. While these laws were designed to reduce the Jewish role in Hungarian economic life, as opposed to the laws of 1944, which were designed to seize their property, the cumulative impact of the legislation was to create serious unemployment in the Jewish community and to cause a drop in the standard of living. Even before 1944, many Jews were supported by community welfare, and economic distress was widespread. By 1942, 300,000 (out of 800,000 Jews in Greater Hungary) were dependent on communal charitable support.[28] The Jews were also affected by the general economic shortages caused by the war effort. Following the German occupation in 1944 there was also looting of Jewish property by German army units and officers, in direct competition with the official Hungarian seizures of Jewish assets.[29] This local looting was in addition to the takeover of the massive Manfred Weiss industrial conglomerate by the SS.[30] The Germans were also able to enrich themselves by demanding the payment of ransom from the various community leaders.[31] In Budapest, ransom payments reached significant proportions and were the cause of an additional conflict over restitution between the Hungarian Jewish community and the international Jewish organizations after the war concerning the Becher deposit (estimated at Sfr 8 million). By the time the Hungarian government began its own legalized expropriation of Jewish bank accounts and valuables, many Jews had already lost most of their savings and possessions. The legislation of April 1944 obliged the Jews to deposit their valuables in local branches of the government Postal Savings Bank. A proportion of their possessions would have been hidden by the victims, or given to Christian friends and neighbors for safe keeping.

The ghettoization and deportations that came soon afterwards were accompanied by widespread local looting of Jewish property. The official attempts to search for and take control of the more valuable assets, together with the Gendarmerie's brutal interrogations of the more prosperous Jews in each community, was an opportunity for theft by local officials.[32] Only in June 1944, two months after the expropriations began, did the Hungarian government attempt to impose some order on the system by the appointment of a Commissioner for Jewish Property.[33] It is not clear what percentage of the movable assets owned by Jews was actually handed over to the central government, and what remained in the hands of the local police and Finance Directory officials.

When the remaining victim loot was eventually sent in from the provincial depots beginning in September 1944, it was sorted and processed in

Obanya and Budapest, and then later in Brennbergbánya and other depots closer to the Austrian border. There was a lot of pilfering at this stage, too. Many of the Financial Directorate officials and guards pocketed gold watches, coins, and items of jewelry,[34] just as Toldi did himself. The processing of the jewelry, breaking it up into its component parts so that the gold could be smelted into bullion and the precious and semiprecious stones sold separately, also caused a serious loss in value.

In addition, account has to taken of a 10 percent commission that Toldi paid in a failed attempt to have the loot taken into Switzerland,[35] the discoveries and spending of the farmers of the town of Schnann who discovered some of the buried crates of valuables immediately after Toldi's men had tried to hide them, the pilfering by American soldiers, and, one can confidently assume, the loot not surrendered to the French authorities by Toldi and his associates. Together with the deterioration of the furs and carpets in the warehouse, and the losses caused in the process of the smelting of silver items and gold fragments during the inventory and appraisal, the combined value of the victim assets handed over to the Jewish Agency and the Joint (these organizations received the money raised from the sale of the better items of the victim loot) and the value of the nonmonetary gold returned to the Hungarian government by France in 1948 was much less than the value of the cargo when the Gold Train began its journey. And the cargo itself was worth only a fraction of the original conjectured value of goods before they were taken from their legitimate owners.

All of the participants in this story were influenced by the fantasies of fabulous wealth. The reality was the opposite—of value, wealth, and prosperity destroyed and dispersed in the process of ethnic cleansing and despoliation. Only very few artifacts of exceptional worksmanship and rarity have a value that remains constant outside of the social context in which they were obtained, used, and cherished. It was the people that used them that gave real value to the items on the Gold Train; the value was not inherent to the objects themselves.

There are various ways of ascribing monetary worth to objects of value. They have a purchase price, a sale price, an insurable value, and a sentimental value. While there are significant differences in these values, they are all much larger than the sale price of the raw materials used in making the jewelry, the religious silverware and tableware, and the coin and stamp collections that made up the bulk of the victim loot. The real value of these items was not the market price but the value given to them by the original owners. However, the sentimental value of a wedding ring, or of Sabbath candlesticks passed from mother to daughter for generations, would be reduced to very little when the owners were deported to Auschwitz. There was not a large market for Judaica in Europe when the war ended. And the impure gold of the wedding rings or dentures fetched very little after the costs of storage, safekeeping, smelting, transportation, and sale were factored in.

The assets of the Hungarian Gold Train may well have been worth $350 million in the circumstances of 1938, or even in those of 1944, when the owners of the items of value were still alive. By 1945, after the items had been vandalized and broken up, and the original owners could no longer be traced, the expropriated goods were worth very much less. It was a fantasy to believe that the prosperity of a community could be seized and redistributed, or evacuated to the Reich. The only thing that could be transferred were household effects and valuable possessions of questionable marketability.

The destruction of European Jewry during the Holocaust took place over a wide geographic area, beginning in Germany with the rise of the Nazis to power in January 1933 and ending with the Allied victory in Europe in May 1945. The motives of the perpetrators included genocide, the exploitation of forced labor, and economic spoliation. Some degree of wealth could be transferred from one population to another by organized plunder, especially where that wealth was concentrated in a few hands. But the roots of popular wealth and prosperity are social, and they were destroyed when the societies that sustained them were laid waste. This was the madness of genocide. Although justice demanded that the material damage of the Holocaust be undone, the real damage were the individual lives lost and the devastation of a vibrant community and that could not be made good again.

Notes

1. Cf. Yehuda Don, "The Economic Effect of Antisemitic Discrimination: Hungarian Anti-Jewish Legislation, 1938–1944," in M. Marrus, ed., *The Nazi Holocaust: Historical Articles on the Destruction of European Jews*, vol. 4 (London, 1989), 507.
2. From Kállay's memoirs, *Hungarian Premier*, cited by Nathaniel Katzburg in *Hungary and the Jews* (Ramat Gan, 1981), 192–93.
3. Detailed accounts of the creation of the Sztójay government can be found in R. L. Brahm, *The Politics of Genocide: The Holocaust in Hungary* (New York, 1994) vol. 1, 421–26; and G. Ránki, *1944 március 19. Magyarország német megszállása* [19 March 1944. The German Occupation of Hungary] (Budapest, 1978). Veesenmayer gave his own account of the German role in the creation of the Sztójay government to American intelligence interrogators immediately after the end of the war. (NARA, RG 226, Field Station Files, London X-2, Box 55, "Interrogation Report: Edmund Veesenmayer," 5 July 1945.) He also testified at various war crimes trials in Hungary. (See L. Karsai and J. Molnár, *Az Endre-Baky-Jaross per* (Budapest, 1994).)
4. For a detailed account of the Sztótay government's policies toward the Jews in March–April 1944, see Braham, *Politics of Genocide*, vol. 2, chapters 14–17; see also C. Gerlach and G. Aly, *Das letzte Kapitel. Der Mord an den ungarischen Juden* (Stuttgart, 2002).
5. See Braham, *Politics of Genocide*, vol. 2, chapters 2–7.
6. Toldi's speech was reported verbatim in the local newspaper, *Fejérmegyei Napló* [Diary of Fejér County], 12 May 1944.
7. For a detailed account of the despoliation in the Szeged region, see J. Molnár, *Zsidósors 1944-ben az V. (szegedi) csendőrkerületben* [Jews in the Fifth Gendarme District (Szeged) in 1944]. See also Braham, *Politics of Genocide*, vol. 2, chapter 16 for an account of events across Hungary.
8. C. A. Macartney, *October Fifteenth. A History of Modern Hungary 1929–1945* (Edin-

burgh, 1956), vol. 2, 452–53.

9. For a detailed description of the processing of the looted goods, see R. Zweig, *The Gold Train*, (London, 2002), chapters 3–4.
10. *New York Times*, 18 May 1945, 8.
11. Ernest Marton to Leon Kubowitzki, 15 March 1946, American Jewish Archives, World Jewish Congress, Series H, File 174, "Hungary 1946."
12. "Report on Conferences with U.S. Forces, Austria, Officials in Vienna and Salzburg, 14–23 January and 26 January 1947" (Abba Schwartz to Sir Herbert Emerson, International Refugee Organization, JDC Archives, New York, AR45/64, Files 532A).
13. International Refugee Organization Press Release, "Reparations Funds Disbursements, 1 April 1949" (ibid.).
14. See Interview with Minister of Finance, Miklós Nyárádi, *Szabadság*, 6 June 1948; and budget speech by Minister of Transport, Ernő Gerő, reported in the *New York Times*, 30 December 1948.
15. Cf. Report by U.S. Political Advisor's Office, Vienna to State Dept., 5 October 1946 (NARA, RG 260, USFA, USACA, Property Control Division, Box 21.)
16. See, for example, the account by Miklós Merenyi, *Népszabadság*, 13 August 1992.
17. In September 2005, a federal judge approved a $25.5 million settlement between the U.S. government and Hungarian Jews who lost jewelry, artwork and other property from the so-called "gold train." The agreement will distribute money through Jewish social service agencies to needy Hungarian survivors around the world. The amount of the settlement was considerably less than the $300 million initially claimed by the plaintiffs.
18. See Zweig, *The Gold Train*, chapter 4.
19. A full account is given in *The Gold Train*.
20. French diplomatic presence in Budapest was reestablished as early as June 1945, and within a year the first of a number of commodities-bartering agreements was signed between Budapest and Paris. French-Hungarian economic relations grew from Fr 100 million to Fr 3 billion between 1946 and 1949. (*Le Monde*, 7 December 1949.)
21. See Transcripts of United States-Hungarian Negotiations, meeting 1–25, in NARA, RG 59, Entry A15398, Box 1, "Hungarian Claims."
22. U.S. Embassy, Budapest, to State Dept., 20 November 1967, *Foreign Relations of the United States, 1964–1968*, Vol. XVII – Eastern Europe, 315–17.
23. On the tension between Zionists and non-Zionsts, see the interview with Shimshon Nathan, head of the Zionist Office in Budapest in the immediate postwar years, Oral History Project, Institute of Contemporary Jewry, Hebrew University, 30 August 1967, 103, no. 4.
24. Rafael (Ruffer), Geneva, to Moshe Shertock (Jerusalem), 14 July 1947, *Political Documents of the Jewish Agency*, vol. II, January-November 1947, ed. Nana Sagi (Jerusalem, 1998), 446–47.
25. Budget and Research Department Report, No. 53, September 1948, European Executive Council, Joint Distribution Committee, JDC Archives, New York.
26. Interview with Péter Feldmájer, *Szombat*, July 1999.
27. See G. Lengyel, "The Ethnic Composition of the Economic Elite in Hungary in the Interwar Period," in *A Social and Economic History of Central European Jewry*, ed. Y. Don and V. Karady (New Brunswick, NJ, 1992), 229–48; G. Ránki, "The Occupational Structure of Hungarian Jews in the Interwar Period," in *Jews in the Hungarian Economy, 1760–1945*, ed. M. K. Silber (Jerusalem, 1992), 274–86; Don, "Economic Effect."
28. Don, "Economic Effect," 517-18.
29. Braham, *Politics of Genocide*, vol. 2, 545–56.
30. Ibid., 556–65; E. Karsai and M. Szinai, "A Weiss Manfréd vagyon német kézbe kerülésének története," [History of the takeover of the Manfred Weiss factories by the Germans] in *Századok* 95, No. 4–5 (1961): 680–719.
31. Braham, *Politics of Genocide*, vol. 1, 516, and E. Lévai, *Black Book on the Martyrdom of Hungarian Jewry* (Zurich, 1948), 110.
32. See the account by a member of the Hungarian Parliament who protested against the

involvement of local officials and citizens in shameful scenes of looting in: Aladár Vozáry, *Így történt!* (Budapest, 1945), 22–75.

33. Zweig, *The Gold Train*, 63.
34. In October 1946 Sandor Ercse, one of the most senior Property Directorate Officials on the train, surrendered 2 kg of gold and 250 gold Napoleon coins to the Hungarian Restitution Commission in Innsbruck. (Report of 25 October 1946 to Hungarian Foreign Ministry, HNA, XIX, J-1-k, 23/g tétel.) Presumably Ercse wanted to benefit from an amnesty offered by the Hungarian government. It is safe to assume that the other "guardians" of the loot on the train also took steps to protect against future contingencies before they left it.
35. Zweig, *The Gold Train*, chapter 5.

RELUCTANT RESTITUTION

The Restitution of Jewish Property in the Bohemian Lands after the Second World War

Eduard Kubů und Jan Kuklík Jr.

The problems surrounding the restitution of Jewish property in Czechoslovakia after 1945 are inextricably linked with the complex political, social, and economic developments of the postwar period. The years immediately after the war were shaped by the transition from a limited democracy to a communist-installed authoritarian regime that brought fundamental changes to the system of property ownership and the principles of property valuation. Before proceeding, we must first define the terms of reference of our enquiry. When addressing this issue, which neither the legal nor the historical literature has examined in any detail, we must largely leave Slovakia aside, despite the fact that it again became part of the Czechoslovak state after 1945. Restitution, however, inevitably had to be performed with reference to the preceding expropriation of Jewish property, which took a different course in the German-allied territory of Slovakia under Tiso's regime than in the Protectorate or in the border areas incorporated into the Reich.[1] After the Germans retreated from Slovakia in 1944 questions concerning the administration of abandoned property,[2] the confiscation of enemy property, and restitution there came under regulations laid down by the new Slovenská národní rada (Slovakian National Council). Not only the legislation regulating restitution, therefore, but also the practice of restitution differed greatly in Slovakia from that in what is today the Czech Republic. Third, we must concede certain limitations to our analysis within the Bohemian Lands. From 1945, restitution for assets that had been expropriated on racial grounds was claimed by legal entities as well as by natural persons. Procedures differed depending on the type of assets and, in the case of businesses, on their size. The various categories of property (e.g., farmland, real estate, businesses, industrial firms, banks, mines, securities, insurance policies, gold, or works of art) were often

Notes for this section begin on page 238.

treated very differently; a thorough investigation of this phenomenon is beyond the scope of our article.

First Steps toward the Restitution of Jewish Property during the Second World War

At a very early stage the Czechoslovak government in exile nullified all property transfers that had been conducted "under pressure from the enemy occupying forces." In October 1938, the Czechoslovak government announced that it "had not acknowledged, did not acknowledge and would never acknowledge"[3] any such transfers or transactions involving movable or immovable property executed after the Munich Agreement. This applied whether the property had been transferred into the ownership of a national of Czechoslovakia or of any other state and whether it concerned public or private property. Even "apparently voluntary" transfers were invalidated. This decree applied also, but not exclusively, to Jewish property, although the government reserved the right to impose a case-by-case limit to the extent of restitution performed.

From the summer of 1944, when liberation became imminent, the first presidential decrees laying the foundations for the reorganization of property ownership, which included measures regarding "enemy property," were issued. A decree of 1 February 1945 concerning special measures for the preservation of economic life in the liberated territories facilitated, first, the restitution of property that had changed hands after the Munich Agreement by reason of persecution on grounds of race, political affiliation, or nationality, and second, the securing of all private and public enemy property and the property of what the state deemed so-called unreliable persons on Czechoslovak territory. The concept of "provisional administration" was introduced for companies, businesses, and assets held or administrated by "persons considered officially unreliable." When securing enemy property, the Czech government made explicit reference to British and American laws on securing and confiscating German property on Allied territory and to subsequent international negotiations on reparations.[4] Such property issues, including the task of defining who was officially "reliable" or "unreliable," were the responsibility of the *národní výbory* (people's councils), newly established organs of public administration that were vested with far-reaching powers.

Developments in the Legal Regulation of Restitution, 1945 to 1989

The Czechoslovak government issued the first orders regulating property ownership on a country wide basis in their Kashau Program.[5] Articles X and XI of this program announced that the property of citizens of enemy states, of German and Hungarian nationals who were guilty of crimes against the Czechoslovak state, and of traitors and collaborators, was to be seized and held in trust. The restructuring of land ownership was to form the basis for a new land reform with the aim of "once and for all rescuing Czech and Slovak soil from the hands of the foreign, German and Hungarian, aristocracy and traitors, and placing it in the hands of Czech and Slovak farmers and the landless." At the same time, however, the government ratified the principle of restitution for property that had been expropriated during the Second World War as a consequence of persecution on the grounds of nationality, political affiliation, or race. Even though there was as yet no specific law concerning the property of Jewish victims of persecution, this formulation certainly alluded to it. However, the government simultaneously resolved to restructure the economy, which in concrete terms meant placing "the entire monetary and credit system, basic industry, the insurance system, and natural and energy resources under general state control and in the service of national economic recovery and the revival of production and trade."

The first decree of this program, "On the Invalidity with Respect to Property Rights of Certain Acts Committed at the Time of Subjection and on the National Administration of the Assets of Germans, Hungarians, Traitors and Collaborators, as well as Certain Organizations and Institutions," was issued on 19 May 1945.[6] This stipulated that "every transfer of property[7] and every transaction in respect of property rights, whether concerning movable or immovable property is invalid insofar as it was executed under pressure from the occupying forces or as a result of persecution on grounds of nationality, race or political affiliation." Subsequent regulations continued in a similar vein, as did the decree of 14 May 1945 on the repeal of anti-Jewish measures issued by the Ministry of Finance.[8]

Conversely, the government's regulation of the property of "persons classified as unreliable" entailed the restriction of private property rights, which in certain cases also affected Jews. This decree was directed towards legal entities as well as natural persons. The state regarded the following persons as "unreliable": "(a) persons of German or Hungarian nationality; and (b) persons who engaged in activities running counter to state sovereignty, independence, unity, the democratic republican state system, and the security and defense of the Republic of Czechoslovakia, or who incited or strove to encourage other persons to take part in such activities, or who in any way intentionally supported the German and Hungarian occupying forces." More specifically, such persons were defined as members of "Vlajka" (The Flag), the "Czech League against Bolshevism," the "Board for Youth Education," the national head office of the employees' union, and the farmers' and forestry association. The legal entities that the state deemed unreliable were those "whose leadership intentionally and wilfully supported the German or Hungarian war effort or served Fascist and Nazi purposes."

The "unreliable persons" category was based on the results of the 1930 national census, for which citizens had been required to declare their (sole) nationality. As well as ethnic Germans, a large group of German-speaking Jews had at that time declared German nationality.[9] This criterion of nationality had been chosen partly with the ethnic Czechs of the border areas in mind, who had involuntarily become citizens of the Reich following the Munich Agreement in 1938.[10] This decree made provisions for workers, farmers, persons carrying on a trade or industry, owners of small- or medium-sized businesses, or officials and their heirs to apply for the release of their property from state administration, if they had lost it due to persecution on grounds of nationality, political affiliation, or race. The local authorities' people's councils were usually entrusted with the enforcement of this law. Theoretically, it was possible to appeal to the next level of the people's councils if necessary.

The most important decree regulating the confiscation of enemy property was that of 25 October 1945.[11] Pursuant to this decree, the Republic of Czechoslovakia confiscated movable and immovable property, and legal claims to property (i.e., debts due and owing, securities, deposits, and intangible rights such as royalties), which on the day of the de facto cessation of the occupation had been in the possession of the following three categories of persons: (1) legal persons of the German Reich or the Kingdom of Hungary and members of the Nazi Party, Hungarian political parties, and other German and Hungarian legal entities, including insurance companies and other corporations under public law; (2) natural persons of German or Hungarian nationality, with the exception of those persons who had proven their loyalty to the Republic of Czechoslovakia; and (3) natural persons engaged in activities running counter to state sovereignty, independence, unity, the democratic republican state system, or the security and defense of the Republic of Czechoslovakia. The only property exempted from confiscation was that which was immediately necessary for day-to-day survival (clothing, bedding, household implements, food, and tools). Confiscated property was administered by the *Fond národní obnovy* [National Renewal Fund], which was to guarantee that it actually would be "held for the benefit of the state." One of the fund's main tasks was to record the amount of assets confiscated and ensure their safekeeping. It worked in cooperation with the regional people's councils that also drew up concrete lists of assets and participated in their allocation to new owners.

The above-mentioned confiscation decrees were issued in connection with a number of nationalization measures. In July 1945, the parties of the Popular Front agreed to implement nationalization by presidential decree, even before the provisional National Assembly had been summoned. The government was obviously under a great deal of pressure from an increasingly radicalized population, to whom the idea of nationalization had become very appealing. Preparations for nationalization were accompanied by political and legal discussions on the extent and pace of the process, as well as on the form compensation should take. While communists and social democrats defended a course of immediate, comprehensive nationalization,[12] a compromise was struck that involved the nationalization of key enterprises in the energy sector, foundries, rolling mills, metal-processing, and electro-technical industries with more than 500 employees; the chemical and armaments industries; and a number of other branches with a maximum of 150 to 500 employees (e.g., glass and porcelain manufacturers and textile businesses), which was enacted by four decrees issued in October 1945. These made provision for the Czech state to take into ownership all significant elements of the means of production. All assets, with the exception of the property of the German Reich, the Kingdom of Hungary, and Nazi legal entities, as well as of natural persons who had been deprived of their Czech nationality, were in principle to be nationalized in exchange for compensation. Later decrees extended the process of nationalization to include the distilling industry, and joint stock companies and private banks. In addition, the government resolved to carry out a comprehensive land reform.

The presidential decrees basically facilitated the restitution of property that had been confiscated on grounds of racial persecution. However, they contained restrictions that frequently had negative repercussions for Jewish claimants. For example, property could only be released from national administration to those applicants who fulfilled the criterion of relative poverty. In addition, they had to provide evidence of their Czech nationality and "reliability" in the eyes of the state.

The constitutional decree regulating nationality for persons of German or Hungarian nationality provided that all former nationals of Czechoslovakia who had become nationals of the German Reich or of Hungary after the Munich Agreement or after 15 March 1939 (when the Germans occupied and dissolved the Czech state) would be deprived of their Czech nationality.[13] The only members of these minorities who were permitted to retain their nationality were those who could prove that they had remained loyal to the Republic of Czechoslovakia. Among these were persons who: (1) for political or racial reasons had been confined in a concentration camp or prison or who "on account of their loyalty to the Republic and to the Czech or Slovak people had been persecuted by the Nazis in any other manner"; (2) had been actively involved in the struggle against the Nazi regime and in support of the Czechoslovak Republic; (3) had served in Czechoslovak or allied units or had fought for the resistance in the country itself; and (4) had not been a member of the SS, the SA (Sturmabteilung) [Nazi Stormtroopers], the Sudeten German Party, the NSDAP, or any other Nazi organization. Political activity in exile and financing the resistance were also regarded as proof of loyalty. The Ministry of the Interior or, where necessary, the people's councils determined who could keep their Czech nationality.[14] Those Germans and Hungarians "who at a time when the Republic was under severe threat professed their Czech or Slovak nationality in an official declaration" were also permitted to keep their citizenship.[15] For this reason, one cannot speak of an indiscriminate application of the principle of collective guilt.

There was in fact one group of persons who could reapply for Czechoslovak citizenship within six months of being expatriated. However, the final ruling was made entirely at the discretion of the Ministry of the Interior and followed the "general regulations on naturalization."[16] Applications for the recovery of Czechoslovak citizenship were not accepted "if the applicant has not observed the duties of a Czechoslovak citizen, has spoken out publicly against the Czechoslovak state or drawn economic or financial profit from [the German and Hungarian] occupation or tried to profit from it."[17] In concrete terms, the majority of Jewish applicants who had declared German nationality in 1930 (because German was their everyday language) nonetheless fulfilled the formal criteria for being recognized as Czech citizens. However, the lower levels of the people's councils put considerable obstacles in their path to restitution. A number of German-speaking Jews were forcibly resettled as Germans even before the Potsdam Agreement, which signalled large-scale expulsions of ethnic Germans.

The first definitive regulation of postwar restitution, including that of "Jewish" property, was formulated in a law passed by the National Assembly on 16 May 1946 on the Invalidity of Certain Actions Regarding Rights of Ownership during the Period of Subjection and on Claims Resulting from this Invalidity and from Other Violations of Property Rights.[18] This law envisaged two basic methods of performing restitution: (1) restitution by order of the authority of the national administration;[19] and (2) judicial restitution when applications were not accepted or processed by the national administration within three months of their submission. Applications were to be filed at the relevant district court no later than three years after the expropriation. Restitution could take the form of a restoration of rights of ownership or other means of restoring the applicants' former condition (so-called restitution in kind) or a payment of monetary restitution under the terms of §6 of the law. This paragraph also made provision for monetary restitution in cases where restitution in kind conflicted with important public interests.

With regard to the restitution of Jewish property, the Ministry for Social Welfare played the most significant role. On 8 June 1945, this ministry set up a temporary national administration for assets, once held by the German "property agency" and the "emigration fund," which these institutions had confiscated during the war on the basis of the victims' nationality, race, or political affiliation. On 30 November 1945, the Ministry for Social Welfare also established a national administration under the supervision of the Jewish "Council of Elders," which was entrusted with real estate originally belonging to the Jewish communities, societies, funeral associations, funds, and foundations; their bank accounts; and precious objects and religious artifacts, which had been brought to Prague from provincial religious communities and Jewish museums on the orders of the German occupation authorities.

Restitution claimants were required to produce certificates of nationality, "reliability," and citizenship; the heirs to deceased owners had to provide a certificate of inheritance, an official declaration, and a witness; where there may have been uncertainty about the identity of movable objects, a detailed description of the object in question was required. Notifications of restitution consisted of two parts: the restitution award and a short statement of the grounds. Heirs were charged a fee for tracing the objects of restitution and for their temporary administration. This restitution by no means covered all forms of transfer or transmission of ownership of Jewish property to Czech citizens. So-called voluntary property transfers following the Munich Agreement or after 15 March 1939, fictitious sales, and pressure put on refugees to emigrate were not considered for restitution under the law. Within this latter category, so-called gifts made in exchange for export permits for works of art and other valuables and the strict implementation of currency regulations during the Second Republic form another chapter of their own.

Any assessment of the restitution of Jewish property after 1945 or 1948 must also consider the problem of victims of the Holocaust who became citizens of other states—namely the United Kingdom, the United States, and Canada—and whose property was affected by the Czech nationalization law. This problem was not solved until the early 1970s, in connection with the issue of Czech gold reserves. Negotiations on this issue included discussion of property that had not been restituted after the Second World War. As a consequence, monetary restitution was paid for property that had been nationalized, amounting to only part of the value of the claimed assets.

The Practice of Restitution and Compensation, 1945 to 1989

The practice of restitution deviated considerably from the legal principles it was based on. This was primarily due to the communist-led political, economic and social reconstruction of state and society, and the continuous weakening of the rights of ownership that this entailed. The nationalization of key industries and the banks, as well as businesses with between 150 and 500 employees (the figure differed according to the type of business), which began on 24 October 1945, prevented the restitution of all kinds of large-scale property in these branches. This process of nationalization was presented to the people as an act of social justice, breaking up big business, which the government accused of being partly responsible for Czechoslovakia's decline. The communists and their allies, particularly the newly unified trade unions with more than two million members, went even further, speaking of the crushing of big agricultural speculators and banking profiteers, and the introduction of a new era of so-called people's democracy.[20] In the countryside land reform played a key role in transforming property relations.

It soon became evident that differentiating between persons the nation and the state deemed reliable who were at least to be offered some compensation for nationalized assets no longer made sense. The state's financial situation cast doubt on the rationality of making compensation payments; the relevant rules and regulations were not even issued. The Communist Party's seizure of power in February 1948 finally put an end to compensation payments to Czechoslovak citizens. Nationals of the former allied states and neutral states were forced to claim compensation by means of laborious and protracted bilateral international negotiations.

With regard to the restitution of small- and medium-sized Jewish property—movable, immovable, and business assets—a considerable number of claims were resolved between 1945 and 1948. The state of research so far, however, does not allow any overall conclusions to be drawn. The restitution of these assets was mainly the responsibility of the lower branches of public administration, whose activities in this field were not well coordinated (the main agencies involved were the local and district people's councils and administrative committees in the border areas), and, after 1946, the district courts. On the regional level, restitution encountered a number of obstacles. In several cases it was actually ruled out with the argument that the property transfer was a "fait accompli," i.e., expropriation had taken place in the first weeks after liberation.

Frequently, the agencies responsible even failed to give special consideration to those returning from the concentration camps. The Ministry of Justice wrote to the cabinet office informing it that "even persons who must be officially considered unreliable today could have been forced to perform property transfers or other actions in respect of the rights of ownership under pressure from the occupying powers or owing to persecution on the grounds of nationality, race or political affiliation at that time," but that awarding restitution to these persons "would certainly not correspond with the people's idea of justice."[21] The law and its interpretation were already being used for political ends.

One device for delaying restitution payments was the process of recognizing citizenship. The fact that restitution was explicitly limited to small- and medium-sized businesses also offered plenty of scope for arbitrariness. The authorities looked into the class backgrounds of claimants and checked to see if restitution would change their social status. If, for example, a claimant owned other businesses and was categorized as a capitalist or man of independent means who was not even active in business, his property was not returned.[22] The May 1946 law on restitution did not speed up the process either, as it envisaged costly proceedings in the courts, which were already completely overburdened. Problems were also posed by the need to identify confiscated or otherwise lost assets and to prove one's right of ownership or succession. Furthermore, applicants had to provide evidence that property transfers had actually taken place as a result of pressure exerted by the occupying forces or racially motivated persecution. At the same time, the law protected people who had had acquired Jewish property "in good faith." Where this was the case, only claims to monetary compensation could be asserted. The renewal of the restitution law was severely criticized by the Council of Jewish Communities. It objected to the unequal treatment of Jewish and non-Jewish claimants and the discriminatory time limits for filing applications, which were so short that foreign applicants could not possibly adhere to them.[23] Thus the majority of cases pending in court remained unresolved up to the communist seizure of power in February 1948.

Many businesses, farmsteads, and houses had, moreover, been allocated to new users (in the Sudeten regions, to new settlers) directly after their expropriation and could, therefore, not be simply restored to their original owners without further complications. In practice, Aryanized property was usually treated as German. Consequently, the original Jewish owners had to contend with the interests of the *Fond národního majetku* (National Property Fund), which administered confiscated property; the inscrutable interests of local, regional, and national politics and individual party members who were involved in national administration; as well as the beneficiaries of the property's original confiscation. Attempts at restitution came up against widespread reluctance and inadequate cooperation.

The former owners of small- to medium-sized businesses were caught in the crossfire of general disputes over Czechoslovakia's political and economic future. The postwar nationalization campaign threatened the future of small- and medium-sized businesses that had been confiscated by the Germans, Hungarians, or their collaborators. This concerned a total of 3,391 businesses, or as much as 13 percent of industrial employees and of the country's productive capacity.[24] Among these firms were a number of Aryanized Jewish companies. After the dissolution of the transitional administration, the question arose of whether the government should hand these businesses over to private persons or to the public sector, or make them the subject of restitution. In the end, the communists and their allies insisted on further restricting capitalist production in order to weaken their opponents economically. This dispute over "confiscations" formed an important chapter in the history of the power struggles leading up to February 1948, and was characterized as a legitimate part of the class struggle right up until the end of the Communist era in 1989.

One case, which served as a model for Communist propaganda, was the restitution of a textile factory in Varnsdorf owned by Emil Beer. This case offers a clear example of the politicization of the restitution of Jewish property in Czechoslovakia. Emil Beer sold his mechanical weaving mill to Josef Eichler, a Reich German, within the context of the Nazi administration's Aryanization program for far less than its value and clearly under duress. Yet on his return from exile after the war, Beer faced a lengthy tug-of-war with the state administration over his property. He finally succeeded in having his rights recognized by the Varnsdorf district court, which repealed the confiscation ruling and ordered the return of the business to its original owner. The Communist Party of Czechoslovakia (CPC) and the trade unions wasted no time in reacting. A staff meeting was called by the factory party chairman, Marek, together with the factory workers' council. In cooperation with the CPC district committee and the regional trade union council, the workers of the entire district prepared for a general strike.[25]

The factory workers' council and employees blocked Beer's return from the outset. As soon as they heard of Beer's arrival, the workers' council quartered Slovak workers in his villa. On 5 March, the day on which his factory was to be handed over to him, one member of the CPC, blacksmith František

Havlas, grasped seventy-year-old Beer "by the throat" and with the words, "So, you want the factory" led him forcibly, together with other strikers, to his home, in front of which a guard had been stationed.[26] Meanwhile, the various processions of demonstrating strikers came together on Varnsdorf's town square. A telegram sent to the chairman of the *Ústřední rada odborů* [Trade Union Central Council] (ÚRO), Antonín Zápotocký, contained the following statement: "The employees of all industries in the district of Varnsdorf have laid down their work and assembled on the town square in Varnsdorf in order to protest categorically the handing over of the factory to Mr Beer. By his behaviour during the First Republic, Mr Beer has revealed himself to be a Germanizer and an asocial employer, and the working people of Varnsdorf, therefore, will not allow his reinstatement as a capitalist."[27]

None of the characterizations of Beer were true. The alleged Germanizer had attended only Czech schools, was a member of the north Bohemian national society with Czech-national leanings (*Národní jednota Severočeská*), had financially supported the Czech minority in Varnsdorf, and during the war openly declared his affiliation with the Czechoslovak émigré community in London.[28] He was nevertheless reproached for declaring Jewish rather than Czech nationality in the national census. Communist Party propaganda ignored the fact that Beer's textile factory had been sold during Aryanization and even stated untruthfully that he had obtained a good price.

The events in Varnsdorf took place in the context of the Communist struggle for supremacy in Czechoslovakia. The Communist Party leader, Kliment Gottwald, declared in Liberec in 1946: "We will not hand over one single factory to the industrialists."[29] Consequently, conflicts over the means of production intensified during the winter of 1946–1947. The plenary meeting of the ÚRO on 14 December resolved that the trade unions would not permit the return of property from state administration to former owners.[30] In a radio broadcast in February 1947, trade union leader Antonín Zápotocky said: "It is simply inadmissible for property that has already been nationalized to be returned to the ownership of independent capitalists. ... The ÚRO demands that confiscated German property be converted into publicly owned companies."

The Varnsdorf incident gained public attention due to investigations by an all-ministry commission, questions in parliament, and the subsequent court proceedings against some of the demonstrators and agitators, who were accused of committing a public disturbance, damaging the property of a third party, restricting the personal freedom of a third party, and extortion; but this did not alter the fact that restitution had been deferred,[31] a costly delay since after February 1948 there could be no talk of restitution.

At a Popular Front conference just one week after the Varnsdorf incident, representatives of the CPC and trade unions managed to put through a resolution on the prioritized allocation of confiscated property to state-owned companies. After this no decision concerning objects under temporary administration could be made without the prior agreement of the ÚRO and factory workers.[32] This resolution for the first time granted workers' councils significant influence not only in the running of businesses but also in questions of restitution. Thus the door was opened for political manipulation. Communist propaganda did not portray Jewish victims of Nazi persecution as people who had lived through hell during the Second World War. Jewish beneficiaries of large-scale restitution were branded as unscrupulous capitalists, parasites who lived off the labor of others, a section of society that had no place in a people's democracy. At a plenary meeting of the CPC in Moravian Ostrava on 29 February 1947, for example, Gottwald argued that "the fragmentation of the trade unions serves the cause of reaction, and only the Rothschilds, Larischs, Pecheks and all those who the people of Ostrava have long since eliminated, capitalize on it."[33] The horror of the Holocaust and the reality of Aryanization were covered up by populist stereotypes that also echoed certain antisemitic notions.[34] None of the other political parties were in a position to come up with any arguments to counter the Communist propaganda or to enforce restitution.

The proportion of former Jewish property among the assets nationalized in Czechoslovakia has never been quantified. An examination of the lists of temporarily administered businesses, which were earmarked to become state-owned companies,[35] however, makes it clear that such cases were not exceptional. The fact that these lists do not differentiate between property that was originally German and that which had been Aryanized makes their evaluation problematic. The extent of restitution, which was performed only provisionally or reversed—even before February 1948—has also never been quantified. It is possible, however, to cite further cases very similar to that of Emil Beer that simply did not stir up so much publicity.

A fundamental conflict of principles concerning the nature of Jewish restitution broke out between the government and the Council of the Jewish Communities with the passing of the act on the *Likvidační fond měnový* (Currency Liquidation Fund) in July 1947. The contentious issue was that the majority of Jewish property was to pass into state ownership. The Supreme Administrative Court ruled that it was not possible to perform restitution in respect of assets that could not be attributed to individual owners. Consequently, all property passed to the state if it had not been claimed after the war because the original owners and their heirs had been killed. Intense debate was also sparked by the question of how much money had been confiscated and mixed with German assets during the Second World War. The upshot was that not only confiscated assets, but also property that could not be returned to individual owners, or that belonged to Jewish associations or other legal entities that were not reestablished after the war, were incorporated into the fund. It was an obvious case of breach of promise on the part of the government, which had pledged to use such assets to support the victims of racially motivated persecution.[36]

Citizenship regulations also became an instrument working against some potential recipients of restitution. The Petschek family, for example, declared German nationality in 1930. Later, all members of the family acquired foreign citizenship, mostly American, without actually renouncing their Czechoslovak citizenship. The Ministry of the Interior (led by the Communist Václav Nosek) judged this act, committed at a time when "the Republic was under increased threat," to be a violation of wartime regulations—in other words, an act of treason. On the basis of this, the Ministry of the Interior prepared the nationalization of the family's property.[37] After February 1948, the state did not even shrink from actually depriving people of their citizenship. Jewish emigrants to Israel were forced to submit a "declaration of the renunciation of property in favour of the Czechoslovak state," which cancelled all restitution and inheritance claims. Research so far shows that in many cases, the objects for which restitution claims had been filed had not been identified, nor had the restitution proceedings been concluded by February 1948.

The second phase of restitution, instituted in February 1948, reduced the scope for restitution to basically nothing. Citizens of the former allied countries were still to be paid compensation, but, in general, the government imposed a blockade on information on all matters concerning property ownership.

Problems of Restitution since 1990

The political revolution that began in November 1989 precipitated a long-term process of fundamental changes in the legal system. It is only on the basis of these changes that a real solution to the problem of the restitution of property confiscated by reason of persecution on the grounds of political affiliation, nationality, or race during the Second World War was found. The first steps were taken by the federal parliament as early as 1990–1991, when the basic principles of restitution in the Czech Republic were established. These were gradually added to and amended in the years that followed. Among these amendments were certain corrections made to the original expansion of the Czechoslovak (and Czech) law on restitution, which mainly concerned property stolen on racial grounds during the Second World War.[38] Some general conditions for entitlement to restitution in Czechoslovakia, and since 1993 in the Czech Republic, remained in place, including the criterion of Czechoslovak (or Czech) citizenship and the limitation to property nationalized after February 1948. After forty years of Communist rule it once again became clear that, because of the far-reaching changes that had taken place in the country's social and economic structure, complete restitution to the original owners or their heirs would in most cases not be possible.

The first postrevolution law concerning restitution was the Act on Relief for Individual Cases of Violation of Property Rights.[39] This applied to the property of small business owners or homeowners that had either been nationalized or confiscated by the state as a result of political persecution after February 1948. Restitution or financial compensation was granted to the original owners, their spouses, or their descendants. This law did not make specific provisions for victims of earlier racial persecution, but it nevertheless facilitated the restitution of their property. The return of real estate was made possible by a special law, the so-called Land Act of 1991,[40] which was renewed several times, with the time limit for filing claims extended. Restitution in kind was not possible in the case of large state-owned businesses, earmarked for privatization, but a certain number of stocks were set aside for the settlement of restitution claims. The first phase of restitution legislation was concluded with the passing of an act on out-of-court rehabilitations.[41] This law did not contain any specific provisions for the victims of racist persecution during the Second World War, but it facilitated the restitution of their property, insofar as they had been deprived of it again after February 1948. Eligible claimants were those who had suffered "political persecution" or persecution owing to affiliation "with a certain religious group or social or property class, or other group or class." This act also facilitated the return of property or the payment of financial compensation to original owners, their spouses, or their heirs and descendents. Claims could still only be filed for property expropriated after February 1948, and claimants still had to be Czechoslovak citizens and long-term residents of the Czech Republic. Those not eligible for restitution were people who had previously received any other kind of compensation (this condition was directed mainly at the recipients of payments made subsequent to the bilateral negotiations), "officially unreliable persons," and those who had acquired their property through Aryanization.

In 1994, Resolution No. 164/1994 of the Constitutional Court eliminated the condition of permanent residency, making it possible to perform restitution for property of claimants with dual citizenship and those who were permanently resident outside the Czech Republic. The most significant change from the point of view of "Jewish restitution," however, was brought about by the revision of Law No. 87/1991 on out-of-court rehabilitations under Law No. 116/1994 (*Collection of Laws*) [CL]. This law made provision for persons to reclaim property or compensation if they had been deprived of their assets during the Second World War and had been entitled to restitution under postwar regulations.[42] The only condition was that no restitution had taken place due to political persecution after February 1948. Pursuant to this law, restitution in kind was performed in the cases of a number of important art collections (e.g., those of J. Waldes and F. Moravetz) and state-owned real estate.

Despite all this, problems surrounding the practical application of restitution continue to this day. For example, after 1989 privatized property could not be returned to the original owners (only financial compensation was offered), the situation being further complicated by the fact that a number of real estate properties in particular had passed into the hands of the local authorities. The so-called Mixed Working Commission was set up under government Order No. 773 of 25 November 1998 to deal with both individual cases and the problematic nature of "Jewish restitution" in general. The commission's research culminated in two reports—one focusing on the fate of Jewish gold and other precious metals,[43] the other on works of art.

A definitive regulation of the restitution process as it concerned victims of the Holocaust was achieved by the Law of 23 June 2000,[44] which consisted of two parts. The first part opened up the possibility for the restitution of real estate belonging to Jewish communities, foundations, and associations that had remained in state hands until that time. It also provided that works of art be transferred from state collections to the Jewish Museum in Prague and that the state undertake to return other works of art to the original owners or their descendents. The February 1948 cut-off date was finally jettisoned for the benefit of victims of the Holocaust. For the restitution of works of art it is no longer necessary to provide evidence of Czech citizenship, and an amending law extended the original one-year limit for filing restitution claims, as several claimants had not been able to identify their artworks in time.

In place of a summary, which would necessarily have to remain open-ended, the case of restitution concerning the Waldes family seems a fitting conclusion, being in many ways typical of restitution attempts in Czechoslovakia that have not yet been finally resolved.[45] This case involves various types of property (a house, a factory, works of art, a museum for different kinds of robe-clasps) and presents an example of restitution that was not completed before February 1948 and therefore, its most important parts, dragged on until after 1996.

The factory-owner Jindřich Waldes (Waldes and Co., manufacturers of buttons and fasteners) was one of Czechoslovakia's leading businessmen. As well as his holdings of General Mercantile Partnership stock, he also owned a number of real estate properties (two villas in the Vinohrady District and an apartment block in the Nusle District of Prague). Waldes was an important collector and patron of Czech art.[46] After 15 March 1939, Waldes arranged for his family to migrate to the United States, but Waldes himself stayed behind in the Protectorate. The Germans arrested him immediately and detained him in Pankrác. On 22 October, he was transferred to Jena and subsequently to the Buchenwald concentration camp. His family in the United States paid for his release from the camp, but he died in May 1941 under mysterious circumstances when his ship arrived in Cuba. All the personal property that he had left behind in the Protectorate was seized by the German Reich. This included his private art collection, which was stored in the State (later, National) Gallery, and the real estate properties mentioned above, along with the furniture and paintings they housed. The factory went into compulsory receivership. The national administrator E. Waller saw to the confiscation and subsequent sale of objects from Waldes's personal property "to recover his allegedly unpaid taxes."[47]

After the end of the Second World War, the Waldes family first had to prove their right of inheritance. This prevented Waldes's widow, Hedvika, from actually filing for restitution until 1946. The family's claim to the factory was now invalid, as it had been nationalized under the name Koh-i-noor. Only some selected items could be retrieved from the Craft Museum and the National Gallery, but the Craft Museum confirmed that there were some exhibits from Waldes's former Museum for Buttons and Robe-clasps in its collection that had not been affected by nationalization.[48] Hedvika Waldes's restitution claim to the house in Nusle and the villas in Vinohrady was conceded without a court hearing. Pursuant to Law No. 128/1946 (CL), the lawyer J. Klouda asserted a claim in Hedvika Waldes's name to the restitution of one of the villas in Vinohrady, to a collection of works of art from the National Gallery, and to the Museum for Buttons and Robe-clasps.[49] The family was able to prove their "official reliability" by means of a testimonial from the Ministry of the Interior on 13 July 1947.[50] Nevertheless, restitution had not been completed by February 1948 and the claim was lodged again under the changed conditions of Law No. 79/1948 (CL). Mrs Hedvika Waldes and her children left the country for the United States, while their lawyer, J. Klouda, who had himself become the object of persecution, had to abandon the case. Without her knowledge, a legal guardian was appointed for Hedvika Waldes, who alleged before a court that he did not know where Hedvika Waldes and her children were. Her claim was refused for the first time on 1 October 1953, by a district court, on the politically influenced grounds that considerable wealth was at issue and the Waldes family had been leading capitalists during the First Republic. This judgment was confirmed by the regional court on 20 November 1953.[51]

Restitution proceedings for the Waldes family were resumed after 1989. Thanks to the new legal regulations introduced in 1994, the collection of artworks from the National Gallery and the objects deposited in the Craft Museum were restored to the children of the late Jindřich and Hedwika Waldes, Jiří, Miloš, and Anna. Of the family's real estate, only one of their two villas in Vinohrady was returned, as the second had already been approved for a privatization project. The family was awarded financial compensation for this property. Legal disputes with the Glass and Jewelry Museum in Jablonec over the Waldes's Museum for Buttons and Robe-clasps and with Prague's fourth district over the house in Nusle, which was the subject of restitution after the war but had been confiscated again in the 1960s, had still not been settled by 2000. The children of Jindřich Waldes, who have dual citizenship—Czech and American—did not attempt to claim their father's factory.

The example of the Waldes family's attempts to obtain restitution shows that, despite the complexity of the problems, the amendments made to legal regulations during the 1990s have made it possible to assert successfully valid restitution claims, with the help of an independent judiciary that has been depoliticized in accordance with European standards. One may assume that most of the remaining disputes will be resolved in the foreseeable future.

Translated from German by Charlotte Kreutzmüller

Notes

1. On the confiscation of Jewish property in Slovakia, see the essay in this volume by Tatjana Toensmeyer.
2. In principle this was a trustee administration, which in the case of large-scale properties was exercised by collective bodies and for smaller properties by individuals.
3. *Úřední věstník československý* [Czechoslovak Official Gazette], year 3, no. 2 (London, 1942).
4. See the unpublished decree on the securing of enemy property of 24 May 1944, published in: *Dekrety prezidenta republiky 1940–1945* [Decrees Issued by the President of the Republic], ed. K. Jech and K. Kaplan (Brno, 1995), part 2, doc. No. 37.1.
5. *Dokumenty moderní doby* [Contemporary Documents] (Prague, 1978), no. 97, 474– 94.
6. See *Collection of Laws* (CL), No. 5/1945.
7. According to Nespor, this refers specifically to confiscations and forced sales resulting from judicial and administrative decisions. See Z. Nespor, *Komentář k dekretu presidenta republiky ze dne 19. května 1945* [Commentary on the Decree of the President of the Republic of 19 May 1945] (Prague, 1945), 5.
8. See *Official Gazette*, no. 1, 15 May 1945. The definitive regulation of postwar restitutions came with Law No. 128/1946; see CL.
9. See the arguments of P. Meyer et al., *The Jews in the Soviet Satellites* (Syracuse, NY, 1953), 78–79.
10. Nešpor, *Komentář*, 9.
11. See CL, No. 108/1945.
12. *Dekrety*, part 2, doc. no. 32.1–32.25, 496–97.
13. On this issue, see the introductory article by V. Pavlíček in: *Dekrety prezidenta republiky*, part 1, 7-8. See also Decree No. 33/1945, CL.
14. The individual definitions are cited from V. Verner, *Státní občanství podle ústavního dekretu presidenta republiky z 2. srpna 1945* [Citizenship According to the Constitutional Decree of the President of the Republic on 2 August 1945] (Prague, 1945), 44.
15. Ibid.
16. *Dekrety*, part 1, doc. no. 21.10, 380–81.
17. Verner, *Státní občanství*, 20–21.
18. See CL, 28/1946 and the text of the law in no. 79/1948, CL of 7 April 1948.
19. On implementation, see the guideline issued by the Ministry of Industry, CL, no. 519/1945.
20. See Všeodborový archiv Praha [Trade Union Archive, Prague] (VAP), Central Council of the Trade Unions – Organizational Section, 1945–1950, Carton 6, Inventory No. 46/2.
21. Confidential Report of the Justice Ministry for the Cabinet Meeting on 27 September 1945, VAP, Fond of the Central Council of the Trade Unions – Commission on the National Economy (ÚRO-NK), Carton 20, Inventory No. 55.
22. Letter of the Ministry for Worker Protection to the Central Council of the Trade Unions on 22 December 1945, VAP, Carton 45, Inventory No. 138.
23. See the objections of the Council of Jewish Communities in the Bohemian lands to the draft of the Settlement Office and of the Fund for National Renewal on a revision of the Restitution Law of 15 February 1948, Archiv ministerstva zahraničních věcu [Archive of the Czechoslovak Foreign Ministry] (AMZV), subject area A, 1945–1949, Carton 38.
24. Activity report of the Central National Committee in the capital Prague regarding National Property Administration on 20 April 1946. Published in: Růžena Hlušičková et al., *Národní výbory v Praze v letech 1945– 1960, sborník dokumentů*, díl 1. [The National Committees in Prague 1945–1960, Documentary Volume, part 1] (Prague, 1985), doc. no. 18, 133–34.
25. Recollections of Marie Rauch-Exner (participant in the Varnsdorf strike), VAP, Section, History of the Trade Unions, Carton 81, Inventory No. 475, Seminar on the 40th anniversary of the Varnsdorf strike, 5.

26. Recollections of Jaroslav Peterka (participant in the Varnsdorf strike), ibid., 8.
27. VAP, ÚRO, Secretariat, Carton 19, Inventory No. 84.
28. Šárka Nepalová, "Židovská menšina v Čechách a na Moravě v letech 1945–1948" [The Jewish Minority in Bohemia and Moravia, 1945–1948], in: *Terezínské studie a dokumenty* [Terezin Studies and Documents] (1999): 321.
29. Recollections of Plechatý (participant in the Varnsdorf strike), VA, Section, History of the Trade Unions, Carton 81, Inventory No. 475, Seminar on the 40th anniversary of the Varnsdorf strike.
30. Karel Růžička, *ROH v boji o rozšíření moci dělnické třídy (1945–1948)* (Prague, 1963), 148.
31. List of criminal cases on 15 May 1947, VAP, ÚRO, Secretariat, Carton 19, Inventory No. 84.
32. *Nástin dějin československého odborového hnutí* [Outline of the History of the Czechoslovak Trade Union Movement] (Prague, 1963), 369–70; *Přehled dějin československého odborového hnutí* [Overview of the History of the Czechoslovak Trade Union Movement] (Prague, 1984), 359.
33. *Dekrety*, part 2, doc. no. 36.1.–36.10., 359–60.
34. See also Meyer, *The Jews in the Soviet Satellites*, 98–99.
35. List of temporarily administered businesses (confiscations) from October 1946, 51 pages, VA, ÚRO-NK, Carton 45, Inventory No. 139.
36. See also K. Wehle, "The Jews in Bohemia and Moravia 1945–1948," in *The Jews of Czechoslovakia*, ed. A. Dagan (V. Fischl) (Philadelphia, 1984), vol. 3, 517–21.
37. List prepared for the Minister of Finance Jaromír Dolanský and the Deputy Head of the Government Zdeněk Fierlinger on 27 September 1947, AMZV, GS, 1948–1954, Carton 39, Fasc. Property Confiscations.
38. See also the critical assessment in E. Barkan, *The Guilt of Nations: Restitution and Negotiating Historical Injustices* (Baltimore MD, 2000), 149–55.
39. See CL, No. 403/1990.
40. See CL, No. 229/1991.
41. See CL, No. 87/1991.
42. This affected above all those covered by Presidential Decree No. 5/1945 and also Law No. 128/1946, CL.
43. The report of the team of experts was published with the title: *Jewish Gold, Other Precious Metals and Objects from the Bohemian Lands 1939–1945: Illegal Violations of Property Rights, their Scale and the Subsequent Fate of this Property* (Prague, 2001).
44. See CL, No. 212/2000.
45. A brief sketch on the restitution was published with the approval of Jiři Waldes, whom the authors wish to thank for his friendly cooperation and for making available the documents cited below.
46. See also F. Kupka, Kupka-Waldes, *malíř a jeho sběratel* [The Painter and his Collector] (Prague, 1999), 27–28.
47. See, for example, the letter of the Director of the Cibulka Gallery to the Ministry for Education on 6 November 1939 on the seizure of the J. Waldes collection by the Gestapo. A copy of the document resides in the family archive.
48. The dispute with the Glass and Jewelry Museum in Jablonec nad Nisou, which refused to surrender the items in the museum, had (at the time of writing [in 2003]) not yet been resolved.
49. Documents Tb. no. 2749/49 and 79 no. 93/52. The documents reside in the family archive.
50. Ibid.
51. Ibid.

THE POLISH DEBATE ON THE HOLOCAUST AND THE RESTITUTION OF PROPERTY

Dariusz Stola

The question of the restitution of the property of victims of the Holocaust in Poland undoubtedly deserves special attention. Any consideration of the genocide of the European Jews committed by the Third Reich must take into account the fact that the Jewish population of Poland was the largest in Europe—over 3 million people—that the proportion of Jews among Poland's total population—about 10 percent—was also higher than in any other country on the continent, and that their survival rate was very low indeed: fewer than 10 percent of Polish Jews lived to see the end of the war.

Furthermore, the question of the restitution of the property of victims of the Holocaust in Poland is unusually complex. First, beside the extermination of Polish Jewry and the expropriation or destruction of their property, the Second World War also resulted in massive losses among Poland's non-Jewish population and general destruction on an unprecedented scale. Genocide, destruction, and expropriation affected Polish Jews most intensively, but not exclusively; to a lesser, but still extraordinary degree they also affected the Polish population. Differences in the German conduct of the war and occupation policies between Western and Eastern Europe also marked the question of property. Second, the war heralded the expansion of the USSR and the communist system into Central Europe, which had a decisive influence on property relations over the next fifty years. Thus the issue of Jewish property is part of a wider question, namely that of the restoration of private property—or reprivatization. The last, but by no means least important aspect of the complexity of the Polish case is the complexity and tension of Polish-Jewish relations before, during, and after the war, a problem that extends far beyond mere material possessions.

This chapter will present the variety of circumstances affecting the restitution question in Poland. Pointing them out does not in any way justify the

Notes for this section begin on page 254.

delay in the restitution of property belonging to victims of the Holocaust, or of the property of other citizens that passed into state or private ownership after 1939 in undeniable violation of established property rights. On the contrary, this chapter will demonstrate how far the question of property is a part of the dramatic and cruel history of the twentieth century, how far it was dependent on the nature of totalitarian regimes, and for that reason, how it remains an aspect of their legacy that is most difficult to overcome. When people die and cities lie in ruins, the abstract title to property paradoxically remains in place—precisely because it is an abstraction.

The question of the restitution of property stolen from the Jews during the Second World War was or is a subject for debate almost everywhere in Europe, yet the manner and circumstances in which the transfer to state ownership, or to the ownership of private or legal persons, took place, varied greatly. On the whole, Polish Jews lost their possessions to foreign occupation authorities or as a consequence of destruction caused by invading armies. In west and central Poland, which fell under German occupation in September 1939, almost all kinds of Jewish property, such as enterprises, bank accounts, securities, real estate, gold, jewelry, and works of art, passed into the ownership of the Third Reich. At subsequent stages of ghettoization, deportations, and eventually extermination, Jewish victims were gradually deprived of everything. In addition to this systematic expropriation, local occupation authorities exacted many ad hoc contributions; there was also robbery and extortion committed independently by German officials and the military.[1] In eastern Poland, Germany took Jewish property indirectly, for the most part, as the rightful owners had already lost it before these territories fell to the Third Reich.[2] The Soviet Union, which occupied eastern Poland in September 1939, had nationalized all larger private property there, including that belonging to Jews. Thus, when the Polish state gained indirect possession of the property of Holocaust victims after the war, it was coming from second or third hands, classified as "former German" or "abandoned."

Some of the property of Holocaust victims went into in the hands of Polish individuals, who acquired the objects either directly or from the (occupying) state. Most often they simply took possession of it as the owners were deported or murdered. Sometimes the German authorities sold to the local population remnants of Jewish property that they found to be useless for the German state. Polish criminals acquired it by theft, extortion, or other dubious means from Jews who were still alive, but defenseless and outlawed. Wartime memoirs often describe instances of Jews giving possessions to their Christian neighbors for safekeeping, which were never returned to their owners. Systematic research that would enable us to estimate the extent and results of such forms of exploitation of Nazi anti-Jewish policies and preying on the victims of the Jewish catastrophe remains to be done. Compared with the transfer of property such as enterprises, securities, real estate, and valuable objects taken by the German state, the amount of goods stolen by Polish individuals cannot be described as large, but for those affected, it certainly had severe consequences. The victims were deprived of their last remaining means, urgently needed for survival, whose value can only be appreciated in the context of a life-and-death struggle. A different channel of property transfer by which the last remnants of property still in Jewish hands ended up in the hands of Poles was black-market trading. Large-scale trade (illegal and punishable by death or the concentration camp) between the ghettos and the "Aryan side" constituted the basic source of food in the ghettos from 1940 to 1942. For many inmates of the ghettos, selling one's remaining property was the only way to avoid, or postpone, starvation.

The Second World War brought enormous material destruction. In Poland's combined prewar and postwar territory the war lasted longer than in any other European country. Heavy bombing and protracted, bitter battles took place here, reducing whole cities to rubble, such as Warsaw in 1944 or German Breslau in 1945. Even after the fighting had ceased, the deliberate and systematic destruction often continued, as in Warsaw after the end of the uprising in autumn 1944, or as a consequence of the tolerated vandalism that often followed the Soviet invasion of German-inhabited areas in the last stage of the war. Ruthless robbery by the state or individuals completed the destruction. In this way, property of inestimable value was irrevocably lost, including the equipment of entire factories. In this general destruction, Jewish property, in particular symbols of Jewish religion and culture such as synagogues, cemeteries, and books, underwent the most systematic and complete devastation.

When assessing the losses caused by the war, we should take into account not only the material damage but also the intangible, yet indubitably tremendous, losses caused by the profound disorganization of the economy. This kind of loss affected both individual businesses and the entire national economy, and therefore the entire population of the country. Ronald Zweig points out elsewhere in this volume the essential difference between prosperity and material wealth, emphasizing that prosperity cannot be taken over in the same way that material possessions can. The situation is similar with economic advantages: flows of income that disappear in the chaos of war, human capital, and other intangible assets, which are more fragile than factory walls. The expropriation, exclusion from economic activity, and subsequent physical extermination of Polish Jewry could not but cause enormous losses of this kind. The Nazi anti-Jewish policy in occupied Poland did not consist of a zero-sum game, in which the losses on the Jewish side came up as profits elsewhere. The destruction of Polish Jewry meant discontinuing its contribution to the national economy, the overall effect of which had to be negative, so that not only the Jews were the losers. Only given the antisemitic prejudice that Jews were parasites could their removal from the economy be portrayed as beneficial.

When the war ended, reconstruction began and continued for many years, but, paradoxically, the reconstruction of houses, factories, and other buildings further complicated the question of their restoration to the original owners. It turned out to be most difficult, particularly in the case of buildings that had been severely damaged, to estimate reliably and compare their value after the war and the value of reconstruction work done with public or private means and manpower. Between the end of the war and the end of the Communist regime in 1989, which opened the door for the restitution of private property, and thus represents a new "year zero," more than four decades passed, during which buildings were rebuilt, expanded, or demolished. On the other hand, many buildings that were taken over by the state were not renovated, but left to fall into disrepair, so that in 1989 they were in a pitiable condition. Besides the material changes, throughout these four decades the remaining property of Holocaust victims was also subject to changes of ownership. Property was merged, divided, or transferred one or more times, to various state institutions and enterprises, cooperatives, or sometimes, particularly since the 1980s, sold into private hands.

Another factor in the complex question of Polish restitution is the consequences of the great territorial changes after the war. The border alterations were so radical that even the very concept of "Poland" was in a state of flux—a problem that other countries struggling with the question of restitution did not have to face. Under the agreements made between the Great Powers at Yalta and Potsdam, Poland, a country that was among the war's victors, declined 20 percent in territory (from 389,000 to 312,000 square kilometers) and was shifted 200 km to the west. It lost almost half of its prewar territory to the USSR and acquired large areas that in 1938 had belonged to Germany and the Free City of Danzig (Gdansk), that make up about a third of Poland today.

In the territories that fell to the Soviet Union or, more precisely, the Soviet Republics of Ukraine, Belorussia, and Lithuania, there had been important Jewish centers such as Wilno (Vilnius) and Lwow (Lviv), and hundreds of *shtetlekh*, little towns with significant, sometimes majority Jewish populations. One could say that, in view of Poland's changed borders, the restitution of the property that had belonged to the roughly 1 million Jews who lived in these regions before the war has become a problem for Lithuania, Belorussia, and Ukraine, but the matter seems to be more complicated than that.[3] Much of the Polish population from the areas annexed to the USSR resettled into the former German territories in the West. The Polish resettlers took over the (officially so named), "post-German" farms, houses, and workshops there. They exercised the right to compensation in kind for property they had left in the East. This right was laid down in the treaties of September 1944 between the Polski Komitet Wyzwolenia Narodowego [Polish National Liberation Committee] (PKWN)—the new, communist government of Poland—and the Lithuanian, Belorussian, and Ukrainian Soviet Socialist Republics.[4] Those who were deprived of this right for political reasons (for example, large landowners) began after 1989 to claim an adequate compensation from the Polish government in the Polish courts. To make things more complex, the real estate awarded after the war to the resettlers as compensation was rarely made their property. Instead they were given the "perpetual usufruct," a legal innovation that the communists substituted for property ownership.

Although the real estate and other property awarded to the resettlers as compensation was rarely officially transferred to their ownership, the provisions of the treaties of 1944 and the regulations implementing them nevertheless serve as the basis for claims against the Polish state.[5]

The Polish-Soviet agreements on population transfers and repatriation from the USSR across the new Polish-Soviet border applied to ethnic Poles and Jews but not Belorussians, Ukrainians, Lithuanians, or others.[6] Notably, the largest group of Polish Jews who survived the war spent it in Siberia, the Urals, and Central Asia, where they had been deported from the Soviet-occupied parts of Poland in 1940 and 1941. After the war, many of those who returned to Poland settled in the newly acquired western territories, mainly in Silesia, receiving material compensation on the same basis as Polish resettlers from the East. Thus, in the event that they received no compensation or inadequate compensation under the communist regime, since 1989, Jewish proprietors from former eastern Poland and their heirs may have claims similar to the dissatisfied Polish resettlers and they may seek compensation from the Polish, rather than the Ukrainian, Belorussian, or Lithuanian governments.

At the end of the war, only an estimated 250,000 Jews were in (or passing through) Poland, a mere fragment of the prewar Jewish population. Most of these survivors emigrated soon afterwards.[7] As entire families were murdered in the Holocaust, there were in many cases no direct heirs to a substantial proportion of the property left behind. Furthermore, regulations introduced in the immediate postwar period to facilitate property restitution limited the number of persons eligible for simplified procedures to the prewar owners and their directly related heirs. The decrees of 1945 and 1946 on "property which is abandoned or left behind" ("post-German and abandoned property") established a procedure by which the heirs of deceased owners—spouses and siblings as well as relatives in ascending and descending line of succession (grandparents, parents, children and grandchildren)—could gain possession of their inheritance (i.e., practical use, not the title to the property). More distant family members and other heirs had no choice but to start proceedings in accordance with regular inheritance procedures. This was, however, very difficult under the conditions at the time, when many documents and eyewitnesses were missing, public archives had been destroyed, and so on.[8]

The authors of the decrees did not conceal the fact that these restrictions had been imposed with, among other things, the possessions of murdered Jews in mind. During the debate in the *Krajowa Rada Narodowa* [National Council] (KRN), a temporary legislative body set up by the communists, the restrictions were justified, among other reasons, by a warning that without them there was a danger of enormous wealth being concentrated in a few hands. Such a concentration of wealth would, the proponents of the restrictions claimed, firstly be unjust and economically unproductive and, secondly, cause a rise in antisemitism.[9] Therefore, the combination of low survival rates (i.e., the efficiency of the Nazi "Final Solution" in Poland) and the restrictions imposed by the 1945 decree meant that most of the property of the victims of the Holocaust was classified as "abandoned." Consequently, it came under state administration and after a time (five to ten years) was nationalized.

Even if someone from the restricted circle of direct heirs had survived the war, there were many difficulties preventing them from regaining their inheritance. First of all, claimants had to prove that they were the only surviving person entitled to inherit, which was no easy task when no official death records were available. One way of getting around this obstacle was to produce an (alleged) witness who would confirm that the last owner had, before his death, bequeathed his property to this one person who had survived the war and was now applying for the recognition of their rights before the court, or confirm that the other family members entitled to inherit had definitely all been killed. The cases of restitution using this type of procedure known to this author ended with the immediate sale of the inherited property by the heir and his or her subsequent emigration. Recent research on Polish-Jewish history has brought to light many cases of abuse and forgery in these procedures.[10] Complications related to such cases continue to this day, and the Polish press still carries legal notices that appear to be invoking ghosts. One district court, for example, sought "Chaja Rozenblat, Chilelel Rozenblat, Abram Sucher Rozenblat, Ezjel Rozenblat. … who were in the camp at Treblinka during the Second World War. The above mentioned persons are requested to reply to this notice within two months, after which they will be presumed to have died."[11] The Rozenblats clearly have not come back to reclaim their property since the war. As the Rozenblats' Polish neighbors have also passed away, probably nobody remembers them in their home town anyway. But their property title remains, land registers keep their names, and civil law forces a local court to publish their names before a new owner can be confirmed.

The case of the Rozenblats' real estate points to the large discrepancy between what is recorded in the land register, the formal nationalization of "abandoned property," and its actual use by private persons. Many court cases on property claims in the 1990s have shown that the prewar owners often remain on the books because the communist officials did not pay attention to such trivia as the land register. Concerning the actual use of the property, many "abandoned" Jewish apartments were simply inhabited by Polish individuals, who often did not care about the formal ownership of the property. Over four decades it was, in practice, "their" apartment, regardless of whose name was inscribed in the prewar books. As under the communist regime private property was far from sacrosanct, what mattered was actual possession. The use of such "formerly Jewish" assets, which was not necessarily accompanied by the formal transfer of property title, was probably the most common way in which ordinary Poles became entangled in the problem that is the subject of this essay.

The term *pożydowski*, which one can translate as "formerly Jewish" (or "post-Jewish") is in itself remarkable. Words beginning with the Polish prefix *po-* refer to a kind of legacy involving something that is no longer present in a certain place. Thus, for example, the expression *zabudowania poklasztorne* is used to describe buildings (*zabudowania*) in which formerly (*po-*) a monastery (*klasztor*) was situated. In postwar Poland the terms *pożydowski* and *poniemiecki* quickly gained widespread usage as they described things that had previously belonged to Jews or Germans respectively. It should be noted that the expression conveys first the explicit information that the object in question is no longer someone's property, second, that the former owner was Jewish (or German); and third, for every Pole familiar with the historical context, it implies that the owner had lost the property as a consequence of the Second World War. Thus, the Holocaust in a sense remains hidden within the term.

The fact that various persons took over "formerly Jewish" property without acquiring a legal title had a fundamental influence on Polish-Jewish relations after the war. Jewish people who returned to their apartments or shops often came up against the open hostility of those who had taken over these assets at the time of German occupation, convinced that the Jewish owners would never return. Accounts of homecoming Jews being threatened, assaulted, and even murdered are sufficiently frequent in survivor accounts and official reports published by Jewish organizations in the first years after the war that one may assume that such events were quite common. Nevertheless, they should not be interpreted as simply a continuation of prewar anti-Jewish behavior.

In the first years after the war, Poland was the scene of uncontrollable banditry, bloody political battles, and a widespread ethnic hatred. The background was a general moral decline caused by the ruthless war, the depreciation of the value of human life in particular, the ease with which weapons could be obtained, and more. Jews were subjected to attacks by ordinary criminals, as actual or imagined participants in the political conflict (which Krystyna Kersten brilliantly describes in her book *Poles, Jews, Communism*), as well as simply for being Jewish—in other words, the object of prejudices and resentments, which were doubtless rife at that time. This hostility was one of the factors that drove surviving Jews to emigrate. This, in turn, led to an increase in the amount of property categorized as "abandoned."[12]

The issue of "formerly Jewish" property certainly contributed to the postwar wave of hostility towards Jews, which reached a climax in the Kielce Pogrom on 4 July 1946, although this was by no means its only cause. This hostility, and later on the inability to tackle it as a historical problem, probably hinged more on the question of "restitution" than anything else; still it remains an unresolved mystery. Political emotions excited by a civil war, ordinary greed, and deep-rooted ethnic prejudice and resentment were certainly present, yet they do not explain satisfactorily the violent resentment against a handful of survivors. The intensity of emotion that actual and imagined "Jews" aroused requires a closer look at irrational factors, side effects of witnessing the Holocaust. This is the claim of two authors who suppose, paradoxically, that the rise in anti-Jewish resentment came not despite the

Holocaust but because of it. As Michael Steinlauf and John Hartman convincingly argue, the Holocaust left an indelible, if not always consciously felt, mark on all those who had witnessed the cruel, unimaginable death of their Jewish neighbors during the war. Moreover, when the occupation ended, instead of being able to process this dreadful past symbolically and emotionally, people experienced further upheavals as communist rule was violently imposed upon Poland.[13] With their proposal to apply theories of individual psychology to Polish society, which most directly witnessed the crimes committed against the Jews, Steinlauf and Hartman introduce an interesting new perspective to the discussion of Polish reactions to the Holocaust.

Not only individual survivors but also Jewish organizations encountered problems when trying to get back their property. This was despite a sound legal foundation for their claims. Many real estate properties that had belonged to Jewish organizations before the war were now in the hands of powerful institutions such as the *Urząd Bezpieczeństwa* [Security Office] (UB) or Communist Party newspapers. Applications for the return of these buildings were either simply ignored or rejected with reference to a clause that allowed the state to take over businesses of "national importance." Such treatment of Jewish property was by no means exceptional. And, as a historian of Jews in postwar Poland has noted, the unscrupulous conduct of the state authorities in appropriating private property could have also rubbed off on ordinary citizens.[14] Like those individuals who took possession of Jewish property without acquiring a legal title, under the general policy favoring nationalization, the authorities and other state institutions often seized real estate properties without doing anything about the legal title, leaving the legal position unresolved for many years. Such property became de facto state property, even if the (former) owner's name remained inscribed in the Land Register—until the regime imploded and private property once again became a key word in public discourse.

Thus the process of nationalization by the communist authorities, which affected more than just productive assets, was the fourth major upheaval to have an impact on the question of Jewish property and its restitution—following the systematic expropriation by the two occupying powers, destruction resulting from the war, and changes in Poland's postwar borders. Starting with big business and large landed estates, practically all trade and industry was expropriated, so that only the smallest stores and workshops remained in private hands. Also the above-mentioned law on "abandoned property" should be viewed within the context and as a part of this massive state-organized expropriation. The general process of nationalization relied on more than twenty different laws and decrees. It was described as land reform and the collectivization of agriculture; the nationalization of industry and the reconstruction of destroyed cities; the economic integration of the newly acquired Western Territories and the democratization of education; the fight against the armed Ukrainian underground and the fight against "speculators"; but one goal was always the same: to eradicate private property, the root of all evil, in communist belief.[15]

At the end of the 1950s, the regime entered a phase of stabilization, during which the property situation established over the previous turbulent decade was consolidated. Over the decades that followed, the Poles gradually grew accustomed to the communist order. Similarly, as Cold War tensions began to ease and international relations normalized, the West also recognized the property dimension of the new order in Poland. In the 1960s, the government of the People's Republic of Poland signed a number of treaties on compensation and made compensation payments to some Western governments for property of their citizens that had been nationalized. Although the sum paid in each case was below the actual value of the property in question, as the communist regime was firmly in control and there was nothing to indicate that it would collapse in the foreseeable future, the affected parties contented themselves with this limited compensation. This has legal consequences for some claims today. To cite one example, Warsaw's Supreme Administrative Court dismissed an action brought by a U.S. citizen who had demanded the return of an apartment block in Kraków as she had already received compensation in the past under the provisions of the earlier Polish-American treaty, under which the People's Republic of Poland had paid $40 million to the U.S. government.[16]

What is the situation concerning the restitution of Jewish property in Poland today? As mentioned above, this issue is only one aspect of the more general question of restoring property rights in Poland, that is reprivatization. This general question has not yet been solved and so it remains. Although there are some 170,000 former owners or their heirs in Poland, it is the only country in post-communist Europe not to have an effective law on reprivatization. This issue became a political bone of contention as early as 1990, when it was first put on the agenda of the Polish Senate. Over the course of the next decade, various government coalitions put forward proposals for resolving the issue, but none of them were adopted by the Parliament. They were usually initiated by right-wing parties, who referred to the importance of private property rights and the scandalous injustice of nationalization by the communists. Their proposals envisaged the physical return of property where possible, or compensation in cash or in government bonds. The parties of the left reacted with reluctance, referring to the considerable costs such measures would entail for the state (i.e., the taxpayer); the impossibility of compensating for any of the other kinds of losses, apart from property, which many people had suffered over the last fifty years; and the growing displeasure of voters with the idea of reprivatization, which they regarded as a loss of "common property" in favor of private owners. For these reasons, the left put a brake on legislative initiatives and introduced bills to limit the extent of reprivatization. During a recent attempt to pass a law, it was calculated that the return or compensation of only half of all nationalized property would cost about 11 billion U.S. dollars. In view of the social tensions in the country and the high budget deficit, even those in favor of reprivatization acknowledged the considerable political and financial obstacles to be overcome.

As further proposals for reprivatization ended up in the wastepaper basket and time passed by, the chances of property being returned grew ever slimmer. In particular, state-owned real estate was sold and thus no longer able to be returned. In the 1990s, state enterprises were sold to private investors; national institutions and organs of self-government disposed of some of their real estate, and other properties were transferred to third parties in payment of debts. The result was that the state's property reserves, which could have been used for the restitution of property in kind, melted away. Whereas in 1993 it still would have been possible to settle about 80 percent of claims by return in kind, seven years later this was possible for only about 30 percent, partly reflecting the fact that the number of restitution claims had risen in the meantime. The legally guaranteed "reprivatization reserves," that is, the amount of equity in privatized enterprises that was set aside to meet possible claims, proved too small. Reprivatization plans inevitably gave priority to compensation in the form of securities over the return of property in kind. This implied putting further strain on the budget (in other words, on the taxpayer), which, in turn, was grist to the mill of all reprivatization opponents—those who were against it in principle as well as those who wanted it restricted. Public opinion surveys helped to gauge the effects this strain had on the population. While in 1991, 65 percent of those questioned agreed that "what was stolen has to be returned" and only 28 percent were against the return of nationalized property, in 1999, only 40 percent were still in favor of reprivatization.[17]

As mentioned, the failed legislative initiatives aimed at the property of all private persons; a law was passed, however, on the restitution of the property of Jewish communities.[18] This law is based on a special procedure, that—even if it did not live up to the expectations of the Jewish organizations in all cases—still allowed for the return of a considerable portion of their property. This success would certainly not have been possible if laws concerning other religious bodies, particularly the Roman Catholic Church, had not paved the way.

It should be stressed that a considerable number of Jews who raised claims to property in Poland and who were potential beneficiaries of the return of Jewish property are foreign nationals, not Polish citizens. This international dimension of the restitution question has become an essential part of public discussions, owing to the pressure exerted by claimants and by media attention. The best-known case is that of the class action brought against Poland (the Republic of Poland, the Polish government, and other Polish persons and institutions) in 1999 before a New York court in the name of eleven American Jews and "others similarly situated."[19] The statement of complaint demanded the return of property and compensation for loss of use during the period when the defendant administered this property. It opened with a very peculiar historical introduction, intended to prove that over the preceding 54 years Poland has pursued a policy aimed at the destruction of the Jews, that Nazi Germany set up extermination camps in Poland because of the "antisemitic climate" that prevailed there, and that after the war the communist authorities, hand in hand with the anti-communist underground, tried to implement a diabolical plan to drive out the last remaining Jews. After nearly three years the court dismissed the class action on the grounds that Poland has immunity by reason of its state sovereignty.[20]

Jewish persons with foreign citizenship who file claims against Poland also exerted or continue to exert pressure in other ways: members of the U.S. Congress and other public figures write to the Polish government; Polish airlines are threatened with exclusion from landing rights at New York airports; hearings are organized in U.S. state assemblies and Congress; investment in Poland by American companies is discouraged; threats were made to block the expansion of the North Atlantic Treaty Organization (NATO) and the European Union. Information about such forms of pressure reaches the Poles quickly, as the initiators of foreign claims deliberately publicize their grievances, following American lobbying patterns, and the Polish media provide extensive coverage of their actions. However, not all claimants favor high-profile campaigns in order to exert pressure; there are also those who work for restitution in a more discreet and conciliatory manner.[21]

With regard to the restitution of Jewish property, there is another difficulty, which should not be overlooked, on top of all the obstacles blocking the path of general reprivatization and specific reprivatization in favor of foreign nationals: the prejudice against and antipathy toward Jews still present in Polish society.[22] This is fed by marginal, but obsessively active antisemitic organizations and publishers, and it is sometimes exploited or tolerated by more prominent factions and political figures. Dark emotions and paranoid ideas that sometimes surface reveal only too clearly that the psychological problems detected by Hartman and Steinlauf are not entirely a thing of the past; nor do they only afflict the war generation.[23] Regardless of the causes and mechanisms by which such prejudices against the Jews spread, the fact remains that they exist and influence the actions of politicians.

It is an unfortunate but nevertheless unsurprising coincidence that xenophobic tendencies—a dislike of Jews and resentment at foreign pressure—are particularly visible among those who vote for right-wing parties, which in principle are in favor of reprivatization. In order to keep their electorate on board, some right-wing politicians try to use subterfuge; an illustration of such tactics is the renewed attempt to pass a law on reprivatization in 2000–2001. Members of the *Zjednoczenie Chrześcijańsko-Narodowe* (Christian-National Union) revised the government bill in a way to restrict entitlement to reprivatization to current Polish citizens. This was to exclude foreign nationals, including emigrants who had changed their citizenship, and their heirs. Since a considerable proportion of Jewish claims were brought by foreign nationals the introduction of this apparently neutral condition of citizenship constituted nothing less than ethnic discrimination. This restriction, together with the tremendous costs involved in the planned process of reprivatization, were reason enough for the left-wing president to reject the bill in March 2001.[24] Since then, the general process of reprivatization has been put on hold, although cases are still being pursued privately in the courts and have enabled several thousand people to get back their property.

The question of restitution is in many ways connected to the question of Polish-Jewish relations, their history and remembrance, but particularly to the attitude of the Poles to the Holocaust. Since the late 1980s, Poland has witnessed at least eleven significant public debates on the Holocaust and Polish attitudes toward Jews. These debates were fought out over a long period in frequent articles and commentaries in the press or other national media, dealing either directly with an event in the past or with publications on the issue. Among these were the arguments over the construction of a supermarket and discotheque in Oświęcim (Auschwitz), the erection of crosses at the gravel pit there, which sparked a debate on the title to symbolic sites, and discussion of Jan T. Gross's book *Neighbors* on the mass crime committed in Jedwabne, to mention just some of the debates that also attracted interest outside Poland. The range and intensity of these and other discussions and, to an even greater degree, the emotions released in the course of these debates, are sufficient proof that the genocide of the Jews and Polish reactions to it were not just events in the distant past, but are highly charged issues of the present day.[25]

The question of "former Jewish" property most probably contributed to the inflamed emotions. By its material presence and special status it has the power to awaken hitherto merely subconscious disquiet, not only among the older generation who experienced the war directly, but also among younger people who inherited such property. Here it is less a question of legal status than of the property's "moral" status. Awareness of the fact that "former Jewish" property did not come into the possession of its new owners by the usual means of legal sale or inheritance, and that a terrible and unimaginable crime is entangled in its history, can be a source of inner anxiety, even when the new owner is in no way responsible for the tragic fate of the previous owner. Psychologist John Hartman believes that the material benefit that some Poles drew from the Holocaust contributed to the development of the tense relationship between Jews and Poles, and awakened in the latter a more or less clearly perceived sense of guilt as well as paranoid fears about the return of the rightful owners, which continue to this day.[26]

If one takes shadows as a metaphor for the past, one could say that "former Jewish" objects cast a deeper, darker shadow than others, as almost every one of them has a dramatic history. It must be stated, however, that this view is merely a hypothesis. Historians are sensitive to the shadows of the past for professional reasons, but it is not safe to assume that this awareness is also shared today by those who live in "former Jewish" houses or use "former Jewish" furniture. The theory that collective, yet subconscious knowledge of the crimes against the owners clings to "former Jewish" property is interesting and certainly convincing for a psychologist, but it remains very difficult to verify empirically. Despite these reservations, examining the question of former Jewish property together with Polish reactions to the Holocaust and the perplexing attitude of Poles toward Jews after the war seems worthwhile, as it enables one to explain how these three difficult questions affected each other, and thereby to make some progress toward demystifying all of them.

The problem of returning "former Jewish" property to the original owners was not a dominant issue in most Polish debates about the Holocaust. Although the connection between this problem and Polish attitudes toward Jews frequently became apparent, the property question was usually seen as an example of the phenomenon to be explained, rather than its explanation. Ambitions to take over property or unwillingness to give it back were, in particular, referred to as factors influencing the attitudes of Poles toward Jews during the war and afterwards. The question of "formerly Jewish" property was not alien even to the proponents of an apologist version of Polish history. Yet they accused those in favor of a critical analysis of Polish attitudes of serving an influential Jewish lobby, which wanted to take over a considerable amount of property in Poland or force Poland to pay compensation, similar to the compensation paid recently by Swiss banks.

To a certain extent, the Polish debates can be viewed as part of a more general phenomenon of a European coming to terms (or settling of accounts) with the history of the Second World War and, particularly, with the Holocaust. Debates similar to these were held in France, Switzerland, the Netherlands, Italy, Hungary, and other countries as well as, of course, Germany. It is notable that the liveliest debates on World War II have taken place in states that were once allied to or satellites of the Third Reich, as well as in formerly occupied and neutral countries. They were difficult everywhere. Polish discussion of reactions to the Holocaust took place in a country that had been the site of the largest ghettos and extermination camps and where Jews from many countries had been deported to die. Dutch, French, and Hungarians had witnessed discrimination against their Jewish neighbors and their "resettlement to the East," but in Poland knowledge of the genocide was fundamentally more direct, intimate, and widespread—practically unavoidable—and therefore demanded a reaction, if only a mental one.

The situation was also aggravated by the fact that the Communist government had blocked open discussion of Polish-Jewish relations and the Holocaust for more than forty years and, like other issues of recent history, it manipulated public memory of these events for political ends. Under these circumstances, the psychological wounds described above could not heal. Fear and feelings of uncertainty reinforced Poles' defensive attitudes. It was no coincidence that discussion of the Holocaust intensified after freedom of speech was regained. In certain respects, the numerous debates in the 1990s made up for lost time during the previous forty years.

In the communist era, a widening gulf between the collective Polish and collective Jewish memory of the war and the German occupation grew. While discrepancies in perception can already be detected in wartime documents, later mechanisms of social communication and remembrance as well as the "politics of memory" made Polish and Jewish visions of the past even harder to reconcile. In particular, many Jews accuse Poles of indifference toward or even of satisfaction at the Jewish catastrophe, of having benefited from it, and, in some (but rather numerous) cases, of having directly participated in the persecution. These views conflict with the common conviction among Poles that they themselves were innocent victims of the Nazi regime who did what they could to help the Jews.

It is worth pointing out again that the first of the big debates on Polish-Jewish relations was sparked by Jan Blonski's article calling on the Poles to perform "moral compensation" for their indifference to the plight of Jews, which caused them to die in isolation. This demand was met with a hail of criticism, emphasizing Poland's victim status and the fact that Poles had nonetheless helped the Jews. As Anthony Polonsky noted, the fact that Jews and Poles were both victims of Nazi German policies, albeit to varying degrees and in different ways, in no way promoted their mutual understanding.[27]

A settling of accounts with the war is all the more filled with tension and emotion in Poland because the Polish national consciousness seems fixated on the past; the sense of attachment to previous generations seems to be stronger here than in many other countries, and the Second World War is the most dramatic and tragic event in Polish national history. In the case of Poland, the "imagined community," to quote Benedict Anderson, is a community with "our dead," particularly those of the wartime generation. Merely permitting the thought that among this generation, among the heroes and martyrs, there were also criminals who persecuted Jews or exploited their misfortune is very difficult for many Poles. In this context, one speaks of a Polish "obsession with innocence." Of course, this obsession combined with the peculiar status of "former Jewish" property makes the use of this property even more problematic. The recurring debates on Polish-Jewish relations and the Holocaust have made some progress in broadening public understanding of the problems involved, which may also facilitate finding a solution to the question of property. However, the prospects for reprivatization remain poor.

Translated from German by Charlotte Kreutzmüller

Notes

1. On the seizure of property by the occupation authorities see, for example, A. Dmitrzak, *Hitlerowskie kontrybucje w okupowanej Polsce 1939–1945* [Nazi Contributions in Occupied Poland] (Pozna'n, 1983); C. Łuczak, *Polityka ludnościowa i ekonomiczna hitlerowskich Niemiec w okupowanej Polsce* [The Demographic and Economic Policy of Nazi Germany in Occupied Poland] (Poznan, 1979); C. Madajczyk, *Die Okkupationspolitik Nazi-Deutschlands in Polen 1939–1945* (Berlin, 1987).
2. On the Soviet occupation from 1939 to 1941, see, for example, J. Gross, *Revolution from Abroad: The Soviet Conquest of Poland's Western Ukraine and Western Belorussia* (Princeton, NJ, 1988).
3. Figures from the Główny Urząd Statystyczny [Main Statistical Office] (GUS) in A. Wyczaski et al., eds., *Historia Polski w liczbach: Ludność i terytorium* [History of Poland in Numbers: Population and Territory] (Warsaw, 1993).
4. See the relevant documentation, for example, in S. Ciesielski (ed.), *Przesiedlenie ludności polskiej z kresów wschodnich do Polski 1944–1947* [The Resettlement of the Polish Population from the Eastern Territories to Poland, 1944–1947] (Warsaw, 1999), 55–60 and from 94. See also P. Ther, *Deutsche und Polnische Vertriebene. Gesellschaft und Vertriebenenpolitik in der SBZ/DDR und in Polen 1945–1956* (Göttingen, 1998), 46–48 and 77–82.
5. See J. Kochanowski, "Eine andere Schuldrechnung. Die polnischen Umsiedler und ihr Kampf um Entschädigungen," *Zeitschrift für Geschichtswissenschaft* 1 (2003): 65–73.
6. See K. Kersten, *Repatriacja ludności polskiej po II wojnie światowej* [The Repatriation of the Polish Population after the Second World War] (Wrocław, 1974).
7. Up to 1947 about 200 to 250,000 Jews lived in Poland; after 1956 a few thousand more Jewish "returnees" arrived from the Soviet Union. Experts point out that an unknown number of Jews who survived in Poland did not reassume their original names and concealed their Jewish identity; see J. Adelson, "W Polsce zwanej Ludową," [In Poland, when it was called the People's Republic] in *Najnowsze dzieje Żydów w Polsce* [Contemporary History of the Jews in Poland], ed. J. Tomaszewski (Warsaw, 1993), 398 and following. The main waves of emigration were in the years 1946 and 1947, when more than 150,000 Jews left the country; in the years 1949–1950, when more than 25,000 left, and 1956–1960, when more than 50,000 emigrated; see D. Stola, *Emigracja z Polski 1948–1989* [Emigration from Poland 1948–1989], (forthcoming).
8. The Decree of May 6, 1945, which was ammended in 1946, concerned "abandoned and former German" property or "abandoned and left behind" property. The decrees granted temporary relief until the end of 1947.
9. See M. Pisarski, "Emigracja Żydów z Polski w latach 1945–1951" [The Emigration of Jews from Poland, 1945–1951) in *Studia z dziejów i kultury Żydów w Polsce po 1945 roku* [Studies on the History and Culture of the Jews in Poland after 1945], ed. J. Tomaszewski (Warsaw, 1997), 39. At the same time there was also a harmonization of the civil law, including the law of inheritance, which during the interwar period had retained some contradictory elements from the era of the partitions.
10. The investigation into the crime in Jedwabne (where a large group of Poles participated in the mass murder of their Jewish neighbors in summer 1941) revealed that immediately after the war in the Białystok region (and undoubtedly in other regions as well), organized groups assisted by bribed witnesses acquired the property of murdered Jews, which they then resold as soon as possible. On this, see K. Persak, "Akta postępowań cywilnych z lat 1947–1949 w sprawach dotyczących zmarłych żydowskich mieszkańców Jedwabnego" [Documents from Civil Proceedings in the Years 1947–1949 Concerning the Deceased Former Jewish Inhabitants of Jedwabne], in *Wokół Jedwabnego* [About Jedwabne], ed. P. Machcewicz and K. Persak (Warsaw, 2002), Vol. 2, 375–414.
11. *Gazeta Wyborcza*, 29 January 2002, 13.

12. K. Kersten, *Polacy-Żydzi-komunizm: Anatomia półprawd, 1939–1968* [Poles, Jews, Communism: An Anatomy of Half-Truths, 1939–1968] (Warsaw, 1992); J. Adelson, "*W Polsce zwanej Ludową*"; the key documents are cited in A. Cała and H. Datner-Śpiewak, eds., *Dzieje Żydów w Polsce 1944–1968: Teksty źródłowe* [History of the Jews in Poland, 1944–1968: Source texts] (Warsaw, 1997) from 23; on the discovery of the crimes committed against a group of surviving Jews in the town of Kańczuga, see *Gazeta Wyborcza*, 2–3 March 2002.
13. M. Steinlauf, *Bondage to the Dead: Poland and the Memory of the Holocaust* (Syracuse, NY, 1997), 57–58; J. Hartman, "Polish-Jewish Relations and the Holocaust: A Psychohistorical Perspective," in *I Remember Every Day ... the Fates of the Jews of Przemyśl during the Second World War*, edited by J. Hartman and J. Krochmal (Przemyśl, 2002): 283–302.
14. M. Pisarski, "Emigracja Żydów," 41.
15. Ultimately only the history of private agriculture took a different course. The circumstance that Poland was an exception within the Soviet Bloc, as a large proportion of peasant farms remained in private hands, did not, however, have any influence on the fate of Jewish property, as in prewar Poland there were virtually no Jews who owned their own small farms.
16. "Odszkodowanie i nic więcej" [Compensation and nothing more], in *Rzeczpospolita*, 16 January 2001.
17. Many articles on reprivatization appeared in the Polish daily and weekly press; see the articles in *Rzeczpospolita*, 2–3 December 2000; *Polityka*, 27 January 2001; *Gazeta Wyborcza*, 27-28 January 2001.
18. Law of 20 February 1997 on the Relationship of the (Polish) State to the Jewish Religious Communities (Ustawa z 20 lutego 1997 r. o stosunku państwa do gmin wyznaniowych żydowskich).
19. Extensive quotations from and commentaries on this lawsuit were published, for example, in the *Gazeta Wyborcza* on 5 August 1999; a copy of the complaint brought before the U.S. District Court for the Eastern District of New York, Garb et al. v. Republic of Poland, 99 Civ. 3487 (ERK), is in the possession of the author.
20. See *Rzeczpospolita* and other newspapers on 25 June 2002; the complaint in New York did not set a precedent. The first complaint in this matter was already rejected by a court in Chicago two years earlier.
21. For example, the Holocaust Restitution Committee, as reported in *Rzeczpospolita* on 22 May 2002.
22. See, for example, *Czy Polacy są antysemitami? Wyniki badania sondażowego* [Are Poles Antisemites? Results of Public Opinion Polls], ed. I. Krzemiński (Warsaw, 1996).
23. For a penetrating analysis of this topic, see the series of articles by A. Mencwel, "Gwiazda na starej chałupie" [The Star of David on the Old Cottages], in *Gazeta Wyborcza* on 15 and 22 June 2002.
24. The issue was commented upon extensively in the media in the period from January to March 2001; some key articles are available on the internet (under "reprywatyzacja," for example, at http:/www.rzeczpospolita.pl and http:/www.wyborcza.pl.). Incidentally, it should be noted that the envisioned restriction to Polish citizens produced negative reactions not only among Jewish emigrants, but also in the large Polish diaspora, especially in the United States.
25. See Introduction to A. Polonsky and J.B. Michlic, eds, *The Neighbors Respond. The Controversy over the Jedwabne Massacre in Poland* (Princeton and Oxford, 2004).
26. J. Hartman, "Polish-Jewish Relations and the Holocaust."
27. A. Polonsky, ed., *"My Brother's Keeper?": Recent Polish Debates on the Holocaust* (London, 1990), 289.

– Part IV –

Concluding Remarks

Reflections on the Restitution and Compensation of Holocaust Theft

Past, Present, and Future

Gerald D. Feldman

In dealing with the intractable and painful subject of this volume, one encounters the problem that the theft to be inventoried is as numbing in its dimensions, albeit not as horrifying, as the murder that accompanied it, and that the tasks of *Wiedergutmachung* ("making good again") seem more and more complex and even insurmountable the more one learns and the more time passes. There appears to be an increasingly inverse relationship between the outcomes of historical research and the capacity to take fair and effective action to right historical wrongs. There is a struggle between those who call for legal peace and who argue, as was done elequently by Jürgen Kocka in the concluded discussion that the conference on which this volume is based, that at some point one has to have a statute of limitations on restitution and compensation lest injustices be committed in the name of justice; and those on the other side of the debate who insist that the frontier has not been reached. Thus, in a letter to the *New York Times* in response to an article on the pillage of Jewish assets in Vienna, distinguished law professor and Jewish leader Harry Reicher pointed out that "for virtually every Jew whose property was seized, there was a non-Jew who benefited." He went on to argue that "many personal fortunes were built up in that way, and were transferred to second- and now third-generation heirs. While there has been some restitution, it has been limited to assets actually confiscated. What has been left unconsidered is the moral and legal right to the profits from those assets, which continue to accrue to this day. In the panoply of Holocaust-era compensation, this may well be the last frontier."[1] As Frank Bajohr convincingly demonstrates in his contribution to this volume, the extent to which Aryanization was a social

---

Notes for this section are found on page 268.

process involving a host of direct and indirect intermediaries cannot be underestimated. This, however, hardly makes the tasks of restitution simpler. Although there are cases in which profits from stolen assets have been taken into account in compensation cases, the notion that the sins of the parents shall be visited upon the children from generation unto generation is grist for the mills of those who argue that the unlimited quest for justice can lead to new injustice and that it is legitimate to demand that compensation be brought to a reasonable termination.

Indeed, some of those who feel, or find themselves, beleaguered by restitution claims wonder if there really will ever be a "last frontier." Why this can be the case can be illustrated by a personal anecdote. In a recent conversation with a person whom I greatly admire and who has spent a good deal of his life dealing with restitution issues, I responded to his question about why a major German insurer was resisting the idea of computerizing and listing the names of the million-plus insurance policies in its files by pointing out that, aside from the privacy issues involved, this was an issue of cost-benefit analysis and that the number of unpaid or uncompensated Jewish insurance policies to be found was likely to be very low and that it would be better to use the money to help impoverished Jews than to pay auditors. My experience going through such policies was that it was very difficult to distinguish Jewish from non-Jewish policies and that those that could be identified had been compensated under the German compensation legislation of the 1950s. What these Jews did receive, I admitted, was pitifully small thanks to the currency reform of 1948, which reduced all RM values by 90 percent, but this was the fate of all paper assets. At this point, my interlocutor shot back that Allianz and the other insurance companies could well afford to do the whole compensation of Jewish policyholders all over again. I believe that this was stated more in frustration than in seriousness, and that he was well aware that one could not undo the now recognizable injustices of the restitution that took place a half century ago any more than people will be able to correct the inadequacies of our present efforts in the year 2150. There is, in fact, something terribly unjust about Jews being forced to accept a ten-to-one RM-DM exchange rate for Hitler's and Germany's war, but the historical context is important and one should remember that the American occupiers of Germany, while certainly insisting that Jews receive restitution and compensation, were no less insistent that this be done in strict accordance with the currency reform.

To be sure, no one involved in the discussions at our conference argued for drawing a final line under these events, although certainly public voices were raised elsewhere in support of the alleged virtues of forgetting, and there has always been the wish, publicly unexpressed for reasons of political correctness by most of those who entertain it, that the entire business would just go away. Peter Novick's seriously researched but rather cynical *The Holocaust in American Life* has had the unfortunate function in Europe of providing a convenient but actually illegitimate explanation of the persistence of Holocaust issues since the book is neither concerned with the historical study of the Holocaust nor restitution issues.[2] Of much greater concern is the totally unjustified attention paid in Europe to Norman Finkelstein's *The Holocaust Industry: Reflections on the Exploitation of Jewish Suffering*.[3] Little more than a pamphlet, and certainly not based on serious research, Finkelstein's polemic, which seriously distorts historical fact, is an odd mixture of personal resentment against the alleged misappropriation of funds by Jewish organizations as illustrated by the purported undercompensation of his mother, and of anti-Zionist screed. At the same time, it charges that the Jewish organizations have been blackmailing Swiss and other European banks and industries, and it does so with singular disregard of what the issues are. While it is hardly surprising that such a diatribe would be welcomed in certain quarters, it is unfortunate that serious commentators should devote attention to such a self-serving polemic that is founded neither on serious research nor on a command of the substantial historical literature.

This does not mean that pleas for a timely legal peace and an expeditious settlement of outstanding claims, neither of which concern Finkelstein, should not be taken seriously. There is nothing incompatible about arguing on the one hand, that there should be a peaceable legal statute of limitations on restitution and compensation claims at some suitable point; and on the other that the spoliation of European Jewry and the effort to exterminate the Jews have permanent consequences for European consciousness and for our understanding of the obligations of civil society in dealing with these terrible events. As Regula Ludi's discussion of Switzerland shows, the dormant accounts question was in truth the tip of an iceberg of collaboration with the National Socialists in which Swiss governments pursued "liberal" policies that made an unoccupied Switzerland more useful to Germany than an occupied one would have been. What was most dormant in the period between 1946, when Allied efforts to call the Swiss to account began to fall victim to the Cold War, and 1996, when the issues of the Swiss past fully erupted, was the consciousness of how much the practices of Swiss neutrality had served the interests of the Third Reich. As the voluminous findings of the Bergier Commission demonstrated, restitution also required a changed understanding of the Swiss past.

In discussing these issues, I think it important to consider Holocaust restitution in the plural terms rather than singular. There were, as Constantin Goschler spells out in his article, a number and variety of restitutions, and these did not take place at a single time or a single place. In our preoccupation with the mountain of new research made possible by the opening of the archives that followed the collapse of the Soviet Bloc and the claims, court cases, and settlements that began with the charges against the Swiss banks in 1996, it is easy to overlook or dismiss the first efforts to deal with issues of compensation and restitution in the years immediately following the end of the Second World War.

As Ronald Zweig has reminded us in the important second edition of his most instructive work on the Claims Conference, "it is doubtful that the current wave of assets negotiations will lead to settlements that will provide more than a small fraction of what has already been paid out following the 1945–1952 agreements."[4] It is all too easy to dismiss the achievements of the late 1940s and the 1950s when the Americans in particular forced a very substantial amount of restitution and compensation that later found extensive legal formulation in the German compensation and restitution legislation of the 1950s. Goschler and Bajohr have pointed out how much resistance there was to restitution and compensation in Germany, and the obstacles that needed to be overcome. The German agreements with Israel led to a very substantial reparations program that constituted a vital German contribution to Israel at a very crucial time in its existence, and to a significant program of aid and reconstruction on the part of the Claims Conference. As Zweig rightly reminds us, the pressing problems of this period were helping survivors whose lives had been devastated by Nazi persecution, as well as reconstruction of Jewish life and Jewish communities—what Zweig calls the "Jewish World." This is an aspect of restitution that is often overlooked, but it was after all precisely the world National Socialism sought to liquidate. One of the most important contributions of Zweig's new edition, however, is to reveal for the first time in public that nearly half the money spent by the Claims Commission went to the highly secret "relief-in-transit" program designed to provide aid to Jews living behind the Iron Curtain, many of whom continued to be the victims of what was now communist persecution and oppression.[5]

While the discovery of new historical facts is of obvious importance, what also concerns us is the recovery of history that was repressed or suppressed. As Jürgen Lillteicher's discussion of German restitution argues, there is a relationship between Wiedergutmachung and the formation of a civil society, on the one hand, and the coming to terms with the past (*Vergangenheitsbewältigung*) on the other. He argues, perhaps too strongly, that the German reparations, restitution, and compensation programs of the years following the war were too much the product of Allied, especially American, pressure and too fraught with self-pity and the sense of victimization on the part of the Germans, as well as bureaucratic stalling and resistance, to be viewed as a genuine reflection of the formation of a civil society in Germany. Nevertheless, he concedes that these programs entailed positive consequences beyond their material benefits to the recipients. They did so in the first instance by creating new standards for international and national law, since the acceptance of German reparation or compensation—Wiedergutmachung—entailed the moral and legal obligation to restitute one's own national victims. The number of nations thus obligated has of course increased substantially with the German compensation payments since 1989. However, there is a second positive consequence of the postwar Wiedergutmachung, namely that it entailed engagement in a *Vergangenheitspolitik* (politics of dealing with the past) in Germany that has not only continued to this day but that has spread to other European nations. Certainly the West German Vergangenheitspolitik of the first two decades after the war left much to be desired, which helps to explain many of the flaws of the Wiedergutmachung; but West Germany's willingness to acknowledge itself as the legal successor of the Third Reich—with all the moral as well as material burdens thus entailed—contributed mightily to the transformation of Vergangenheitspolitik over time and to the creation of the robust civil society that characterizes Germany today.[6] This is in marked contrast to Austria, which was not only allowed but also encouraged by the Allies to consider itself the "first victim" of National Socialist German expansion, and could thus, at least until recently, evade responsibility for its own role in Nazi crimes, including the spoliation of the Jews.

At the same time, however, Lillteicher makes the very important point that Vergangenheitspolitik involves more than some vaguely evolving responsibility for the past, but rather entails as precise a knowledge as one can muster of what actually happened in the past and what it is that needs to be or can be acknowledged as deserving of restitution.

Much research on the spoliation of European Jewry has been done over the past decade by individual historians, and by historians working for national commissions or for private enterprises that have commissioned historians to look into their record during the National Socialist period. One of the great achievements of this vast research effort has been to document the extent to which Jewish spoliation was international in scope and was anything but the exclusive domain of Germany as the hegemonial power. To be sure, as Martin Dean demonstrates in his chapter, both the methods and mechanisms of plunder and the inspiration to plunder were provided by German intiative, but the history is far more multifaceted than previously imagined. Quite aside from the variety of means by which Jewish property was stolen and Jews were excluded from economic life, much attention has recently been given to the networks of spoliation, which involved government officials and occupation authorities, German and non-German officials charged with the registration of Jewish assets, agencies or banks used to collect Jewish property, private banks engaged in the transfer of Jewish assets, and the government agencies or private persons and institutions into whose possession these assets came.

The functioning of these networks varied considerably. Leaving aside the great difference between Western and Eastern Europe (to be discussed shortly), as Jean-Marc Dreyfus notes and as the individual country papers attest, one finds considerable variation among the Western European countries. As the work of Gerard Aalders has shown, the looting in the Netherlands—like the murder of the Dutch Jews—was extraordinarily efficient and "successful," thanks in good measure to the experience and enthusiasm of the Austrians in the Nazi civilian administration, the pliancy of the Jewish victims, the collaboration of the Dutch civil service and police, and the organized rapacity of various private German banks and enterprises.[7] In Belgium, by contrast, as Rudi van Doorslaer explains, there was a good deal of slippage—the great exception being the Antwerp diamond market—because the German military administration was simply less interested in Jewish asset seizure. Belgian officialdom was both less controlled and less cooperative, and both private banks and the Jews were less willing to report assets. The most complex case was France, where the Vichy regime became massively engaged and sought to bend the Aryanization process to its own interests while the German military administration in the Occupied Zone played a more ambivalent role.

In each of these three countries, the history of postwar restitution underwent a two-stage process that reflected its wartime history. In the case of the Netherlands, the murder of the overwhelming majority of the nation's Jews tended to reduce the attention given to the Jewish plight and the pressure for restitution so that the primary emphasis was only on the legal restoration of property rights. This by all accounts was a protracted and bureaucratic process that dragged on until the early 1970s. While various types of restitution were made, the process left a legacy of bitterness and dissatisfaction that has more recently moved official commissions to recommend more substantial donations to the Jewish community on the part of the Dutch government.[8] In Belgium, as Rudi van Doorslaer reports, restitution proved very effective in the most spectacular instance of theft, namely, of diamonds from the Antwerp Jewish community, a theft that was also accompanied by the most significant part of the deportations in Belgium. The restitution record was much less impressive in other sectors, and only recently has an effort been made to compensate for the failures of the past.

The happiest record, as it turns out, is that of France, where, as Claire Andrieu argues, a number of propitious circumstances favored fairly rapid restitution. One of these was the survival of 75 percent of France's Jews, while another was the repudiation of Vichy and its works, entailing in turn a clear government commitment to restitution. As she notes, postwar compensation was based on the clear principle that "what had been taken had to be given back," and this simple materialistic principle, whatever deficiencies existed in its implementation, produced a high rate of success. She then raises the significant question of why a second round of compensation in the 1990s was necessary. The answer, she argues, lies not simply in the post-Cold War situation and the raising of these issues in the context of unfinished business in Central and Eastern Europe, but far more in a greater awareness of the full scope and criminality of the Holocaust since the 1970s, and particularly of France's role in it, a consciousness magnified by economic and cultural globalization. It is this new consciousness, for example, that puts the issue of stolen art on the table in a new way and that creates the demand for restitution in current rather than past values. It is not simply the monetary values that have changed, but the political and cultural values have changed as well. From this perspective, Holocaust restitution today reflects the development of civil society in a globalizing world.

One may of course share Constantin Goschler's view that the handling of restitution "is not an encouraging example for the role played by civil society in overcoming the consequences of historical injustice." Such scepticism is fed by Ilaria Pavan's utterly depressing account of the indifference and insensitivity shown by the Italian state and society toward the victims of Fascist persecution, a crudeness that went so far as to demand that the victims pay the administration costs of restitution. Obviously, in the Italian case the emphasis was on forgetting rather than remembering, demonstrating the fragility of Italian democracy and civil society then.

The Italian case notwithstanding, the societies discussed so far were all advanced societies and well-developed nations that had enjoyed democratic rule since 1945. The picture presented by the essays on the East presented in this volume is quite different, both with respect to the modes of spoliation and the attitudes toward restititution. While spoliation and Aryanization in the Czech lands followed the pattern of Austria in being "legally" and systematically implemented—albeit without being as "wild" as in Austria—direct expropriation, theft, and outright looting characterized the spoliation in Poland, the Baltic States, and the occupied territories of the Soviet Union. As Dieter Pohl argues in dealing with this issue, expropriation and looting of Jewish property, increasingly accompanied by population transfers and murder, were motivated by ideological rather than economic motives and were closely connected to the settlement and resettlement of ethnic Germans (*Volksdeutsche*). To be sure, bureaucratic organizations also played a role, as exemplified by the notorious Haupttreuhandstelle Ost (Central Trusteeship Agency for the East), which was charged with the expropriation and transfer of Jewish and Polish property in the annexed areas of Poland. But robbery and looting in the poorer areas of the "wild" East were characterized far more by violence and corruption than by the effort at "legal" and systematic expropriation found in the West or in Central Europe.

Another peculiarity of East Central Europe is stressed in the important chapter by Tatjana Tönsmeyer, namely that antisemitism and expropriation measures were not necessarily German imports, and that many such actions were undertaken before the Germans undertook measures of their own. Jews played an important role in the economies of the states allied to Nazi Germany, Slovakia, Hungary, and Romania, and these states sought a delicate balance between giving vent to their native societal antisemitic tendencies and indulging in a certain moderation of their expropriation measures for domestic political and economic reasons, even when increasingly trying to please the Germans with harsher measures. Thus, the expropriation of Jewish assets in Slovakia had its roots in nineteenth-century notions about the Jews and was considered a matter of "justice" quite independent of German influences. Recent research on Romania by Jean Ancel has shown that much of the Romanian plundering of the Jews was undertaken autonomously and had as its goal the enrichment of Romanians and the Romanian economy.[9] Until the German invasion of March 1944, Hungary was undoubtedly the most autonomous in its treatment of the Jews, creating an odd mixture of restrictions on Jewish economic life and dependence on continued Jewish economic activity. From this perspective, the measures inspired by the German invasion were terribly disruptive of Hungarian economic life, a situation noted in a chilling but illuminating report by an Austrian businessman from Vienna in May 1944:

> Currently the removal of the Jews dominates politics and the economy in Hungary. This can be seen from the fact that the greater part of the businesses in the capital, which as is known were in Jewish hands, are now closed. Only very few shops, whose owners were ethnic Hungarians, are open. On the streets there is a very lively commotion; the yellow sunflowers on the clothes of the Jews predominate. But also the employees, waiters, and others who have been made unemployed by the closing of the businesses can be seen on the streets. In a word, the Jews are being removed, but nobody is working. As a man of the economy, this strikes me immediately, and I think that the leading circles need to be reminded that simply removing the Jews does not suffice at all.[10]

While clearly the author of these brutal lines did not so intend them, they reinforce the powerful lessons to be learned from Ronald Zweig's discussion of the "Hungarian Gold Train" and of the mythology and fantasies connected with it. The prolonged fixation on the Hungarian Gold Train illustrates the limitations on the possibilities of restitution in two respects. On the one hand, the legal actions undertaken in American courts with respect to the train were based largely on misinformation, because the facts have been buried in the mythology surrounding the train. Given what we now know, who is really responsible to make restitution, to whom, and for how much? On the other hand, to borrow a phrase from the quoted Nazi businessman, "simply restoring Jewish property does not suffice at all" ("*mit der Restitution allein noch nichts getan ist*"), because what Zweig calls the cultural attributes connected with Jewish material assets could neither be redistributed to those who sought to gain from the thievery nor restituted later to the victims. Indeed, as Bajohr shows in his moving discussion of the loss of social and cultural capital and the psychological damage done to the despoiled and the exiled, Wiedergutmachung in these spheres is an utterly hopeless task.

What made matters worse in Central and Eastern Europe, however, was that the thievery was perpetuated by the successor regimes after 1945; neither the loss of the Jewish world nor the restitution of its material assets, were ever really confronted. The emergence of a different social system from that of the West is only part of the explanation, since, as Kubů and Kuklík point out, restitution was viewed in Czechoslovakia as a burdensome and undesired problem even before the Communists took over. Indeed, recent Czech research suggests that the pre-Communist government ended up trading off certain Jewish assets in their possession in the hope of gaining specific concessions from the Soviets.[11] This being said, the triumph of socialist systems in portions of Central and Eastern Europe had odious consequences for the cause of restitution and was tantamount to the sanctification of the National Socialist theft that preceeded them. Thus in East Germany Nazi expropriated Jewish enterprises were not only denied restitution but this expropriation was viewed as an action that helped pave the way for the nationalization program of the communist regime.[12] In Czechoslovakia after 1948, as Kubů and Kuklík report, restituted assets were actually reexpropriated by the regime, and this in a political environment in which antisemitic stereotypes were used in the fight against capitalism.

Needless to say, the same burying of the problem took place in Poland as well, which served to compound the extremely complex situation described by Dariusz Stola. In any case, insofar as Jewish assets were concerned, socialism was theft. These regimes not only failed to restitute assets, they also sought to bury memory by denying access to the important archives that would reveal how the Jews were expropriated and who benefited.

It is thus no surprise that the issues of opening archives and providing restitution have proven so extremely difficult in the cases of Central and Eastern Europe, and especially in Poland, which experienced massive border changes and where Jews suffered the worst consequences of the policies of expropriation and extermination, but where Poles were especially devastated by Nazi rule. Matters are made worse by the difficulties of Jewish-Polish relations, recent charges that Poles were perpetrators, and the very real question of what to do about Jewish property without Jews, the "Post-Jewish Question," as Stola terms it. At the same time, Poles feel surrounded by claimants—Jews, the Church, Diaspora Poles, and ironically, also postwar German expellees and their heirs—and while it is unfortunate that Poland is the one country without a restitution act, it is not entirely surprising.

This volume puts more problems on the table than can possibly be solved, and whether one wishes to accept the fact or not, much that has been lost will never be recovered and such recovery as is taking place will come to an end in the forseeable future by sheer force of circumstances. What has been gained and what might be gained in the future from this second wave of restitution? Certainly it reflects a major change in our consciousness since the years immediately following the war, and the Holocaust has now become a central event in European consciousness.[13] It also, I would submit, reflects a changed attitude toward property and property rights that recognizes the relationship between property and liberty and the role of property as an expression of human personality and value. There is, as a consequence, a much fuller awareness of the criminality of the National Socialist regimes and the emptiness of the communist dictatorships, which could neither explain the past nor confront the issues in trying to deal with the future, and even often instrumentalized antisemitism themselves. What has been gained and can continue to be gained, however, is historical knowledge and understanding. This is important to the victims and their heirs, who thereby recover at least some connection to what had once been part of their lives or their family's history. At the same time, the historical consciousness thus created is essential for the anchoring of civil societies in an expanding European community.

Notes

1. Letter to the editor, "Heirs of the Holocaust," *New York Times*, 11 March 2002.
2. Peter Novick, *The Holocaust in American Life* (Boston, 1999).
3. Norman Finkelstein, *The Holocaust Industry: Reflections on the Exploitation of Jewish Suffering* (London, 2001).
4. Ronald W. Zweig, *German Reparations and the Jewish World: A History of the Claims Conference*, 2nd edition (London, 2001), 9.
5. Ibid., chapter 5.
6. An outstanding discussion of the positive consequences of West Germany's acceptance of its role as the successor to its National Socialist predecessor is Helmut Dubiel's *Niemand ist frei von der Geschichte. Die Nationalsozialistische Herrschaft in den Debatten des Deutschen Bundestages* (Munich, 1999). For the early years, see the classic study of Norbert Frei, *Vergangenheitspolitik: Die Anfänge der Bundesrepublik und die NS-Vergangenheit* (Munich, 1996).
7. The paper given at the conference has not been included in this volume.
8. See Gerard Aalders, *Geraubt! Die Enteignung jüdischen Besitzes im Zweiten Weltkrieg* (Cologne, 2000); see also Second World War Assets Contact Group, ed., *Second World War: Theft and Restoration of Rights, Final Report* (Amsterdam, January 12, 2000), esp. 94–104.
9. See the essay by Martin Dean in this volume.
10. Josef Mayrhofer an Ministerialrat Joachim Riehle, 11 May 1944, Firmenhistorisches Archiv der Allianz AG, MR, C 2/23.
11. See Expert Report, *Jewish Gold and Other Precious Metals, Precious Stones, and Objects Made of Such Materials—Situation in the Czech Lands in the Years 1939 to 1945. Unlawful Infringement of Property Rights and its Scope; Subsequent Fate of the Jewish Assets Affected by this Infringement* (Terezin Initiative Institute, 2001), esp. Ch. VI–VII.
12. See Karin Hartewig, *Zurückgekehrt. Die Geschichte der jüdischen Kommunisten in der DDR* (Cologne, 2000), 296–97.
13. See Dan Diner, "Die Holocaust in den politischen Kulturen Europas: Erinnerung und Eigentum," in *Auschwitz. Sechs Essays zu Geschehen und Vergegenwärtigung*, ed. Klaus-Dietmar Henke (Dresden, 2001), 65–74.

Notes on Contributors

Claire Andrieu, born 1952, is Professor of Contemporary History at the Institut d'études politiques in Paris. From 1998, she was also a member of the Mission d'étude sur la spoliation des Juifs de France (Mattéoli Commission). Her publications include: *La Banque sous l'Occupation. Paradoxe de l'histoire d'une profession, 1936–1946* (Paris, 1990); *La persécution des juifs de France (1940–1944) et le rétablissement de la légalité républicaine. Recueil des textes officiels 1940–1999*, 2 vols. (Paris, 2000); and *La spoliation financière*, 2 vols. (Paris, 2000).

Frank Bajohr, born 1961, is a Researcher at the Forschungsstelle für Zeitgeschichte in Hamburg and Lecturer at the Department of History at the University of Hamburg. His publications include: *'Aryanisation' in Hamburg: The Economic Exclusion of Jews and the Confiscation of their Property in Nazi Germany 1933–1945* (New York, 2002); *Parvenüs und Profiteure. Korruption in der NS-Zeit* (Frankfurt am Main, 2001); and *"Unser Hotel ist judenfrei." Bäder-Antisemitismus im 19. und 20. Jahrhundert* (Frankfurt am Main, 2003).

Martin Dean, born 1962, is an Applied Research Scholar at the United States Holocaust Memorial Museum's Center for Advanced Holocaust Studies in Washington, DC. His publications include: *Robbing the Jews: The Confiscation of Jewish Property in the Holocaust, 1933–1945* (New York, 2008); *Collaboration in the Holocaust: Crimes of the Local Police in Belorussia and Ukraine, 1941–44* (London, 2000); and "Jewish Property Seized in the Occupied Soviet Union in 1941 and 1942: The Records of the Reichshauptkasse Beutestelle," *Holocaust and Genocide Studies*, 14, no. 2 (Spring 2000), 83–101.

Rudi van Doorslaer, born 1951, is Director of the Centre for Historical Research and Documentation on War and Contemporary Society (CEGES/SOMA). His publications include: *Enfants du ghetto. Juifs révolutionnaires en Belgique, 1925–1940* (Bruxelles, 1997); and with Jean-Philippe Schreiber, *Les curateurs du ghetto. L'Association des Juifs en Belgique sous l'occupation nazie* (Bruxelles, 2004).

Jean-Marc Dreyfus, born 1968, was a Junior Professor at the Institut d' études politiques in Paris. A former Alexander von Humboldt Fellow at the Centre Marc Bloch in Berlin, he is a Researcher at the German Historical Institute in Paris. His publications include: *Pillages sur ordonances. L'aryanisation des banques en France et leur restitution, 1940–1953* (Paris, 2003); with Sarah Gensburger, *Des camps dans Paris: Austerlitz, Lévitan, Bassano, juillet 1943 – août 1944* (Paris, 2003); and *Ami si tu tombes. Les déportés-résistants, des camps au souvenir, 1945–2005* (Paris, 2005).

Gerald D. Feldman, born 1937, Professor of History and Director of the Institute of European Studies at the University of California, Berkeley; his many publications include: "Introduction" and "The Deutsche Bank from World War to World Economic Crisis," in Lothar Gall et al., *A History of the Deutsche Bank, 1870–1995* (London, 1995), iii–ix, 129–276, 817–35; *The Great Disorder: Politics, Economics, and Society in the German Inflation, 1914–1924* (New York, 1997); and *Allianz and the German Insurance Business, 1933–1945* (New York, 2001).

Constantin Goschler, born 1960, is Professor of Contemporary History at the Ruhr-University Bochum. His publications include: with J. Lillteicher (eds.), *"Arisierung" und Restitution. Die Rückerstattung jüdischen Eigentums in Deutschland und Österreich nach 1945 und 1990* (Göttingen, 2002); *Rudolf Virchow. Mediziner, Anthropologe, Politiker* (Cologne, 2002); and *Schuld und Schulden. Die Politik der Wiedergutmachung für NS-Verfolgte nach 1945* (Göttingen, 2005).

Eduard Kubů, born 1951, is an Associated Professor and Deputy Director at the Institute of Economic and Social History, Faculty of Arts, Charles University Prague. His publications include: *Německo – dilema zahraniční politiky E. Beneša. Hospodařské vztahy s Německem v československé zahraniční politice let 1918–1924* [Germany – the Dilemma in the Foreign Policy of E. Beneš. Economic Relations with Germany in Czecholslovak Foreign Policy, 1918–1924] (Prague, 1994); and as co-editor: *Konkurrenzpartnerschaft. Deutsch-tschechoslowakische Beziehungen in der Zwischenkriegszeit* (Essen, 1999) and *Tschechen und Tschechinnen, Vermögensentzug und Restitution* (A publication of the Austrian Historical Commission) (Vienna, 2004).

Jan Kuklík, Jr., born 1967, is a Lecturer in Legal History at the Law Faculty of the Charles University in Prague. His publications include: *Londýnský exil a obnova československého statu 1938–1945* [The Exile Government in London and the Renewal of the Czechoslovak State, 1938–1945] (Prague, 1998); and *Vznik československého národního výboru a prozatímního státního zřízení ČSR v emigraci v letech 1939–1940* [The Creation of the Czechoslovak National Committee and the Preliminary Construction of the Czechoslovak Republic in Emigration, 1939–1940] (Prague, 1996).

Jürgen Lillteicher, born 1968, is a Historian at the Simon-Dubnou-Institute for Jewish Culture and History at Leipzig University. His publications include: (ed.), *Profiture des NS-Systems? Deutsche Unternehmen und das "Dritte Reich"* (Berlin, 2007); Raub, Recht un Restitution. Die Rückevstattung judischen Eigentums in der frühen Bundesrepublik (Göttingen, 2007); and *"Arisierung" und Restitution. Die Rückerstattung jüdischen Eigentums in Deutschland und Österreich nach 1945 und 1989*, ed. with Constantin Goschler (Göttingen, 2002).

Regula Ludi, born 1965, is a Researcher at the Karman Center for Advanced Studies in the Humanities, University of Berne, and Lecturer at the University of Berne. Her publications include: *Die Fabrikation des Verbrechens. Zur Geschichte der modernen Kriminalpolitik 1750–1850* (Tübingen, 1999); and with Thomas Huonker, *Roma, Sinti und Jenische. Schweizerische Zigeunerpolitik zur Zeit des Nationalsozialismus*, Publication of the Independent Commission of Experts: Switzerland – Second World War, vol. 23 (Zurich, 2001).

Ilaria Pavan, born 1972, is a Researcher in contemporary Jewry at the Scuola Normale Superiore in Pisa. Her publications include: *Gli ebrei in Italia tra persecuzione fascista e reintegratzione postbellica* (Florence, 2002); and *Tra indifferenza e ablio. Le consequenze economiche della leggi razziali in Italia 1938-1970* (Florence, 2004).

Dieter Pohl, born 1964, is an Historian at the Institut für Zeitgeschichte in Munich. His publications include: *Nationalsozialistische Judenverfolgung in Ostgalizien 1941–1944* (Munich, 1996); *Justiz in Brandenburg 1945–1955* (Munich, 2001); and *Verfolgung und Massenmord in der NS-Zeit* (Darmstadt, 2003).

Dariusz Stola, born 1963, is a Fellow at the Institute for Political Studies of the Polish Academy of Sciences, and Professor of History and vice-president at the Collegium Civitas in Warsaw. He focuses on the history of Polish-Jewish relations, international migrations in Central Europe and the Communist regime. His publications include: *PRL: trwanie i zmiana* [Communist Poland: Continuity and Change] (Warsaw, 2003); *Kampania antysyjonistyczna w Polsce 1967–1968* [The Anti-Zionist Campaign in Poland, 1967–1968] (Warsaw, 2000); *Nadzieja i zaglada* [Hope and the Holocaust] (Warsaw, 1996).

Philipp Ther, born 1967, is Junior Professor at the Europa-University Viadrina in Frankfurt an der Oder. His publications include: *Deutsche und Polnische Vertriebene. Gesellschaft und Vertriebenenpolitik in der SBZ/DDR und in Polen 1945–1956* (Göttingen, 1998); *Redrawing Nations: Ethnic Cleansing in East Central Europe*, ed. with Ana Siljak (Lanham, 2001) (Harvard Cold War Studies No. 1).

Tatjana Tönsmeyer, born 1968, is a fellow at the Berliner Kolleg für Verleichende Geschichte Europas in Berlin. Her publications include: *Das Dritte Reich und die Slowakei, 1939–1945. Politischer Alltag zwischen Kooperation und Eigensinn* (Paderborn, 2003).

Ronald W. Zweig, born 1949, is Marilyn and Henry Taub Professor for Israel Studies at New York University. His publications include: *Britain and Palestine during the Second World War* (London, 1988); *German Reparations and the Jewish World: A History of the Claims Conference* (London, 2001); *The Gold Train: The Destruction of the Jews and the Looting of Hungary* (New York, 2002).

Select Bibliography

Aalders, Gerard, and Cees Wiebes. *The Art of Cloaking Ownership: The Secret Collaboration and Protection of the German War Industry by the Neutrals – The Case of Sweden.* Amsterdam: Amsterdam University Press, 1996.

Aalders, Gerard. *Geraubt! Die Enteignung jüdischen Besitzes im Zweiten Weltkrieg.* Cologne: Dittrich, 2000.

________. *Nazi Looting: The Plunder of Dutch Jewry during the Second World War.* Oxford, UK: Berg, 2004.

Adam, Uwe Dietrich. *Judenpolitik im Dritten Reich.* Düsseldorf: Droste, 1972.

Adler, H. G. *Der verwaltete Mensch: Studien zur Deportation der Juden aus Deutschland.* Tübingen: J.C.B. Mohr, 1974.

Aglan, A., M. Margairaz, and P. Verheyde, eds. *La Caisse des dépôts et consignations, la Seconde Guerre mondiale et le XX° siècle.* Paris: A. Michel, 2003.

Aly, Götz. *Hitlers Volksstaat: Raub, Rassenkrieg und nationaler Sozialismus.* Frankfurt am Main: S. Fischer, 2005.

Ancel, Jean, ed. *Documents Concerning the Fate of Romanian Jewry during the Holocaust.* 3 vols. New York: Beate Klarsfeld Foundation, 1986.

________. *Transnistria, 1941–1942.* 3 vols. Tel Aviv: Goldstein-Goren Diaspora Research Center, 2003.

Anderl, Gabriele, Dirk Rupnow, and Alexandra-Eileen Wenck. *Die Zentralstelle für jüdische Auswanderung als Beraubungsinstitution.* Vienna: Historikerkommission, 2002.

Andrieu, Claire. *La persecution des Juifs de France (1940–1944) et le rétablissement de la légalité républicaine: Recueil des texts officiels 1940–1999,* with the participation of Serge Klarsfeld and Annette Wieviorka, and the cooperation of Olivier Cariguel, and Cécilia Kapitz. Mission d'étude sur la spoliation des Juifs de France. Paris: La Documentation Française, 2000.

________. *La spoliation financière,* with the cooperation of Cécile Omnès, David Charron Murat, Christophe Dubois, Fleur-Hélène Lebreton,

Jean-Gabriel Matsrangelo, Karine Royer, Babacar Sarr, Flavie Telles. Mission d'étude sur la spoliation des Juifs de France. Paris: La Documentation Française, 2000.

Arad, Yitzhak. "Plunder of Jewish Property in the Nazi-Occupied Areas of the Soviet Union." *Yad Vashem Studies* XXI (2000): 109–48.

Authers, John, and Richard Wolffe, *The Victim's Fortune: Inside the Epic Battle over the Debts of the Holocaust.* New York: HarperCollins, 2002.

Bähr, Johannes, and Ralf Banken eds. *Das Europa des "Dritten Reichs": Recht, Wirtschaft, Besatzung, Das Europa der Diktatur.* Vol. 5. Frankfurt am Main: Klostermann, 2005.

_______. *Der Goldhandel der Dresdner Bank im Zweiten Weltkrieg.* Leipzig: Kiepenhauer, 1999.

Bajohr, Frank. *"Arisierung" in Hamburg.* 2nd ed. Hamburg: Hans Christians, 1997. Also available in English translated by George Wilkes: *"Aryanisation" in Hamburg: The Economic Exclusion of the Jews and the Confiscation of their Property in Nazi Germany.* New York: Berghahn, 2002.

_______. "The Beneficiaries of 'Aryanization': Hamburg as a Case Study." *Yad Vashem Studies* XXVI (1998): 173–201.

_______. *Parvenüs und Profiteure: Korruption in der NS-Zeit.* Frankfurt am Main: S. Fischer, 2001.

Banken, Ralf. "Kurzfristiger Boom oder langfristiger Forschungsschwerpunkt? Die neuere deutsche Unternehmensgeschichte und die Zeit des Nationalsozialismus." *Geschichte in Wissenschaft und Unterricht* 3 (2005): 183–96.

_______. "Die nationalsozialistische Goldreserven und Devisenpolitik 1933-1939." *Jahrbuch für Wirtschaftsgeschichte* 1 (2003): 49–78.

Barendregt, Jaap. *Securities at Risk: The Restitution of Jewish Securities Stolen in the Netherlands during World War II.* Amsterdam: Aksant, 2004.

Barkai, Avraham. *Vom Boykott zur "Entjudung": Der wirtschaftliche Existenzkampf der Juden im Dritten Reich 1933–1943.* Frankfurt am Main: S. Fischer, 1987.

Barkan, Elazar. *The Guilt of Nations: Restitution and Negotiating Historical Injustices.* New York: Norton, 2000.

Bazyler, Michael J. *Holocaust Justice: The Battle for Restitution in America's Courts.* New York: New York University Press, 2003.

_______, and Roger P. Alford, eds. *Holocaust Restitution: Perspectives on the Litigation and Its Legacy.* New York: New York University Press, 2006.

Beiträge zur Geschichte des Nationalsozialismus 20, Die Deportation der Juden aus Deutschland: Pläne – Praxis – Reaktionen 1938–1945. Göttingen: Wallstein, 2004.

Beiträge zur Geschichte des Nationalsozialismus 19, Kooperation und Verbrechen: Formen der "Kollaboration" im östlichen Europa 1939-1945. Göttingen: Wallstein, 2003.

Belgium: Commission d'étude des biens juifs, ed. *Les biens des victimes des persécutions anti-juives en Belgique: Spoliation – Rétablissement des droits. Résultats de la Commission d'étude. Rapport Final de la Commission d'étude sur le sort des biens des membres de la Communauté juive de Belgique spoliés ou délaissés pendant la guerre 1940–45*. Brussels: Services du Premier Ministre, July 2001.

Benz, Wolfgang, ed. *Die Juden in Deutschland 1933-1945: Leben unter nationalsozialistischer Herrschaft*. Munich: C.H. Beck, 1993.

Bertz, Inka. "Ein Karteiblatt für jeden abgeschobenen Juden erleichtert die Übersicht," in *Zehn Brüder waren wir gewesen ... : Spuren jüdischen Lebens in Berlin-Neukölln*, ed. Dorothea Kolland, 372–86. Berlin: Edition Hentrich, 1988.

Biella, Friedrich, et al. *Das Bundesrückerstattungsgesetz*. Munich: C. H. Beck, 1981.

Billig, Joseph. *Le Commissariat Général aux Questions Juives, 1941-1944*. 3 vols. Paris: Editions du Centre, 1953, 1955, and 1960.

Bindenagel, J. D., ed. *Washington Conference on Holocaust-Era Assets: November 30–December 3, 1998 Proceedings*. Washington, DC: U.S. Government Printing Office, 1999.

Bonhage, Barbara, Hanspeter Lussy, and Marc Perrenoud. *Nachrichtenlose Vermögen bei Schweizer Banken: Depots, Konten und Safes von Opfern des nationalsozialistischen Regimes und Restitutionsprobleme in der Nachkriegszeit*. Zurich: Chronos, 2001.

Bopf, Britta. *"Arisierung in Köln": Die wirtschaftliche Existenzvernichtung der Juden 1933-1945*. Cologne: Emons, 2004.

Bower, Tom. *Blood Money: The Swiss, the Nazis and the Looted Billions*. London: Macmillan, 1997.

Bradsher, Greg, ed. *Holocaust-Era Assets: A Finding Aid to Records at the National Archives at College Park, Maryland*. Washington, DC: National Archives Trust Fund Board, 1999.

Braham, Randolph L. *The Politics of Genocide: The Holocaust in Hungary*. Condensed Edition. Detroit: Wayne State University Press in association with the United States Holocaust Memorial Museum, 2000.

Brüns-Wüstefeld, Alex. *Lohnende Geschäfte: Die "Entjudung" der Wirtschaft am Beispiel Göttingens*. Hannover: Fackelträger, 1997.

Buomberger, Thomas. *Raubkunst – Kunstraub. Die Schweiz und der Handel mit gestohlenen Kulturgütern zur Zeit des Zweiten Weltkriegs*. Zurich: Orel Füssli, 1998.

Cała, A., and H. Datner-Śpiewak, eds. *Dzieje Żydów w Polsce 1944–1968: Teksty źródłowe*. Warsaw: Zydowski Instytut Historyczny, 1997.

Cesarani, David, ed. *Genocide and Rescue: The Holocaust in Hungary 1944*. Oxford: Berg, 1997.

The Commission on Jewish Assets in Sweden at the Time of the Second World War. *The Nazigold and the Swedish Riksbank: Interim Report.* Stockholm: SOU, 1998.

Confiscation of Jewish Property in Europe, 1933–1945: New Sources and Perspectives. Washington, DC: Center for Advanced Holocaust Studies, United States Holocaust Memorial Museum, 2003.

Dean, Martin. *Collaboration in the Holocaust: Crimes of the Local Police in Belorussia and Ukraine, 1941–44*. London and New York: Macmillan and St. Martin's, in association with the United States Holocaust Memorial Museum, 2000.

_______. "The Development and Implementation of Nazi Denaturalization and Confiscation Policy up to the Eleventh Decree to the Reich Citizenship Law." *Holocaust and Genocide Studies* 16, No. 2 (Fall 2002): 217–42.

_______. "Jewish Property Seized in the Occupied Soviet Union in 1941 and 1942: The Records of the Reichshauptkasse Beutestelle." *Holocaust and Genocide Studies*, 14, No. 1 (Spring 2000): 83–101.

_______. "Multinational Jewish Businesses and the Transfer of Capital Abroad in the Face of 'Aryanization,' 1933-39," in *European Business, Dictatorship and Political Risk: 1920–1945*, ed. by Chris Kobrak, and Per Hansen, 103–21. New York: Berghahn, 2004.

_______. "Seizure, Registration, Rental and Sale: The Strange Case of the German Administration of Moveable Property in Latvia (1941–1944)," in *Latvia in World War II: Materials of an International Conference, 14-15 June 1999, Riga*, 372–78. Riga: Latvijas Universitates Latvijas vestures instituts, 2000.

Dehnel, Regine, ed. "Jüdischer Buchbesitz als Raubgut." *Zeitschrift für Bibliothekswesen und Bibliographie* Sonderheft 88 (2005)

Douzou, Laurent. *Voler les Juifs*. Paris: Hachette Littératures, 2003.

Dreßen, Wolfgang, ed. *Betrifft: "Aktion 3." Deutsche verwerten jüdische Nachbarn: Dokumente zur Arisierung*. Berlin: Aufbau Verlag, 1998.

Dreyfus, Jean-Marc, and Sarah Gensburger. *Des camps dans Paris: Austerlitz, Lévitan, Bassano, juillet 1943 – août 1944*. Paris: Fayard, 2003.

_______. *Pillages sur ordonnances: Aryanisation et restitution des banques en France, 1940-1953*. Paris: Fayard, 2003.

Dubiel, Helmut. *Niemand ist frei von der Geschichte: Die Nationalsozialistische Herrschaft in den Debatten des Deutschen Bundestages*. Munich: C. Hanser, 1999.

Eichwede, Wolfgang, and Ulrike Hartung, eds. *"Betr.: Sicherstellung" – NS-Kunstraub in der Sowjetunion*. Bremen: Temmen, 1998.

Eizenstat, Stuart E. *Imperfect Justice: Looted Assets, Slave Labor, and the Unfinished Business of World War II*. New York: Public Affairs, 2003.

Feilchenfeld, Werner, Dolf Michaelis, and Ludwig Pinner, *Haavara-Transfer nach Palästina und Einwanderung deutscher Juden 1933–1939*. Tübingen: J.C.B. Mohr, 1972.

Feldman, Gerald D. *Die Allianz und die deutsche Versicherungswirtschaft 1933-1945*. München: C. H. Beck, 2001. Also available in English as *Allianz and the German Insurance Business, 1933–1945*. Cambridge, UK: Cambridge University Press, 2001.

Feliciano, Hector. *The Lost Museum: The Nazi Conspiracy to Steal the World's Greatest Works of Art*. New York: Basic Books, 1997.

Fichtl, Franz, Stephan Link, Herbert May, and Sylvia Schaible. *"Bambergs Wirtschaft Judenfrei": Die Verdrängung der jüdischen Geschäftsleute in den Jahren 1933 bis 1939*. Bamberg: Collibri, 1998.

Francini, Esther Tisa, Anja Heuss, and Georg Kreis. *Fluchtgut – Raubgut: Der Transfer von Kulturgütern in und über die Schweiz 1933–1945 und die Frage der Restitution*. Zurich: Chronos, 2002.

Frech, Stefan. *Clearing: Der Zahlungsverkehr der Schweiz mit den Achsenmächten*. Zurich: Chronos, 2001.

Frei, Norbert. *Vergangenheitspolitik: Die Anfänge der Bundesrepublik und die NS-Vergangenheit*. Munich: Beck, 1996.

Friedenberger, Martin. "Das Berliner Finanzamt Moabit-West und die Enteignung der Emigranten des Dritten Reichs 1933-1942." *Zeitschrift für Geschichtswissenschaft* 49:8 (2001): 677–94.

________, Klaus-Dieter Gössel, and Eberhard Schönknecht, eds. *Die Reichsfinanzverwaltung im Nationalsozialismus: Darstellung und Dokumente*. Bremen: Edition Temmen, 2002.

Fritz Bauer Institut, ed. *Legalisierter Raub: Der Fiskus und die Ausplünderung der Juden in Hessen 1933–1945*. Frankfurt am Main: Ausstellungskatalog, 2003.

Genschel, Helmut. *Die Verdrängung der Juden aus der Wirtschaft im Dritten Reich*. Göttingen: Musterschmidt Verlag, 1966.

Gerlach, Christian, and Götz Aly. *Das letzte Kapitel: Der Mord an den ungarischen Juden*. Stuttgart: DVA, 2002.

Goschler, Constantin, and Jürgen Lillteicher, eds. *Die Rückerstattung jüdischen Eigentums in Deutschland und Österreich nach 1945 und 1989*. Göttingen: Wallstein, 2002.

________. *Schuld und Schulden: Die Politik der Wiedergutmachung für Verfolgte des Nationalsozialismus in Deutschland nach 1945*. Göttingen: Wallstein, 2005.

________. *Wiedergutmachung: Westdeutschland und die Verfolgten des Nationalsozialismus 1945–1954*. Munich: Oldenbourg, 1992.

Grimsted, Patricia Kennedy. "Twice Plundered or 'Twice Saved'? Identifying Russia's 'Trophy' Archives and the Loot of the Reichssicherheitshauptamt." *Holocaust and Genocide Studies*, 15, No. 2 (Fall 2001): 191–244.

Händler-Lachmann, Barbara, and Thomas Werther. *Vergessene Geschäfte – verlorene Geschichte: Jüdisches Wirtschaftsleben in Marburg und seine Vernichtung im Nationalsozialismus*. Marburg: Hitzeroth, 1992.

Hartman, John J. "Polish-Jewish Relations and the Holocaust. A Psychohistorical Perspective," in *I Remember Every Day ... the Fates of the Jews of Przemyśl during the Second World War*, eds. J. J. Hartman, and J. Krochmal, 283–302. Przemyśl: Towarzystwo Przyjaciół Nauk w Przemyślu, 2002.

Hayes, Peter. *From Cooperation to Complicity: Degussa in the Third Reich*. Cambridge, UK: Cambridge University Press, 2004.

Heim, Susanne. "Vertreibung, Raub und Umverteilung: Die jüdischen Flüchtlinge aus Deutschland und die Vermehrung des 'Volksvermögens.' " *Beiträge zur Nationalsozialistischen Gesundheits- und Sozialpolitik* 15 (1999): 107–38.

Henke, Klaus-Dietmar, ed. *Die Dresdner Bank im Dritten Reich*. 4 vols. Munich: R. Oldenbourg, 2006.

Henry, Marilyn. *The Restitution of Jewish Property in Central and Eastern Europe*. New York: American Jewish Committee, 1997.

Hepp, Michael, ed. *Die Ausbürgerung deutscher Staatsangehöriger 1933–45 nach den im Reichsanzeiger veröffentlichten Listen*. 3 vols. Munich: K.G. Saur, 1985.

Herbert, Ulrich, ed. *National Socialist Extermination Policies: Contemporary German Perspectives and Controversies*. New York: Berghahn, 2000.

Herbst, Ludolf, and Thomas Wiehe, eds., *Die Commerzbank und die Juden 1933–1945*. Munich: C. H. Beck, 2004.

________, and Constantin Goschler, eds. *Wiedergutmachung in der Bundesrepublik Deutschland*. Munich: R. Oldenbourg, 1989.

Heuss, Anja. *Kunst-und Kulturgutraub: Eine vergleichende Studie zur Besatzungspolitik der Nationalsozialisten in Frankreich und der Sowjetunion*. Heidelberg: Universitätsverlag C. Winter, 2000.

Hilberg, Raul. *Die Vernichtung der europäischen Juden*. 3 vols. Frankfurt am Main: S. Fischer, 1982. Also available in English as *The Destruction of the European Jews*. (Third Edition) New Haven: Yale University Press, 2003.

Hockerts, Hans Günter. "Wiedergutmachung in Deutschland: Eine historische Bilanz 1945–2000." *Vierteljahrshefte für Zeitgeschichte* 49 (2001): 167–214.

Holzbauer, Robert. "Einziehung volks- und staatsfeindlichen Vermögens im Lande Österreich: Die 'VUGESTA' – 'die Verwertungsstelle für jüdisches Umzugsgut der Gestapo.'" *Spurensuche*, 1–2 (2000): 38–50.

Independent Commission of Experts: Switzerland – Second World War. *Switzerland and Gold Transactions in the Second World War*. Bern: EDMZ, 1998.

________. *Switzerland, National Socialism and the Second World War: Final Report*. Zurich: Pendo, 2002.

Ioanid, Radu. *The Holocaust in Romania: The Destruction of Jews and Gypsies under the Antonescu Regime, 1940–44*. Chicago: Ivan R. Dee in association with the United States Holocaust Memorial Museum, 2000.

Jabloner, Clemens, et al., eds. *Vermögensentzug während der NS-Zeit sowie Rückstellungen und Entschädigungen seit 1945 in Österreich: Schlussbericht*. Vienna: Historikerkommission, 2003.

James, Harold. *The Deutsche Bank and the Nazi Economic War against the Jews*. Cambridge, UK: Cambridge University Press, 2001.

Jančík, Drahomir, and Eduard Kubů. *"Arizace" a arizátoř:. Drobný a střední židovský majetek v úvěrech Kreditanstalt der Deutschen 1939–1945*. Prague: Nakl. Carolinum, 2005.

_______, et al., eds. *Jewish Gold, other Precious Metals and Objects from the Bohemian Lands, 1939–1945: Illegal Violations of Property Rights, Their Scale and the Subsequent Fate of this Property*. Prague: Sefer, Institute of the Terezin Initiative, 2001.

Jelinek, Yeshayahu A. *The Parish Republic: Hlinka's Slovak People's Party*. New York: Columbia University Press, 1976.

Joly, Laurent. *Vichy dans la solution finale: Histoire du Commissariat general aux questions juives*. Paris: Grasset, 2006.

Junz, Helen. *Where Did All the Money Go? The Pre-Nazi Era Wealth of European Jewry*. Bern: Staempfli, 2002.

Kádár, Gábor, and Zoltán Vági, *Self-financing Genocide: The Gold Train, the Becher Case and the Wealth of Hungarian Jews*. Budapest: Central European University Press, 2004.

Kaiser, Johann. "Die Politik des Dritten Reiches gegenüber der Slowakei 1939–1945: Ein Beitrag zur Erforschung der nationalsozialistischen Satellitenpolitik in Südosteuropa." PhD diss. Bochum, 1969.

Kamenec, Ivan. *Po stopách tragédie*. Bratislava: Archa, 1991.

Kaplan, Marion A. *Between Dignity and Despair: Jewish Life in Nazi Germany*. Oxford, UK: Oxford University Press, 1998.

Kenkmann, Alfons, and Bernd-A. Rusinek, eds. *Verfolgung und Verwaltung: Die wirtschaftliche Ausplünderung der Juden und die westfälischen Finanzbehörden*. Münster: Oberfinanzdirektion Münster, 1999.

Knight, Robert, ed. *"Ich bin dafür, die Sache in die Länge zu ziehen": Wortprotokolle der österreichischen Bundesregierung von 1945–1952 über die Entschädigung der Juden*. Frankfurt am Main: Athenäum, 1988.

Kolbe, Christian, and Stephan Wirtz, eds. *Enteignung der jüdischen Bevölkerung in Deutschland und nationalsozialistische Wirtschaftspolitik 1933-1945: Annotierte Bibliographie*. Frankfurt am Main: Fritz Bauer Institut, 2000.

Kratzsch, Gerhard. *Der Gauwirtschaftsapparat der NSDAP: Menschenführung – „Arisierung" – Wehrwirtschaft im Gau Westfalen-Süd*. Münster: Aschendorffsche Verlag, 1989.

Kubu, Eduard, and Gudrun Exner, *Tschechen und Tschechinnen: Vermögensentzug und Restitution*. Vienna: Oldenbourg, 2004.

Lagrou, P. *The Legacy of Nazi Occupation: Patriotic Memory and National Recovery in Western Europe, 1945–1965*. Cambridge, UK: Cambridge University Press, 2000.

Laloum, Jean. *Les Juifs dans la banlieue parisienne des années 1920 aux années 1950*. Paris: CNRS Editions, 1998.

Leesch, Wolfgang, et al., eds. *Geschichte der Finanzverfassung- und verwaltung in Westfalen seit 1815*. Münster: Oberfinanzdirektion Münster, 1998.

Lehmann, Rosa. *Symbiosis and Ambivalence: Poles and Jews in a Small Galician Town*. New York: Berghahn, 2001.

Le Masne de Chermont, Isabelle, and Didier Schulmann, eds. *Le pillage de l'art en France pendant l'occupation et la situation des 2000 oeuvres confiées aux musées nationaux: Contribution de la direction des Musées de France et du Centre Georges-Pompidou aux travaux de la Mission d'étude sur la spoliation des juifs de France*. Paris: Documentation française, 2000.

Levi, Fabio. *Le case e le cose: La persecuzione degli ebrei torinesi nelle carte dell'EGELI, 1938–1945*. Turin: Compagnia di San Paolo, 1998.

Levin, Itamar. *The Last Chapter of the Holocaust?* Israel: Jewish Agency for Israel in cooperation with The World Jewish Restitution Organization, 2nd and revised ed. 1998.

_______. *Walls Around: The Plunder of Warsaw Jewry during World War II and Its Aftermath*. Westport, CT: Praeger, 2004.

Lillteicher, Jürgen "Die Rückerstattung jüdischen Eigentums in Westdeutschland nach dem Zweiten Weltkrieg: Eine Studie über Verfolgungserfahrung, Rechtsstaatlichkeit und Vergangenheitspolitik, 1945–1971." PhD diss. Freiburg Univ., 2002.

Lipscher, Ladislav. *Die Juden im Slowakischen Staat 1939–1945*. Munich: Oldenbourg, 1980.

Longerich, Peter. *Politik der Vernichtung: Eine Gesamtdarstellung der nationalsozialistischen Judenverfolgung*. Munich: Piper, 1998.

Lorentz, Bernhard. "Die Commerzbank und die 'Arisierung' im Altreich: Ein Vergleich der Netzwerkstrukturen und Handlungsspielräume von Grossbanken in der NS-Zeit." *Vierteljahrshefte für Zeitgeschichte* 50. Jhrg., 2. Heft (2002): 237–68.

Łuczak, Czesław. *Polityka ludnościowa i ekonomiczna hitlerowskich Niemiec w okupowanej Polsce*. Poznan: Wydawn. Poznanskie, 1979.

Ludi, Regula. "Waging War on Wartime Memory: Recent Swiss Debates on the Legacies of the Holocaust and the Nazi Era." *Jewish Social Studies* 10.2 (Winter 2004): 116–52.

Ludwig, Johannes. *Boykott – Enteignung – Mord: Die "Entjudung"der deutschen Wirtschaft*. Hamburg: Facta, 1989.

Machcewicz, P., and K. Persak, eds. *Wokół Jedwabnego*. Warsaw: Instytut Pamieci Narodowej, 2002.

MacQueen, Michael. "The Conversion of Looted Assets to Run the German War Machine." *Holocaust and Genocide Studies* 18, No. 1 (Spring 2004): 27–45.

Maissen, Thomas, *Verweigerte Erinnerung: Nachrichtenlose Vermögen und die Schweizer Weltkriegsdebatte 1989–2004*. Zurich: Neue Zürcher Zeitung, 2005.

Margairaz, Michel, ed. *Banques, Banque de France et Seconde Guerre mondiale*. Paris: Albin Michel, 2002.

Marrus, Michael R., and Robert O. Paxton. *Vichy France and the Jews*. New York: Basic Books, 1981.

Mehl, Stefan. "Das Reichsfinanzministerium und die Verfolgung der deutschen Juden 1933–1943," in *Berliner Arbeitshefte und Berichte zur Sozialwissenschaftlicher Forschung* No. 38. Berlin, 1990.

Meinl, Susanne, and Jutta Zwilling, *Legalisierter Raub: Die Ausplünderung der Juden im Nationalsozialismus durch die Reichsfinanzverwaltung in Hessen*. Frankfurt am Main: Campus, 2004.

Michman, Joseph. "Planning for the Final Solution Against the Background of Developments in Holland in 1941." *Yad Vashem Studies* XVII (1986): 145–80.

Möllenhoff, Gisela, and Rita Schlautmann-Overmeyer, eds. *Jüdische Familien in Münster 1918 bis 1945, Teil 1: Biographisches Lexikon*. Münster: Westfälisches Dampfboot, 1995.

________. *Jüdische Familien in Münster, Teil 2,1: Abhandlungen und Dokumente 1918–1935*. Münster: Westfälisches Dampfboot, 1998.

________. *Jüdische Familien in Münster, Teil 2,2: Abhandlungen und Dokumente 1935–45*. Münster: Westfälisches Dampfboot, 2001.

Musial, Bogdan, ed. *"Aktion Reinhardt": Der Völkermord an den Juden im Generalgouvernement 1941–1944*. Osnabrück: Fibre, 2004.

________. *Deutsche Zivilverwaltung und Judenverfolgung im Generalgouvernement. Eine Fallstudie zum Distrikt Lublin 1939-1944*. Wiesbaden: Harrassowitz, 1999.

Mussgnug, Dorothee. *Die Reichsfluchtsteuer 1931-1953*. Berlin: Duncker and Humblot, 1993.

Nicholas, Lynn. *The Rape of Europa: The Fate of Europe's Treasures in the Third Reich and the Second World War*. London: Macmillan, 1994.

Novick, Peter. *The Holocaust in American Life*. Boston: Houghton Mifflin, 1999.

Offenburg, Mario, ed. *Adass Jisroel, Die Jüdische Gemeinde in Berlin, 1869–1942: Vernichtet und Vergessen*. Berlin: Museumspädagogischer Dienst, 1986.

Pavan, Ilaria, and Guri Schwarz, eds. *Gli ebrei in Italia tra persecuzione fascista e reintegrazione postbellica*. Florence: Giuntina, 2001.

________. *Tra indifferenza e oblio: Le conseguenza economiche delle leggi razziali in Italia, 1938–1970*. Florence: Le Monnier, 2004.

Perz, Bertrand, and Thomas Sandkühler, "Auschwitz und die 'Aktion Reinhard' 1942–1945: Judenmord und Raubpraxis aus neuer Sicht." *Zeitgeschichte* 26. Jg., H. 5 (Sept./Okt. 1999): 283–316.

Petropoulos, Jonathan. *Art as Politics in the Third Reich*. Chapel Hill: University of North Carolina Press, 1996.

Pezechkian, Johanna. "La Möbelaktion en Belgique." *Cahiers d'Histoire du Temps Présent* 10 (2000): 153–180.

Pohl, Dieter. *Nationalsozialistische Judenverfolgung in Ostgalizien 1941-1944*. Munich: Oldenbourg, 1996.

_______. "Schauplatz Ukraine: Der Massenmord an den Juden im Militärverwaltungsgebiet und im Reichskommissariat 1941-1943," in *Ausbeutung, Vernichtung, Öffentlichkeit: Neue Studien zur nationalsozialistischen Lagerpolitik*, ed. Norbert Frei, Sybille Steinbacher, and Bernd C. Wagner, 135–74. Munich: K.G. Saur, 2000.

_______. "Ukrainische Hilfskräfte beim Mord an den Juden," in *Die Täter der Shoah: Fanatische Nationalsozialisten oder ganz normale Deutsche?* ed. Gerhard von Paul, 205–34. Göttingen: Wallstein, 2002.

_______. *Von der "Judenpolitik" zum Judenmord: Der Distrikt Lublin des Generalgouvernements 1939-1944*. Frankfurt am Main: Peter Lang, 1993.

Potthast, Jan Björn. "Antijüdische Massnahmen im Protektorat Böhmen und Mähren und das 'Jüdische Zentralmuseum' in Prag," in *'Arisierung' im Nationalsozialismus: Volksgemeinschaft, Raub und Gedächtnis*, ed. Irmtrud Wojak and Peter Hayes, 157–201. Frankfurt am Main: Campus, 2000.

_______. *Das jüdische Zentralmuseum der SS in Prag: Gegnerforschung und Völkermord im Nationalsozialismus*. Frankfurt am Main: Campus, 2002.

Presidential Advisory Commission on Holocaust Assets in the United States, Plunder and Restitution: The U.S. and Holocaust Victims' Assets; Findings and Recommendations of the Presidential Advisory Commission on Holocaust Assets in the United States and Staff Report. *Washington, DC: U.S. Government Printing Office, 2000.*

Presidenza del Consiglio dei Ministri, ed. *Rapporto Generale Allegati: Commissione per la ricostruzione delle vicende che hanno caratterizzato in Italia le attività di acquisizione dei bene dei cittadini ebrei da parte di organismi pubblici e privati*. Rome: Dipartimento per l'Informazione e l'Editoria, 2001.

Prost, A., R. Skoutelsky, et al. *Aryanisation économique et restitutions: Mission d'étude sur la spoliation des Juifs de France*. Paris: Documentation française, 2000.

Rathkolb, Oliver, ed. *Revisiting the National Socialist Legacy: Coming to Terms with Forced Labor, Expropriation, Compensation, and Restitution*. Innsbruck: Studien Verlag, 2002.

Reichel, Peter. *Vergangenheitsbewältigung in Deutschland: Die Auseinandersetzung mit der NS-Diktatur von 1945 bis heute*. Munich: Beck, 2001.

Reisel, Berit and Bjarte Bruland. *The Reisel/Bruland Report on the Confiscation of Jewish Property in Norway*. Part of Official Norwegian Report 1997: 22. Oslo, 1997.

Republique Française. *Summary of the work by the Study Mission on the spoliation of the Jews in France*. Paris: Documentation française, 2000.

Reschwamm, D. "Die Vertreibung und Vernichtung der Juden im Spiegel der Akten des Finanzamtes Nordhausen." *Geschichte, Erziehung, Politik* 7, 7/8 (1996): 404–13.

Rings, Werner. *Raubgold aus Deutschland: Die 'Golddrehscheibe' Schweiz im Zweiten Weltkrieg*. Munich: R. Piper, 1996.

Robinson, Nehemiah, ed. *Indemnification and Reparations: Jewish Aspects*. New York: Institute of Jewish Affairs of the American Jewish Congress and World Jewish Congress, 1944.

________. *Spoliation and Remedial Action: The Material Damage Suffered by Jews under Persecution, Reparations, Restitution, and Compensation*. New York: Institute of Jewish Affairs, World Jewish Congress, 1962.

Rosenkötter, Bernhard. *Treuhandpolitik: Die "Haupttreuhandstelle Ost" und der Raub polnischer Vermögen 1939-1945*. Essen: Klartext, 2003.

Rosenkranz, Herbert. *Verfolgung und Selbstbehauptung: Die Juden in Österreich 1938-1945*. Wien: Herold, 1978.

Roth, Karl Heinz. "Hehler des Holocaust: Degussa und Deutsche Bank." *1999*, 13 (1998): 137–44.

Rummel, Walter, and Jochen Rath, eds. *"Dem Reich verfallen" – "den Berechtigten zurückzuerstatten": Enteignung und Rückerstattung jüdischen Vermögens im Gebiet des heutigen Rheinland-Pfalz, 1938–1953*. Koblenz: Verlag der Landesarchivverwaltung Rheinland-Pfalz, 2001.

Ryan, Donna F. *The Holocaust and the Jews of Marseille: The Enforcement of Anti-Semitic Policies in Vichy France*. Urbana: University of Illinois Press, 1996.

Safrian, Hans. *Eichmann und seine Gehilfen*. Frankfurt am Main: Fischer, 1995.

________. "Expediting Expropriation and Expulsion: The Impact of the 'Vienna Model' on Anti-Jewish Policies in Nazi Germany, 1938." *Holocaust and Genocide Studies* 14, No. 3 (Winter 2000): 390–414.

Schilde, Kurt. *Bürokratie des Todes: Lebensgeschichten jüdischer Opfer des NS-Regimes im Spiegel von Finanzamtsakten*. Berlin: Metropol, 2002.

Schwarz, Walter, ed. *Rückerstattung nach den Gesetzen der Alliierten Mächte*. Munich: C. H. Beck, 1974.

Second World War Assets Contact Group, ed. *Second World War: Theft and Restoration of Rights. Final Report of the Second World War Assets Contact Group*. Amsterdam, 2000.

Seibel, Wolfgang. "A Market for Mass Crime? Inter-institutional Competition and the Initiation of the Holocaust in France, 1940-42." *International Journal of Organization Theory and Behavior* 5, Nos. 3 and 4 (2002): 219–57.

_______, and Gerald Feldman, eds. *Networks of Nazi Persecution: Division-of-Labor in the Holocaust.* New York: Berghahn, 2005.

Simmert, Johannes ed. "Die nationalsozialistische Judenverfolgung in Rheinland-Pfalz 1933 bis 1945," in *Dokumentation zur Geschichte der jüdischen Bevölkerung in Rheinland-Pfalz und im Saarland von 1800 bis 1945*, ed. die Landesarchivverwaltung Rheinland-Pfalz in Verbindung mit dem Landesarchiv Saarbrücken, vol. 6. Koblenz: Landesarchivverwaltung Rheinland-Pfalz, 1974.

Steinberg, Jonathan *The Deutsche Bank and its Gold Transactions during the Second World War*. Munich: C. H. Beck, 1999.

Steinberg, Maxime. *L'etoile et le fusil: La Question Juive 1940–42.* 4 vols. Brussels: Vie ouvrière, 1987.

_______, "The Judenpolitik in Belgium within the West European Context: Comparative Observations," in *Belgium and the Holocaust: Jews, Belgians, Germans.* ed. Dan Michman, 199–224. Jerusalem: Yad Vashem, 1998.

Steiner, Hubert, and Christian Kucsera. *Recht als Unrecht: Quellen zur wirtschaftlichen Entrechtung der Wiener Juden durch die NS-Vermögensverkehrsstelle. Teil I: Privatvermögen, Personenverzeichnis.* Vienna: Österreichisches Staatsarchiv, 1991.

Steinlauf, Michael C. *Bondage to the Dead: Poland and the Memory of the Holocaust.* Syracuse, N.Y.: Syracuse University Press, 1997.

Strzelecki, A. "Der Raub des Besitzes der Opfer des KL Auschwitz." *Hefte von Auschwitz* 21 (2000): 7–99.

Tanner, Jakob, and Sigrid Weigel, eds. *Gedächtnis, Geld und Gesetz: Vom Umgang mit der Vergangenheit des Zweiten Weltkriegs*. Zurich: Vdf, Hochschulverlag AG an der ETH, 2001.

Ther, Philipp. *Deutsche und Polnische Vertriebene: Gesellschaft und Vertriebenenpolitik in der SBZ/DDR und in Polen 1945–1956.* Göttingen: Vandenhoeck and Ruprecht, 1998.

Tönsmeyer, Tatjana. *Das Dritte Reich und die Slowakei, 1939-1945: Politischer Alltag zwischen Kooperation und Eigensinn*. Paderborn: Ferdinand Schöningh, 2003.

Tomaszewski, Jerzy, ed. *Studia z dziejów i kultury Żydów w Polsce po 1945 roku*. Warszawa: Wydawn. Trio, 1997.

Unabhängige Expertenkommission Schweiz – Zweiter Weltkrieg, ed. *Die Schweiz und die deutschen Lösegelderpressungen in den besetzten Niederlanden: Vermögensentziehung, Freikauf, Austausch 1940–1945: Beiheft zum Bericht Die Schweiz und die Flüchtlinge zur Zeit des*

Nationalsozialismus. Bern: Unabhängige Expertenkommission Schweiz – Zweiter Weltkrieg, 1999.

________, ed. *Die Schweiz, der Nationalsozialismus und das Recht,* Band I, *Öffentliches Recht*. Zurich: Chronos, 2001.

U.S. and Allied Efforts to Recover and Restore Gold and Other Assets Stolen or Hidden by Germany during World War II: Preliminary Study, coordinated by Stuart E. Eizenstat. Washington, DC: Department of State, 1997.

U.S. and Allied Wartime and Postwar Relations and Negotiations With Argentina, Portugal, Spain, Sweden, and Turkey on Looted Gold and German External Assets and U.S. Concerns about the Fate of the Wartime Ustasha Treasury, coordinated by Stuart E. Eizenstat. Washington, DC: Department of State, 1998.

van der Leeuw, A. J. "Der Griff des Reiches nach dem Judenvermögen," in *Studies over Nederland in oorlogstijd*, ed. A. H. Paape, 211–36. 's - Gravenhage: Martinus Nijhoff, 1972. First published in *Rechtsprechung zum Wiedergutmachungsrecht* (1970): 383–92.

________. „Reichskommissariat und Judenvermögen in den Niederlanden" in *Studies over Nederland in oorlogstijd*, ed. A. H. Paape, 237–49. 's-Gravenhage: Martinus Nijhoff, 1972.

van Laak, Dirk. "Die Mitwirkenden bei der 'Arisierung.' Dargestellt am Beispiel der rheinisch-westfälischen Industrieregion 1933–1940," in *Die Deutschen und die Judenverfolgung im Dritten Reich*, ed. Ursula Büttner, 231–58. Hamburg: Christians, 1992.

Vasek, A. *Die Lösung der Judenfrage in der Slowakei*. Bratislava: Globus, 1942.

Veraart, Wouter. *Onrechting en rechtherstel in Nederland en Frankrijk in de jaren van bezetting en wederopbouw*. Rotterdam: Sanders Institute, Kluwer, 2006.

Verheyde, Philippe. *Les mauvais comptes de Vichy: L'aryanisation des entreprises juives*. Paris: Perrin, 1999.

Verse-Herrmann, A. *Die Arisierungen in der Land und Forstwirtschaft 1938–42*. Stuttgart: Franz Steiner, 1997.

Walk, J., ed. *Das Sonderrecht für die Juden im NS-Staat*. Heidelberg: C. F. Müller, 2nd ed. 1996.

Wehle, K. "The Jews in Bohemia and Moravia 1945–1948," in *The Jews of Czechoslovakia*, ed. A. Dagan (V. Fischl), vol. 3, 517–21. Philadelphia, 1984.

Weiss, George, ed. *Einige Dokumente zur Rechtsstellung der Juden und zur Entziehung ihres Vermögens 1933–1945: Schriftenreihe zum Berliner Rückerstattungsrecht VII*. Germany: G. Weiss, 1950.

Weissberg-Bob, Nea, and Thomas Irmer, *Heinrich Richard Brinn (1874–1944) Fabrikant-Kunstsammler-Frontkämpfer: Dokumentation einer „Arisierung."* Berlin: Lichtig, 2002.

Wieviorka, Annette. *Les Biens des Internés des Camps de Drancy, Pithiviers et Beaune-la-Rolande*. Paris: Documentation française, 2000.

_______. *Le pillage des appartements, Mission d'étude sur la spoliation des Juifs de France*. Paris: Documentation française, 2000.

Willems, Susanne. *Der entsiedelte Jude: Albert Speers Wohnungsmarktpolitik für den Berliner Hauptstadtbau*. Berlin: Hentrich, 2000.

Wojak, I., and P. Hayes, eds. *"Arisierung" im Nationalsozialismus: Volksgemeinschaft, Raub und Gedächtnis. Jahrbuch 2000 zur Geschichte und Wirkung des Holocaust*. Frankfurt am Main: Campus, 2000.

Wolf, Herbert. "Zur Kontrolle und Enteignung jüdischen Vermögens in der NS-Zeit: das Schicksal des Rohtabakhändlers Arthur Spanier." *Bankhistorisches Archiv*, 16, Heft 1 (1990): 55–62.

Wolf, Kerstin, and Frank Wolf, eds. *Reichsfluchtsteuer und Steuersteckbriefe 1932–42*. Berlin: Biographische Forschungen und Sozialgeschichte, 1997.

Zabludoff, Sidney. *"And It All But Disappeared": The Nazi Seizure of Jewish Assets*. Policy Forum No. 13. Jerusalem: Institute of the World Jewish Congress, 1998.

Zweig, Ronald W. *German Reparations and the Jewish World: A History of the Claims Conference*. London: Frank Cass, 2001.

_______. *The Gold Train: The Destruction of the Jews and the Looting of Hungary*. New York: Morrow, 2002.

Index

T

U

V

W

Y

Z

Book Shelves
D804.3 .R37513 2007
Robbery and restitution :
the conflict over Jewish
property in Europe

DATE DUE

Demco, Inc. 38-293

Printed in the United States
205052BV00004B/99/P

CANISIUS COLLEGE LIBRARY